About the Author

Grace Selous Bull has a BA (Hons) in History of Art, Religious Studies
and Theology, which she studied at Leeds University. She went on to complete an MA in
Fine and Decorative Arts at Sotheby's Institute of Art in London. She has worked for an
international art consultant and auction house, Bonhams. After marrying, she gained a teaching
assistant qualification and was shocked at the lack of art and art history taught
at Primary Schools. Determined to show teachers, parents and children alike the vast
co-curricular expanse one can gain from learning about Art Education, she has gone on
to start writing books. She has a blog – https://therainbowtree.squarespace.com – that is full of arts
and crafts activities from toddlers all the way up to young teenagers.

Potty About Pots

Arts And Crafts For Home And School

Grace Selous Bull

AUSTIN MACAULEY PUBLISHERS™
LONDON • CAMBRIDGE • NEW YORK • SHARJAH

A CIP catalogue record for this title is available from the British Library.

ISBN 9781787105829 (Paperback)
ISBN 9781787105836 (E-Book)

www.austinmacauley.com

First Published (2018)

Austin Macauley Publishers™ Ltd.

25 Canada Square

Canary Wharf

London

E14 5LQ

Printed and bound in Great Britain

Dedication

I would like to dedicate this book to the teachers throughout my life, whose
love of Art History and teaching ignited my passion for the subject. To the nay-sayers
that believe Art History is not a proper subject. To my parents, without whom this would not
have been possible. And lastly, to my husband and two beautiful daughters, Ariana and
Tabitha, for whom this book is written. Let no one tell you your dreams are too big.

CONTENTS

Illustrations

Image one: Getty image, canopic jars, March 6 2009 Paris, Louvre, opening day of exhib 'Les Portes du Clei' doors to the sky

Image two: Papyrus with a depiction of the 'weighing of the heart' of the deceased, From the papyrus of Ani, in the British Museum

Image three: Pitcher (oinochoe), Greek late Geometric Period 740-730 BC, Boiotia, MFA Boston

Image four: The Elgin Amphora. Greek, made in Athens circa 760-750 BC. Late Geometric period. Attributed to artist Dipylon Painter. World History Archive

Image five: Detail of 7th c BCE amphora, Anicent Thera, Santorini, Archaeological Museum, Thera

Image Six: Peru, Pre-Inca civilization, Nazca culture, Double spout and bridge vessel with painted monkey figures
Credit: DEA/G. DAGLI ORTI

Images seven and eight: Tomb figure of a horse, Tang Dynasty, 618-906AD, Getty Images, Photographer Werner Forman

Image nine: Rare sancai-glazed pottery dish, Christies, Fine Chinese Ceramics and Works of Art, 21 March 2002, New York, sold for $88,125

Image ten: Ewer, Tang Dynasty. (618-907), 7th Century, Earthenware, Metropolitan Museum

Image eleven: A panel composed with tiles in shape of eight pointed stars and crosses, stone paste lustre painted, c.260-70, Iran, Metropolitan Museum, New York

Image twelve: A star-shaped tile, Iran, Varamin, made from stone paste with lustre-painted on opaque white glaze. 1262-63, Metropolitan Museum

Image thirteen: John Frederick Lewis, Intercepted Correspondence, 1869

Image fourteen: Bottle with purple splashed blue glaze (Yuhuchunping), Jun stoneware Northern Song Dynasty, AD 1000-1127, British Museum

Image fifteen: Shallow plate with thick opalescent blue glaze with copper pigment of purple splashes
Jun ware, Northern Southern Song, AD 1115-1234, British Museum

Image sixteen: Jun ware dish with opalescent blue and lavender splashed glazes, Jin dynasty, 1115-1234, British Museum

Image seventeen: Jar, Ming Dynasty (1368-1644), Xuande mark and period (1426-1435) , Metropolitan Museum, NY.

Image eighteen: A large blue and white porcelain 'Phoenix' bowl Jailing Mark and Period, Sold at Sotheby's in Important Chinese Art, 13 May 2015, London

Image nineteen: A blue and white Kraak porcelain dish with bird and flowers, China, Wanli period. © 2011 Nagel - Auctions

Image twenty: Anonymous Painter, circle of Joachim Credit National Maritime Museum, Greenwich, London, Caird Collection

Image twenty-one: A Kraak bowl from the Ming Dynasty, Wanli period, 1573-1619, From sale Paintings, Varia & Carpetsby, Lot 247, Bruun Rasmussen, Sept 28, 2010, Denmark

Image twenty-two: Still Life with an Oriental Rug, Willem Kalf, (1619-1693), Ashmolean Museum

Image twenty-three: Apothecary jar, c.1480, Italian, Maiolica, Metropolitan Museum

Image twenty-four & five: Italian Maiolica bowl, Workshop of Fontana Family, c.1540-60, Urbino. British museum

Image twenty-six: A pair of figures of Shishi, Japanese, late 17th Century, Burghley House

Image twenty-seven: Earthenware Tile, attributed to Christopher Dresser, Factory of Minton Hollins & Co, Stoke-on-Trent, 1880, British Museum.

Image twenty-eight: Rare Minton Aesthetic Movement, tile attributed to Christopher dresser c.1870 (Found on Ebay)

Image twenty-nine: Tile, William De Morgan, Victoria & Albert Museum, London

Image thirty: Dish, 1888-89, William De Morgan, Victoria & Albert Museum, London

Image thirty-one: Porcelain vase with crystalline glaze, mounted with silver, c.1900, Siegfried Bing (1838-1905), France, Victorian and Albert Museum London

Image thirty-two: Plate with sliced circle designs, Bizarre ware, c. 1930, Bonhams sold for £660

Image thirty-three: Meiping vase with sliced circle design, Bizarre ware, c.1930, Bonhams sold for £5400 in 2009

Image thirty-four: Auction assistant at Bonhams with set of 'Yo-Yo' vases by Clarice Cliff. There was an auction of 100 pieces of Clarice Cliff's ceramics in London on March 16, 2009. These pieces are rare and are dated c.1930. The seller, Sevi Guatelli 's collection was thought to be the best quality of pieces to have come onto the market. (Photo by Oli Scarff/Getty Images)

Image thirty-five: Spanish artist Pablo Picasso portrayed while decorating with paint and paintbrush one of his ceramic dishes, Paris, 1948. (Photo by Archivio Cameraphoto Epoche/Getty Images)

Image thirty-six: Dish, c.1957 Pablo Picasso, France, Victoria & Albert Museum

Images thirty-seven: Five piero fornasetti (1913-1988) transfer printed ceramic plates circa 1950 Christie's, Sale The Art of Food and Drink, Thursday 16 Jan 2014, lot 79

Image thirty-eight: Untitled (Blade cup)
Ruth Duckworth (Germany, Hamburg, active England and United States, 1919-2009) United States, 1994 Sculpture

Image thirty-nine: A Cycladic Marble Head of a Goddess, Early Bronze Age II, circa 2500-2400 B.C. Sotheby's sale, 07 JUNE 2007, New York

Ancient Egypt
History of the Canopic Jars
c.2575BCE–664BCE

Religious Belief

The afterlife was a huge part of the religious belief system in Ancient Egypt. They believed that after you died, you would travel to the afterlife and live another life. This meant that they had to preserve their bodies so that they could return. This process was called Mummification. All major organs are removed from the body and placed into Canopic Jars.

What Are Canopic Jars?

Canopic jars held and preserved major organs in each of them - the liver, intestines, lungs and stomach. These Canopic jars were then put into a special box, like a coffin, with the mummifed body.

Image one: Getty image, canopic jars, March 6 2009 Paris, Louvre, opening day of exhib 'Les Portes du Clei' doors to the sky

Evolution of the Canopic Jar

- The earliest Canopic jars were made in the Old Kingdom c.2575-c.2130BCE and had plain lids.
- From the Middle Kingdom c.1938-1630BCE, the jars were decorated with sculpted human heads.
- From 19th dynasty to the end of the New Kingdom 1539-1075BCE, the lids became heads representing the sons of Horus.
- During the 21st-25th dynasties 1075-664BCE, they began putting the organs back into the body so dummy Canopic jars were made with no interior space.

Image two: Papyrus with a depiction of the 'weighing of the heart' of the deceased, From the papyrus of Ani, in the British Museum.

The Heart

The heart was never removed from the body as it was believed in the afterlife, it would be weighed on scales with a feather on the other scale to determine whether the person had led a good life or not. If the feather was heavier than the heart, they could pass into the afterlife.

What Are They Made Of?

Wood, stone or pottery depending on the era. With a sculpted top.

SONS OF HORUS

Each of the four sons protects a major organ in their jar on their journey to the afterlife.

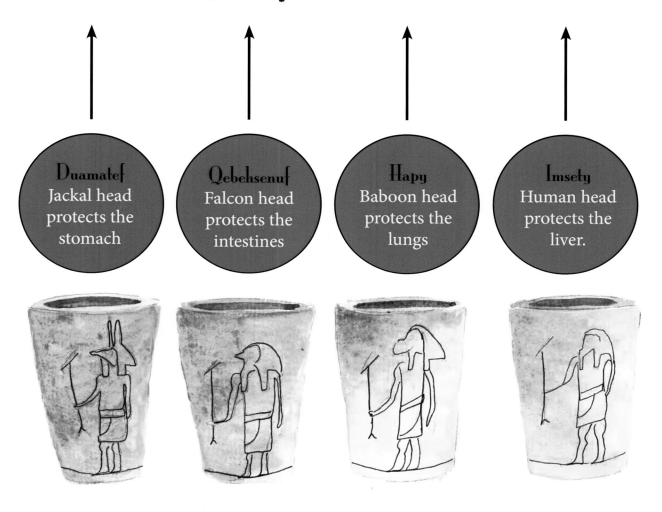

Duamatef
Jackal head protects the stomach

Qebehsenuf
Falcon head protects the intestines

Hapy
Baboon head protects the lungs

Imsety
Human head protects the liver.

Draw the correct organs in the boxes below the jars.

Art Activity

What you will need:
- A long terracotta plant pot (Homebase has some, shown to the right)
- Some terracotta coloured air drying clay (Amazon or Hobbycraft sells it)
- Any type of poster paint.
- PVC tablecloth
- Rolling pin
- Knife

Instructions:

1. First, you will need to roll out your clay with your rolling pin on the PVC tablecloth. Roll it out to the depth of a £1 coin, not too thin.

2. Place your pot face down on the clay (so that it is upside down) and with a knife cut a circle around it. It should be the same size as the pot hole as it will make the bottom of the stopper for your Canopic jar.

3. Using the rest of the clay create a head for your jar. It is up to you which you chose, just make sure you pick either a human, falcon, jackal or baboon head.

Why not draw it out on paper first?

4. Once you are happy with your head, with the knife, criss cross the bottom of it and do the same for the base circle part. Brush both with a bit of water and gently press the head onto the base so they stick together. Let them dry in a safe place for 48 hours.

5. Once dry, you can paint it with your poster paints. Once it is all dry, you can hide things inside it!

Create Your Own Canopic Jar!

On later Canopic Jars, there were sometimes images or writing in hieroglyphics on the body of the jars. Why not write your name in hieroglyphics on it to make sure everyone knows it's your jar?

Hieroglyphics is the language ancient Egyptians used to write. A symbol can mean a letter, word, adjective or noun. Some of the symbols have the same picture because they sound the same. In English, this would be like if you say 'C' and 'K', for example, Coat and Kite.

Tip:
If your name has double letters, you need to stack them as shown below. What name does this spell?

Glossary

Baboon – Some of the world's largest monkeys, they can be found in Africa or Arabia.

Evolution – Charles Darwin (1809-1882)'s theory of evolution is that all species have developed and changed over time from simple organisms.

Falcon – Part of the speices Falco, it is a type of bird of prey and can be found all over the world.

Hieroglyphics – Ancient Egyptian writing that used pictures to represent objects, actions, sounds, ideas and whole words. There are 700 hieroglyphs. The word is two Greek words put together: hieros, which means holy, and glyphe, meaning writing – so holy writing. We understand them from the Rosetta Stone in the British Museum.

Jackal – Small mammals that are part of the Canis species, which includes the wolf and dog. Can be found in Africa, Asia and some parts of Europe.

Mummification – A mummy is a body that has been preserved after death. Mummification is the process of preserving the body.

Organ – The human body works through semi-dependent organs, each doing specific things. Examples of organs are the heart, lungs, kidneys, intestines, brain, etc.

Using the words in the glossary, find them in the word search below

S	C	N	D	F	X	Y	T	V	S	Q	S	F	Y	E
H	H	Q	Y	P	B	L	L	P	L	H	N	E	U	Z
P	U	P	R	M	Y	H	V	L	A	K	O	M	P	R
P	B	W	Y	D	T	G	M	T	R	F	I	K	T	Q
Y	Y	G	W	L	A	Q	T	W	O	J	T	O	P	M
X	Q	U	U	G	G	T	B	N	X	T	U	P	L	Q
E	R	M	D	B	Z	O	Z	P	Z	N	L	O	M	N
N	A	W	P	W	K	Q	R	P	J	T	O	G	E	T
N	O	T	O	Q	A	C	K	E	T	C	V	B	N	N
P	S	Q	Q	W	K	M	U	X	I	G	E	A	F	R
C	L	N	E	H	U	B	G	L	P	H	G	V	P	S
Z	S	J	K	Z	J	J	T	N	J	R	V	I	B	H
R	D	V	O	M	X	D	E	G	O	G	F	Q	Z	T
W	N	O	I	T	A	C	I	F	I	M	M	U	M	P
V	P	S	C	E	Y	R	S	L	I	J	H	O	I	I

Organ Hieroglyphs Falcon Jackal

Mummification Evolution Baboon

ANCIENT GREECE

The Ancient Greeks believed the goddess Athena created the potters wheel

Geometric Pottery 900BCE-700BCE

Art Facts:

- ✦ The use of geometric shapes makes it distinctive.

- ✦ Common patterns painted – <u>circles, semi-circles, horizontal lines, zig-zags, keys, meander rays.</u>

- ✦ Circles were painted with multiple brushes fixed to a compass.

- ✦ Every space is filled with patterns.

- ✦ Horizontal bands filled with patterns cover the entire pot.

- ✦ There were only a few shapes of pottery at this time. Most were made to hold liquids and oils.

- ✦ Some of the shapes of pottery used were hydria, volute krater, lekythos, kylix, amphora and oinochoe.

- ✦ From the 8th Century BCE, geometric pottery decoration began to include human figures and animals.

Image three: Pitcher (oinochoe), Greek late Geometric Period 740-730 BC, Boiotia, MFA Boston

Common pot shapes in geometric pottery

AMPHORA
Storing liquids

OINOCHOE
Wine jug

KRATER
For mixing wine and water

PYRIS
Holds cosmetics and jewellery

KYLIX
Drinking cup

HYDRIA
Water pitcher

Art and Design Activity:

What you will need:

- Brown or orange card

- Pen and a pencil

- Clay garden pot

- Black acrylic paint

- Paintbrush

- OR - if you are feeling more adventurous, why not buy some scratch paper and scratch out your design and pot on that.

1. First, decide which shape of pot you want to design. Once you have decided, cut out your pot shape in the card you have.

2. With your black pen, using the patterns you have seen on the pots, create your own designs. Remember to make your designs in horizontal sections.

3. Once you are happy with your design, you can get your paint and clay pot ready and draw and paint the designs you have chosen onto your pot.

4. Once you have finished and it is dry (best to leave it for 24 hours), why not use it to store your paint brushes and colouring pens? Why not display your paper drawing also? Draw and cut out a white column, stick it on a wall and place your pot on top.

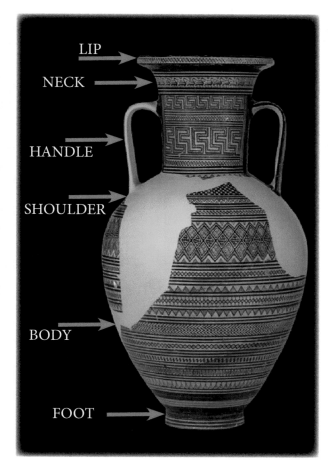

Image four: The Elgin Amphora. Greek, made in Athens circa 760-750 BC. Late Geometric period. Attributed to artist Dipylon Painter. World History Archive

Greek Geometric Pottery Patterns

Greek Vase Patterns in Geometric Pottery

Pottery was used in Ancient Greece as vessels to carry liquids and solids. They liked to decorate their pottery, and it became an art form in its own right. Most of the pottery shapes remained the same over many centuries, so painters showed their skills by decorating them.

Image five: Detail of 7th c BCE amphora, Anicent Thera, Santorini, Archaeological Museum, Thera

Finish the patterns on each line

COMPLETE THE SYMMETRY OF THE OTHER SIDE OF THE POT

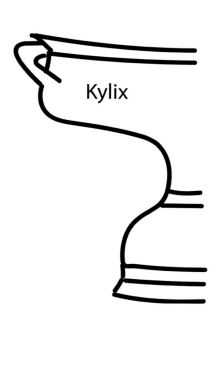

Kylix

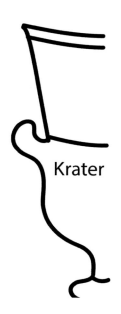

Krater

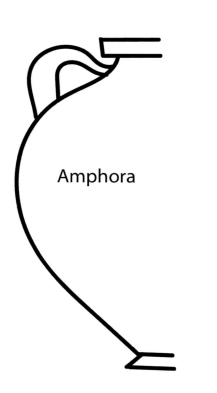

Amphora

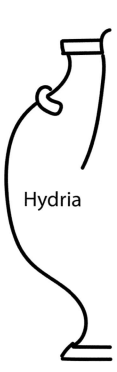

Hydria

Glossary:

Acrylic - A type of plastic used to make paint

Compass - An instrument with two legs that is used to create circles.

Distinctive - Something that is unusual or set apart from the normal.

Geometric - Pattern that is created using shapes such as circles, triangles or straight lines. Shapes that are repeated to make a pattern.

Horizontal - People sleep in a horizontal position in their beds.

Pattern - Something that is repeated more than once. (Like the activity above)

Using the words in the glossary, find them in the word search below

Q	M	O	C	P	T	W	E	K	N	W	A
Q	X	Y	Y	H	A	K	V	E	L	M	C
U	H	U	W	Y	A	T	I	A	I	J	R
M	M	Y	V	E	L	A	T	Y	E	Q	Y
I	U	P	O	A	L	N	C	E	P	Z	L
Q	Y	I	N	H	O	O	N	N	R	J	I
J	E	A	M	Z	M	J	I	L	R	N	C
J	L	D	I	P	Y	W	T	F	K	V	I
O	D	R	A	H	H	B	S	R	V	J	A
U	O	S	S	F	F	B	I	W	H	Q	F
H	S	O	D	P	A	Z	D	K	E	H	I
G	E	O	M	E	T	R	I	C	C	O	F

Geometric   Compass   Distinctive

Pattern   Horizontal   Acrylic

NAZCA POTTERY

Pre-Columbian 100BCE-800AD

Human & Art Facts:

In the western world, children are given outlined images to colour in. In Nazca pottery decoration, the colour is painted in first and then the black outline afterwards.

- ✦ On the south coast of Peru from 200BCE-600AD, the Nazca civilisation grew.
- ✦ They are now famous for their pottery, textiles and geoglyphs.
- ✦ Made a variety of vessel shapes. They were mostly used for storage or cooking.
- ✦ Some of the pottery shapes include bowls, vases, goblets, jars, plates and double spout bottles. The double spout bottle is one of the most prestigious shapes.
- ✦ Potters used a shallow plate or bowl as the support; unlike other pre-Columbian potters, they never used moulds in making their ceramics.
- ✦ The pottery decorations you will see are animals, geometric patterns and mythical creatures.

- ✦ Their pottery is polychrome (more than one colour) and made from slip paints (paint put on a pot before it is fired).
- ✦ The colours you will see are black, white, purple, red, dark red, light red, orange, light orange, yellow, grey, brown, violet and pink.
- ✦ These slip paints were made from minerals, like iron oxides, kaolin and carbon.
- ✦ Potters used paint brushes made from human hair, Alpaca or Llama wool.
- ✦ Vessels are painted with as many as eight to twelve colours!

Image Six: Peru, Pre-Inca civilization, Nazca culture, double spout and bridge vessel with painted monkey figures
Credit: DEA/G. DAGLI ORTI

POLYCHROME PAINTING is unique to Nazca Pottery.

No other ancient Peruvian ceramic art uses the variety and quantity that they did.

Designs Taken from Some Nazca Pottery

Geoglyphs

- Geographical Facts
- 400AD-650AD people from Nazca, Peru began to etch a number of lines and pictures into their desert plateau.
- They scraped away the top layer of reddish soil and pebbles. This left behind the light under layer.
- More then 30 animals have been found. For example, a hummingbird, a monkey, a spider, fish, shark or a llama, as well as patterns of triangles, trapezium, quadrangles, single and parallel lines.
- The geoglyphs are very similar to the designs decorated on their pottery.

Fun Fact
Over the years, scholars have argued over the reasons why Geoglyhs were made.
Some ideas:
They had primitive hot air balloons to look at them from above.
Road signs for travellers.
Irrigation system for collecting rain water.
Landing strips for aliens!

The spider

The Monkey

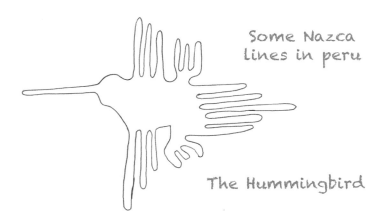

Some Nazca lines in peru

The Hummingbird

Activity One   Make Your Own Nazca Lines

Nazca lines and pottery decoration have the same cartoon styling. There is a clear focus on lines, whether etched into the ground or outlined on pottery. This activity focuses, therefore, on LINES.

You will need:

- A Sketchbook/white paper
- A black sheet of card
- Glue - PVA is fine
- A roll of white string
- Pencil

Instructions:

1. Do some research on the different animals and creatures the Nazca Civilisations created and pick your favourite one. On your white sheet of paper, or in your sketchbook, draw the design out, then go over it in thick black pen.

2. Once you are happy with the design, draw it on to your black card.

3. Cut a long piece of string from the roll (it will need to be long enough to go all around the shape). Now, dip the string into the pot of glue, get it really wet. Carefully, start to place the string over the lines you have drawn. Continue all around the shape until you cannot see any of your drawing and are left with the image, which is now made up from the string.

4. You should now be left with a Nazca drawing. See how the creature, now made from string, stands out from the black card. Just like how the Nazca Lines pop out from the sky.

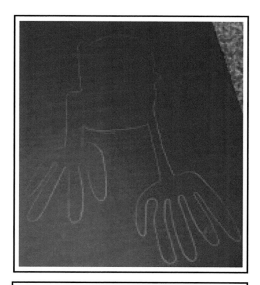

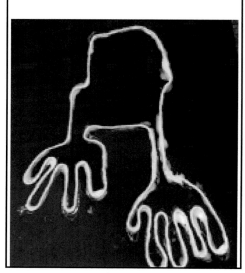

Activity Two

Astronaut Nazca Geoglyph, Aerial image taken 7 Sept 2010.

What you will need:

- White T-shirt (an old one is fine)
- Your hand drawn Nazca image
- A food bag/clingfilm
- Elmer's Washable No Run School Glue Gel (Amazon)
- Fabric dye (colour is your choice)
- Bucket or bowl
- Kitchen gloves
- Water

Step One

Instructions:

1. Choose a design and draw it on a white piece of paper. Use a black pen to draw out your design and then colour it in with black.
2. Wrap your paper in clingfim and insert it into the middle of your T-shirt, so that the design faces out through the front of your T-shirt.
3. With your glue, trace over the drawing design. Make sure to go over your entire design, don't miss any of it! I have decided to only do the outline. It's up to you whether you fill it in or just do the outline.
4. Now, you will need to let your T-shirt dry. The glue needs to be completely dry. Mine took about 24 hours to dry.
5. The next day, put on your kitchen gloves, and fill up your bucket or bowl with your fabric dye (follow the instructions on the box). Dunk your T-shirt into it and swirl it around. Leave it in there for as long as the instructions tell you to.
6. Get out your T-shirt and let it dry. And there you have it, your very own watermark Nazca line T-Shirt!

Step Two

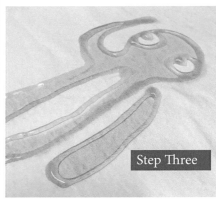

Step Three

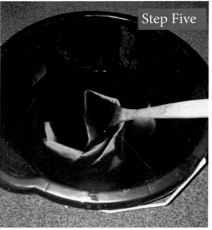

Step Five

Tip – Make sure to wash your T-shirt on its own after you wear it as there will be some dye that will come off in the wash. You don't want your other clothes turning that colour!

Step Six

Glossary

Geoglyph – Designs made by the Nazca people in the desert on the ground that can be seen from the sky.

Polychrome – Something painted and decorated in many different colours.

Parallel lines – Two lines that run along side each other, like an equal sign.

Quadrangle – A two-dimensional geometric shape that has four sides, like a square or rectangle.

Trapezium – A two dimensional geometric shape with four sides, two of which are parallel.

Using the words in the glossary, find them in the word search below

P	W	H	Q	L	Q	I	W	D	Q	O	T	R
O	O	Y	Y	P	M	Z	T	K	U	R	Q	A
G	H	L	J	L	Y	H	T	F	A	Z	W	K
I	I	T	Y	E	G	E	P	P	D	V	O	F
C	R	J	C	C	T	O	E	A	R	P	X	C
W	O	U	N	R	H	Z	E	G	A	S	U	T
S	A	V	S	Y	I	R	N	G	N	E	E	J
T	R	A	G	U	J	G	O	B	G	N	T	E
L	Z	X	M	L	S	J	O	M	L	I	H	Y
O	M	Y	W	L	A	B	S	L	E	L	Q	P
B	W	G	P	A	N	E	N	N	N	V	P	C
K	N	R	R	K	I	Z	V	C	L	M	Y	B
L	E	L	L	A	R	A	P	S	H	C	G	I

Geoglyh   Trapezium
Polychrome   Quadrangle
Parallel Lines

23

TANG DYNASTY

China 618-906 AD (7th-9th Century)

ART Facts :

- The Tang dynasty saw, for the first time, the use of ceramics as a decorative art.
- The most popular design was <u>sancai</u> which in Chinese literally means, 'three colours'. Potters used three mixed colours for decorating.
- The glaze runs and shows a splash effect.
- The most common colours used were green (copper), Amber (iron) and brownish-yellow-blue (cobalt).
- Famous for its coloured tomb figurines. These included horses, camels and dogs, as well as people.
- The sancai technique went all the way to Syria, Cyprus and Italy and was used in their pottery from the 13th-15th centuries.

Images seven and eight: Tomb figure of a horse, Tang Dynasty, 618-906AD, Getty Images, Photographer Werner Forman

Art Activity One

In this activity, we will try and create the same effect as the plate on the right. Using liquid watercolours and masking fluid, we can recreate the decoration.

What you need:
- Watercolours
- Watercolour paper
- Paint brush
- Masking fluid and paint brush
- Pencil

Instructions:

1. Choose a Tang Dynasty design, any type or shape of ceramic. Draw out the shape on your paper.

2. Using a paint brush, dip it into the masking fluid and paint the white parts of the ceramic design onto the paper. It is worth doing it by a light so that you can see where you have put the fluid. It dries quickly and dries waxy, so you will be able to see the reflection. Leave to dry for a few minutes.

3. Pick out a few colours and have some fun, painting the rest of the design. You can paint straight over the masking fluid. The paint will just run straight off it! Professional watercolourists would then rub the masking fluid off with a special rubber, but there is no real reason in this activity.

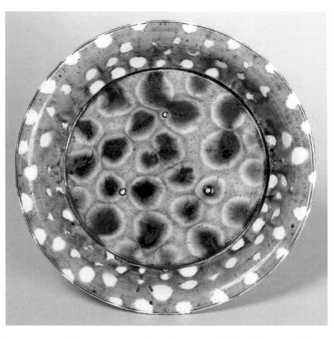

Image nine: Rare sancai-glazed pottery dish, Christies, Fine Chinese Ceramics and Works of Art, 21 March 2002, New York, sold for $88,125

Watercolour tip:

To get the 'bleeding' paint effect as seen in the middle of the plate, top right, you need to make sure that you work quickly. Paint the background one colour and then while still wet, use another colour and make dots by touching your paintbrush to the paper. It should spread into the background colour. While this colour is still wet, use another colour and dot on top of those dots. This paint will then bleed into the under dot.

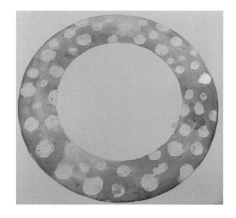

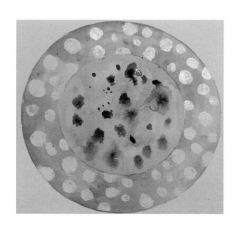

Art Activity Two

In this activity, we will be concentrating and learning from the dripping technique that is used in some Sancai pottery.

What you will need:

- A clay or plastic plant pot (B&Q/Homebase)
- Something to stand the pot upside down on
- Three different colours of acrylic paint
- Cardboard or a splatter mat
- If you are thinking of using your finished pots outside, you will need to have either a terracotta pottery spray or clear polyurethane spray

Instructions:

1. Put your splatter mat or cardboard down and place your pot on top of the item you chose to balance it on. The pot ideally needs to be off the ground so that the paint can flow properly off the ends and not pool.

2. Start with one of your paints and squirt it straight from the bottle to the bottom of the pot (now, face upwards).

3. On top of that colour, squirt the next colour, and then the next and so on. Soon, you will see the paint overflow the top bit and start to flow down the sides. Watch the dripping paint and compare to the Sancai pottery. You may notice that acrylic paint is much thicker than the glazes that they used in the Tang Dynasty. Glazes are more watery and transparent than acrylic paint. Think how you might be able to create that effect still using acrylic paint. When the paint flows down the pot, try blowing hard on it to encourage the paint to flow downward.

4. Once you are happy, leave your pot to dry for 24 hours. Now you can do whatever you would like with it. If you are putting it outside with plants in it, you will need to apply a spray to protect the paint. Otherwise, if it rains the paint will wash off and make a big mess!

Image ten: Ewer, Tang Dynasty . (618-907), 7th Century, Earthenware, Metropolitan Museum

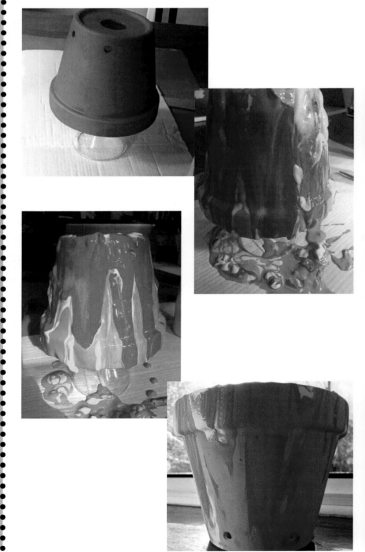

Glossary

Figurines - A small statue in the shape of a human or animal. They can be made of clay, plastic, wood, glass or metal.

Glaze - Glaze for pottery is a layer that seals the decoration on a ceramic body through firing in a hot kiln (an oven that bakes pottery). Glaze can not only waterproof a piece of pottery but decorate and colour them too.

Masking fluid - A liquid that watercolour painters use. You use it when you want certain areas of your paper to remain white. For example, if you want to paint a brick wall brown but you want the cement lines in between each brick to be white, you can paint the masking fluid as the brick lines. When you paint over it, the paint will not settle on these lines.

Sancai - A Chinese word that means three colours. It is a type of decoration that was used on pottery in China.

Using the words in the glossary, find them in the word search below

L	D	I	D	L	C	N	F	R	K	S	G	X	M
Z	E	M	A	B	N	G	O	I	H	M	vO	A	L
X	C	D	L	C	N	T	O	M	U	Z	S	X	K
E	O	R	N	T	N	B	M	B	O	K	K	F	O
F	R	E	A	E	Q	A	R	P	I	I	O	Q	R
L	A	J	D	W	I	U	S	N	Y	N	I	D	E
E	T	L	S	B	A	U	G	J	A	M	K	M	A
P	I	A	B	D	X	F	L	D	J	F	V	J	T
F	V	P	Y	Q	L	R	D	W	I	L	H	C	X
H	E	O	J	U	S	E	N	I	R	U	G	I	F
E	A	I	I	X	B	Z	F	I	U	E	U	T	E
B	R	D	G	M	E	A	S	M	K	R	V	N	L
H	T	Y	V	A	M	L	T	F	I	F	X	C	F
L	R	M	F	H	G	G	W	S	X	D	Y	O	K

Glaze   Masking fluid

Sancai   Figurines

ISLAMIC CERAMICS

From the 9th–14th Century

Art Facts

✦ Pottery in the Middle East was only considered an art after contact with China's pottery at the end of the 8th century.
✦ The most important creation of Iraqi pottery was <u>lustre painting</u>.

Islamic Pottery Decoration:

✦ Inscriptions
✦ Geometric patterns
✦ Plant designs
✦ Animal designs
✦ People designs

Islamic Tiles

FROM THE 9TH CENTURY, TILES WERE MADE TO DECORATE IMPORTANT BUILDINGS LIKE PALACES, MOSQUES, HOLY SHRINES AND GRAVES.

Image eleven: A panel composed with tiles in shape of eight pointed stars and crosses, stone paste lustre painted, c.260-70, Iran, Metropolitan Museum, New York

Image twelve: A star-shaped tile, Iran, Varamin, made from stone paste with lustre-painted on opaque white glaze. 1262–63, Metropolitan Museum

Geometrical shapes used in Islamic art

Hexagon

Octagon

Decagon

Square

Triangle

Six point star

Eight Point star

Ten point star

Circle

Parallelogram

Six fold rosette

Eight fold rosette

Ten fold rosette

In this pattern, which three geometric shapes can you see?

Activity One   Making a Lattice Wall Hanging

What you will need:
- White canvas
- A craft knife
- Cutting mat
- Pencil
- Black Pen
- Coloured card of your choice. Big enough to fit the back of your canvas.

Instructions:

Stage one:
Design in pencil, a repetitive pattern using one of the shapes shown on the last two pages. Once you are happy with it, go over the pencil with black pen. Now, sellotape it face down onto the front of the canvas.

Stage two:
Turn your canvas over so that you can see the wooden frame and your pattern showing through. With a pencil, trace over your design and then remove the paper design from the front.

Stage three:
Put your canvas front down on your cutting mat and with your craft knife, start to carefully cut out your design. Once you have finished, turn it over and hang it up.
If you fancy having colour, why not put coloured paper in the back.

Feeling adventurous? Why not try doing a lampshade and watch the pattern that appears when the light is on!

John Frederick Lewis' painting, 'Interior of a School, Cairo', 1865, watercolour, Victoria and Albert Museum

Islamic art uses a lot of geometric repetition. It can be seen in mosaics, paintings, carpets and even wooden fretwork in their housing. See how the light shines through them.

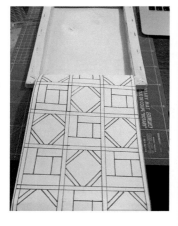

Activity Two

Repetition, Pattern, Colour & Rotational Symmetry

What you will need:

✦ Small rectangular or square rubbers
✦ Permanent Black markers (fine)
✦ Linoleum carving tools
✦ Watercolour pens or paint

Instructions:

1. In your sketchbook, draw a grid of rectangles that are the size of your rubber.

2. Using a pen, draw a simple pattern on your rubber and with the carving tool, carefully carve out parts of the design that you want to be white. Remember what you leave on the rubber is what the colour part will show.

3. Once you are happy, use watercolours and gently paint parts of the rubber in one colour and some other parts in another.

4. Now, gently and carefully, turn it and firmly press it down in the first, top left hand drawn rectangle in your sketchbook.

5. Continue to paint the rubber and print.

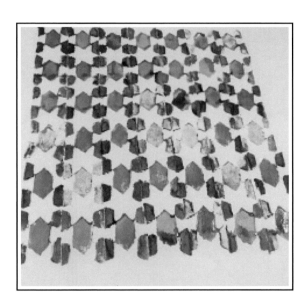

What shapes has your design created?

What shape can you see that has been made in white in the pattern above?

This is a common Islamic geometrical design.

Using the already coloured square section, fill in the rest with the correct colours.

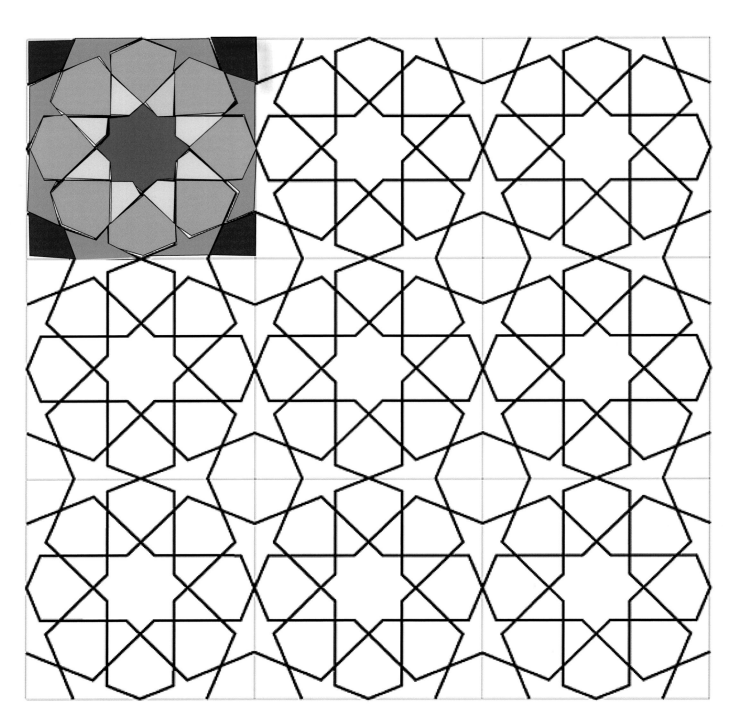

How many different variations of stars can you see?

How many stars are in this image?

How many eight fold rosettes can you see?

Glossary

Geometric - In this case, a design that is made up of shapes, often circles, squares, rectangles and triangles.

Inscription - Writing that is painted, cut or imprinted onto paper, brick, stone or any other hard surface.

Lustre Painting - A way of painting glazed pottery with metallic powder (pigment). It was first invented in Persia (now Iran).

Mosque - A place of worship for people of the religion of Islam, the equivalent in Christianity would be a cathedral.

Rosette - A formation of shapes that make up something that looks like a flower, often a rose.

Shrine - A specific place where the remains of a holy person or an object they used is kept. People will often make pilgrimages (travel far distances) to see them.

Using the words in the glossary, find them in the word search below

X	Y	X	C	G	R	C	J	Z	M	O	R	K	G
H	Z	Z	B	X	E	M	P	Y	Y	F	H	N	G
C	T	B	E	V	O	O	J	V	K	A	I	K	D
I	P	U	T	S	I	L	M	T	Q	T	N	M	R
J	D	L	Q	X	S	M	K	E	N	X	B	K	O
V	L	U	N	H	U	F	Q	I	T	Y	Z	D	S
M	E	S	X	W	Z	M	A	F	P	R	H	F	E
G	E	T	Q	C	K	P	Q	F	S	S	I	S	T
J	E	T	P	X	E	K	U	M	R	D	T	C	T
G	O	Z	Z	R	T	U	S	A	D	D	C	R	E
Y	W	S	T	H	T	Q	C	L	S	P	A	S	Z
W	I	S	T	K	I	R	O	S	P	T	E	P	Z
Q	U	I	N	S	C	R	I	P	T	I	O	N	L
L	E	N	I	R	H	S	I	I	K	D	M	I	C

Lustre Painting	Geometric	Mosque
Inscription	Rosette	Shrine

SONG DYNASTY

China 960–1279 (10th–13th Century)

Art Facts:

- Jun ware was created in the Tang Dynasty and reached a high point of production in the Song dynasty.
- Jun ware is one of the <u>five great wares</u> of China; the others are Ding, Ru, Guan and Ge.
- There are four colour types of Jun ware: green, lavender-blue, lavender-blue with purple splashes and purple-and-blue streaked.
- A chemical reaction that happens while firing and cooling means that the colours we see are an optical illusion.
- The purple splashes are made from copper oxide in the glaze.
- Some were fired twice to perfect the glaze.
- There were very strict rules for making these ceramics. If they were not perfect, they were destroyed.
- Ceramics from the Song dynasty are fairly rare and therefore are precious pieces that go for thousands of pounds at auction.

Image fourteen: Bottle with purple splashed blue glaze (Yuhuchunping), Jun stoneware Northern Song Dynasty, AD 1000-1127, British Museum

34

Art Activity One

What you will need:

✦ Watercolour paper
✦ Plastic container, big enough for your paper
✦ Dropper (Amazon)
✦ Liquid watercolours (Amazon, Hobbycraft)
✦ Paintbrush
✦ Water

Instructions:

1. Fill your container with a couple of inches of water and choose a couple of watercolours.
2. With your dropper, drop a few drops of a watercolour into the water. Don't do too many. Now, add a few of another colour.
3. With the end of your paintbrush, gently swirl the paint around into a pattern.
4. Slowly lower a sheet of watercolour paper onto the top of the water and leave it there for a few seconds. Now, gently lift it out and put it face up to dry. Does your pattern have the swirls like the Jun ware on these pages?
5. Once dry, you may need to put it under something heavy to stop the paper from curling. What you do next is up to you. You could draw a vase on it and cut it out, make it into a card to send someone or draw birds on it (mine looks like the sky).

Image fifteen: Shallow plate with thick opalescent blue glaze with copper pigment of purple splashes. Jun ware, Northern Southern Song, AD 1115-1234, British Museum

Step one

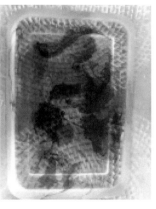

Step two & three

Step four

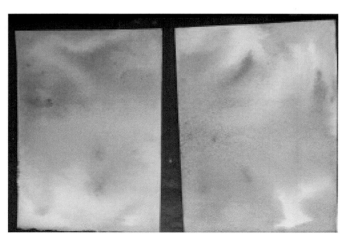

Step five

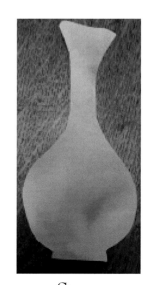

Step six

These Chinese pottery shapes were popular during the Song dynasty.

Meiping Vase   Yuhuchunping Vase   Huluping Vase

Using each half of the pottery shown here as a starter, complete the other side.

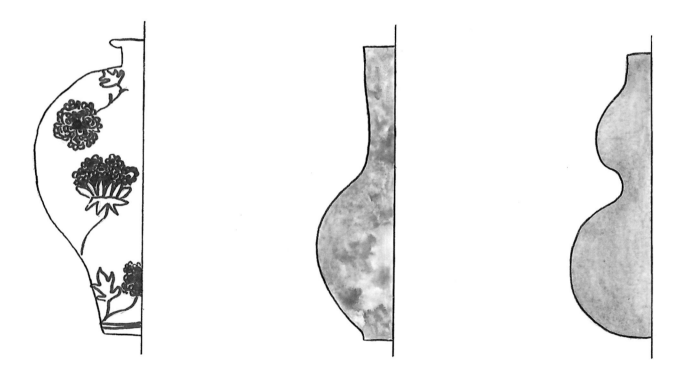

Using the examples in this chapter, copy one of the patterns off the pottery piece.

Art Activity Two

What you will need:

✦ A compass
✦ A pencil if your compass doesn't have one attached
✦ Three liquid watercolours (I've chosen colours like those used in Jun ware)
✦ Water
✦ Paintbrushes
✦ Watercolour sketchbook

Jun ware reminds me of pictures of planets in space. The way the glazes mix and merge with each other gives a beautiful sense of harmony. The swirl-like colours remind me of clouds and moving gases. With this in mind, we are going to create three different planets of our own.

1. Firstly, have a look through the images in this chapter. If you look carefully, you will be able to see three slightly different ways the glazes settle on the ceramics. Now, look at some planets on the internet. Earth is a good example to look at with its clouds.
2. In your watercolour sketchbook, draw three different sized circles with the help of your compass.
3. I have chosen to let the different ways the glazes appear on Jun ware be my inspiration for my planets. Some Jun ware is subtle and the colours beautifully harmonise. Others are more of a deep, dark blueish purple with freckling all over. Lastly, some Jun ware has distinct cloud-like shapes that contrast in colour.

Image sixteen: Jun ware dish with opalescent blue and lavender splashed glazes, Jin dynasty, 1115-1234, British Museum

Tips for using watercolours

- With a paint brush soaked in water, wet your paper first before painting, this will give your paint something to sink into.
- Build your layers slowly with light paint washes done one at a time. Leave them to dry for a few seconds and then build on that colour.
- If you want the paint to swirl into each other, you will need to work quickly so that the paint can mix on the paper and dry naturally together.

Step one

Step two

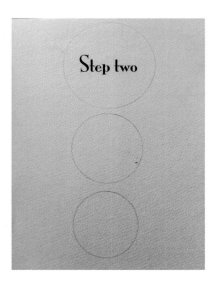

Step three

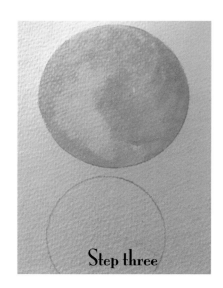

finished product

Glossary:

Dropper - A plastic suction device used to suck up a liquid. It has a thin long nozzle and a bulbous end. When dipping in the liquid, you squeeze the bulb and then release it. The liquid will then rise into the tube. To use the liquid, simply squeeze the bulb gently and it will come out.

Huluping - A vase described as double-gourd, which means it looks like the figure of 8.

Meiping - A vase described as shaped like a plum.

Optical illusion - The use of colour, light or patterns that make images that trick your eyes into seeing something different than what actually exists.

Paint Wash - A diluted paint or ink wash, meaning a little paint or ink watered down. This means it just stains the paper lightly with colour. Once this dries for a few seconds, one can build the colour up gradually.

Yuhuchunping - A vase described as shaped like a pear.

Using the words in the glossary, find them in the word search below

N	F	X	F	A	P	M	P	G	V	M	U	Y	I	U
Z	O	I	P	C	C	C	U	N	Z	E	Z	F	S	G
D	M	I	Q	X	F	R	B	I	V	H	J	M	K	G
B	Y	J	I	U	I	L	D	U	Y	J	W	C	V	A
V	A	K	R	P	L	D	M	L	G	A	O	H	A	G
H	D	M	X	K	I	L	Z	U	S	T	B	J	D	F
U	Y	G	V	Q	A	N	I	H	T	E	G	V	B	W
J	Z	A	X	C	A	D	G	S	P	T	R	A	G	I
U	G	N	I	P	N	U	H	C	U	H	U	Y	P	H
P	Y	T	G	L	T	Y	D	I	Z	Z	Z	F	A	E
Y	P	I	S	J	Q	D	X	E	I	W	M	H	I	U
O	D	R	O	P	P	E	R	O	N	I	M	D	N	D
S	Z	E	S	B	R	S	E	P	V	M	M	A	T	P
E	Q	I	R	D	O	M	V	H	O	H	Y	F	X	Y

Optical illusion   Paint Wash   Yuhuchunping
Dropper   Meiping   Huluping

MING DYNASTY

China (1368–1644) 13th–16th Century

The Facts:

✦ 18 different emperors ruled throughout the Ming dynasty!

✦ Design styles and pottery shapes changed with every new emperor.

✦ By the 14th century, development of blue and white porcelain was popular.

✦ Blue and white decoration was made by painting the blue under the glaze.

✦ By 1430s, enamels (the colours) were applied over the glaze and their ceramics became very colourful.

✦ You can also see greens, reds and yellow colours in some of the ceramics.

✦ During this dynasty, China began to trade worldwide. Europe was their biggest buyer. This porcelain was called Kraak Ware.

✦ Most Of the designs on their pottery had some sort of symbolism.

✦ The Chinese believed that dragons were warm hearted with the power to bring rain, floods and even hurricanes to the land. They were a symbol of power, strength and good luck.

Image seventeen: Jar, Ming Dynasty (1368-1644), Xuande mark and period (1426-1435), Metropolitan Museum, NY.

SYMBOLISM
THE DRAGON AND PHOENIX: MALE & FEMALE: EMPEROR AND EMPRESS

In the Han Dynasty (206BC-220 AD), the Chinese Emperor decreed that he was a descendant of the dragon. Since then, most emperors claim this too. Calling themselves 'The True Dragon, Son of Heaven'. The symbol of the dragon became recognised as the ruler. Soon the Phoenix symbolised his partner, the Empress. These mythical animals can be seen decorating all types of art in China.

Image eighteen: A large blue and white porcelain 'Phoenix' bowl Jailing Mark and Period, Sold at Sotheby's in Important Chinese Art, 13 May 2015, London

Art Activity One:

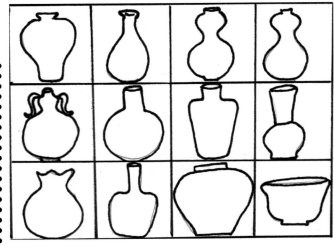

Some Chinese pottery shapes to choose from

What you will need:

✦ Sketchbook paper

✦ Oil pastels: blue and green

✦ Toothpick

✦ White and green acrylic paint

✦ Scissors

✦ Paintbrush

✦ Pencil

Instructions:

1. Have a look at some Chinese vases and choose a shape. Draw the shape of your vase on your sketchbook paper.

2. Look at different designs on Ming dynasty pottery and decide what pattern you want your vase to have on it.

3. Go back to your pottery shape, decide whether your pot is going to be a blue and white vase or a green and yellow vase. Using your oil pastel, colour in the vase shape.

4. With your paint, paint over the oil pastel colour and let it dry.

5. Once dry, look at the design you drew and with your toothpick scrape the design out on the paint. It will come off revealing the blue or yellow.

6. Once you have finished, cut it out and there you have it your own Ming vase!

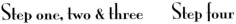

Step one, two & three   Step four

Step five & six

Kraak porcelain

Kraak porcelain was a special type of ceramics that were made especially for the European export market.

Image nineteen: A blue and white Kraak porcelain dish with bird and flowers, China, Wanli period. © 2011 Nagel - Auctions

Kraak ware was made from mid 16th-mid 17th century. The Portuguese transported them in huge ships called 'Carracks'. This is where the word Kraak comes from.

Image twenty: Anonymous Painter, circle of Joachim Credit National Maritime Museum, Greenwich, London, Caird Collection

A striking feature on Kraak porcelain is the panelled decoration. All the decoration is in separate boxes that are generally filled with plants and flowers. The middle scene is very often animals in a landscape.

Image twenty-one: A Kraak bowl from the Ming Dynasty, Wanli period, 1573-1619, From sale Paintings, Varia & Carpetsby, Lot 247, Bruun Rasmussen, Sept 28, 2010, Denmark

Art Activity Two:

In this activity, we will be making blue and white plate designs. In the 17th and 18th century, Europeans loved to decorate their houses with Chinese porcelain. Aristocrats would line their walls and fireplaces with them.

Instructions:

1. Using the basic design of Kraak porcelain, create some designs to draw onto your plates and bowls. Use pencil first to draw the design.
2. Using paint, pen or crayon, decorate your plates.
3. If you are using paint, you will need to wait for them to dry. If you have used pen or crayon, you can then display them on a blank wall with blue tack and experience what it would have felt like to live in the 17th century.

Aristocrats all over Europe began to collect porcelain and began making what soon became known as 'China Cabinets'. These were rooms with porcelain displayed everywhere! Like this room in Charlottenburg Palace, Berlin, called the 'Porcelain Chamber', finished in 1706.

This image is computer manipulated to highlight and easily draw your attention to the sheer number of porcelain pieces in the room.

Image twenty-one: Still Life with an oriental rug, Willem Kalf, (1619-1693), Ashmolean Museum

Notice the Chinese Kraak porcelain

17th century Dutch painters began to paint Kraak porcelain in their still lifes. Why not create a still life with the plates and bowls you made and take a picture. Or better yet draw it!

Glossary

Carracks - Large Portuguese ships that could withstand heavy seas and could hold large amounts of foods and goods.

Export market - A country foreign to your own that you are selling goods and services to. For example, the Chinese and Japanese sold porcelain to Europeans.

Emperor - A supreme ruler of an empire. They have more power then a king or queen; their rule is undisputed.

Empress - In China and Japan, the Empress was married to the Emperor.

Still life - A painting genre that depicts mostly foods or inanimate objects like musical instruments or carpets and glasses.

Using the words in the glossary, find them in the word search below

T	S	K	S	K	B	C	K	C	Z	C	U	I	I	K
R	J	M	V	S	O	C	M	Z	A	N	D	B	M	Q
O	H	O	V	Q	E	K	Y	R	K	R	D	J	R	U
P	O	H	O	J	I	R	R	O	F	H	T	B	F	Z
X	W	U	X	P	I	A	P	W	H	E	N	L	D	Y
Q	W	L	B	K	M	C	L	R	E	G	U	W	H	H
B	D	M	S	W	A	I	I	D	T	I	L	Y	W	X
Q	Q	C	K	V	K	M	G	Y	M	X	N	I	C	T
R	O	R	E	P	M	E	J	S	T	I	L	L	F	Q
N	G	J	D	T	N	C	T	U	G	W	X	G	H	E
S	T	U	O	K	H	O	J	R	Q	E	V	Q	V	P
U	M	Q	P	Q	J	R	K	U	V	X	G	A	A	C
U	H	M	W	G	X	D	U	Y	M	M	U	H	T	Y
R	T	E	U	G	D	Z	U	F	I	K	T	S	Y	J

Still   Life   Carracks   Export   Emperor   Empress

43

Italian Maiolica
Story Painting
15th–16th Century

ART FACTS

What is Maiolica?

Maiolica is a type of Italian pottery made of tin-glazed earthenware. It was popular during the 1400s-1600s. The tin in the glaze meant the glaze would be less likely to run in the kiln. This meant the designs were intricate and detailed. It also preserved the colours over time, which means the vibrant colours we see now would be exactly the same as when they were first painted! Wow!

Where did it come from?

Tin-glaze is commonly thought to have come across the sea from the Majorcan island port in Spain. See map

Popular ceramic shapes

- Tableware-plates, bowls, etc.
- Tiles
- Candlesticks
- Marriage plates
- Sculptural pieces
- Coat of arm plates
- Drug jars that stored herbs and medicines

Image twenty- three: Apothecary jar, c.1480, Italian, Maiolica, Metropolitan Museum

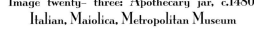

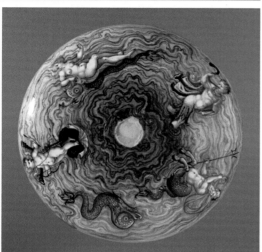

Image twenty-four & five: Italian Maiolica bowl, Workshop of Fontana Family, c. 1540–60, Urbino. Both sides are painted with Roman mythological subject matters. Front, soldiers on horseback, and reverse, cupid on a shell, naked woman on sea monster, a Triton with a horn, a centaur and another sea monster. Scene on the front possibly refers to the Punic wars. British Museum.

- In 1500, a new style of painting pottery emerged. It was called istoriato, which literally means story painting.
- The painters used the whole surface of the plate or vessel to paint the story as if it were a canvas.
- Some popular subject matters were Greek/Roman mythology, Biblical stories, Coat of Arms, wedding portraits or decorative patterns.

Some Italian Maiolica Designs

Art Activity

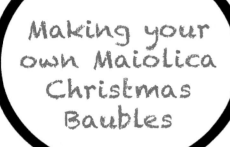

Making your own Maiolica Christmas Baubles

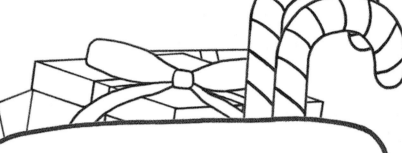

What you'll need:
- Ceramic or cardboard craft baubles
- Porcelain pens or paint
- Pencil
- Rubber/Nail Varnish remover
- Christmas tree

It is up to you whether you do the activity with cardboard craft baubles or ceramics. The ceramic baubles are more likely to end up looking like Italian Maiolica, as they will have the same vibrant colours that 15th century ceramics would have.

Instructions:

1. First, you will need to design your baubles, which you can do on the next page.
2. If you are making ceramic baubles you will need your porcelain pens; if you are doing cardboard ones, a pencil. In pencil, draw your design on the cardboard; on the ceramic bauble, draw your design using a black porcelain pen or paint. If you make a mistake, use a little nail varnish remover on a cotton pad to rub it off.
3. Once you are happy with your design, colour or paint the design using your pens or paint.
4. Carefully leave it to dry in a safe place for at least 24 hours. Once dry, decorate your tree!

Design Your Baubles

Glossary

Preserve – To keep something as it is.

Apothecary – A profession that can be dated back to 2600BCE! The term describes someone in the medical profession, so a doctor or pharmacist. An apothecary jar is where herbs, spices and medicines were stored.

Coat of Arms – An image that identifies a certain family. In England, at this time, people began to wear coat of arms on their armour and helmets that cover their faces so that people would know what side they were fighting on. Created in Tudor times when people began to wear armour and helmets that covered their faces. People began to have them displayed on their armour.

Istoriato – Literally meaning 'story painting'. Originated in 1500 in Faezna, Italy and was a way of painting on ceramics. Pottery painters began to paint narrative scenes onto plates as if they were like canvases.

Use the words in the Glossary and find them in the Word Search below

C	O	Q	T	V	T	C	Q	Y	N
O	T	S	N	T	E	U	A	R	B
A	A	P	Z	M	V	F	Z	A	L
T	I	R	N	Z	X	D	F	C	W
O	R	E	L	L	T	X	J	E	W
F	O	S	I	Z	D	R	Q	H	C
A	T	E	X	L	O	Z	J	T	U
R	S	R	S	E	E	M	L	O	X
M	I	V	P	P	Z	Q	H	P	C
S	B	E	T	G	Q	K	G	A	J

Preserve   Apothecary   Coat   Arms   Istoriato

Japanese Kakiemon Porcelain
1680-1725

![A pair of figures of Shishi]

Image twenty-six: A pair of figures of Shishi, Japanese, late 17th Century, Burghley House

Shishi, Komainu, Lion of Buddha, Foo Dog

What are they?

The Britannica describes their original significance to be a guardian presence in Buddhist Temples. They are stylised figures of snarling lions. They are generally created in pairs of a male with a paw on a ball and a female playing with a cub. They soon became depicted in Chinese and Japanese pottery as well as western imitations. They are popularly believed to have powerful mythical protective powers.

Where can they be seen?

Buddhist Temples, Imperial Palaces, porcelain, and door knockers as well as often seen in front of Chinese or Japanese restaurants in the west.

History

After the Ming dynasty in China collapsed in 1644, Japan took over as the main exporter of porcelain to Europe. Porcelain was transported on either large Chinese ships called Junks, or Dutch ships.

Europe, to begin with, wanted the old Chinese blue and white porcelain wares; however, a new style of bright enamel colours on a creamy white porcelain body rapidly took over. Notably, England fell in love with this style from 1660-1700.

Colours used in Kakiemon

Cerulean blue, soft-coral red, green, yellow and black enamels

Kakiemon Animals

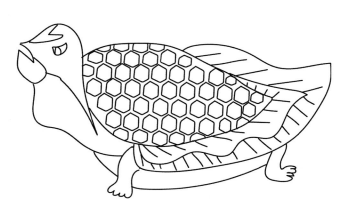
Why not try looking on the internet for a lion dog like me and try drawing it? Google images will have some, but why not try to find some on porcelain pots too?

Kakiemon animals became very popular in the west. Various types began to be made.

Most popular were the lion dogs and elephants; others that can be found are tigers, ducks and animals from myths. You can even find monkeys.

For images, have a look at the Christie's Auction House website, they often sell these pieces for a lot of money. One sale in particular has some good pieces:

Courtly Display: The Somlyo Collection of Japanese Ceramics

Activity

Making a Decoupage Kakiemon Animal

What you will need:

- Either a mache animal or a polystyrene animal
- Decoupage paper, at least two different types (try and find some with the colours used in Kakiemon pottery)
- Mod Podge (decoupage glue can be found online or in craft stores)
- Decoupage paintbrush/normal paintbrush is also fine.

Instructions:

1. Cut or tear your paper into pieces. Spread the glue with your paintbrush onto one part of your mache or polystyrene animal.
2. Place a piece of your cut-up paper onto the glue and press down with your fingers. Then, with the paintbrush, apply more glue on top of the paper to seal it onto the animal. Brush the excess glue off.
3. Continue this process, making sure the paper pieces overlap each other until the whole piece is covered. You do not want any empty areas.
4. Leave to dry.

Seasonal Decoupage Ideas

- Easter - Mache or polystyrene eggs
- Summer - Mache boxes covered in floral paper
- Halloween - Mache Pumpkins, cats and masks for costumes
- Christmas - Mache or polystyrene baubles, advent calendars, gift boxes and decorations.

Glue

Paintbrush

Hobbycraft mache animals

Decoupage paper

Glossary

Buddhist – Someone that follows the teachings of the Buddha.

Decoupage – The art and craft of decorating an object with paper, cuts and glue.

Exporter – A person, company or country that sends something or services to another country for sale.
For example, like China or Japan sending pottery to the West.

Imperial Palace – Relating to an empire. China and Japan has empires with Emperors and Empresses.
They lived in Imperial Palaces.

Mythical – Something that is in a myth or folklore. Can be idealised and fictitious (not real).

Using the words from the glossary above, find them in the word search below.

E	D	C	D	S	Y	R	R	T	M
P	G	N	G	E	S	E	D	S	A
M	I	A	D	Q	T	L	L	I	W
K	Y	M	P	R	M	Q	M	H	P
E	B	T	O	U	H	V	O	D	A
X	Z	P	H	D	O	Q	U	D	A
C	X	R	U	I	L	C	C	U	A
E	H	I	S	S	C	B	E	B	C
H	J	N	R	N	O	A	N	D	E
I	M	P	E	R	I	A	L	N	C

Buddhist   Decoupage   Exporter   Imperial   Palace   Mythical

The aesthetic movement was a late nineteenth century movement that championed pure beauty and 'art for art's sake', emphasising the visual and sensual qualities of art and design.

Tate Museum

Image twenty-seven: Earthenware Tile, attributed to Christopher Dresser, Factory of Minton Hollins & Co, Stoke-on-Trent, 1880, British Museum. Transfer-printed in blue underglaze on a white ground. The design is three flying cranes above waves with four small circles with stars above.

The movement became popular in the 1870s-1880s and was important in the decorative arts. This was revolutionised by William Morris in the 1860s with his company Morris & Co. These ideals were taken up by the famous London shop Liberty and widely commercialised. This was made more popular through the Art Nouveau movement later on.

History

- Victorians' use of ceramic tiles was a way of combining art with mass production.
- Good design began to be regarded over poor design and over-production.
- Led by William Morris, his ideas began to influence the production of beautiful products for the middle-class buyer.
- This became known as the Aesthetic Movement and later developed into the Arts & Crafts style.

Themes and Patterns

Design themes were heavily influenced by Japanese motifs:

- Bamboo
- Carp
- Cranes
- Waves

Ceramic backgrounds in 1870s-80s were often partly covered with:

- Fans
- Half circles
- Fretwork
- Prunus blossoms
- Zig-zags

These are twinned with abstract background designs like fret work, zig-zag borders, fans, half circles, prunus blossoms.

Image twenty-eight: Rare Minton Aesthetic Movement, tile attributed to Christopher dresser c.1870 (Found on Ebay)

Makers:

- Royal Worcester
- Christopher Dresser
- Wedgewood
- Doulton
- Minton

Colours used:

As to the surface decoration on pottery, it is clear it must never be printed...Think of your material. Don't paint anything on pottery, save what can only be painted on pottery; if you do, it is clear that however good a draughtsman you may be, you do not care about that special art.
William Morris, *The Lesser Arts of Life*, in Lectures in Art, 1882, p.195

The popular response to the reforms in art and design was superficial. It was decoration that was fashionable and there was little concern for the object or how it was made.
Victorian Ceramic Tiles, Julian Barnard, p10

V S

Many decided to decorate their tiles by hand, which gave them ultimate artistic freedom. However, the most popular way to decorate tiles was by transfer-printing.

Unfortunately for Morris, this new fashion for decoration meant that industrial manufacturers responded and therefore guaranteed the future of mass-produced ceramics and decorations for the masses.

Artistic Freedom Activity

What you will need:
- White candle- pillar is probably easiest, but you could use a round ball candle or even tea lights if you want.
- Henna tube (Amazon)

Instructions:
- William Morris encouraged hand done creations, as he believed this was where true beauty in art flourished. Think about what sort of design you would like to draw onto your candle. You will be using the henna tube like a paint brush.
- Experiment with your design on paper until you are satisfied with the result.
- Ideally, you want to draw straight onto the candle with the henna, but if you are not feeling confident, there is no reason why you can't use a pen to sketch on the design first and go over it with henna.
- You only need to cut a really small hole at the top of the henna tube for the henna to come out from. Too big and it will come out too fast and thick.
- Leave it to dry for a few hours and then test gently by touching some of the henna to see whether it is dried. Then you can light it!

Alternatively, why not take turns with a friend to create henna designs on each other's hands. Please ask your parents before doing this, it might be best to wait for the holidays to do this activity as the henna will stay on your hands for a couple of weeks.

Transfer Printing

What and How?

One way of transfer-printing was for the design to be inked onto tissue paper.

This was put on the surface of the raw tile and rubbed to move the ink from the tissue paper to the tile. The tile was then fired in the kiln at a low temperature, which fixed the ink to the tile. It was then glazed, colour could be added now, and then fired again.

Process

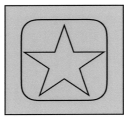  

Transfer Printing Activity

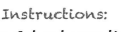

What you will need:
- One or two white pillar candles
- A coloured sharpie pen
- Wax cooking paper
- White tissue paper
- Heat tool
- Print-out of your design

Instructions:
- Cut out your tissue paper so that it is just the size of your design and trace over it with your sharpie pen. Once you have the outline drawn, take the tissue paper off the print-out and carefully block colour it all in. You don't want there to be any spaces or gaps.
- Make sure your tissue paper is the size of the candle height-wise. Trim if necessary. Then cut a large size piece of wax paper. You need to be able to wrap it around the whole candle, covering the tissue paper and candle. If you have excess at the back it will make it easier to hold.
- With your heat gun, heat up the area where the tissue paper is. After a minute or two, the candle wax and the wax on the wax paper will melt and perfectly transfer the tissue paper and pen work onto the candle! Let it cool and then gently remove the wax paper. If the tissue paper comes off, it means you haven't left it under the heat long enough. Put the wax paper back and do it again. Remember the wax side needs to be facing the candle to help fuse the tissue onto the candle.
- Once the wax paper is off, gently heat the candle again to make sure the sides of the tissue paper are melded onto the candle. And there you have it! Your own transfer printed candle!

Glossary

Commercialise – Something designed especially to make money and earn a profit.

Emphasis – Giving something special importance or value.

Henna – A reddy brown dye made from leaves of a Henna tree found in the Middle East and Asia. Used to decorate the hair and body.

Industrialisation – When a country or city develops industries very quickly on a wide scale.

Revolutionise – Completely change or overthrow something in favour of a brand new system.

Superficial – Something fake, only on the surface does it appear true, go deeper and it will reveal itself false.

Overproduction – Too much production or a certain item that is not needed.

Using the words from the glossary above, find them in the word search below.

N	S	E	J	J	H	H	Q	P	D	B	L	Y	A	O
M	O	S	M	L	Y	E	X	S	G	D	P	X	G	E
V	U	I	W	P	X	N	K	S	H	H	L	I	S	N
M	N	L	T	K	H	N	R	C	P	O	D	I	D	O
W	C	A	A	C	V	A	K	N	Z	P	N	I	F	P
X	C	I	G	S	U	F	S	U	R	O	G	F	X	H
Y	V	C	G	V	P	D	K	I	I	I	K	Y	J	M
A	Y	R	W	W	R	W	O	T	S	T	H	G	A	B
J	B	E	M	I	D	M	U	R	F	I	P	U	L	I
T	I	M	F	C	S	L	Y	C	P	N	I	N	L	M
R	Z	M	Q	Q	Q	H	H	Q	W	R	Z	B	W	U
R	Z	O	H	V	J	X	V	Q	C	T	E	N	C	E
D	P	C	E	E	B	H	W	Q	H	H	E	V	W	H
G	Q	R	P	W	J	B	O	Q	I	M	P	U	O	E
S	U	P	E	R	F	I	C	I	A	L	D	C	C	F

Commercialise	Revolutionise
Emphasis	Superficial
Henna	Industrialistion
Overproduction	

Arts & Crafts Movement
Britain 1880–1910

William F. De Morgan (1839–1917)

Image twenty-nine: Tile, William De Morgan, Victoria & Albert Museum, London

People

William Morris (1834–1896)

Morris, Marshall, Faulkner & Co.
-Made furniture, textiles, wallpaper, jewellery.

William F. De Morgan (1839–1917)
-Made glass, tiles, pottery

CFA Voysey (1857–1941)
-Made wallpaper, textiles, silverware

Characteristics of the Arts & Crafts Movement

1. Used and emphasised natural materials.
2. Simple forms are used, nothing extravagant. Construction is often exposed.
3. Nature is a main source of motifs. Patterns were flora and fauna from the British countryside, championing the country.
4. Many workshops were opened in the rural countryside and old techniques were revived.

Image thirty: Dish, 1888–89, William De Morgan, Victoria & Albert Museum, London

Motifs & Designs of the Arts & Crafts & De Morgan Ceramics

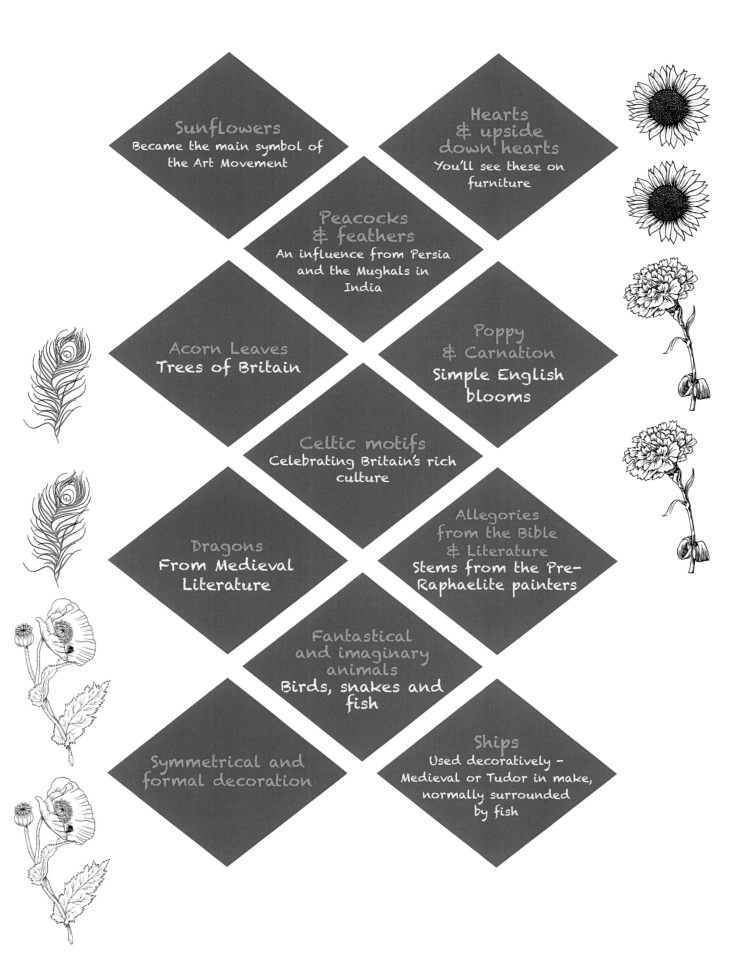

Sunflowers
Became the main symbol of the Art Movement

Hearts & upside down hearts
You'll see these on furniture

Peacocks & feathers
An influence from Persia and the Mughals in India

Acorn Leaves
Trees of Britain

Poppy & Carnation
Simple English blooms

Celtic motifs
Celebrating Britain's rich culture

Dragons
From Medieval Literature

Allegories from the Bible & Literature
Stems from the Pre-Raphaelite painters

Fantastical and imaginary animals
Birds, snakes and fish

Symmetrical and formal decoration

Ships
Used decoratively – Medieval or Tudor in make, normally surrounded by fish

A Two-Step Art Activity

Making Your Own Arts & Crafts Coasters and Creating a Ceramic Top Table

What you will need:

Step One
- Ceramic coasters – up to you how many (Amazon)
- Porcelain pens or sharpies (Amazon)
- Nail varnish remover with cotton pads
- Protective enamel finish

Step Two
- Second hand table
- Tile adhesive and spreader (to stick tiles down)
- Grout and spreader (for filling in between tiles)
- Furniture paint (chalk paint is an easy one to use)

Step One

Some Arts and Crafts tile designs

1. Begin by choosing an Arts & Crafts Design for each of your coasters and draw them out on paper. Now, with your pens, carefully draw them on the ceramic coasters.

2. Once you are happy with them, use the protective enamel finish to seal them. If you are only doing step one, then you have finished! Make your mum and dad happy by using them around the house for your hot and cold drinks. No more excuses for heat or water mug stains!

3. If continuing to step two, get your furniture paint and paint your table in your chosen colour, then leave to dry. Once dry, you should make sure you have enough coasters to cover the top of your table. If you do, design the pattern you want them to be in, take a picture or remember the order and then put tile adhesive on to the top of the table and carefully place the tiles down one by one. Leave to dry.

Step Two

4. Now insert the grout to fill in the spaces between the tiles. Smooth with a grout smoother and shine with a sponge to get the remainder off.

5. If you are not happy with seeing the edges of the tiles, then why not go to Homebase or B&Q and buy some wood trim moulding. Paint it the same colour as the table, put glue on the outer side of the tiles and press together.

Glossary

Celtic – Relating to the Celts or their languages, which constitute a branch of Indo-European family and include Irish, Scottish Gaelic, Welsh, Breton, Manx, Cornish, and several extinct pre-Roman languages such as Gaulish.

Decorative arts – The arts concerned with the production of objects that are both useful and beautiful.

Flora – The plants of a particular region, habitat or geological period.

Fauna – The animals of a particular region, habitat or geological period.

Industrialisation – The development of industries in a country or region on a wide scale.

Victorian – The time period during Queen Victoria's region in England.

Using the words from the glossary above, find them in the word search below.

N	B	O	A	S	M	A	S	P	E	G	I	C	V	Y
I	A	F	P	E	V	I	T	A	R	O	C	E	D	P
T	X	I	O	S	Q	P	P	K	H	S	O	C	Z	P
J	O	A	R	A	P	Y	C	Y	R	S	F	U	U	T
H	A	V	R	O	I	O	L	Z	C	E	F	O	U	N
I	O	O	B	E	T	M	H	P	I	Q	A	V	K	Z
U	L	L	D	L	U	C	P	O	T	F	A	U	N	A
F	Q	A	U	Q	U	O	I	I	L	P	K	U	U	E
A	W	E	P	H	M	V	D	V	E	M	B	I	K	R
S	R	S	B	A	S	P	S	Y	C	K	Q	P	J	A
J	Z	T	Q	R	B	A	S	D	S	Z	A	N	P	K
V	A	G	I	Z	E	E	Y	A	O	V	W	Z	X	O
S	M	R	O	H	Q	O	V	E	Y	A	P	U	R	F
B	M	T	T	Z	B	U	E	V	I	M	P	L	I	M
A	G	W	F	S	X	N	M	H	I	O	Q	E	P	B

Industrialisation   Decorative arts
Victorian   Flora
Celtic   Fauna

ART NOUVEAU
c.1890-1914

Image thirty-one; Porcelain vase with crystalline glaze, mounted with silver, c.1900, Siegfried Bing (1838-1905), France, Victorian and Albert Museum London

Europe: During the early 1890s, a new style of art and design was born. Born simultaneously in multiple countries under different names and areas of art. We now refer to it as the Art Nouveau.

Every art discipline was affected – architecture, illustration, fabric, jewellery, painting, ceramics and glass art. By 1895, the style was in full effect.

By 1900, at the Paris International Exhibition, the Art Nouveau style marked its belonging as the first global decorative style of the modern era.

Unlike the Arts & Crafts Movement, Art Nouveau artisans embraced new materials and used mass production to their benefit.

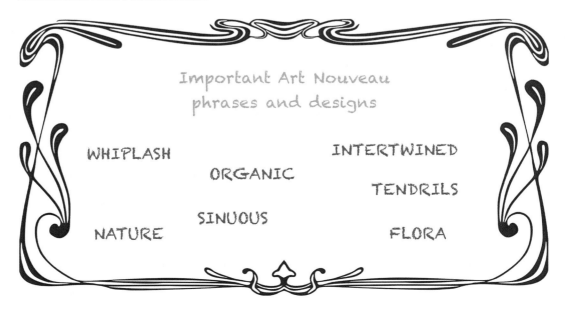

Important Art Nouveau phrases and designs

WHIPLASH   INTERTWINED

ORGANIC

TENDRILS

SINUOUS

NATURE   FLORA

Activity One

You will need:

- Two A4 sheets of white paper
- Two A4 sheets of white printer card
- Scissors
- Pencil
- Sharpies/felt tip pens/colouring pencils
- Some Art Nouveau tile designs
- Laminator - optional
- Photocopier/scanner and printer

Instructions:

- Looking on the internet/through some art nouveau books, pick out some designs on tiles that you like. You will need to pick 8-10 designs. Why not design some of your own?
- On equal sized squares, draw out each of the designs with pencil and then colour them in.
- Once you have finished, take them to a photocopier/scanner and copy/scan the pages. This way, you will have two of each design. Print two copies on white cards.
- Cut them out.
- If you want, you can laminate them to make them last longer.
- Now grab a partner and play!

Make Your Own Memory Game!

For two players

Rules:

Once you have created all your pairs of cards, you must face them down on the table or floor. Take turns to turn over two cards. If they are different, turn them back over. As the game goes on, remember which cards are where so when you turn over a card, you have already seen elsewhere you will be able to make a pair! Once you get a pair, take them out and put them on your side. The player with the most pairs wins at the end of the game!

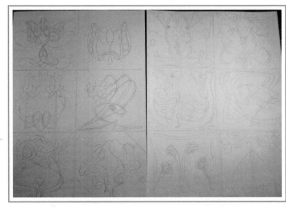

For inspiration: Google Art Nouveau Jewellery

You will need:
- Jewellery plier tools - I used 3 in 1 pliers and flat nose pliers

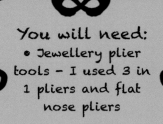

- Silver/copper jewellery wire 1.0-1.5mm size
- Ribbon/cord to use for the necklace part/ball and spring earring wire hooks - depending on whether you are making earrings or a pendant for a necklace
- Paper to draw your design on and a pencil or pen

Instructions:

1. Firstly, draw out some designs. Don't make them too difficult, as it can be a bit tricky using the tools.
2. Draw out your piece of jewellery to the actual size you want it and then measure and note down how long the sides are, etc. This will help you when making the piece. Why not try something simple to begin with?
3. Using your tools, cut, twist and curl the wire to the design you are happy with. It can be quite time consuming and you may not be happy to begin with so buy enough wire to experiment with first.
4. Once you are happy, make sure you have a little loop at the top of your design to thread a necklace or spring and ball earring hooks. Why not try doing a ring or a bracelet?

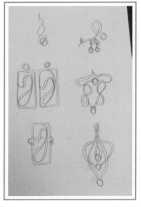

Art Nouveau jewellery is some of the most beautiful you can find. Designs have the same organic and flowing theme as the rest of the movement with stunning enameling and stones such as agate, garnet, and opal.

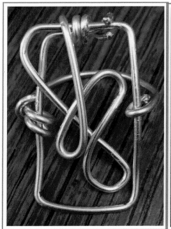

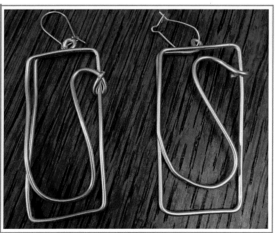

Think about Art Nouveau shapes, take your time but most of all have fun with it!

Glossary

- **Artisan** – A worker who has a skilled trade and generally works with their hands.
- **Intertwine** – Something twisted or twined together.
- **Organic** – Something that is living matter.
- **Simultaneously** – At the same time.
- **Sinuous** – Something that has many turns and curves.
- **Tendrils** – Something like a growing plant that grows in spirals, and stretches out.
- **Whiplash** – The visual effect of something moving forward very fast and then jerking back the other way.

Using the words from the glossary above, find them in the word search below.

G	B	M	Z	U	Y	N	Y	Z	N	Y	N	K	E
E	T	E	N	D	R	I	L	S	G	Y	S	N	Q
W	Y	W	B	O	O	O	S	G	C	A	L	A	S
Q	F	F	H	F	J	U	U	I	H	Z	T	A	N
X	R	F	S	I	Q	W	O	S	C	F	E	R	K
S	U	M	R	R	P	R	E	W	Q	N	I	T	K
M	L	E	N	L	G	L	N	X	I	B	F	I	S
I	I	F	O	A	F	I	A	W	F	S	W	S	K
D	S	X	N	U	D	R	T	S	D	X	O	A	I
U	E	I	B	C	X	R	L	R	H	H	Q	N	X
E	C	P	M	M	E	S	U	O	U	N	I	S	Q
A	Y	U	Q	T	Q	O	M	U	G	Z	G	A	E
V	D	F	N	Y	G	P	I	U	R	X	H	Y	T
M	T	I	L	W	L	A	S	M	P	D	P	V	R

Artisan   Intertwine   Organic   Simultaneously   Sinuous   Tendrils   Whiplash

ART DECO

CLARICE CLIFF 1899-1972
Shape, Colour, Form and Line

Art Facts:

✦ Clarice's drawing ability was noticed while working at A. J. Wilkinson's Royal Staffordshire pottery.

✦ In 1927, she was allowed to design and paint 60 pieces of old 'ghost' or white ware. 'Ghosts' are second pieces that have small imperfections and were not up to company standards. In 1929, they were called 'Bizarre Ware'. Her designs were an immediate success with all selling quickly.

✦ They were in the Art Deco style and were affordable for anyone to buy.

✦ Girl power – factories began to employ thousands of women and young girls to paint the pottery made. Each piece is unique with some being painted free hand and colours varying.

✦ Her early work was made up of simple geometric shapes and patterns.

✦ Colours used in the Art Deco movement were BLUE, BLACK, ORANGE, RED, GREEN, YELLOW, PINK AND BEIGE.

✦ The designs consist of combining fun shapes together.

✦ Though they stopped production in 1941, her pieces are still popular and collectable to this day.

Image thirty-two: Plate with sliced circle designs, Bizarre ware, c. 1930, Bonhams sold for £660

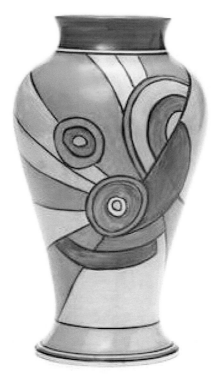

Image thirty-three: Meiping vase with sliced circle design, Bizarre ware, c.1930, Bonhams sold for £5400 in 2009

Some shapes used

Yo-Yo Vase

Conical sugar sifter

Conical odilion

Tea and saucer odilion

Tube vase

Bowl

Stepped candlestick

Sugar indivdual Conical

Activity One
You will need:
- A3 sketchbook paper
- Pencil and rubber
- Acrylic paint
- Paint brush and water
- Sellotape/ masking tape

Instructions:

1. Look at the designs on the ceramics on the pages and using them for inspiration, create your own design of circles, semi-circles, lines, squares and any other design you can see.
2. Pull a page out of your sketchbook and with a compass on the edge of the paper, in the middle, draw a large semicircle. Cut the semi-circle out. Like this:

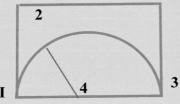

   You will be taking side 3 and wrap it round 1 and to 2 to create a cone shape. Be aware then that the space between 1 and 2 you want be able to see, so maybe draw a line like line 4.
3. Now, fill the entire piece with your design. You might want to once you have finished pick four colours of acrylic paint and paint your design.
4. Once you have finished, paint black outlines around your shapes to give them more definition - like how the painters have done on Clarice Cliff's pottery. Have a look and see if you can see them.
5. You must now wait until your paint dries - maybe a couple of hours. Once dry, bring the corners of the semi-circle together to form a cone. Now, tape them together to form the cone. And there you have it your own sugar sifter shaped cone just like Clarice Cliff's designs. If you are feeling adventurous, why not do another cone and try and re-create the Yo-Yo vase!

Image thirty-four: Auction assistant at Bonhams with set of 'Yo-Yo' vases by Clarice Cliff. There was an auction of 100 pieces of Clarice Cliff's ceramics in London on March 16, 2009. These pieces are rare and are dated c.1930. The seller Sevi Guatelli's collection was thought to be the best quality of pieces to have come onto the market. (Photo by Oli Scarff/ Getty Images)

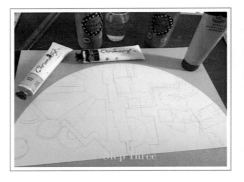

Step One and Two

Step Three

Step four

Step five

Step One

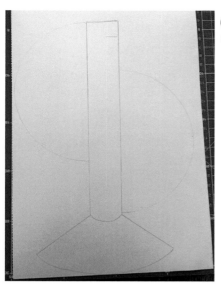

Step Two

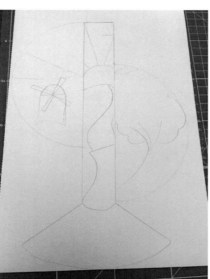

Step Three

Art Activity Two

What you will need:

✦ Paper
✦ Scissors
✦ Peel and stick craft foam sheets
✦ Pencil
✦ Black pen

Instructions:

1. Pick one of the ceramic shapes in this chapter and draw it out on an A4 sheet.

2. Have a look at some of the designs Clarice Cliff created for her ceramics and use them for inspiration to create your own design and fill your ceramic shape of choice.

3. How you do the next part is up to you. Using the different coloured Peel and Stick Craft Foam Sheets, cut them out and stick them on to give your design colour. Remember Clarice Cliff's designs are BRIGHT and fun! Use lots of colour and try and overlap the foam sheets, build on top of them to create a bit of depth. After you have stuck all your pieces down, you can add a bit more detail with a black pen. Why not add some more detailing with a pen, like on the windmill shown in Step Three?

Glossary

Art Deco – An art movement that spanned the 1920s and 30s. The art movement expanded over the fine and decorative arts as well as fashion, furniture, ceramics, film, photography, transport, just to name a few.

Bizarre ware – Clarice Cliff's most famous and first set of pottery designs. They were all seconds, but sold extremely quickly and were very popular.

Free hand – When talking about creating art in 'free hand', it means that you don't use any guiding instruments. Each piece is unique, as there are no two exactly the same as no one can make two pieces exactly the same without using a stencil, for example. It gives the artists more freedom.

'Ghosts' or 'Seconds' – When referring to a ghost or a second in ceramics, it means pieces that are second rate. Pieces of pottery that have some small fault in them and therefore are not acceptable to sell at the normal price. For example, nowadays the company Emma Bridgewater have a section on their online site that sells seconds. These are cheaper then the first rate ones, though to an untrained eye they look fine!

Using the words from the glossary, find them in the word search below.

Z	K	I	S	A	L	M	N	J	Q	I	C	R	W	M
C	G	Q	E	W	R	D	B	R	P	P	T	O	H	Y
T	S	W	C	J	I	T	Q	D	N	J	K	J	P	A
E	F	T	O	Q	J	V	P	D	S	G	C	O	V	B
P	S	U	N	G	D	G	E	J	A	X	H	Z	U	E
D	L	F	D	B	R	Y	Q	C	S	U	P	E	B	E
B	A	G	S	W	A	R	E	P	V	A	P	I	P	R
Y	M	C	V	J	B	X	D	V	H	V	Z	H	W	F
Q	N	G	C	W	K	N	J	V	X	A	C	Z	Z	N
Y	P	F	V	E	A	M	T	O	R	Z	A	P	T	D
H	T	Y	Z	H	S	W	M	R	C	Y	N	V	X	C
X	E	O	G	E	I	F	E	B	W	E	C	R	Q	F
A	F	I	V	S	T	S	O	H	G	P	D	M	P	S
E	N	M	I	M	F	A	I	E	O	Y	W	U	A	U
Y	Y	Y	F	H	N	P	H	A	N	C	N	H	W	U

Art	Bizarre	Ghosts	Free
Deco	Ware	Seconds	Hand

Pablo Picasso (1881-1973)

Cubism, Surrealism & Neo-Expressionism

- Picasso had a long career. From the 1900s onward, a lot of art movements came into being in a short period of time.
- Picasso experimented with a lot of the art movements. He co-founded Cubism and his styles range from Surrealism to Neo-expressionism.
- Picasso is most well known for his paintings, but did you know he did hundreds of ceramics too?
- At the end of the 1940s, he began to create ceramics.
- In 24 years, Picasso created over 633 pieces and has over 3500 designs. Wow!
- He decorated plates, dishes, jugs, pitchers, vases, plaques, tiles and lots of other pottery vessels.
- Some of the decorations he used were faces, still lifes, animals, mythical creatures, Mediterranean landscapes and bull fighting.
- When he did make some pieces, Picasso would mould, twist, stretch, punch and pierce the pottery to make it fit his design. Often, he would mismatch and move the positioning of the handles and spouts to make it look more like the animal he was aiming for.
- As well as using traditional tools, he would use the end of a pencil, or he would use cardboard and chicken wire pressed into wet clay in order to get a certain effect.

Image thirty-five: Spanish artist Pablo Picasso portrayed while decorating with paint and paintbrush one of his ceramic dishes, Paris, 1948. (Photo by Archivio Cameraphoto Epoche/Getty Images)

Image thirty-six Dish, c.1957, Pablo Picasso, France, Victoria and Albert Museum, London

FACT: PICASSO IS THOUGHT TO BE ONE OF THE GREATEST AND MOST INFLUENTIAL ARTISTS OF THE 20TH CENTURY.

Some **SHAPES** Picasso used in his work

Some **FACES** Picasso used in his work

Some **ANIMALS** Picasso used in his work

Activity One – Making Your Own Picasso Plate

What you will need:

1. White or Terracotta air drying clay (Hobbycraft 1kg £4.00)
2. Acrylic paint
3. Paintbrush
4. Pencil
5. Carving tool (could be an icing cake tool, or even just a pencil)
6. Rolling pin
7. Sketchbook

Instructions:

1. Decide what shape of plate you would like to do. Perhaps a simple circle? A rectangular platter? A bowl maybe? Once you have decided on the shape of pottery you will be making, now, decide what design you will have decorating it. Have a look through the images and pick either an animal, a face or perhaps a still life you can make and then draw. Draw out your design in your sketchbook. Really look at how Picasso draws his images. On some pieces, the paint work looks like it has been done quickly, others more carefully; you might be able to see a bit of Cubism in some of them. Think about what colours you want to use. Think of bright colours. Picasso LOVED colour.

2. You will need to knead the clay to make it softer and easier to use. When it is softer, roll out your clay and mould it into the shape you want. If you are struggling, use some clingfilm to cover a plate or bowl you already have and mould the clay on top of the clingfilm so that you make the same shape. When you are happy with the shape, use your pencil or carving tool to draw out the design in your sketchbook. Picasso often used a pencil or carving tool to carve out some parts of the design. If you make a mistake, you can smooth it out again with a bit of water. When you are happy with it, you will need to leave it to dry for at least FOUR or FIVE days. Four or five days later... Time to paint! Remember to use beautiful bright colours. Once the paint has dried, why not display your piece on a mantel piece or on a wall and admire your very own ?version of Picasso's ceramics?

We are going to be making our own piece of pottery with air drying clay. It is easy to use and the end result will look just like the real thing.

What shape do you want to do? If you have a lot of clay you could try more then one. We will stick to just a simple plate.

Colour & Portraiture

Colour phases he went through

1. Blue Period (1901-4); blue colouring

2. Rose Period (1904-6); rose/red colouring

3. Cubist (1907-25); loss of almost all colour, browns

4. **Cubist (1907-25), black and whites**

5. Expressionist (1938-); very colourful with thick black lines that cut the image up

By the time he gets to making his ceramics, we can see influences from all of these periods.

"Colours, like features, follow the changes of the emotions," he said. Continuing: "Why do two colours, put one next to the other, sing? Can one really explain this?"

	Nose	Mouth	Ears	Eye 1	Eye 2
●					
●●					
●●●					
●●●●					
●●●●●					
●●●●●●					

Instructions:

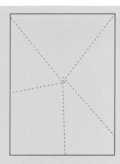

You will need:
Canvas/A3 sketchbook
Pencil
Paint
Paintbrush
Water
Dice

Instructions:

1. Split your canvas into five sections with a pencil and then draw a face shape on it, right in the middle.

2. Now, roll your dice. What ever number it lands on, go across to the Nose column and draw the picture of the nose on your canvas that is shown for that number.

3. Repeat throwing the dice for the Mouth, Ears, Eye 1 and Eye 2. Again, following the number across to the relevant facial feature and draw on to your canvas.

4. Once completed, now choose a colour stage for each section. So a blue one, rose one, brown, black and white one and lastly, a very colourful one.

GLOSSARY

Cubism - Was a brand new movement created by Picasso and Georges Braque in 1907. It was a revolutionary approach of looking at objects by capturing lots of different angles of the item, items, landscape, face in one frame, breaking the image into distinct planes or spaces.

Surrealism - Movement that came into being in the 1920s. Poets, writers and artists such as Salvador Dali experimented with ways to unlock the unconscious mind. Works are known to be slightly crazy!

Neo-expressionism - Major painting revival movement of Expressionism (1905-25) that came about in the 1980s.

Using the words from the glossary, find them in the word search below.

N	H	N	W	D	K	M	M	X	N	Y	W	Z	U	X
E	V	I	E	E	W	S	S	X	Z	C	C	T	U	S
G	O	A	P	O	J	F	I	D	E	W	D	G	K	M
V	S	O	S	S	Y	H	N	I	N	M	X	A	S	A
T	M	S	C	J	F	R	O	T	B	O	W	I	Y	I
C	K	B	X	C	U	B	I	S	M	C	L	P	D	Z
D	U	W	D	Y	V	N	S	C	P	A	Q	F	A	V
Y	M	A	U	M	X	T	S	U	E	G	I	J	P	E
Y	V	R	T	W	G	Z	E	R	I	Z	R	S	I	U
A	M	V	X	E	W	L	R	H	Q	T	H	I	A	N
M	N	E	Y	P	B	U	P	H	V	N	B	K	K	M
O	A	I	L	K	S	E	X	X	U	O	P	I	V	P
B	K	G	M	H	M	E	E	O	R	M	W	X	T	H
N	S	J	Q	I	E	O	P	W	J	N	C	Q	R	R
A	W	K	H	B	O	X	Y	N	A	M	V	K	D	B

Cubism   Neo   Expressionism   Surrealism

75

Piero Fornasetti
(1913-1988)

Surrealism
The 1950-70s

Art Facts:

- Piero Fornasetti was an Italian painter, sculptor, decorator and craftsman.
- His inspiration for his art work was from the great Italian art from the past. He loved using early Renaissance motifs to decorate furniture, scarves, plates and other objects.
- Some of his plates in the 1950s were decorated with vegetables in the form of faces. This inspiration also came from the Renaissance, from an artist called Giuseppe Arcimboldo 1526/7-1593.

Image thirty-seven: FIVE PIERO FORNASETTI (1913-1988) TRANSFER PRINTED CERAMIC PLATES CIRCA 1950

Decorated with various fruits and vegetables, with printed maker's marks Fornasetti Milano Made in Italy, one printed Arcimbodesca and painted initials L. P., one Vegetalia 1955, Christie's, *The Art of Food and Drink* sale, Thursday 16 Jan 2014, lot 79

Summer, 1572, Kunsthistorisches Museum Vienna, Austria

Art Activity for the Family!

What you will need:

- A plate for you, your parents and any siblings you have (plain white plates will do)
- A variety of fun shaped fruit and vegetables
- Sharpies or specific porcelain pens in a variety of colours
- Cotton wool and nail varnish remover for mistakes

1. Set all your fruit and vegetables on a table and create faces out of them. <u>Why not do this as a whole family at the weekend?</u> Each person then takes their plate and draws the face they created with the pens onto their plate. If you are doing it as a group, get everyone to create someone else's face.

2. If you are not confident, draw it out on paper first. When you are happy, draw the outlines first in black on your plate- if you make a mistake you can always remove it with some cotton wool and nail varnish remover. Once you are happy with the outline, you can colour it in.

3. Now leave your plates to dry for 24 hours. If you are using sharpies, after 24 hours put your plates into a cold oven and turn it on to 180 degrees C/ 350F or gas mark 4. This will allow the glaze on the plates to melt and allow the ink to sink into it properly. Leave the plates in the oven for 30 minutes, then turn the oven off and leave them in the closed oven for 15 minutes until cool and then lift out. You can now display them or use them for your meals!

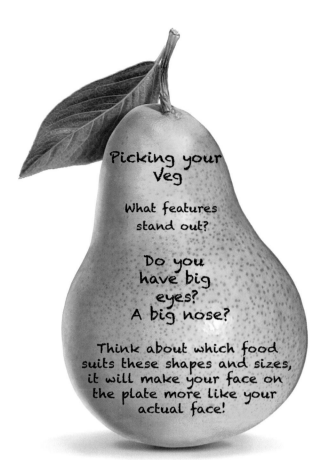

Picking your Veg

What features stand out?

Do you have big eyes? A big nose?

Think about which food suits these shapes and sizes, it will make your face on the plate more like your actual face!

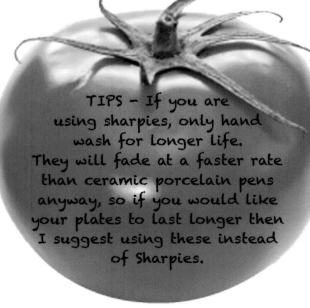

TIPS – If you are using sharpies, only hand wash for longer life. They will fade at a faster rate than ceramic porcelain pens anyway, so if you would like your plates to last longer then I suggest using these instead of Sharpies.

Stage One

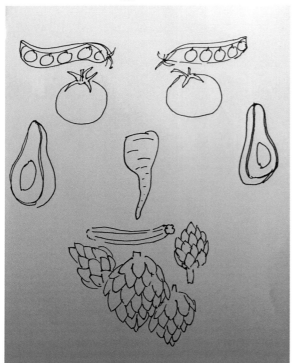

StageTwo

StageThree

Some Examples:

What would make good hair?
- Broccoli
- Rosemary
- Spinach
- Pineapple

What would make good ears?
- Butterbeans
- Avocados
- Mushrooms

What would make good eyes?
- Tomatoes
- Oranges
- Peas
- Kidney beans

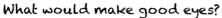

What would make a good beard?
- Artichoke
- Cauliflower
- Kale
- Brussels Sprouts

What would make a good mouth?
- Runner beans
- Leeks
- Bananas
- Courgettes
- Aubergine

What would make a good nose?
- Corn on the cob
- Cucumbers
- Strawberries
- Turnips
- Butternut squash

Glossary

Decorator – A profession that involves decorating the interior of buildings. This would include layout, colour system, paint, furniture, placement and so on.

Early Renaissance – Movement in Italy spanning the 15th century. It was an experimental time for painters and artists.

Giuseppe Arcimboldo – An Italian artist living from 1526-1593. Most famous for his faces made from vegetables and fruit.

Motif – A decorative design or image that may make up part of a pattern.

Porcelain pens – Specific pens made especially for porcelain. Once dry and baked, they are food and dishwasher safe.

Using the words from the glossary, find them in the word search below.

N	E	D	I	U	V	Z	R	H	R	T	X	L	F	J
J	A	R	C	I	M	B	O	L	D	O	W	P	I	V
S	B	N	F	W	B	L	G	F	Y	N	Z	O	B	O
E	U	K	H	Z	P	I	S	R	E	D	W	R	C	M
W	W	S	B	W	U	U	N	F	V	K	M	C	X	K
R	T	L	D	S	P	V	E	R	E	O	X	P	D	Z
L	C	V	E	D	I	P	P	T	Y	B	K	L	Q	V
C	O	P	P	F	E	U	B	P	I	N	K	A	G	M
V	P	G	O	A	I	C	S	F	A	U	O	I	S	T
E	Y	L	R	A	E	T	O	F	R	H	J	N	P	D
L	T	H	Q	L	H	H	O	R	Z	R	E	D	I	B
Z	Z	E	R	U	U	H	V	M	A	C	C	A	B	I
R	S	X	K	U	N	I	T	H	O	T	T	H	M	X
I	X	R	I	I	E	K	A	W	Z	T	O	N	V	B
Z	A	D	Z	D	Z	B	B	L	S	E	D	R	J	O

Arcimboldo   Renaissance   Porcelain

Decorator   Motif   Pens

Early   Guiseppe

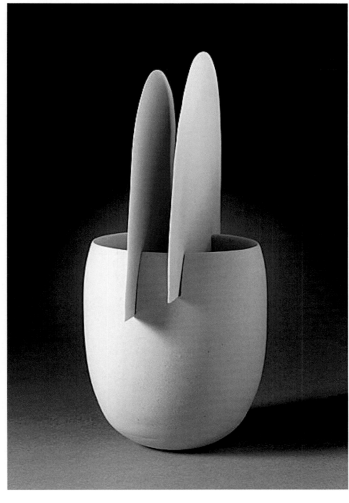

Ruth Duckworth

(British, 1919-2009)
Modernist Sculptor

SHAPE & FORM

"She was a great original, pioneering her own path within ceramics, brilliantly exploring the idea of the figure, the vessel and the more abstract form"
Emmanuel Cooper, a British ceramist

Image thirty-eight: Untitled (Blade cup
Ruth Duckworth (Germany, Hamburg, active England and United States, 1919-2009)
United States, 1994 Sculpture

- Worked with clay like a sculptor not a potter.
- Some pieces were only a few inches, other huge and site-specific.
- It was not until she was in her 40s that she became interested in clay and ceramics.
- Her work looks at the balance between space, shapes and proportions.

Influences:
1. Stylised, figurative Ancient Egyptian sculptures
2. Henry Moore
3. Early Bronze Age Cycladic Sculptures

Image thirty-nine: A Cycladic Marble Head of a Goddess, Early Bronze Age II, circa 2500-2400 B.C. Sotheby's sale, 07 JUNE 2007

Some shapes & forms that Ruth Duckworth made over her career as a ceramicist

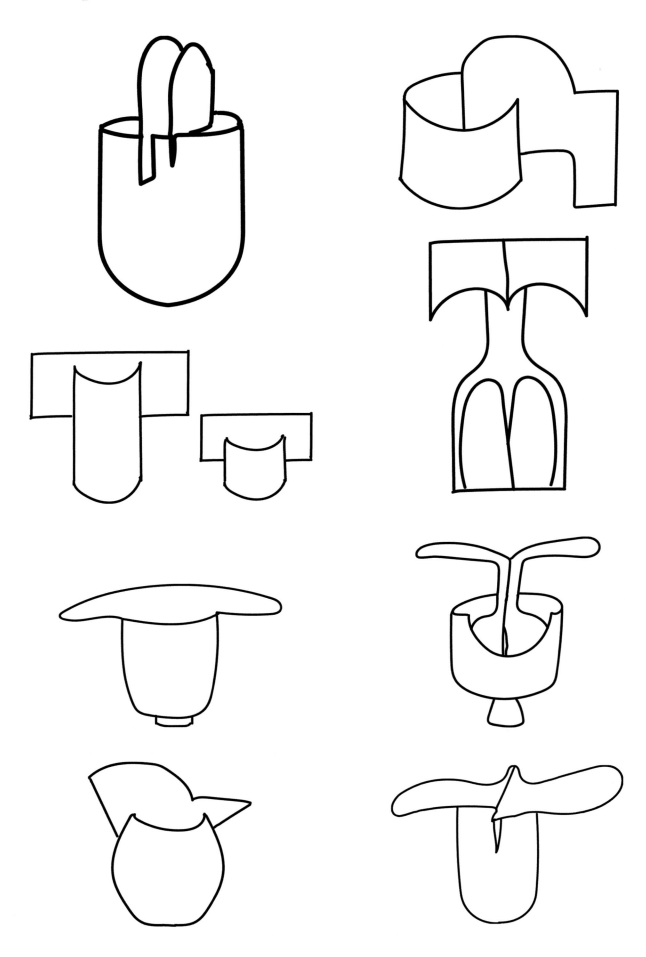

Activities
Exploring Shape, Form & Contrast
Shape & Contrast Activity

What you will need:
- Black paper/card
- White paper
- Pen
- Large needle
- Colourful thread
- Pencil

3. 1. 2. Back Stitch

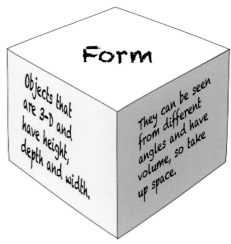
Instructions:
- Choose a ceramic piece of Ruth Duckworth that you like and draw the outline in black pen on the white paper. Around the outline, draw Xs on the lines as these will be your markers to thread the paper.
- Now repeat the shape with the Xs on your black card.
- Thread your needle with a bright-coloured thread and tie a knot at the end of your thread. Start sewing around the outline, using running stitch diagram to help.
- When finished, tie a knot in the other end of your thread and trim. There you have it - your shape design in contrasting thread to the black card. See how it jumps out?

Contrast

Opposites, whether in colour, texture, light and dark, size and so on.

Why not, try sewing your own design on a card and make it a card to send someone?

What you'll need:

- Black or coloured card
- String - natural or coloured
- Scissors
- Pencil
- Two wire hangers

Drawing of the mobile

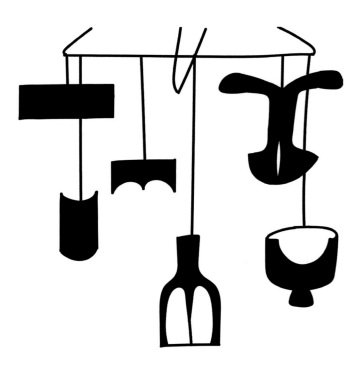

Instructions:

- Choose a few interesting pieces of Ruth Duckworth's ceramics and draw out each of the separate pieces on either your coloured or back card.
- Now cut them out.
- If you are using coloured paper, I would suggest using natural string; if you are using black paper, you can use either natural or brightly coloured string for a vibrant contrast.
- At this point, it is probably a good idea to sketch out how you would like your mobile to look. Where do you want the pieces to hang? What levels should they hang at? How many pieces should you hang on the hangers without it looking cluttered? We want to make a mobile that is striking, one where we can see all the individual pieces for the shapes they are and then see how they become forms if looking at them from another angle.
- Once happy, carefully, with your scissors, make small holes at the top of each of your cut out pieces. If you need an adult, please make sure to ask them to help.
- Thread your string in them and tie a small knot on one side. Remember the string should not all be the same length so take into account whether the top pieces of each object should be higher up on the mobile and therefore have shortened strings. It may help to string each on up as you go along so you can visualise the mobile as you go along.
- Tie the strung shapes to the wire coat hangers. I have done two pieces of two pieces each on each coat hanger. So there are eight separate pieces over all.
- Once you are done, hang it up somewhere central and have a look at the different angles and shapes it makes from different view points. If you have used black card, there will be a fantastic contrast against a white wall, for example.

Glossary

Enclose – Surround or shut off from all sides.

Figurative – An artist or work of art representing forms that are recognisably derived from life.

Organic – Relating to living matter.

Proportions – Comparative measures or size of different parts of a whole.

Stylise – Depicting something in a non-realistic but recognisable way.

Volume – The amount of space an object occupies or is enclosed within.

Using the words from the glossary above, find them in the word search below.

S	S	S	T	Z	V	R	I	C	G	E
H	N	T	Y	C	X	N	T	K	C	V
X	F	O	Y	I	N	J	Q	X	O	I
V	K	O	I	L	J	B	N	O	N	T
O	D	T	P	T	I	P	E	T	R	A
L	Z	F	O	L	R	S	H	R	H	R
U	G	Z	K	C	O	O	E	A	L	U
M	W	G	D	L	O	L	P	E	S	G
E	A	T	C	O	Z	H	D	O	X	I
U	T	N	M	C	R	U	F	M	R	F
Z	E	R	O	R	G	A	N	I	C	P

Enclose   Proportions

Figurative   Volume

Organic   Stylise

85

Where to find materials for the activities

Just a few examples of where you can buy materials for the arts and crafts activities in this book. It is not exhaustive but should give you a big enough range.

Shops

- Hobbycraft
- Homebase
- B&Q
- Wilkinsons
- Poundland
- Tesco
- Sainsburys
- The Works

Websites

- http://www.hobbycraft.co.uk/
- https://www.amazon.co.uk/
- http://www.bakerross.co.uk/
- http://www.theworks.co.uk/
- https://www.craftsuperstore.co.uk/

Where to find more pictures of examples for each chapter online

Chapter One: Ancient Egypt, History of the Canopic Jar c.2575 BCE-664BCE
- www.gettyimages.co.uk/ Instructions: Type into search engine, Canopic Jars
- http://www.britishmuseum.org/ Instructions: Go to - Research, Collection Online, Search the collection, type in Canopic Jars
- http://www.metmuseum.org/ Instructions: Search engine - Canopic Jars
- http://www.fitzmuseum.cam.ac.uk/ Instructions: Collections - Search the Collections - In the Collections Explorer search engine, type in Canopic Jars

Chapter Two: Ancient Greece, Geometric Pottery 900BCE-700BCE
- www.gettyimages.co.uk/ Instructions: Type into search engine, Ancient Greece Geometric Period Pottery
- http://www.britishmuseum.org/ Instructions: Go to - Research, Collection Online, Search the collection, type in Greek Geometric Pottery
- http://www.metmuseum.org/ Instructions: Search engine - Greek Geometric Pottery
- http://www.vam.ac.uk/collections Instructions: Search the collections - Greek Geometric Pottery

Chapter Three: Nazca Pottery, Pre-Columbian 100BCE-800AD
- www.gettyimages.co.uk/ Instructions: Type into search engine, Nazca Pottery
- http://www.britishmuseum.org/ Instructions: Go to - Research, Collection Online, Search the collection, type in Nazca Pottery
- http://www.metmuseum.org/ Instructions: Search engine - Nazca Pottery
- http://www.ancient.eu/article/883/
- http://www.latinamericanstudies.org/nazca/nasca-ceramics.pdf
- http://ngm.nationalgeographic.com/2010/03/nasca/hall-text Very informative article about the Nazca Lines
- http://science.nationalgeographic.com/science/archaeology/nasca-lines/ Another informative article about the Nazca Lines from a Science and Geographical aspect

Chapter Four: Tang Dynasty, China 618-906AD (7th-9th century)
- www.gettyimages.co.uk/ Instructions: Type into search engine - Tang Dynasty
- http://www.vam.ac.uk/collections Instructions: Search the collections - Tang Dynasty
- www.christies.com Instructions: Calendar - Past Auctions - Search Past Lots - Tang Dynasty Pottery
- http://www.christies.com/features/Tang-Dynasty-Sancai-7688-1.aspx?sc_lang=en An article called, 'Collecting guide: Tang Dynasty sancai'. Auction house websites are often fantastic places to find great quality examples of art works.
- http://www.sothebys.com/ Instructions: Search - Tang Dynasty Sancai

Chapter Five: Islamic Ceramics, 9th-14th century
- www.gettyimages.co.uk/ Instructions: Type into search engine- Islamic tiles (an excellent resource for Islamic tiles)
- http://www.vam.ac.uk/collections Instructions: Search the collections - Islamic Tiles
- http://www.metmuseum.org/ Instructions: Search engine - Islamic Tiles
- http://www.britishmuseum.org/ Instructions: Go to- Research, Collection Online, Search the collection, type in Islamic Tiles

Chapter Six: Song Dynasty, China 960-1279 (10th-13th century)

- www.gettyimages.co.uk/ Instructions: Type into search engine – Song Dynasty ceramics
- http://www.sothebys.com/en/auctions/2015/song-ceramics-yang-de-tang-collection-n09338.html
- http://www.christies.com/features/Song-dynasty-ceramics-7642-3.aspx Article called, 'Song-dynasty ceramics – made in China, adored in Japan'.
- http://www.vam.ac.uk/collections Instructions: Search the collections – Song Dynasty
- http://www.metmuseum.org/ Instructions: Search engine – Song Dynasty porcelain

Chapter Seven: Ming Dynasty, China 1368-1644 (13th-16th century)

- http://www.vam.ac.uk/collections Instructions: Search the collections – Ming Dynasty blue and white
- http://www.britishmuseum.org/ Instructions: Go to – Research, Collection Online, Search the collection, type in Ming Dynasty blue and white porcelain
- http://www.metmuseum.org/ Instructions: Search engine – Ming Dynasty blue and white porcelain
- http://www.sothebys.com/en/auctions/2013/important-ming-porcelain-from-a-private-collection-hk0489.html An important sale that happened in 2013 that has a great selection of examples

Chapter Eight: Italian Maiolica 15th-16th century

- http://courtauld.ac.uk/gallery/collection/decorative-arts/renaissance-decorative-arts-highlights Examples of Italian Maiolica
- http://www.vam.ac.uk/collections Instructions: Search the collections – Italian Maiolica
- http://www.britishmuseum.org/ Instructions: Go to – Research, Collection Online, Search the collection, type in Italian Maiolica
- http://www.metmuseum.org/ Instructions: Search engine – Italian Maiolica
- http://www.fitzmuseum.cam.ac.uk/ Instructions: Collections – Search the Collections – In the Collections Explorer search engine type in Italian Maiolica

Chapter Nine: Japanese Kakiemon Porcelain, 1680-1725 (17th-18th century)

- http://www.christies.com/privatesales/2015/The-Somlyo-Collection-of-Japanese-Ceramics Article on 'The Courtly Display: The Somlyo Collection of Japanese Ceramics'. A sale in London, 12-19 December 2016. Some excellent examples of Japanese Kakiemon porcelain animals
- http://www.sothebys.com/ Instructions: Search – Japanese Kakiemon
- http://www.burghley.co.uk/collections/category/exhibitions/kakiemon-porcelain/ Burghley House is in Stamford, Lincolnshire, England. It has one of the biggest and extensive collections of Japanese Kakiemon in the country.

Chapter Ten: Aestheticism, England, 19th century

- http://www.vam.ac.uk/content/articles/s/style-guide-aestheticism/ Victoria and Albert Museum's Style Guide to Aestheticism
- http://www.vam.ac.uk/collections Instructions: Search the collections – Aestheticism pottery. It shows two excellent pots by Edward William Godwin. They show

the Japonisme style shown in this chapter. Aestheticism pottery. It shows two excellent pots by Edward William Godwin. They show the Japonisme style shown in this chapter.

Chapter Eleven: Arts & Crafts, through the work of William de Morgan, England, 19th-20th century

- http://www.vam.ac.uk/collections Instructions: Search the collections - William de Morgan.
- http://www.britishmuseum.org/ Instructions: Go to - Research, Collection Online, Search the collection, type in William de Morgan
- http://www.demorgan.org.uk/collection
- http://williammorristile.com/gallery/william-de-morgan-tiles-gallery.html For a modern reproduction of William de Morgan's tiles

Chapter Twelve: Art Deco, through the work of Clarice Cliff England, 20th Century 1920-1940s

- http://www.claricecliff.co.uk/
- http://andrew-muir.com/ Andrew Muir is a leading ceramics dealer of over 25 years. He sells Clarice Cliff, Moorcroft and 20th century ceramics. There is an excellent selection of examples of Clarice Cliff's work.

Chapter Thirteen: Cubism, Surrealism and Neo-Expressionism through Pablo Picasso 20th century, 1940s-1960s

- http://www.christies.com/features/Collecting-Picasso-Ceramics-7312-1.aspx - Excellent article on 'Collecting Guide: Picasso Ceramics' with some great examples
- www.christies.com Instructions: Calendar - Past Auctions - Search Past Lots - Picasso ceramics. Auction houses are some of the best websites to find examples of Picasso's ceramics. They will be in great condition and have the ability to zoom right up to the details of each piece.
- https://www.theguardian.com/artanddesign/2016/sep/15/Richard-attenborough-pablo-picasso-ceramics-sale-auction
- www.google.com - images, Picasso ceramics

Chapter Fourteen: Surrealism through the work of Piero Fornasetti 20th century, 1950s-1970s

- http://www.bada.org/antiques/d/a-set-of-six-mid-century-piero-fornasetti-arcimboldesca-motif-vegetable-face-pla/ 209123
  Go to Google and type into the search engine 'Piero Fornasetti vegetables'. Click on the 'images' button directly underneath the search engine and lots of images will appear.

Chapter Fifteen: Modernism through the work of Ruth Duckworth, 20th-21st century

- http://www.metmuseum.org/art/collection/search/487053
- http://www.vam.ac.uk/collections Instructions: Search the collections - Ruth Duckworth
- http://www.artnet.com/artists/ruth-duckworth/
  Go to Google and type into the search engine 'Ruth Duckworth'. Click on the 'image' button directly underneath and lots of images will appear.

LONGMAN
*h*OMEWORK *h*ANDBOOKS

KEY STAGE 3

HISTORY

Malcolm Chandler

LONGMAN

HOMEWORK HANDBOOKS

Series editors:

Geoff Black and Stuart Wall

Other titles in the series:

ENGLISH

FRENCH

GEOGRAPHY

GERMAN

MATHEMATICS

SCIENCE

Addison Wesley Longman Limited
Edinburgh Gate, Harlow
Essex CM20 2JE
England
and Associated Companies throughout the world.

© Addison Wesley Longman 1998

First published 1998

ISBN 0582-33247-2

British Library Cataloguing in Publication Data
A catalogue record for this book is available from the British Library.

Set by 34 in 9.5/11pt Stone
Produced by Addison Wesley Longman Singapore Publishers Pte
Printed in Singapore

ACKNOWLEDGEMENTS

I am indebted to my colleague Kerry Burdsey for reading the manuscript and for the suggestions she made to improve it.

We are also grateful to the following for permission to reproduce copyright material: Getty Images Limited for the photograph on p. 10; and ET Archive for the poster 'These women are doing their bit. Learn to make munitions' on p. 48.

CONTENTS

USING THIS BOOK

This book will help with the history that you will study in your Key Stage 3 history lessons.

In this book you will find entries arranged in alphabetical order. These include the names of the people, places and events which you will need to know about if you are going to do as well as possible in history at Key Stage 3. You will also find explanations of some of the types of tasks that you may be asked to do and hints on how to do these. You will also find the meanings explained of words that you may come across.

Most of the entries are short: these give you details about people's lives, inventions, events or places, for instance. But some entries are longer: these tell you about important developments or changes. Sometimes you will find cross-references from one entry to another: these are marked by **bold italics**. For example:

ALBERT, THE PRINCE CONSORT

Prince Albert married Queen **Victoria** on 10 February 1840. He was her first cousin. He played a very important role in advising Queen Victoria on politics and became her private secretary. He was often unpopular in Britain and was once forced to leave the visitors' gallery in the House of **Commons**. His unpopularity was mostly caused by the fact that he was a foreigner and he was believed to be a **Catholic**.

From this entry on Albert, the Prince Consort, we can see that there are separate entries on **Victoria**, the House of Commons under **Commons** and **Catholic**. You may find it helpful to refer to these topics when thinking about **Albert**, Prince Consort.

At the end of some entries you will also find a list of other entries which you might also find useful. The entry on **Reichstag Fire**, for example, ends with the following:

⁘ Hitler, Nazi Germany

Again, it may be useful for you to look at these entries when thinking about the **Reichstag Fire**.

Throughout this book there are self-check questions to help you practise what you have just learned. The answers to these can be found at the back of the book. There are also 'Remember' speech bubbles, giving you interesting or important tips about the topic. For example in the entry on **Essay** the following Remember bubble appears:

> REMEMBER: always plan your essay before you start to write.

TO THE STUDENT

This book is written to help you do as well as possible. It is not a textbook, but it will help you make more and better use of the textbooks that you use in school. It will give you more information and more ideas about how to tackle your school work.

This book is not meant to be read from cover to cover, although some of the entries can be read like that. It is more like an encyclopedia and, therefore, it should be looked at whenever you need extra help. Keep it handy and try to get used to how it is laid out.

TO THE PARENT

Many parents that I meet at parents' evenings in school say how much they enjoyed and still do enjoy history. This book offers you an opportunity to rediscover history, by going through and supporting your son or daughter's work. You may find that some of the entries in this book are a little different from the history that you studied at school: try looking at the entry on **Robin Hood**, for example, and decide for yourself whether he really existed.

It will help you to find out from the school which units in the National Curriculum are being covered and in what order. This will help you to make better use of this book.

The entries in this book cover three years in your child's education. You will find, therefore, that both the language and the detail of the references become more complex as your child progresses from Year Seven to Year Nine.

HISTORY AT KEY STAGE 3

During Key Stage 3 you will study six different units. There are four compulsory units, which are all covered in this book. These are:

- Medieval Realms: Britain 1066 to 1500
- The making of the United Kingdom: 1500 to 1750
- Britain 1750 to 1900
- The Twentieth-Century World

You will also have to study two optional units. These will be chosen by your school and you should ask your teachers what the optional units are.

As well as the units, you will also have to study and understand history in a number of ways. All of these are explained in more detail in the guide. It would be a good idea to look at these explanations and the examples that are given.

1. **Chronology**   This means getting dates and events in the right order and being aware of the changes that have taken place. You will also be expected to use the correct terms and expressions for each of the units you study.
2. **Knowledge** and **understanding**   You will be expected to develop a knowledge of all of the units, but you will be expected to have a detailed knowledge of certain topics.
3. **Interpretations**   This means trying to understand why some events and people have been described or explained in different ways.
4. **Historical enquiry**   This means learning how to use different types of **evidence** to try to find answers to questions. You will find that many different forms of evidence are discussed in the guide.
5. **Organisation** and **communication**   This means being able to explain your ideas to other people. The usual way of doing this will be by writing answers to questions. You will find explanations of the main forms of written work, such as the **essay**, and the best ways of attempting them in the guide.

History Homework

Homework in history can come in a number of forms. You may be asked to read pages from a textbook and make **notes** or answer some questions. You may be given a worksheet with **sources** and questions on it. You may be asked to write a long answer to a question; this is often called an **essay**. You may be asked to do **research**, using books, a CD-ROM, a library or by interviewing people about their experiences. All of these forms of homework are discussed in the guide.

ACCOUNT

An account is one of the simplest forms of history homework. It means that you are being asked to write a story describing and explaining what happened. It is important to make sure that an account makes sense; this will usually mean getting the events in the correct order and explaining how they link together. If you are asked to write an account using more than one book, you need to make sure that you put the information from the different books together, rather than taking information from each book in turn. A good way to do this is to draft your answer first. Use a page in your exercise book to sort the information into the correct order, by writing all the dates in the margin before you start writing your answer. It will help if you word-process your answer, as you will be able to make changes more easily.

> REMEMBER: an account must make sense, so things should be in the correct order.

ACT OF PARLIAMENT

An Act of **Parliament** is a law passed in the United Kingdom. Parliament is made up of three sections, the House of **Commons**, the House of **Lords** and the Monarch. Any Member of Parliament can introduce a bill which, if it is approved by all three sections of Parliament, will become an Act. Once it has been passed by Parliament, an Act must be obeyed by everyone in Britain.

AGINCOURT

The battle of Agincourt was fought on 25 October 1415. It was one of the most important battles of the **Hundred Years' War**. In 1415 **Henry V** invaded France to try to take the French throne. The English army met a much larger French army at Agincourt and destroyed it. The main reason for the English success was the use of the **longbow** as a long-range weapon. Henry had also chosen a narrow muddy battlefield, where the heavily armoured French knights were ineffective.

The importance of the victory was that Henry V became the regent of France and his son **Henry VI** was crowned King of France in 1422 after his father's death. He was the only King of England to be crowned King of France.

This success did not last, however. Henry VI was unable to hold on to his father's conquests and in the 1430s and 1440s most of the English possessions in France were recaptured by the French.

ALBERT, THE PRINCE CONSORT

Prince Albert married Queen **Victoria** on 10 February 1840. He was her first cousin. He played a very important role in advising Queen Victoria on politics and became her private secretary. He was often unpopular in Britain and was once forced to leave the visitors' gallery in the House of **Commons**. His unpopularity was mostly caused by the fact that he was a foreigner and he was believed to be a Roman **Catholic**.

Albert was closely connected with the Great Exhibition of 1851, which he used as a means of increasing his popularity with the British people. He was the chairman of the organising committee and took an active role in the preparations for the Exhibition and the building of the Crystal Palace.

Albert died of disease in December 1861.

ALLIANCE

An alliance is an agreement between two or more countries, usually for military reasons. For example, in the years before the **First World War** two alliances were built up. The Triple Alliance involved Germany, Austria–Hungary and Italy, and the Triple Entente involved France, Russia and Great Britain.

ALSACE-LORRAINE

Alsace and Lorraine are two provinces of eastern France. In 1871, after the Franco–Prussian War, in which the French army was heavily defeated, Prussia (Germany) took Alsace-Lorraine from France. This led to very bitter feelings in France.

- The statue representing the city of Strasbourg in Paris was covered with black cloth every day. Strasbourg was the capital of Alsace.
- Sarah Bernhardt, the most famous actress of her day, refused to appear in Germany. When she received a letter from a German theatre manager asking her to name her price to appear in his theatre, she replied with a two-word telegram, 'Alsace-Lorraine'.
- Politicians in France called themselves 'Revanchistes'. Revanche is French for revenge. Revenge meant recapturing Alsace-Lorraine.
- The main plan of the French army, Plan 17, was based on an attack into Alsace-Lorraine.

At the end of the **First World War** Alsace-Lorraine was returned to France. In June 1940 when France surrendered to Germany at the beginning of the **Second World War**, **Hitler** took back Alsace-Lorraine. At the end of the Second World War it was returned to France again.

Alsace-Lorraine has played a very important role in European history in the last 130 years.

✛ **Treaty of *Versailles***

AMERICAN COLONIES

The American Colonies were the 13 English settlements in North America, which became the basis of the United States of America. The first English colonies in the New World were founded in Virginia in the 1580s, by Sir Walter Raleigh, which he named after Queen **Elizabeth I**; she was known as the 'Virgin Queen'. Raleigh was looking for gold, but instead found tobacco, turkeys and potatoes. It was not until 1607, however, that the first successful colony was founded at Jamestown.

The next attempts were in New England. The Mayflower Pilgrims landed at Plymouth in Massachusetts in 1620; then more settlements were started in New Hampshire in the 1620s. By the 1630s, Massachusetts was the largest colony. At that time Connecticut, Rhode Island, Delaware and Maryland were established.

New York became English when it was captured from the Dutch in 1664 and Pennsylvania was created in the early 1680s. North and South Carolina were first settled in the 1660s, being named

after **Charles II**, and were finally developed by the 1720s. New Jersey became a colony in 1702, and the last English colony, Georgia, was set up in 1733. This brought the number of colonies to 13.

The American Colonies were unlike any other part of the British Empire, or of any other empire, because they were occupied by large numbers of emigrants. Hundreds of thousands of English, Scots, Germans, Swedish and other nationalities left Europe to settle in the New World. This made the American Colonies more and more difficult to govern, and led to the outbreak of the **American Revolution** in 1775.

> REMEMBER: the American Colonies were the only part of the British Empire which had large numbers of Europeans living in them.

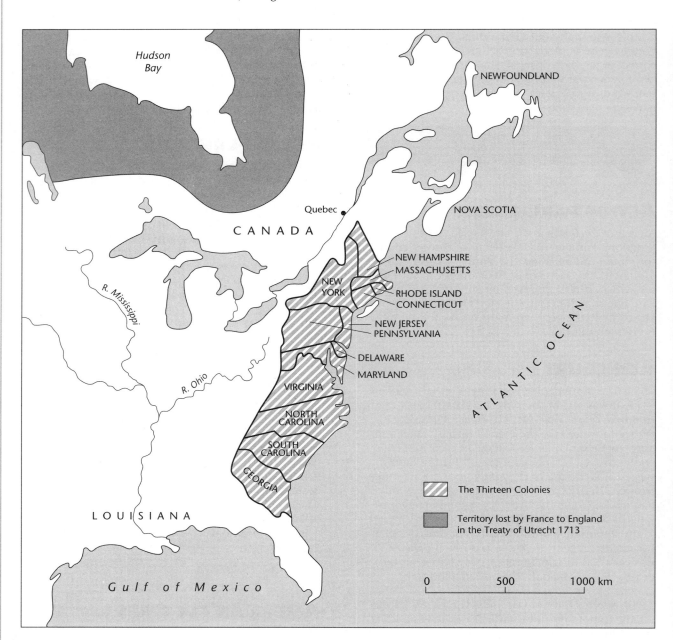

AMERICAN REVOLUTION

The American Revolution was the revolt of Britain's colonies, which began in 1775 and ended in 1783, when the Colonies became independent.

Why did the American Colonies revolt?

- The defeat of the French in North America during the Seven Years War (1756 to 1763). This meant there was no longer a threat to the colonies from another European power. There was also, therefore, less need for British forces to be stationed in the American Colonies.
- Disagreements between the colonists and the British government which began even before the peace was signed. The British government began to raise taxes to try to pay for the cost of the war and for the administration of the new territories gained at the Treaty of Paris in 1763. The Sugar Act (1764), the Stamp Act (1765) and the Townshend Duties (1767) all met great opposition in the Colonies. Although the Stamp Act was abolished in 1766, the Declaratory Act said that the King and the Houses of Parliament had the right to make laws which the colonists had to obey.
- Opposition of the port of Boston in the colony of Massachusetts. Bostonians were merchants and traders and were badly affected by the attempts by the British government to control the trade of the colonists. In 1770 several Bostonians were killed in a brawl with British soldiers; this became known as the Boston Massacre, and was blamed on the British soldiers. There is evidence, however, that the crowd deliberately provoked and attacked the soldiers.
- In 1773 Bostonians, disguised as Indians, threw tea into the harbour, when it arrived from India. The British government had allowed tea from India to be sent to America to be sold in competition to American tea. The following year the port of Boston was closed.

In September 1774, representatives of 12 of the 13 Colonies met at Philadelphia. This was the first time that the Colonies had actually worked together.

War broke out in April 1775 and lasted until 1781, when the last British army surrendered at Yorktown.

Why did the American Colonies win the war?

- During the first years of the war the British forces were very successful, but from 1777 the tide began to turn in favour of the Americans. The British were far from home, reinforcements took a long time to arrive and the British used many German mercenaries, who were often unpopular in the Colonies. This meant that some of the British soldiers had little to fight for, while the Americans knew exactly what they were fighting for.
- The British armies used the same tactics as they did in European battles and sometimes suffered very heavy casualties. The Americans were used to fighting in woods and mountains. They ambushed the British and this led to heavy casualties. Although the Americans were disorganised at first, they adapted quickly and were better at using the countryside.
- In 1778 France declared war on Britain after the surrender of General Burgoyne at Saratoga. This meant that the Americans were supported by French troops and also by the French Navy. Britain had to fight against the French in Europe, the Caribbean and in India. In 1780 Spain also declared war on Britain. This made the war much more difficult for Britain.
- In 1780 and 1781 the British lost control of the sea and so were unable to send supplies to their forces in America. General Cornwallis surrendered in Yorktown in October 1781 and this brought the fighting to an end. The American Colonies became independent in the Treaty of Paris in 1783.

ANNE, QUEEN, 1702–1714

Queen Anne was the younger daughter of *James II* and the last of the Stuarts. Most of her reign was taken up by a war against France and Spain called the War of the Spanish Succession. During this war a series of battles were fought by the English general *Marlborough*, of which the most famous was the battle of Blenheim in 1704. Blenheim Palace was built for Marlborough as a reward for his successes. Sir Winston *Churchill* was a descendant of the family and was born at Blenheim.

Queen Anne had no surviving children, so when she died the crown passed to George, the Elector of *Hanover*, who became *George I*; he was a great-grandson of *James I*. This had been decided by the Act of *Settlement* of 1701.

During Queen Anne's reign the Act of *Union* was passed. This united England and *Scotland* under the name of Great Britain. The Union Flag, made up of the crosses of St George and St Andrew, was created.

ANSCHLUSS

Anschluss is the German word for 'union'. The Anschluss was the name given to the occupation of Austria by *Hitler* in March 1938. This had been banned by the Treaty of *Versailles*, but Hitler had already ignored this in 1935, when he had begun *rearmament*, and in 1936 when he had reoccupied the *Rhineland*.

Unrest broke out in Austria in early March: most of this was the work of Nazis inside Austria. When the Austrian chancellor, Schuschnigg, tried to deal with the crisis, he was forced to resign and the German army invaded. A *plebisicite* (a vote on a particular issue) was held in Austria, and there was a vote of 99.75 per cent in favour of a union with Germany. Events moved so quickly that Britain and France had no time to protest.

The Anschluss was an important step in persuading Hitler that Britain and France would not oppose him in the future.

ANTI-SEMITISM

Anti-Semitism is the name given to the hatred and persecution of Jews. This is normally connected with the policies of the Nazis in Germany in the 1930s, but was in fact much more widespread. Anti-Semitism had occurred in many countries in Europe since the middle ages. Jews were banned from many occupations and sometimes had to live in certain areas in towns; these became known as ghettos. Jews often became involved in money-lending, as Christians were not allowed to make any profit from lending money.

What made the attacks by the Nazis different was that they eventually attempted to kill all Jews in what they called the Final Solution. This became known as the *Holocaust*.

✦ *Nazi Germany*

APPEASEMENT

Appeasement was the name given to the policy adopted by the British governments in the 1930s to deal with the threats from the dictators, such as *Hitler* and *Mussolini*. It meant to give in to the demands of the dictators, in the belief that they would be satisfied and, therefore, make no further demands. The policy of appeasement is most closely connected with Neville Chamberlain who had to deal with Hitler's demands for parts of Czechoslovakia in September 1938. This became known as the *Munich Agreement*.

Why did many British people support appeasement?

- They felt Germany had been very badly treated by the Treaty of *Versailles*. It deserved a second chance.
- They thought that Hitler was helping Germany to recover and he should be supported. They believed that Hitler could be trusted.
- Many people remembered the horrors of the *First World War* and did not want them to be repeated.
- Some people believed that Hitler would protect them from communism. Others were pacifists and did not believe in fighting.

✦ *Manchuria, Rhineland, Anschluss*

ARKWRIGHT, RICHARD

Richard Arkwright was an eighteenth-century businessman, who was one of the first to realise the opportunities offered by the development of new machinery in the textile industries in the 1760s. In 1768 Arkwright built a spinning machine called a water-frame. This was too big to fit into the cottages used in the *Domestic System* and also needed water power, as it was too heavy to be worked by hand. The alternative was to design new buildings to hold the water-frames. At first these were called mills, as they were built beside streams and had water-wheels to drive the machinery.

From 1771, Arkwright developed a new town at Cromford in Derbyshire. Because he needed to attract workers, he not only built factories, but also houses for his workers, churches, shops and a hotel. He also built a school and insisted that children who came to work for him learned to read and write first.

By the time he died in 1792, Richard Arkwright had been knighted and had become very wealthy indeed. His success was not based on his invention of the water-frame. In fact this machine was not ideal for cotton-spinning. The thread it produced was strong, but too coarse, and it had to be mixed with thread produced by the Spinning Jenny. Arkwright's success was his business skill and enterprise. He gambled that factories would work and proved himself to be right. He saw the opportunity that was offered by the increasing supplies of cotton, the new machinery and the rising population and took his chance. Many others followed his example. He was one of the most important figures in the *Industrial Revolution*.

> REMEMBER: *Richard Arkwright was a successful businessman, rather than a great inventor.*

ARMISTICE

The Armistice is the name given to the ending of fighting at 11.00 am on 11 November 1918. This brought the *First World War* to an end.

ARTHUR, PRINCE

Prince Arthur was the eldest child of *Henry VII*. He was married to *Catherine of Aragon*, but died soon afterwards. Catherine later married his younger brother, who became *Henry VIII*. When Henry VIII tried to divorce Catherine, he gave as one excuse that it was against Church law to marry his sister-in-law.

ATLANTIC CHARTER

The Atlantic Charter was signed by Franklin *Roosevelt*, the President of the *United States of America* and Winston *Churchill*, the Prime Minister of Great Britain, on 14 August 1941. It was a declaration of rights for countries and peoples; these included giving up the use of force, disarmament, the freedom to travel and the recognition of the independence of countries. This Charter was later signed by a further 42 countries and became the basis of the *United Nations*, which was set up in 1945.

AUTHORISED VERSION

The Authorised Version, also known as the King James Version, was an edition of the Bible published in 1611 by King *James I* of England and VI of Scotland. This version was part of the attempt by King James I to bring to an end disagreements over religion. These had become more and more common since the creation of the *Church of England* by *Henry VIII*. The Authorised Version became the most popular and widely used edition of the Bible for the next 300 years, and is still in use today.

AUTOBIOGRAPHY

An autobiography is an account of someone's life written by that person. Autobiographies, therefore, need to be used with care. Historical figures will often try to present their actions and the events in which they were involved in the most favourable light.

> REMEMBER: an autobiography is written by the person whose life is being described.

realised that Serbia now represented a major threat to its aim of expanding to the south. This led to increased tension between Austria–Hungary and Serbia supported by Russia.

⚓ *Sarajevo*, **Archduke** *Franz Ferdinand*, *First World War*

BALKANS

The Balkans is the name given to the area of south-east Europe now occupied by the countries of Greece, Romania, Bulgaria, Albania, Serbia, Montenegro and Bosnia. Until the nineteenth century this area was controlled by the Turkish Empire, but gradually one country after another broke away from Turkish control. The first was Greece in the 1820s. As Turkish control collapsed, both Russia and Austria–Hungary attempted to gain influence over the new countries. Austria–Hungary wanted to gain more land to the south, which would give it a Mediterranean coast; Russia wanted to control the entry to the Black Sea and to protect Orthodox Christians.

The two powers clashed over Bosnia–Herzegovina and Serbia. Serbia had finally broken away from the Turkish Empire in 1878 after 50 years of conflict. The Serbs were Orthodox Christians and were supported by Russia. Many of the inhabitants of Bosnia–Herzegovina were also Serbs. This area had been occupied by Austria–Hungary in 1878 and annexed in 1908. Serbia by 1913 was the most powerful state in the Balkans and wanted Bosnia–Herzegovina. Austria–Hungary

BANNOCKBURN

The battle of Bannockburn was fought in 1314 and ended the attempts by the English Kings to take control of **Scotland**. After the death of **Edward I** in 1307 the English were driven out of most of Scotland. By 1313 only Stirling was in English hands. **Edward II** marched into Scotland to try to reach Stirling but was attacked at Bannockburn and heavily defeated.

BATTLE OF BRITAIN

The Battle of Britain was fought between the RAF and the Luftwaffe from 15 August and 15 September 1940. It was part of the attempt by **Hitler** to defeat Britain during the **Second World War**. The battle began with attacks on airfields and at first the RAF was very successful. The RAF had the advantage of radar, which allowed it to work out when attacks were coming. Its main fighter aircraft, the **Hurricane** and the **Spitfire** were more effective than the German fighters. However, by early September British losses outnumbered German. The problem was that Britain did not have enough pilots.

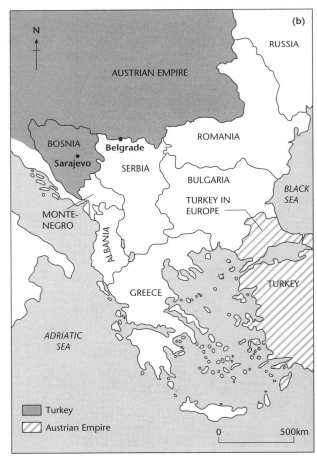

The Balkans before 1912

The Balkans in 1914

On 7 September Hitler ordered the Luftwaffe, the German airforce, to attack London by night. This attack continued for the next seven nights and gave the RAF a chance to recover. When the Luftwaffe attempted to attack London by day on 15 September, 60 German planes were shot down. This was the end of German attempts to invade Britain.

15 September is now remembered as Battle of Britain Day.

BATTLE OF THE ATLANTIC

This began in early 1941 and continued for more than two years. It was an attempt by *Hitler* to force Britain to surrender during the *Second World War* by starving her of supplies by sea. In September 1940 Hitler gave up his attempt to invade Britain and began the *Blitz*. This continued until early 1941, when many bombers were withdrawn from western Europe for the attack on the *Union of Soviet and Socialist Republics*, codenamed Operation Barbarossa. The Battle of the Atlantic began in February 1941 and continued until the middle of 1943.

At first the German submarines (U Boats) were very successful, sinking 321 ships in March to May 1941. There were not enough Royal Navy ships to escort merchant ships across the Atlantic and very little air cover. Later in 1941, American warships began to assist as escorts, even though the USA did not declare war on Germany until 11 December 1941. After that the battle was gradually won, using convoy escorts, escort carriers, long-range aircraft and asdic (a form of underwater radar).

Winston *Churchill* said that the Battle of the Atlantic was the only thing that 'really frightened me'.

BECKET, THOMAS À

Thomas à Becket was appointed Chancellor of England in 1155 by King *Henry II*. He was a close friend of Henry. Henry II had become king in 1154 after the reign of King *Stephen* (1135–1154). During the reign of Stephen there had been a great deal of warfare because Stephen, a grandson of *William I*, was opposed by Matilda, a daughter of *Henry I* and granddaughter of William I. *Henry II* was the son of Matilda.

When Henry II became king the authority of the crown needed to be re-established. Thomas à Becket supported him in trying to restore the power of the royal courts of justice. Henry wanted to reduce the power of Church courts and make sure that clergy were sentenced in royal courts if they committed crimes.

In 1162 Henry appointed Thomas à Becket Archbishop of Canterbury and he resigned as chancellor. Henry expected Becket to support his efforts to bring the Church courts under control, but instead he immediately began to oppose Henry II's plans to extend royal power. When Henry published the Constitutions of *Clarendon* in 1164, Becket fled abroad to France, where he remained for five years. He returned in 1170, but was murdered on 29 December in Canterbury Cathedral by four knights. They apparently believed that Henry wanted Becket murdered after an outburst of anger at a feast after Christmas.

The murder of Becket was important as Henry had to accept the blame for it and was forced to do penance. He also had to accept that clergy should be tried in Church courts. The Pope did not deal very harshly with him, however, as England was the most powerful country in western Europe. Popes also needed support from Crusaders for the defence of Jerusalem against the Muslims.

⧋ *Crusades*

BEER HALL PUTSCH

The Beer Hall Putsch was an attempt by Adolf *Hitler* and the Nazi Party to seize power in the Bavarian city of Munich on 9 November 1923. The attempt was a failure, partly because Hitler had burst into a meeting at the Burgerbraukeller in the centre of Munich on the previous evening, fired a gun through the ceiling and announced that he was going to try to take over the government the following morning.

There are different accounts of what actually happened on the morning of the 9 November. According to a biography of Hitler published by the Nazis in 1934, Hitler's arm was dislocated as he tried to carry a wounded boy to safety. Other versions of events suggest that he fell to the ground, sprained his wrist and then ran away.

Why did the Putsch fail?

- The meeting on the night of 8 November had been a disaster. Some people had escaped and the police had been warned.
- Hitler expected a great deal of support from the people of Munich on 9 November. There was almost none.
- After the events of the night before, Hitler got up late on 9 November and the march did not start until about 11.00 am.
- The police were ready for the marchers and fired at them to make them disperse.
- Hitler apparently ran away.

Hitler had made a mistake. He believed that the government of Germany was so unpopular that many Germans would support him. He was even planning a 'March on Berlin' after his success in Munich. In fact Germany was beginning to recover from the problems caused by the *First World War*. The new chancellor Gustav *Stresemann* had already brought *hyperinflation* under control and most Germans saw him as a much better leader than Hitler.

BEGGARS

Beggars became an increasing problem in England during the reign of *Elizabeth I* (1558–1603). Begging increased for a number of reasons:

- prices rose a great deal during the sixteenth century
- *enclosure* became widespread in some parts of England, forcing labourers off the land

7

the increasing importance of trade attracted people to towns to find work.

These reasons meant that the number of people wandering around the country increased.

Why were beggars and vagrants regarded with suspicion?

- Anyone who wandered around the country was regarded as unreliable. There was no police force and no way of checking on people.
- Beggars were often accused of crimes and causing diseases, even the **Plague**. People believed that the Plague was brought by strangers.
- Beggars were often driven from towns. There are pictures of them being whipped through the streets.

The **Poor Law** of 1601 tried to tackle the problem of begging by making it the responsibility of each **parish** to look after its own poor. This not only meant that beggars could receive some help, but also encouraged them to remain in one place, where they could be checked up on more effectively.

> *REMEMBER: beggars were distrusted because they wandered from place to place.*

BERLIN BLOCKADE

From June 1948 until May 1949, Joseph **Stalin** ordered that all traffic between **West Germany** and **West Berlin** should be stopped. He was able to close the road, canal and rail routes, but was not able to prevent the western Allies, Great Britain, France and the USA from bringing supplies into West Berlin by air. The Berlin airlift lasted ten and a half months and one plane landed in West Berlin every 90 seconds.

Why did Stalin blockade Berlin?

- The main reason for the blockade was that Great Britain and the USA had made it clear that they intended to rebuild the economy in their zones of Germany.
- Stalin believed that Germany should be kept weak to prevent any risk of further trouble. He also wanted to get reparations from Germany to help rebuild the Soviet Union.
- In 1948 the western Allies announced they were going to introduce a new currency in the West to help the economy get going again. This would mean that East and West would be separate economically.
- West Berlin was a temptation to East Berliners. In the West the **Marshall Plan** was beginning to make life much better. Already East Berliners and East Germans were trying to escape to the West.

How did the Allies react?

- They were determined that Stalin should not succeed. General Lucius Clay, the US commander in Berlin, said, 'If West Berlin falls, West Germany will be next.'
- The Allies believed that if they gave in Stalin would behave as **Hitler** had in the 1930s. More and more countries would be taken over.
- The Allies began to bring supplies into West Berlin by air. 4000 tonnes were needed every day. Eventually they were bringing in 8000 tonnes; even coal was brought in by plane.

In May 1949 Stalin gave up. It was obvious that the West was not going to give in, so he ended the blockade.

BERLIN WALL

The Berlin Wall was built in August 1961. It was intended to cut the Soviet sector of Berlin (often called East Berlin) off from the western sectors (**West Berlin**).

Why was the Wall built?

- The Wall was built on the orders of the Soviet leader Nikita **Khrushchev** because so many East Berliners had left East Berlin to live in the much more prosperous West in the years from 1949 to 1961. They left because the West offered better living conditions and much better pay.
- Most of the people who left were highly qualified or skilled. This meant that East Germany was losing many of its most educated people.
- Khrushchev believed that he could get away with it because the new US president John **Kennedy** was very inexperienced. Kennedy had just been made to look stupid when an invasion of Cuba from the USA had ended in disaster at the Bay of Pigs.

How did Kennedy react?

He went to Berlin and made a speech to hundreds of thousands of West Berliners. In it he said, 'Ich bin ein Berliner.' This was meant to show that he was sharing their difficulties, but it actually meant 'I am a doughnut'. 'Berliner' was a slang term for a doughnut.

The Wall remained in place until 1990 and more than 300 people were killed trying to cross it.

Iron Curtain, West Germany

BEVERIDGE, SIR WILLIAM (LATER LORD)

William Beveridge was the most important figure in the development of the **Welfare State** in Britain in the twentieth century. He was a civil servant who advised the Liberal governments in the years from 1906 to 1914, when the first welfare measures were introduced. In 1941 he was asked to head a commission which would investigate how Britain was to be rebuilt after the **Second World War**. The Beveridge Report, which was produced in November 1942, became a best-seller. Beveridge said that the State should protect the people of Britain from five 'Giant Evils': Squalor, Idleness, Want, Ignorance and Disease. This protection should last 'from the cradle to the grave'.

The Beveridge Report was the basis for the reforms introduced by the **Labour Party** in the years from 1945 to 1950, which led to the setting up of the Welfare State. The most important of these were the National Health Service and National Insurance.

Liberal Reforms

BIOGRAPHY

A biography is a life story of an historical figure. It is not written by the person in question. Sometimes biographies are written for a particular reason. They may be intended to attack the subject, or they may be intended to make the person out to be successful. Most biographies are written to explain what the person was trying to achieve.

> REMEMBER: a biography is not written by the person whose life is being described.

SELF-CHECK QUESTION 1

What name is given to a life story written by the person whose life is being described?

BLACK DEATH

The Black Death was an epidemic disease which swept across Europe in the middle of the fourteenth century. The worst outbreaks were in the years from 1348 to 1360, but there were other outbreaks afterwards and the disease returned from time to time until the eighteenth century. There was a major outbreak in London in 1665.

There were two forms of the disease: Bubonic Plague, which was caused by plague fleas carried on black rats; these were brought to Europe from China; and Pneumonic Plague which was an infection of the lungs. The real causes of the plagues were not known at the time and people blamed wild animals, travellers, gypsies or saw it as a punishment by God. The same causes were given in London in 1665.

Some people realised that the Bubonic Plague was linked to rubbish in the streets, although they tended to believe that it was the smell, rather than the fact that it attracted rats. In the city of Milan there were attempts to clean up the streets and King **Richard II** gave orders to clean the River Thames in the 1380s.

What effects did the Black Death have in England?

- The Black Death killed about one-third of the population. This led to many villages becoming abandoned. They can still be seen in some parts of the country.
- There was an increase in the pay-rates of labourers, as population had fallen.
- The Black Death helped to bring an end to the **Feudal System**, which was based on service. More people began to work for wages instead.

- It helped to cause the **Peasants' Revolt** in 1381. The peasants complained about their lords trying to impose feudal taxes, which they said they could not afford.

Historians disagree on how severe these changes were. This is an example of different interpretations of historical changes. Some historians believe that the Black Death led to big changes in England in the second half of the fourteenth century, because it led to an increase in the numbers of people working for wages; others believe it had little effect and that England soon recovered.

> REMEMBER: Bubonic Plague was caused by plague fleas on rats; Pneumonic Plague affected the lungs.

BLITZ

The Blitz was the name given to the prolonged period of bombing of British cities which began in September 1940 and lasted until November. The worst affected city was London, where 13 000 people were killed in 1940. In the rest of Britain 10 000 people were killed. Coventry was hit by a very heavy raid in November 1940, which destroyed the centre of the city and killed about 500 people. Belfast was not bombed until April 1941, when the 'Belfast Blitz' killed nearly 1000 people.

Why did the Germans bomb British cities?

- The Blitz began after Hitler gave up his attempt to invade Britain in September 1940; this had been called 'Operation Sealion'. He was trying to force Britain to surrender.
- The Blitz was really intended to break the morale of the British people. If they saw their homes being destroyed and their loved ones being killed, Hitler believed that they would force the government to come to terms with him.
- The Blitz was also an attempt to destroy industry. In London the docks were attacked regularly and this meant that people living in the East End were often bombed. The Luftwaffe, the German airforce, also tried to hit railway lines and junctions.

What effects did the Blitz have?

- At the time the government would only allow stories to be published in newspapers which said how well the British people were coping. 'Britain can take it' was one slogan. This was an example of **propaganda**.
- In fact there are many examples of people being very near to total despair in the winter of 1940–41. The Blitz had much more devastating effects than the government was prepared to admit.
- In October 1940 Balham underground station was hit by a bomb which burst a water main. Sixty-four people were drowned. This story was not released until after the war, because many people

A man hoists a Union Jack on the ruins of his house the morning after an air raid
Courtesy of Getty Images Limited

sheltered from air-raids in underground stations. If they had found out what had happened there might well have been panic.

Above is an example of a photograph which was published during the war. It shows a man cheerfully coping with the effects of bombing.

How did the British people defend themselves against bombing?

- A blackout went into force in 1939. All lights had to be hidden at night. Windows were taped to prevent people being injured by flying glass.
- Anderson air-raid shelters were distributed; these were dug into the garden and covered with earth. They were designed to protect people against falling brickwork if the houses were bombed.
- All houses had to have a safe room, usually in a cellar or on the ground floor, where people could sleep during a raid if there was no shelter. Some people slept in a Morrison shelter, a steel cage which fitted under a dining-table.
- Air-raid Precaution Wardens were appointed for every street. They had the job of checking everybody's house. They had to be told how many people were sleeping in each house each night.

In 1944 and 1945 Britain was attacked from the air once again. The first attacks came from pilotless rocket planes called V1s. These could be launched from railway trucks which were moved from place to place. Each rocket carried about one tonne of explosive and when it ran out of fuel it fell to the ground and exploded. At first there was little that could be done about these, but eventually many of the anti-aircraft guns around London were moved down to the south coast and used to shoot down the rockets as they came over.

V2s were a much more serious threat. They were real rockets which were fired from sites in Holland. They could not be shot down and there was no defence against them. The attacks were only stopped when the launch sites were overrun in 1945.

> REMEMBER: the Blitz was an attempt to break the morale of the people of Britain.

BLITZKRIEG

Blitzkrieg was the method of fighting developed by the German armed forces in the years leading up to the outbreak of the **Second World War**. The word blitzkrieg means lightning war. It made use of dive-bombers to attack enemy positions from the air and massed formations of tanks to smash through before there was any chance of recovery. Using these methods **Hitler** hoped to avoid the stalemate of the **First World War**.

German forces were sent to take part in the **Spanish Civil War** (1936 to 1939) to practise and perfect Blitzkrieg. It was then used against Poland in September 1939 and Denmark, Holland, Belgium and France in April and May 1940.

Blitzkrieg proved highly effective and the armies of Britain and France were taken by surprise. They had expected that the war would be fought in trenches as it had been from 1914 to 1918.

BOERS

This is the name used to describe the Dutch settlers in South Africa: it means 'farmer'. The settlers had arrived in the seventeenth century and the Cape remained a Dutch colony until 1815, when it was handed over to Britain. In the nineteenth century relations between the British government and the Boers changed many times. After the ending of **slavery** in the British Empire in 1833, the Boers left the Cape and occupied the territory beyond the Orange and Vaal Rivers. These areas eventually became the Orange Free State and Transvaal. This movement became known as the Great Trek.

The Boers set up the South African Republic, but in 1877 this was annexed by the British. After the Zulu War (1879) the Boers revolted against the British and regained their independence in the First Boer War (1880 to 1881).

In 1886 gold was discovered in the Transvaal. This attracted many foreign miners. These were called Uitlanders by the Boers. From 1886 to 1895 tension developed between the Boers and the Uitlanders, who were not allowed to vote, but had to pay heavy taxes. The Uitlanders were encouraged by the Prime Minister of Cape Colony, Cecil **Rhodes**; Rhodes wanted to bring the Boers into a union with the British colony, but the Boers refused. Finally, Rhodes organised an attack on the Boer capital, Johannesburg, in December 1895: the Jameson Raid. It was a disaster. Jameson was captured and Rhodes was forced to resign. Kaiser **Wilhelm II** of Germany sent a telegram to the Boer leader, Paul Kruger, congratulating him on his success. This made the Kaiser very unpopular in Britain.

However, the situation in South Africa soon became worse. In 1897 a new British High Commissioner, Sir Alfred Milner, arrived. He set about provoking a war with the Boers and encouraged the Uitlanders to appeal to Queen **Victoria** for help. In 1899 Milner met the Boer leader, Kruger, and demanded that the Uitlanders be given the vote. Kruger refused, as he knew that this would give the Uitlanders control of the Transvaal. Eventually Kruger decided to declare war on Britain; he knew that the British had only about 25 000 soldiers in South Africa and the Boers outnumbered them two to one.

The Second Boer War

The war lasted from 1899 to 1902. At first the British Army was outnumbered and suffered a series of defeats. The Boers besieged three towns, Mafeking, Ladysmith and Kimberley, but as more forces arrived the sieges were relieved and the tide turned in the British favour. The Boers then began a guerrilla war attacking railway lines. The British replied by building concentration camps and rounding up Boer women and children. About 26 000 people died in these camps. Eventually the Boers signed the Treaty of Vereeniging in May 1902. This set up the union of South Africa made up of Cape Colony, Natal, the Orange Free State and Transvaal. The Boers were given £3 000 000 to help them recover from the effects of the war.

BOLEYN, ANNE

Anne Boleyn was the daughter of a wealthy and influential landowner, Thomas Boleyn, who lived at Hever Castle in Kent. The family was well known at **court** and Anne's sister Mary had been King **Henry VIII**'s mistress during the early 1520s. By 1527 Henry had fallen in love with Anne and she became involved in his attempts to gain a divorce from Pope Clement VII.

Henry married Anne secretly on 25 January 1533 and she gave birth to Princess **Elizabeth** in the same year. Anne was executed on 19 May 1536 after being convicted of adultery.

It seems that Thomas Boleyn had used his daughters in an attempt to gain influence at court. Anne paid the price for her immaturity and the scheming of her father.

BOLSHEVIKS

The Bolsheviks were the supporters of Lenin in Russia. The name meant 'the majority' and had come about as a result of an argument in 1903, when the Social Democrat Party had split into two sections, the Bolsheviks and the Mensheviks. The Bolsheviks seized power in Russia in October 1917 and remained in control until the collapse of the **Soviet Union** in 1991. In 1921 the name was changed to the Communist Party.

BOROUGHS

Boroughs were towns which had been given a royal charter. In 1265 Simon de **Montfort** summoned two burgesses from each borough in England to Parliament. This was the first time that towns had ever been included in Parliament. Boroughs continued to send two representatives each until the **Reform Acts** of the nineteenth century.

By the eighteenth century boroughs varied considerably. In some, all local ratepayers could vote; in others there were very few voters. The biggest was Westminster with 4000 voters; the smallest were Old Sarum, which had burnt down in the thirteenth century, and Dunwich, which collapsed into the North Sea in the fourteenth century. None of these had any voters. Gatton, in Surrey, had only one voter. Boroughs such as these were the property of the landowner and became known as 'pocket boroughs'. In other boroughs, where there were few voters, it was possible to use bribery to get elected. These were known as 'rotten boroughs'.

The differences between the sizes of boroughs was one of the reasons for the passage of the Great **Reform** Act in 1832.

BOSTON MASSACRE

+ **American Revolution**

BOSWORTH FIELD

+ **Wars of the Roses**

BOYNE, THE BATTLE OF, 1 JULY 1690

The Battle of the Boyne was fought in Ireland between the forces of **James II**, who had invaded in March 1689 with French support, in an effort to regain the throne, and the English under **William III**. James was defeated and fled to France. The war in Ireland continued for another year, but the Boyne was the crucial victory and is remembered as such in Ulster today.

BREDA, THE DECLARATIONS OF

This was a statement by **Charles II**, before his **Restoration**, which tried to reassure the people of England that he did not intend to make great changes if he returned as king. He promised:

- to grant an amnesty to all who had taken part in the civil wars
- to allow Parliament to decide who should be punished for their actions
- to allow Parliament to settle all the problems to do with finance and money.

The Declarations were accepted by Parliament and Charles was proclaimed King on 8 May 1660. He returned on 29 May, his birthday.

BRITISH EXPEDITIONARY FORCE

This was the name given to the British forces sent to the continent at the beginning of the First and Second World Wars. In 1914, at the beginning of the **First World War**, the BEF, as it was known, was able to delay the advance of the German army at the battle of **Mons** and therefore played an important part in preventing the **Schlieffen Plan** being successfully carried out.

In 1940, at the beginning of the **Second World War**, the BEF was forced back on **Dunkirk** and Calais and had to be rescued.

BRUNEL, ISAMBARD KINGDOM

I.K. Brunel was an engineer, who started work with his father, Sir Marc Brunel, working on a foot tunnel

under the Thames at Greenwich. You can still walk under the Thames today using the tunnel, the entrance is near the Cutty Sark.

Brunel next became famous when he won the competition to design a bridge across the Avon near Bristol. His entry beat Thomas **Telford**'s. The success of the bridge meant Brunel was given the chance to build the Great Western Railway, which was completed in 1841. This was nicknamed 'Brunel's billiard table', because he tried to avoid as many hills as possible.

Before he began work on the railway, Brunel carried out tests to find out what would be the best gauge to use. He ended up with seven feet and a quarter of an inch; this became known as 'broad gauge'. But only 8 per cent of the track in Britain was built using Brunel's gauge, against 92 per cent using **Stephenson**'s standard gauge. Although every test showed Brunel's to be safer, the Gauge Act of 1846 made the standard gauge compulsory.

The Great Western Railway ended at Bristol, but Brunel wanted to continue the line by building steamships to cross the Atlantic to the USA. He built three: the Great Western, the Great Britain and the Great Eastern. Although the first was built of wood and used paddles, the second two were made of iron and used screw propulsion. This was a big step forward in steamship design. The Great Eastern was the biggest ship afloat and could carry 4000 passengers. Unfortunately it was too big: there were not that many people who wanted to cross the Atlantic, so it was not a success.

Brunel extended his railway further west into Cornwall. He built the Tamar Bridge and also tried to build a railway near Exeter where the train had no locomotive, but was pushed by atmospheric pressure. Like many of Brunel's ideas, it was ahead of its time.

BUCKINGHAM, GEORGE VILLIERS, FIRST DUKE OF

The Duke of Buckingham was a favourite of King **James I**. He went with James' son, Charles (later **Charles I**) to Spain in 1623 and tried to arrange a marriage for Charles to a Spanish princess. This was very unpopular in England and led people to believe that Charles was a Catholic. Buckingham became even more unpopular when Charles became King in 1625 and was attacked by Parliament in 1626. Charles was accused of giving money to Buckingham – money which was raised illegally, as some taxes had only been granted for one year in 1625.

Buckingham became a symbol of the disagreements between Charles and Parliament, which led to Parliament being dissolved in 1629. This in turn led to Charles' attempt to rule without Parliament from 1629 to 1640.

Buckingham himself was murdered on 29 August 1628. His murderer was John Felton, who was a naval officer. The murder had nothing to do with the disagreements between Charles and Parliament.

CABINET

The Cabinet is the name of the council of ministers, each with their own department or area of policy, appointed by the Prime Minister in a British government. The ministers are linked together by common responsibility for their actions, which is the basis of Cabinet government in Britain. The term has no legal or constitutional status, so there was no one point when the Cabinet first emerged. The first signs of a Cabinet came in the 1660s when the CABAL came to power in 1667. This was made up of five ministers: Clifford, Ashley, Buckingham, Arlington and Lauderdale. They did not form a Cabinet, but this was a sign that groups of ministers were becoming important.

Over the next 50 years the **Prime Minister** and the Cabinet gradually emerged. Sir Robert Walpole is usually said to be the first Prime Minister. He was appointed by **George I** in 1721 and remained in office until 1742, but during the reign of Queen **Anne** (1702–1714) there were signs that the Earl of Oxford was acting as a chief minister and had a council of ministers who acted together. The general election of 1710 was the first which led to a complete change of ministry.

> REMEMBER: legally, the Cabinet does not really exist.

CANALS

Canals played an important part in the development of the **Industrial Revolution** in Britain. The first real modern canal was the Bridgwater Canal, which was built for the Duke of Bridgwater by James Brindley and opened in 1763. It carried coal from the Duke's mines at Worsley to Manchester and it cut the cost of coal by a half.

After that Brindley went on to build his 'Grand Cross'. This linked four rivers – the Thames, Severn, Trent and Mersey – and crossed over near Birmingham. Part of the finance for this was supplied by Josiah **Wedgwood**.

Why were canals important?

- From the 1760s to the 1830s they were the only way of carrying heavy goods from one part of the country to another.
- 4000 miles of canal were built; they linked the new industrial towns with their markets and with their supplies of raw materials and fuel.

- They were cheap and easy to operate; one horse could pull about 60 tonnes on a barge, but only about one tonne on a road.

Why did the canal system collapse after the 1830s?

- The main reason is that they could not compete with railways; these could carry more goods faster and more cheaply.
- Canal builders and owners did not help themselves by building different widths of canals. This meant that goods had to be moved from one barge to another. They also put in unnecessary locks to try to stop water escaping from one canal to another.
- Canals could be unreliable. They froze up in the winter and could flood. The banks could collapse and water could seep out.
- Canals were slow; the maximum speed was about three miles per hour.

> REMEMBER: canals were very good at carrying fragile goods, like pottery, or very heavy raw materials, like coal.

CARTOONS

Cartoons are drawings usually intended to make fun or to criticise. They often exaggerate the physical features of people and are usually published in newspapers or magazines. Cartoons first became popular in the late-eighteenth century and they are important historical sources. They can show the ideas and beliefs that people had at the time, but, because they exaggerate, they can be difficult to interpret. It is important to consider what the artist was trying to say about the subject and also who was expected to see the cartoon. Cartoons in daily newspapers show us ideas which were popular at the time, otherwise they would not have been published.

> REMEMBER: cartoons are intended to make fun of something or someone.

CATHERINE OF ARAGON

Catherine was the second daughter of Ferdinand of Aragon and Isabella of Castile, who united Spain for the first time at the end of the fifteenth century. Catherine was married to Prince **Arthur**, the elder son of **Henry VII**, who died soon afterwards in 1502. Catherine then married **Henry VIII** in 1509. Catherine had one surviving daughter, **Mary**, who was born in 1512, and probably another five children who were either born dead or who did not survive. She was a popular figure in England, but she failed to produce the son and heir that Henry wanted.

Catherine's last pregnancy was in 1518. This meant that Henry VIII's heir was Princess Mary. He was convinced, however, that he needed a son to succeed him, as his father had had to fight for the throne against **Richard III** at Bosworth Field in 1485. Henry became more and more convinced of the need to divorce Catherine and remarry. After a number of mistresses and illegitimate children, Henry fell in love with Anne **Boleyn** and began to seek a divorce in 1527. A divorce could only be granted by the Pope, who was Clement VII.

The divorce was handled by Cardinal **Wolsey**, Henry's chancellor, but it proved very difficult. In 1527 Pope Clement was taken prisoner by the army of Charles V, the Holy Roman Emperor. He was the grandson of Ferdinand and Isabella and was, therefore, Catherine's nephew. Charles objected to Henry's plans and even went so far as to declare war on Henry. Although Pope Clement escaped later in 1527, the divorce was never granted, under pressure from Charles, and the affair dragged on for almost six years. Wolsey was dismissed in 1529.

Henry and Catherine were eventually divorced on 30 March 1533 by Archbishop Thomas **Cranmer**. Catherine retired to a convent and died in 1536.

CATHOLIC

The Catholic Church is the branch of Christianity led by the Pope in Rome. The word Catholic means worldwide and also refers to a member of the Catholic Church. Until the late-fourteenth century there were no real challenges to the authority of the Pope. Increasingly, however, in the fifteenth and sixteenth centuries, **Protestants** appeared, who wanted to reform the Church and limit the influence of the Pope. The most famous of these was Martin Luther, who began to criticise the Pope in 1517. In England the Anglican Church (**Church of England**) was set up in 1534 after the divorce of **Henry VIII** from **Catherine of Aragon**.

From then the term Catholic acquired a new meaning in England and 'Roman Catholic' was used more and more. After the reign of **Mary** (1553–1558), when Protestants were persecuted, Catholics were regarded as potential traitors. A series of laws was passed to prevent them from worshipping, taking up public office, voting, going to university and becoming army officers. The fear of Catholics was made worse by the Spanish Armada in 1588, the Gunpowder Plot in 1605 and the events of the reigns of **Charles I** (1625–1649) and **James II** (1685–1688).

The laws against Catholics remained in force in England until the nineteenth century. Catholics gained the vote in 1829 and were allowed to go to Oxford and Cambridge Universities in 1872.

CENSUS

The first census was held in 1801. It was an attempt to calculate the population of Britain by counting all the people alive at the time. Until the late-eighteenth century little attention had been paid to population figures; it was generally assumed that births and deaths evened out and that, therefore, the population remained more or less stable. In the second half of the eighteenth century the population began to increase rapidly for the first time. This led to the census of 1801.

Since then a census has been held every ten years, with the exception of 1941, during the **Second World War**. In addition to questions about numbers of people, questions are also asked about occupations and consumer goods. In 1851 a question was asked about attendance at church the previous Sunday, and recently questions have been included about ethnic origin.

Accurate statistics about the population are essential, and the census allows trends in life expectancy, marriage and mobility to be identified.

CHARLES I, KING 1625–1649

Charles I was the son of **James I** and was the second of the Stuart kings. He grew up in England and, unlike his father, regarded himself as an Englishman. During his reign he had little to do with Scotland. He was a devout member of the **Church of England** and a sincere husband and father. He was also a firm believer in the Divine Right of Kings. This said that Kings were appointed by God and were only responsible to God. As a result, Charles tended to reject criticisms made of him by **Parliament**. Later in his reign this was to cause serious trouble, as Charles was rarely ready to compromise and, when he did make agreements, he often broke them.

Charles was a patron of the arts, in particular painting. He commissioned a series of outstanding portraits of himself and his family by the Flemish painter Van Dyck. In these Charles appears elegant, serious and immaculately dressed. This is the most common image of him. In fact he could be stubborn and very naïve. He failed to realise that Parliament could not be ignored and in the end paid for his mistakes with his life.

Why did Charles become involved in difficulties with Parliament?

- He was accused of giving too much money to his favourite, **Buckingham**.
- He went on collecting taxes when he had only been granted them by Parliament for one year.
- He was criticised for marrying a Catholic princess, Henrietta Maria.
- He fought two unsuccessful wars: one against Spain in 1626 and another against France from 1626 to 1630.
- Charles arrested MPs and had them put into prison. Sir John Eliot died in prison after four years.

Charles summoned three Parliaments in the years from 1625 to 1629 to try to cover the cost of the war against France; each time he found himself facing more criticism. In fact Parliament had only granted Charles taxes awarded for one year in 1625, and he had continued to collect them ever since. This led Parliament to present a series of demands in 1628, including that taxes could only be collected with the approval of Parliament. This was called the Petition of Right.

Although Charles agreed to the Petition of Right, more trouble broke out in 1629, when Charles was again criticised in Parliament. As a result he dismissed Parliament in 1629 and governed without it until 1640.

Why did Charles become more unpopular during the 1630s?

- He tried to enforce the use of a new Prayer Book, drawn up by the Archbishop of Canterbury, William **Laud**.

- He ordered altar rails to be installed in churches. These would cut the congregation off from the priest and the altar. Both these changes upset the increasing number of **Puritans**, who preferred simpler services and plainer churches.

- He also began to try to raise taxes without Parliament's consent. The most well known of these was Ship Money. This had been collected in the past from ports as a way of financing the Navy. Charles also began to collect Ship Money from inland towns. This was technically illegal, although there was no reason why the Navy should only be paid for by towns on the coast.

- He used the Court of Star Chamber to deal with people who refused to pay. This was a court which had not been used since the previous century. It was not a proper law court.

Charles would probably have got away with all these actions, if he had not tried to force the new Prayer Book on the Scots. This led to war with Scotland in 1639 (a strange event as Charles was also King of Scotland), as many Scots were Presbyterians and refused to accept the Prayer Book.

The cost of the war forced Charles to summon Parliament in 1640. He immediately faced complaints and Parliament refused to vote any money. Charles dismissed Parliament, but when the Scots invaded England, Charles agreed to pay them £850 a day to prevent them advancing any further. This meant that Charles was forced to call another Parliament in November 1640. This became known as the '**Long Parliament**', as it remained in session until March 1660.

Why did relations between Charles and Parliament get worse from 1640 to 1642?

- Charles' attempts to collect Ship Money and other taxes made Parliament demand that all taxes must have the consent of Parliament.

- Puritan MPs were also concerned that Charles appeared to be favouring **Catholic**s. His wife was a Catholic and apparently held Catholic services; the actions of Laud made many people convinced that Charles himself was a Catholic. In fact this was not true, but Charles was forced to dismiss Laud in 1641 and arrest him.

- Charles also faced criticism about his use of the army. Parliament was always reluctant to vote money to finance a standing army – one which was kept in existence in peacetime. Charles had been criticised for this in the 1620s and now found himself in trouble again.

- The central problem was **Ireland**. War broke out in Ireland in 1640 and Charles asked for money to deal with the rebellion. But Parliament distrusted him: an Irish army could be used in England against Parliament. Parliament also distrusted Thomas Strafford, Earl of Wentworth, Charles' commander in Ireland. In 1641 Charles was forced to allow Strafford to be executed after he had been impeached by Parliament. Impeachment was a form of trial where Parliament decided whether someone was guilty or innocent.

- The turning point came at the end of 1641. Parliament produced the Grand Remonstrance, which was a list of all of its complaints against Charles. He replied by ordering the impeachment of five MPs: **Pym**, **Hampden**, Hazelrigg, Holles and Strode. Parliament refused to impeach them so Charles tried to arrest them himself with 300 guards. On 4 January 1642, Charles entered the House of Commons, but found that the 'five members' had fled. Charles left London.

- Charles' actions on 4 January were seen as very serious. First, MPs could not be arrested in the House of Commons; second, the King was not allowed to enter the House. It appeared, therefore, that Charles was deliberately breaking the law.

- A final attempt was made in June to reach a settlement. Parliament sent Charles a list of 19 proposals, which he rejected. On 22 August 1642 Charles raised the royal standard at Nottingham. In effect, he declared war on Parliament.

The **English Civil War** lasted from 1642 to 1645 and ended in defeat for Charles. He surrendered to the Scots on 5 May 1646. They handed him over to Parliament on January 1647, in return for a promise of back pay for their army. Parliament held a series of discussions with Charles throughout 1647 in an effort to reach a solution. Charles rejected all Parliament's proposals and escaped to the Isle of Wight, where he was arrested by the Governor of Carisbrooke Castle in November. Parliament presented Charles with four Bills, which he again rejected. In fact he was playing for time as he had already signed a secret treaty with the Scots, who declared war on England in January 1648. Charles promised the Scots that he would abolish the Prayer Book and allow them to run their Church as they wished.

The Scottish invasion was easily defeated by the Army under Oliver **Cromwell**, and the Army seized Charles. The Army Council (the Council of Affairs) now decided to deal with Charles once and for all. The House of Commons was cleared of all MPs who wanted to try again to reach agreement with Charles (Pride's Purge) and then the remaining MPs, the Rump Parliament, voted to bring Charles to trial. He was found guilty of treason and executed on 30 January 1649.

Why was Charles executed?

- Charles showed he could not be trusted. He broke agreements and tried to involve the Scots in affairs in England.

- Charles refused to make any compromises with Parliament.

- Parliament and the Army disagreed about how Charles was to be treated. The Army wanted Charles to be stopped from causing any further trouble. By 1648 the Army was in control and had lost patience with Parliament.
- Charles refused to have anything to do with the court which was appointed to try him. This annoyed the members of the court.

CHARLES II, KING 1660–1685

Charles II was the son of **Charles I**. He was born in 1630 and took no part in the **Civil War**, but tried to regain the throne in 1650 when there were risings in **Ireland** and **Scotland** in support of him as Charles II. He landed in **Scotland** in June 1650 and invaded England in 1651. The invasion was a total failure. Charles was defeated at the battle of Worcester on 3 September 1651.

Charles was restored as King in 1660. In April he had issued the Declarations of **Breda** and they led to him being invited to become King again on 1 May. He returned to England on his thirtieth birthday, 29 May 1660. This period became known as the **Restoration**.

Charles II proved to be an extremely popular King. His reign was a reaction to the **Protectorate** and he encouraged the arts and sciences, founding the **Royal Society** in 1662 and the Royal Observatory at Greenwich in 1675. He also enjoyed horse-racing: part of Newmarket Racecourse, the Rowley Mile, is named after him. Old Rowley was one of his nicknames. The theatre became very popular and Restoration dramas are still performed today. Samuel **Pepys**, John Dryden, **Christopher Wren** and Isaac **Newton** all worked during Charles' reign.

Unlike his father, Charles appreciated that Parliament was growing in importance. He realised that he could not behave like his father, so his reign saw the beginnings of the **Cabinet**, political parties and the position of **Prime Minister**. In 1679 the **Habeas Corpus** Act was passed: this prevented someone being arrested and held without trial. It became a central feature of the British judicial system.

Charles was almost certainly a **Catholic** and tried to introduce a Declaration of Indulgence in 1672. This would have freed Catholics and **Protestant non-conformists** from legal restrictions. However, Charles was forced to withdraw it in 1673. Charles' decision showed that he had learned from the problems faced by his father. He was not prepared to risk confrontation with Parliament.

Charles was determined, however, to ensure that his brother, James, Duke of York, succeeded to the throne after him. Charles had no legitimate children, so it became increasingly obvious that his successor would be James, who was a Catholic. In the late 1670s two factions appeared in Parliament: the **Tories**, who supported James, and the **Whigs**, who opposed him and wanted an **Exclusion** Bill to prevent James becoming King. In 1681, Charles dismissed Parliament when an Exclusion Bill passed the Commons but was defeated in the Lords. When Charles died in 1685 his brother became **James II**.

-+- **Clarendon Code**

CHARTISM

Chartism was a movement which emerged in the 1830s. Chartists were mostly working men who were not satisfied with the 1832 **Reform** Act and who objected to the effects of the 1834 **Poor Law** Amendment Act. The movement was started by William Lovett, who published the Charter in 1836. This contained six points, or demands:

- no property qualification for MPs
- payment for MPs
- universal manhood suffrage
- electoral districts of equal size
- voting by secret ballot
- Parliament to be elected every year.

These points were not new, but this was the first time they had been put together. All but the last of the points has since become law.

Although Chartism was founded by William Lovett in London, the most important figure was Feargus **O'Connor**, who was the owner of the *Northern Star*, a newspaper based in Leeds. Other leaders included Thomas Attwood in Birmingham and Thomas Cooper in Leicester.

Why was Chartism very popular with working men?

- Many working men had expected they would be given the vote when the Reform Act of 1832 was passed. When they found that the Act had only given the vote to the middle class, they joined the Chartist movement to continue the fight.
- After 1834 there was a great deal of opposition to the **Poor Law** Amendment Act, especially to the workhouses. This led to many people supporting the Charter.
- After the collapse of Robert **Owen**'s Grand National Consolidated Trades Union in 1834, many trade unionists turned to Chartism.
- In the late 1830s the price of bread began to rise. Whenever this happened, people began to protest in one way or another.

The Chartists sent three petitions to Parliament; in 1839 they got 1 250 000 signatures, in 1842 3 000 000 and in 1848 5 000 000. In between these years, support for Chartism tended to die down. Nevertheless, Chartism was the first nationwide political organisation and the first time the working people had combined to try to achieve political aims.

Why did the Chartists fail?

- They asked for too much. The Six Points would have meant too many changes for most people to accept.
- Some Chartists were violent. In 1839 there was an armed uprising in Newport led by John Frost which was put down by the army.
- The movement was divided. William Lovett, the founder, led the 'moral force' Chartists who believed in peaceful methods, and Feargus O'Connor led the 'physical force' Chartists, who

talked about using violence. There was little cooperation between them or the other leaders.

- The movement was not organised and had little money.
- Many of the signatures on the petitions were forged.
- The movement was at its strongest when there was unemployment in 1839, 1841 and 1847. In between there was little support. After 1848 the economy picked up and support for Chartism fell away.

> **REMEMBER: Chartism was the first national organisation of working men.**

SELF-CHECK QUESTION 2

Which of the points of the Charter has never become law in Britain?

CHAUCER, GEOFFREY

Geoffrey Chaucer (*c.* 1340–1400) was the writer of *The Canterbury Tales*, a long poem which is a series of tales told by pilgrims as they travel from Southwark to the shrine of St Thomas à **Becket** at Canterbury. They give a remarkable picture of all aspects of English society at the end of the fourteenth century, with the exception of the nobility.

CHRONOLOGICAL ORDER

Chronological order means the order in which events happened according to time and date. Obviously it is very important to get a clear idea of the sequence of events if we are to work out exactly what happened in the past. You may be asked to sort events into chronological order for an exercise. It may seem easy at first sight, but it can be very difficult, because often books do not give the exact date of every event which is mentioned. If this is the case, you will need to try to work out exactly what happened, perhaps by comparing the accounts in different books.

> **REMEMBER: chronological order means the order in which things actually happened.**

CHURCHILL, SIR WINSTON

Winston Churchill was born at Blenheim in 1874. He was a descendant of the Duke of **Marlborough**. As a soldier he took part in the campaign in the Sudan in 1898 and then went to South Africa as a journalist during the **Boer** War. When he returned from Africa he went into politics as a conservative, but joined the **Liberal Party** and became a minister in the government of Herbert Asquith from 1908 to 1915. He helped organise a number of the **Liberal Reforms**. As President of the Board of Trade, he was responsible for the creation of Labour Exchanges in 1908.

When the **First World War** broke out in 1914, Churchill became First Lord of the Admiralty, but he resigned after the failure of the **Gallipoli** Campaign and went to serve as a Colonel on the Western Front.

In the 1920s and 1930s Churchill played little part in national politics. He became Chancellor of the Exchequer in 1924, a post which he said he had no qualifications for, and edited the *British Gazette*, a newspaper set up by the government during the General Strike of 1926. After 1929, however, he held no further posts in the government and sat as a backbencher in the House of **Commons**.

Churchill's real chance came when the **Second World War** broke out in 1939. He became First Lord of the Admiralty again and then Prime Minister when Neville Chamberlain resigned in May 1940. This was to be his 'finest hour'. For the next five years Churchill led Britain through some of the nation's most difficult times. He is best remembered for his inspiring speeches which were broadcast by the BBC. These defiantly rejected any suggestion of surrender and raised the morale of the British people when it seemed that **Hitler**'s armies would overrun all of Europe. He was often to be seen touring bomb-damaged areas of cities, wearing his homburg hat, smoking a cigar and making the victory sign.

Churchill also made important military decisions. In 1940 he refused to send the Royal Air Force to France to help the French against the German **Blitzkrieg**. This proved to be a vital decision and enabled Fighter Command to defeat the Luftwaffe in the **Battle of Britain** in August and September 1940. He also took the decision to send a major part of the British Army to Egypt in 1941. This led to the victory of El Alamein in October 1942; the first occasion when a German army had been defeated in battle.

Another of Churchill's successes was his friendship with Franklin **Roosevelt**, the President of the USA. Although the USA was neutral until December 1941, Roosevelt did all he could to aid Britain from 1940 and signed the **Atlantic Charter** with Churchill in August 1941, four months before the USA declared war.

Churchill took part in the wartime conferences with Roosevelt and **Stalin** that led to the final defeat of Germany. Unlike Roosevelt he was not convinced about Stalin's sincerity when he promised to allow free elections in the countries in eastern Europe which were liberated by the Red Army. Churchill suggested that the western Allies should 'shake hands with the Russians as far east as possible'. This would mean the allied invasion forces driving east for Berlin as quickly as possible. Roosevelt turned down Churchill's idea. His commanders believed that it would lead to too great a loss of life. They preferred to concentrate on capturing the German industrial area of the Ruhr.

This failure to take Churchill's advice led to the emergence of the communist bloc after the Second World War and to the creation of the **Iron Curtain**. Churchill himself used this term in a speech in 1946.

At the General Election of 1945 Winston Churchill and the **Conservative Party** were defeated, but he became Prime Minister for a second time in 1951 and resigned in 1955. He died in 1965 at the age of 90. He was the first commoner to be given a State funeral since the Duke of **Wellington** in 1852.

CHURCH OF ENGLAND

The Church of England, or Anglican Church, is the name given to the English Church after **Henry VIII** broke away from the **Catholic** Church in 1534. Since then, the Monarch has been the head of the Church of England. The only exception to this was during the reign of **Mary**, when England became Catholic again.

CIVIL WAR

A civil war is a war fought between two sides in the same country. The **English Civil War** was fought between **Parliament** and the King from 1642 to 1646 and the **Spanish Civil War** was fought between the Nationalists and the Republicans from 1936 to 1939.

CLARENDON CODE

The Earl of Clarendon played an important role in the **Restoration** of **Charles II** in 1660. He was appointed Chancellor by the King and was the leading figure in **Parliament** from 1660 until his resignation in 1667. During these years Parliament passed the Clarendon Code, a series of laws aimed at restricting **Non-conformists** or Dissenters. These were **Protestants** who did not belong to the Church of England. There were four main Acts:

- the Corporation Act, which said that all magistrates had to be Anglicans
- the Act of Uniformity, which said that all clergy and schoolmasters had to accept the Prayer Book
- the Conventicle Act, which prevented all religious meetings of more than five people
- the Five-Mile Act, which made anybody who had not accepted the Act of Uniformity stay at least five miles away from any town.

These Acts were examples of the religious discrimination which existed in England from the seventeenth to the nineteenth centuries.

CLARENDON, CONSTITUTIONS OF

These were issued by **Henry II** in 1164. They stated that:

- members of the clergy should be tried in Church Courts, but sentenced and punished in Royal Courts
- bishops should be appointed by the King.

These played an important part in the dispute between Thomas à **Becket** and the King, which ended with the murder of Becket in 1170.

COLD WAR

The Cold War is the name given to the period of hostility between East and West in the years after the **Second World War**. The term meant that the two sides were fighting each other, without actually going to war.

How was the Cold War fought?

- Both sides used propaganda to criticise the other. There were many novels written, as well as films and newspaper articles.
- Both sides used spies to try to find out what the other was up to. There were a number of spy trials in Britain.
- Both the **USA** and the **USSR** tried to influence countries around the world and to persuade them to support their side. They offered financial or military support to countries in Africa and Asia.
- Both sides tried to catch the headlines by getting ahead in the Space Race or in sport. The USSR put a great deal of money into winning as many gold medals at the Olympic Games as possible.

The Cold War eventually came to an end in the 1980s, when the USA and the USSR signed a number of important agreements, like START, the Strategic Arms Reduction Talks. But relations had actually begun to improve long before that.

> REMEMBER: the Cold War was a war of ideas without any actual fighting.

COLONIES

Colonies are territories occupied as overseas possessions. Many European countries acquired colonies around the world from the fifteenth century onwards. The first was Portugal, which gained colonies in the East Indies. Holland, France, Britain, Spain and Belgium all colonised parts of Asia, Australasia and the Americas. During the late-nineteenth century many European countries tried to gain colonies in Africa. This became known as the **Scramble for Africa** and it was one of the causes of the **First World War**.

COMMONS

Commons has a number of meanings. The most widely used is in the House of Commons, the lower house of **Parliament**. The name refers to everyone in Britain who does not have a noble title, such as Lord, Earl, Marquess or Duke. These titled people are represented in the House of **Lords**. Representatives of the Commons were first called to Parliament in 1265 by Simon de **Montfort**.

Commons can also mean areas of land owned in common by people. Before **enclosure** most villages had commons which could be used for grazing by all the villagers. Today many towns and villages still have commons, which are often used for recreation.

COMMONWEALTH

The word Commonwealth has two meanings. It refers to the period from 1649 to 1660 when England was a republic, ruled, in effect, by Oliver **Cromwell**. It is also used to describe the organisation which has replaced the British Empire since the **Second World War**. The Empire was dominated and governed by Britain, but the Commonwealth is a federation of equal partners. There are more than 40 members of the Commonwealth and it is the largest multinational organisation after the **United Nations**. Two countries have joined recently: Namibia and South Africa.

COMMUNICATION

This is one of the ways in which your work will be assessed in history. It is important that you communicate your ideas carefully and accurately. Most communication in history will be in writing. You should try to make sure that you think about and plan your work before you actually put pen to paper. It will help if you can wordprocess your work, as it will be easier to make changes and corrections if you have saved it on disk.

There are different types of written work, for example **notes** and **essays**, and you will need to practise each. You will find help on each of these in this book.

COMMUNISM

✛ **Karl** *Marx*

CONSERVATIVE PARTY

The Conservative Party was the name adopted by the **Tories** in the nineteenth century. The name was intended to show that the members wanted to 'conserve', i.e. retain and protect, the traditional values of Britain.

✛ *Peel, Disraeli*

CONTEXT

This means the historical setting for a piece of evidence, a quotation or an action or event. For any piece of evidence to be used effectively, the background events must be understood and taken into account. This enables us to understand exactly what the speaker or writer intended, or the significance of the events being studied. For example, today it would be unthinkable for young children to be made to work in factories in Britain for 12 hours a day, but in the 1780s it would have been quite common.

> REMEMBER: we can only understand the past if we are aware of the context. We cannot criticise just because the past was different from the present day.

CORN LAWS

The Corn Laws were passed in 1815 at the end of the **Napoleonic War**. They said that foreign wheat could not be imported into Britain when the price in Britain was less than 80 shillings per quarter. This tended to make wheat and bread more expensive than it could have been.

Why were the Corn Laws introduced?

- To protect British farmers from foreign competition after the end of the war. During the war **Napoleon** had tried to starve Britain out by the Continental System. Many farmers had grown more wheat to try to stop this happening. They had invested money in new equipment and ploughed up new fields. The Corn Laws were a sort of reward for all they had done.
- The government believed that foreign wheat was much cheaper than British. If it came into Britain, British farmers would be ruined.
- Many MPs were landowners so they were protecting themselves.

In 1828 the figure was reduced to 73 shillings and in 1842 to 66 shillings. But by then the Corn Laws were having little effect. Many factory owners wanted the Corn Laws repealed. They believed that if Britain bought more foreign wheat, then foreign countries would buy more British goods. In 1838 a group of businessmen formed the Anti-Corn Law League to try to persuade the government to abolish the Corn Laws.

In December 1845 the leaders of the League persuaded the Prime Minister, Sir Robert **Peel**, to repeal the Corn Laws. He realised that most of his party, the **Tories**, did not want the Laws repealed, but he was also aware that there was a famine in **Ireland** caused by the failure of the potato crop. He decided to repeal the Corn Laws to make it possible for wheat to be imported into Ireland to feed the starving.

About one-third of the Tories supported Peel, but the **Whigs** were all in favour. Peel resigned and many of his supporters left the Tory Party and eventually joined the Whigs. The most important MP to change was William **Gladstone**, who became Prime Minister four times in the second half of the nineteenth century.

CORT, HENRY

Henry Cort developed a way of making wrought iron cheaply and easily in 1781. He was trying to produce cannon for the Royal Navy, when he invented the puddling process. This involved stirring molten iron by hand to bring impurities to the top. Puddling was said to be the hardest physical work ever undertaken by human beings.

Why was Cort's puddling process important?

- Before this process, most iron had been cast. Cast iron was weak and tended to break too easily. It was also very heavy.
- Wrought iron was lighter and stronger. It could also be finished more accurately, which meant it was much better for parts of machines, like steam engines.
- Cort's invention came in the same year as **Watt**'s sun and planet gear. It helped to speed up the **Industrial Revolution**.

COTTON

Cotton was the material which began the **Industrial Revolution** in Britain. It comes from a plant which only grows in hot climates, such as the southern states of the **USA**, Egypt and India.

In the middle of the eighteenth century, increased supplies of cotton began to arrive in Britain from the new colony of Georgia. This had been developed as a penal colony and had been named after George II (1727–1760). The cotton was brought back to Liverpool on the last leg of the Triangular Trade.

During the 1760s and 1770s a series of inventions were made which speeded up the spinning of thread. These inventions were used in the manufacture of cotton before they were used in the other main textile industry, wool.

Why did the cotton industry develop more quickly than the woollen industry?

- Cotton was a new industry and manufacturers were more ready to try new ideas.
- Cotton had been expensive up till then and many people wanted to buy cotton clothing.
- Cotton was lighter, more comfortable and easier to keep clean than wool.

By chance, Liverpool, the main port in the Triangular Trade, was in Lancashire. This county had an ideal climate for cotton-spinning. The rain which fell on the western slopes of the Pennines kept the air damp, which prevented the threads from drying out when they were spun.

Cotton became even more profitable when Eli Whitney invented his cotton gin in 1793. This extracted the cotton seeds mechanically, before this had been done by hand.

⤙ Slavery

COURT

This word has two meanings. It can be a law court, where legal cases are heard. It can also mean the people who attend a Monarch and the procedures they follow. The first Monarch to establish a real court in England was Queen **Elizabeth I** (1558–1603). She realised that one way of controlling her nobles was to keep them at court. This meant they would have to follow her from place to place. This enabled her to check up on them. Elizabeth also began to insist that members of the court had to behave in certain ways and to wear certain clothes; they were also given duties to perform. This was all intended to prevent them from becoming involved in plots against her. Becoming a courtier was very important, however. It meant that you had the opportunity to talk to the Queen and to influence her. If a member of the court was sent away, it was a sign that the Queen was displeased.

Louis XIV of France (1643–1715) took the idea of the court to extremes. He gave his nobles duties which they had to perform at certain times of each day, such as carrying the King's candle, or the King's night-shirt. Nobles were also allowed to watch the King going to bed or having breakfast. These duties and privileges were intended to ensure that the nobles had no time to themselves.

CRANMER, THOMAS, ARCHBISHOP OF CANTERBURY

Thomas Cranmer was the Archbishop of Canterbury who divorced **Henry VIII** from **Catherine of Aragon**. He told Henry in 1532 that if Henry declared himself to be the head of the Church in England, then Cranmer would be able to carry out the divorce. Cranmer suggested that Henry should refer the matter to the universities of England for a decision. When some universities decided in Henry's favour, Cranmer agreed to Henry's divorce.

Cranmer later drew up the first English Prayer Book and the 42 articles which were to become the basis of the **Church of England**. They were reduced to 39 in the reign of **Elizabeth**.

Cranmer was the most important figure in the development of the Church of England in the 1530s and 1540s. But when **Mary** became Queen in 1553, after the death of her brother **Edward VI**, Cranmer became a victim of the Catholic revival. He was forced to admit that he was wrong. But he then reversed his decision, and was burnt at the stake on 21 March 1556.

CROMWELL, OLIVER

Oliver Cromwell was born in 1599 and was elected MP for Huntingdon. In 1642 he was appointed to command a force of Parliamentarian soldiers recruited from the eastern counties. These later became known as the Ironsides and played an important part in the victories of **Marston Moor** in 1644 and **Naseby** in 1645.

In January 1645 Cromwell was appointed Lieutenant-General of the Parliamentary Army, which was under the overall control of Sir Thomas **Fairfax**. The **New Model Army**, as it was called, was reorganised on the lines of the Ironsides and Cromwell became the Cavalry Commander. Cromwell was the only Member of Parliament who was allowed to take up a post in the Army.

In 1647 a dispute broke out between the Army and Parliament. The main reason for this was that Parliament wanted to reduce the size of the Army, but this was rejected as the Army had not been paid. Cromwell sided with the Army and became its spokesman.

In 1648 war broke out again when the Scots invaded England in support of **Charles I**. Cromwell defeated the Scots at Preston in August 1648. Cromwell and the Army commanders were now determined to deal with the King once and for all. The King was arrested, moderate members of the House of Commons were forced to leave (Pride's Purge) and the King was tried and executed.

From 1649 to 1660 Britain became the **Commonwealth** and was ruled as a **republic**. In fact all decisions were taken by the Army led by Oliver Cromwell. He spent the years from 1649 to 1652 dealing with uprisings in **Ireland** and **Scotland** and the invasion by Prince Charles, the son of Charles I. When he returned to London he found that the Army and the Rump Parliament (the Members of the Parliament elected in November 1640, who had survived Pride's Purge) could no longer work together. He closed the Rump in April 1653 and set up the Barebones Parliament. In December 1653 he was appointed Lord Protector.

For the next five years Cromwell tried to find a satisfactory way of governing England. However, he continually clashed with Parliament and on a number of occasions ordered Members to be excluded. These actions by the Army became more and more unpopular.

In 1655 Cromwell divided the country into 12 military districts: each was to be commanded by a Major-General. **Puritans** began to control people's behaviour: the theatre and sports were banned, as was going out on Sunday, except for going to church. These seemed to be worse than the changes introduced by Charles I in the 1630s.

Oliver Cromwell died on 3 September 1658. His son, Richard, succeeded him as Lord Protector.

CROMWELL, RICHARD

Richard Cromwell was Lord Protector from September 1658 until 25 May 1659, when he was forced to resign. He was incapable of carrying out his duties and his incompetence made the **Restoration** of **Charles II** all the more likely.

CROMWELL, THOMAS

Thomas Cromwell was one of **Henry VIII's** ministers in the 1530s. He had no official title, but took charge of the affairs of the Church of England after the disgrace of **Wolsey** in 1529 and the execution of Sir Thomas **More** in 1535. He suggested to Henry that the monasteries could be closed and their wealth taken by the Crown. He set up a commission which inspected the monasteries and published reports on each.

There had been accusations made about **monasteries** for many years: monks were said to live in luxury, to keep wives and mistresses, and to have forgotten their vows. Cromwell produced reports which supported these accusations and then used them as reasons for the closing of the smaller monasteries in 1536 and the larger monasteries in 1539. Many of the reports were false: Cromwell was merely looking for an excuse to take their wealth.

Cromwell was also responsible for the Act of **Union** with **Wales** in 1536.

Cromwell suggested a fourth wife for Henry VIII, Anne of Cleves. Unfortunately Cromwell had only seen a portrait of her, which proved to be very flattering. Henry was furious and divorced Anne after six months. Cromwell was charged with treason and executed in 1540. His failing was that he had overreached himself: he had begun his career as a secretary to Cardinal Wolsey and had not realised his limitations.

CRUSADES

The Crusades were a series of campaigns to try to recover the Holy Land from Muslim control. The first was a response to an appeal from Pope Urban II in 1095. He had received a letter from the Byzantine Emperor Alexius I in Constantinople asking for help against the Muslims. Three groups of knights responded. Godfrey of Bouillon and his brother Baldwin led one group from Lorraine, Raymond of Toulouse led a second from Provence and Bohemund of Otranto led the third made up of Normans from southern Italy.

This was the First Crusade, probably about 30 000 men in all. It was typical of the later crusades. Most of the Crusaders were French and they were almost always divided and often quarrelled among themselves. Consequently the Muslims called the Crusaders the 'Franj' or Franks. A chronicle describing the First Crusade was called 'Gesta Francorum': the Deeds of the Franks.

The First Crusade recaptured Jerusalem and established four Christian States. A second Crusade, which set out in 1147, failed. Some of the Crusaders attacked the Greek cities of Athens, Thebes and Corinth, which were easier targets than the Muslim armies. This became another trend in the Crusades. The Fourth Crusade in 1204 occupied Constantinople.

Jerusalem remained in Christian hands until 1187 when it was recaptured by the Muslims. This led to the biggest crusade, the Third, which was led by **Richard I** of England, Philip II of France, Leopold of Austria and the Emperor Frederick Barbarossa. They managed to recapture Acre, but failed to take Jerusalem. After this attempt Crusades continued for another 200 years, but with less and less success.

Why did people go on Crusades?

- Because they believed it was their Christian duty.
- Because they were younger sons who had no inheritance.
- To seek wealth: this became more and more important in the later Crusades.
- To fight: knights did little other than train for battle, so a Crusade was an excellent opportunity for some practice.
- Many Crusaders were Normans, descendants of the Norsemen or Vikings. They had already occupied Normandy, Sicily and southern Italy, so a Crusade was an opportunity to gain more land.

Why did the Crusades fail?

- The Crusaders were often divided. During the Third Crusade the leaders quarrelled so much that Philip II returned home early. Leopold of Austria arrested Richard I on his way home and held him to ransom.
- They depended on long lines of supply. The Holy Land was more than 1000 miles away and the journey could take a year.
- They underestimated their opponents. They thought of the Muslims as heathen barbarians, when in fact Muslim technology was much more advanced than in Christian Europe. They had better steel, clothing and medicine. They even used gunpowder in hand-grenades.
- The Muslim armies used different tactics from the Crusaders. The Crusaders' main weapon was the knight on horseback in heavy armour. The

Muslims used lightly armed horsemen armed with bows and arrows and usually avoided set-piece battles. This meant that the Crusaders rarely got the chance to charge at the Muslim armies. Most set-piece battles were sieges.

- The Crusaders had to survive in the deserts of the Middle East. Muslims used camels to travel long distances, which the Crusaders ridiculed, and often disappeared into the desert when they were attacked.

What did the Crusades achieve?

- The Holy Land remained in Muslim hands.
- The Crusaders gained very bad reputations. They attacked and destroyed many Christian cities.
- Many people in western Europe became tired of the behaviour of the Crusaders.
- Jerusalem was recaptured briefly in the 1220s, but lost again soon afterwards.

- The idea of the Crusade began to be used against people in Europe. In 1208 20 000 people in southern France were killed as heretics in the Albigensian Crusade.
- The Crusades made little difference to Christian pilgrims wanting to visit Jerusalem. They had been allowed by Muslim rulers before the First Crusade and continued during the Crusades. Christians living in the Middle East found Muslim rulers to be tolerant, providing they paid extra taxes.
- The Crusades led to the founding of orders of knights. The most well known was the Knights of St John, the Hospitallers. They were the forerunners of the modern St John's Ambulance.

REMEMBER: to the Muslims the Crusades were invasions by foreigners.

DARBY, ABRAHAM, I, II AND III

The Darby family were ironmasters at Coalbrookdale on the river Severn in Shropshire. Abraham Darby I discovered a way of using coal in iron-smelting, by coking it first: that is, he turned it into pure carbon. His son and grandson developed the business, producing bigger furnaces and complicated cast-iron work. In 1779, Abraham Darby III completed the Iron Bridge across the Severn. This was the first bridge to be built completely of iron and still stands today. Darby did not know how to construct it, so he cast the iron in woodworking joints, dovetails and mortice and tenons and slotted it together.

Why were the Darbys important?

- They made possible the mass-production of cast iron, by developing the use of coke in iron-smelting. Before only charcoal could be used and this was in short supply as it consumed large quantities of wood.
- They made possible the development of steam power, as this needed iron as a raw material.
- They showed that iron could be used for large structures. The iron bridge became world famous and the town of Ironbridge, about a mile from Coalbrookdale, grew up around it. The Tontine Hotel was built at one end of the bridge for the many visitors who came to see it.

Coalbrookdale iron work became world famous and the company built the central fountain for the Crystal Palace in 1851. By then, however, the company was in decline. Like many British companies it was too small to survive against much bigger German and American companies in the late-nineteenth century.

The Ironbridge Gorge museums celebrate the work of the Darbys and Coalbrookdale. They can be visited all year round just west of Telford in the west Midlands. The Museum of Iron tells the story of the Darby family and iron-working, Blists Hill is a recreated nineteenth-century industrial town and you can also visit the Coalport pottery works and other sites.

✦ *Industrial Revolution*

SELF-CHECK QUESTION 3

What sort of iron did the Darby family produce?

D DAY

D Day was 6 June 1944, the day that Allied forces invaded France to begin the defeat of Germany in the *Second World War*. The D apparently stood for Day. The landings were planned for 4 June, but had to be cancelled on two occasions because of bad weather. The tides meant that 6 June was the last possible day for the invasion that month.

The landings took place in Normandy on five beaches: Sword, Juno and Gold beaches were attacked by British and Canadian troops, Omaha and Utah beaches were American. The Allies went to great lengths to ensure that the landings were a success.

- A big diversion was staged to persuade the Germans that the landings were going to be near Calais. Imitation camps were built from plywood and canvas.
- The biggest naval fleet ever assembled was to escort the invasion force and bombard the German defences.
- 10 000 aircraft were available to provide air cover.
- A pipeline was laid across the Channel to supply oil to the invasion force, PLUTO, Pipe Line Under The Ocean.
- Floating harbours were built which could be towed across the Channel to enable supplies to be landed.
- Seasick pills were invented to try to ensure that the invasion force was fit to fight.
- Paratroops were to be landed the night before the invasion to knock out enemy positions.
- Gliders carrying 40 soldiers each were to be towed across to France to land behind the German defences.

Despite these and other precautions the landings did not go as planned.

- Many of the gliders crashed and about half the soldiers in them were killed.
- Some of the aeroplanes carrying the paratroops lost their way and dropped them in the wrong places. One unit fell into a marsh and drowned. Another fell into the middle of a town and all the soldiers were killed immediately.
- The naval bombardment did not destroy all the German defences.
- The American beaches were very heavily defended and the invaders were unable to make quick progress.
- The Germans were able to bring up reinforcements to stop the Allies making much progress. It was not until mid-July that they were able to break out of Normandy and advance on Paris.

D Day was a very important event in the Second World War. It led to the liberation of France and then to the final defeat of Germany in May 1945.

DECLARATION OF RIGHTS

✦ *Glorious Revolution*

DEPRESSION

The Depression, or Great Depression, is the name given to the period in the 1930s when industry in the **USA** and Europe slumped after the **Wall Street Crash**.

The main effects of the Depression in Britain were:

- high unemployment in the heavy industries, such as ship-building, coal, steel and textiles. Ship-building collapsed as the Depression led to falls in imports and exports throughout the world. Coal and steel depended heavily on shipbuilding for sales. Textiles, cotton and wool, suffered because of the development of man-made fibres, such as dacron and rayon. These were cheaper, easier to wash and longer-lasting. The collapse of these industries led to extreme hardship in the areas of Britain where these industries were concentrated, such as south Wales, the north-east around Newcastle, central Scotland, the north-west in Lancashire and Cumbria.

The worst affected towns were places such as Maryport, Whitehaven, Abertillery, Merthyr Tydfil and the most well known, **Jarrow**. The Depression led to the formation of a **National Government** in 1931, which lasted until 1940. The Depression was only finally cleared up by the outbreak of the **Second World War** in September 1939.

The Depression in Germany

Germany was the country most affected by the Depression. This was because Germany depended on loans from the **USA** to help repay the reparations set by the Treaty of **Versailles**. Unemployment in Germany rose very quickly, reaching 6 000 000 by the end of 1932. This gave Adolf **Hitler** and the Nazi Party the chance they had been waiting for.

DISRAELI, BENJAMIN, EARL OF BEACONSFIELD

Disraeli was the leader of the Conservative Party and was Prime Minister twice in the years from 1868 to 1880. He was the rival of **Gladstone** and helped to establish the two-party system in Britain.

Disraeli first became important after the **Repeal of the Corn Laws** in 1846, which he opposed. Most of the leading **Tories**, like Gladstone, supported Peel and left the party. Disraeli remained and became the leader of the party in the House of **Commons**. He did not get the chance to be Prime Minister until 1868 but, when he did, he wanted to bring the Tory Party up to date and attract more working people to vote for it.

What did Disraeli achieve?

- He passed the Second Reform Act, which gave the vote to working men in towns. He hoped they would vote for the **Conservative** Party.

- He passed Acts of Parliament which improved **public health** and housing for working people.

- He also made peaceful picketing legal, which made it possible for **trade unions** to persuade workers to join a strike.

- But he was most concerned with foreign affairs and the **Empire**. In 1876 he made Queen **Victoria** Empress of **India** and he also bought shares in the Suez Canal Company. This meant that British ships would be able to use the canal to get to India. It also got Britain involved in Egypt. This was to last until 1956.

DOMESDAY BOOK

The Domesday Book was compiled in 1086 as a result of a survey of most of England carried out by **William I**. Teams of commissioners were sent to groups of counties. They took evidence on oath from juries from each village. London and Winchester were not covered and there is little information north of Yorkshire and Lancashire.

What were the aims of the Domesday Book?

- to find out who held land in England and how big each landholding was. This was because almost all the land in England had changed hands since the Conquest

- to find out about liability for Geld, a national tax on land

- to find out about incomes from woods, mills and pastures

- to find out about military service. Landowners had to provide knights in return for the right to their land: this was the basis of the **Feudal System**, as set up by William I. The number of knights was based on the amount of land held.

Why is the Domesday Book important?

- It is the only record of its kind from any country during the medieval period.

- It provides detailed information about almost every village and town in England.

- It gives a clear idea about how royal administration worked and how efficient it was. The findings for each village were redrafted and published under counties. These drafts were then corrected and altered.

William apparently planned to revise and update the survey, but the task was never undertaken; he died on 9 September 1087.

> REMEMBER: the Domesday Book is the only book of its kind from the eleventh century.

DOMESTIC SYSTEM

The domestic system, or cottage system, was the main method of manufacture before the **Industrial Revolution**. It gained its name because workers usually worked in their own homes or in the homes of their employer. The usual image of the domestic system is of a family working together in the cotton or woollen industries, the young children preparing the raw material, the mother and elder daughters spinning it and the father and elder son weaving it.

In fact there were many different forms of the domestic system. In Yorkshire master clothiers worked with apprentices in their own homes; in south Wales there were merchants who had workshops attached to their houses; in central Scotland there were woollen businesses which employed 3000 families all working at home. The domestic system also operated in many other industries: nail-making for example.

The domestic system is often portrayed as an ideal way of working. Workers could take breaks when they wanted, could work at their own pace and did not have to travel to work.

The truth must have been very different.

- Workers were paid piece-rates by merchants, who forced rates down as low as possible.
- Workers' homes would have been polluted by textile fibres: 'fly' it was called.
- Workers had little security: at any moment the merchant might cut off the supply of raw material and leave the family destitute.
- Workers often had to rent machinery from the merchant. He could charge whatever he liked.
- Merchants often tried to cheat their workers by underpaying them. They would wet the raw wool when they brought it, so that it weighed more, then accuse them of stealing some when they came to collect it at the end of the week. By then, of course, it would have dried out.

To many workers the *factories* of the late-eighteenth century, however unpleasant they appear to us, must have meant an improvement in standards.

> REMEMBER: most pictures of the domestic system were drawn by people who knew very little about it.

DUNKIRK

In May 1940, the *British Expeditionary Force* in Belgium was attacked by the German Army. The aim of the Germans was to separate the British from their French allies and to pin the BEF against the French and Belgian coasts. The plan worked perfectly. The Allies were taken by surprise by the Germans who sent tanks through the Ardennes, a wooded hilly area in north-eastern France. This had been believed to be impossible. The BEF retreated and had to be rescued from the beaches of Dunkirk by the Royal Navy. The government appealed to the owners of small boats to sail to Dunkirk to help evacuate the Army from the beaches to the warships offshore.

Why was the BEF able to escape?

- Many owners of boats risked their lives to pick up soldiers from the beaches.
- The RAF patrolled the skies over Dunkirk and prevented the Luftwaffe from attacking the soldiers.
- *Hitler* ordered the German army to hold back from attacking Dunkirk. He believed that his tank crews were exhausted and he wanted to give Britain a chance to surrender.

The defeat of the BEF was a disaster. All of its equipment was lost, but 310 000 men were saved. Instead of being a blow to the morale of the people of Britain, the newspapers described it as the 'miracle of Dunkirk'. However, if Hitler had ordered an invasion of Britain in the month after Dunkirk, there would have been little that could have been done to prevent it. To the people of Britain it was a sign that all was not lost and that right was indeed on their side.

EASTERN FRONT

This is the name given to the fighting between Germany and Russia during the *First World War*. In August 1914 the Russian armies advanced rapidly, expecting to win easy victories. They were defeated at the Battles of Tannenberg and the Masurian Lakes, suffering very heavy casualties. The German armies then advanced into Russia, but by 1916 the war had reached stalemate. The Germans concentrated most of their efforts on the Western Front, and the Russians were unable to break through the German defences in a series of attacks in 1916 and 1917.

The failure of the Russian armies and the numbers of casualties was a factor in the collapse of support for Tsar Nicholas II and the revolutions of 1917.

Bolsheviks, Russian Revolution

EDWARD I, KING, 1272–1307

Edward I was the eldest son of *Henry III*. He came to the throne after a period of civil war between the barons, led by Simon de *Montfort*, and the King's forces led by Edward. Edward had defeated Simon de Montfort at the Battle of Evesham in 1265 and he was in fact the ruler of England from that year. Edward wanted to re-establish royal authority, which had suffered during the reign of his father *Henry III*.

What did Edward achieve?

- From 1276 Edward attacked Llywelyn ap Gruffydd, Prince of *Wales*, and killed him in 1283. Edward built a series of castles in Wales, Conwy, Harlech, Carnarfon, Criccieth and Beaumaris, to ensure his control of the mountains of north Wales. He gave his fourth son, Edward, later to be *Edward II*, the title of Prince of Wales. This began a tradition which survives today. Edward adopted the *longbow*, used by the Welsh archers; this was used by English armies until the sixteenth century.

- In 1296 Edward invaded *Scotland*, declared himself King of Scotland and removed the stone of Scone. This was only returned in 1997. A rebellion by William Wallace in 1297 was crushed and Wallace was captured and executed in 1305. Edward was on his way to Scotland to fight Robert Bruce when he died in 1307.

- During Edward's reign *Parliament* gained more power. In 1275 it was asked to approve an increase in taxation for the first time. Edward continued to summon knights of the shire and burgesses from towns to Parliament. This had

been begun by Simon de *Montfort*. Parliament also met frequently and the word 'statute' began to be used regularly. It usually meant a royal proclamation, however, rather than an Act passed by Parliament.

- For the first time the royal *courts* of law were organised into separate divisions dealing with different kinds of cases. For the first time records began to be kept of legal proceedings.

Edward's reign was an important step towards the creation of the kingdom of England.

SELF-CHECK QUESTION 4
Which new weapon did Edward I use in his wars with the Scots?

EDWARD II, KING, 1307–1327

Edward II was the fourth son of *Edward I*. He had little experience of government and was a poor military commander. He had to deal with opposition from his barons, his nephew Thomas, Duke of Lancaster, and invasions by the Scots under Robert Bruce. The situation was made worse by Edward's favouritism for Piers Gaveston, who was murdered in 1312, and later for Hugh le Despenser, who was hanged in 1326.

The central event of Edward's reign was the Battle of Bannockburn in 1314. Edward advanced north to try to relieve the castle of Stirling. He was faced by the Scottish army commanded by Robert Bruce. The result was a massacre of the English knights by the Scottish infantry. Edward did not make use of the *longbow*, which his father had adopted from the Welsh.

Edward's wife, Isabella, turned against him and in 1327 Edward was forced to abdicate. His son, *Edward III*, was crowned on 1 February 1327. Edward II was murdered in Berkeley Castle in September 1327.

EDWARD III, KING, 1327–1377

Edward III became King at the age of 15. Until 1330 England was ruled by his mother, Isabella, and her lover, Roger Mortimer. Then Edward took power himself and had Mortimer hanged.

Why was Edward III's reign important?

- He began the *Hundred Years' War* in 1338, winning the battles of Poitiers in 1346 and Crecy in 1356. Many of the conquests had been lost by 1377, however.

- In the 1340s *Lords* and *Commons* began to sit separately in *Parliament* for the first time.

- The post of 'speaker' in the Commons emerged for the first time.

- The *Black Death* broke out in 1348 and led to shortages of workers and higher prices and wages. Edward attempted to control wages and prices by the Statute of Labourers in 1351.

- *Justices of the Peace* were given powers to hear legal cases and were allowed to control wages and prices.

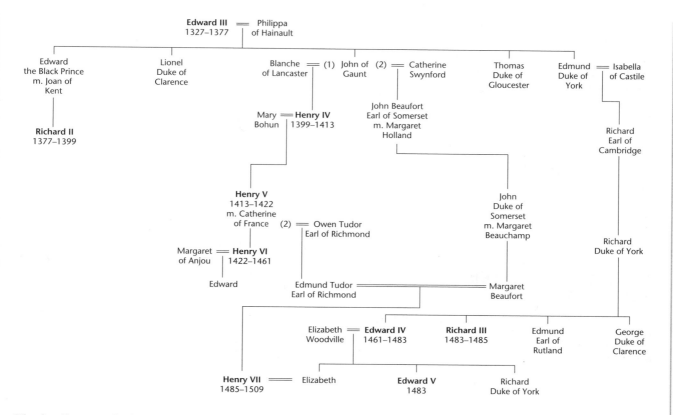

The family tree of Edward III

● John Wycliffe produced the first Bible in English in 1376.

Edward's eldest son, Edward the Black Prince, who had won many of the successes of the Hundred Years' War, fell ill and died in 1376. The most powerful person in England was John of **Gaunt**, Edward's third son. He had become Duke of Lancaster in 1367.

John of Gaunt became the leader of the council which ruled England when Edward the Black Prince's son, **Richard II**, became King at the age of 11 in 1377. His position led to a split in the **Plantagenet** family into the Houses of **Lancaster** and **York**.

EDWARD IV, KING, 1461–1483

Edward IV was the first of the Kings of the House of **York**. He was descended from Edmund of York, the youngest son of **Edward III**. He became King after six years of warfare between **York** and **Lancaster**: the **Wars of the Roses**. The fighting continued for another 12 years until 1471 when Edward finally defeated Queen Margaret, the wife of **Henry VI**, at the Battle of Tewkesbury. Henry VI had been captured by Edward in 1465 and had been in the Tower ever since. He died in 1471 and was probably murdered.

There was now only one surviving member of the Lancastrian family, Henry Tudor, Earl of Richmond, the great, great grandson of John of **Gaunt**. He was 14 years old and in exile.

When Edward died in 1483 at the age of 40, he left two sons: the elder was Edward, aged 12, and the younger was Richard, aged nine. They became known as the **Princes in the Tower**.

EDWARD V, KING, 1483

Edward V was the elder son of **Edward IV**. He became King on the death of his father in April 1483, but was never crowned. He and his brother were taken to the Tower by their uncle, Richard of Gloucester, and never emerged. Richard was crowned King in July. Rumours soon spread that Richard had had the princes murdered, although there was no conclusive evidence.

Richard III

EDWARD IV, KING, 1547–1553

Edward VI was the only surviving son of **Henry VIII**. His mother was Jane Seymour, Henry's third wife, who died after Edward's birth on 24 October 1537. Edward became King at the age of nine and his uncle, the Duke of Somerset, was appointed Lord Protector. Somerset, like the Duke of Northumberland, who succeeded him in 1550, was a **Protestant**. They brought in a series of changes to the **Church of England**:

1547   Abolition of the Six Articles, which had been introduced by Henry VIII in 1539. This meant that priests could marry.

1549   The First Book of Common Prayer, so called because it was meant to be used in all churches. A second was introduced in 1552. This meant that the whole church service would now be in English.

1551   Publication of the 42 Articles (reduced to 39 in the reign of Elizabeth I). These formed the basis of the Church of England and cut it off completely from Rome.

The Church of England was now changed from a **Catholic** Church to a Protestant Church.

Before any further changes could be made, Edward died at the age of 15. He named as his successor his cousin, Lady Jane Grey, who was the grand-daughter of Mary, the younger sister of Henry VIII. Henry had left orders in his will that if his children all died childless, Mary's heirs should succeed. Lady Jane Grey was married to the son of the Earl of Northumberland, who had been Edward's protector since 1550. Northumberland tried to make Lady Jane queen, but was arrested by **Mary** Tudor. He was executed, along with Lady Jane and her husband.

ELIZABETH I, QUEEN, 1558–1603

Elizabeth I was the younger daughter of **Henry VIII** and became Queen at the age of 25, when her sister **Mary** died. Elizabeth had been brought up a **Protestant**, but wanted to avoid the extremes of the reigns of **Edward** and Mary. She wanted to re-establish the authority of the Monarchy, rebuild royal finances and eliminate opposition, both at home and abroad.

How did Elizabeth tackle the problems caused by religion?

- Elizabeth adopted a policy which became known as the 'Middle Way'.
- An Act of Supremacy made Elizabeth the 'Governor of the Church of England'. The title was chosen as a compromise.
- A revised Prayer Book was published and an Act of Uniformity passed, which made use of the Prayer Book compulsory.
- The 39 Articles were published in 1563 but, as these were often vague, many people were able to accept them, even if they did not call themselves Anglicans. Only **Catholics** and some extreme Protestant groups were excluded.
- There was no widespread persecution. Elizabeth was prepared to leave people alone if they did not worship in public. Maps were prepared which showed where all the important Catholic families lived, in case there was any trouble.

How did Elizabeth try to restore the authority of the Monarchy?

- Elizabeth insisted on being called by a new title, 'Your Majesty', instead of the traditional, 'Your Grace'. This emphasised that she was more important than a Duke, who was also addressed as 'Your Grace'.
- She created a **court**, where her courtiers were made to attend her regularly. They were expected to dress as expensively as possible; Lord Burleigh, her Secretary of State, wore a suit made of silver wire on one occasion. To be banished from court was a sign of the Queen's displeasure.

- Elizabeth had many portraits of herself painted, all in the same pose, which she thought made her look at her best. As many people as possible were encouraged to buy these portraits and hang them in their houses as a sign of loyalty. Public houses called the 'Queen's Head' still have pictures of Elizabeth on their inn signs.
- She went on progresses through the country so that people could see her. On her way she stayed at the country houses of her courtiers and lived at their expense.
- She encouraged poets and painters to dedicate their works to her, or even to write about her. This became known as the cult of 'Gloriana'. This was a name by which she was known.
- William **Shakespeare** was encouraged to write a series of history plays which showed that **Richard III** had murdered the **Princes in the Tower**. This meant that **Henry VII**, Elizabeth's grandfather, had been right to kill Richard and take the throne.

How did Elizabeth try to rebuild the royal finances?

- She tried to avoid wars, with Spain in particular, and forbade attacks on Spanish shipping in an effort to prevent a Spanish attack.
- She encouraged her courtiers to give her gifts: the more expensive the gift, the more she appeared to favour the giver.
- On her progresses she stayed at the houses of courtiers, which was intended to be seen as a great honour. It was also an attempt to save money, by living at someone else's expense. Elizabeth always travelled with many courtiers and servants, sometimes more than 1000, and she expected to be entertained while she stayed. Visits by the Queen usually ruined a family for many years.
- She encouraged explorers to sail to the New World (the Americas), by providing ships and financial support, and then took a share of the profits.

How did Elizabeth try to create a new sense of order in England?

- She had a network of spies throughout the country who checked up on anyone she did not trust. These were mostly used to spy on Catholics. In the 1580s there were at least three plots to kill the Queen.
- She was prepared to execute anyone she believed to be a threat. **Mary, Queen of Scots** was beheaded in 1587.
- The **Poor Law** was passed in 1601. This made parishes responsible for looking after the poor. One reason for this law was to try to make beggars stay in one place where they were known, rather than wandering around the country and possibly causing trouble. This remained a major problem in Britain until police forces were set up in the nineteenth century.

Elizabeth tried to control her powerful nobles by keeping them at court, but also by having favourites. Some of them were encouraged to believe that she might even marry them. She followed the same policy with foreign rulers, including Philip II of Spain, who had been married to her sister, Mary.

Why is Elizabeth I remembered so much today?

- She was a woman. Her father Henry VIII had believed that women could not govern; he had wanted a son. There were very few women rulers in the sixteenth century.
- She defeated the Spanish Armada, which was sent to invade England in 1588.
- She encouraged the development of the arts and the theatre. During her reign there were many poets, playwrights and composers.
- She survived for 45 difficult years and died at the old age of 70 in 1603. She never married, as she had stated that she was married to her country.

EMPIRE

An empire is overseas land which a country has conquered and occupied. Many European countries, including England, created empires in the far east and the Americas in the sixteenth and seventeenth centuries. There was a further expansion in the nineteenth century, mostly in Africa, when the British Empire reached its peak.

✦ *American Colonies, India, Scramble for Africa*

ENCLOSURE

Enclosure was the name given to the destruction of the Open Fields and the **Commons**, which surrounded many English villages in medieval times. They were replaced by enclosed farms, where each villager could farm as they pleased. The open fields and the commons were divided up between the villagers and made into compact farms. Before this, each villager would have owned land in different areas of the open fields.

Enclosure began in the sixteenth century when many areas were enclosed for sheep-farming. It continued into the eighteenth and nineteenth century, when many arable villages in the south and midlands were enclosed.

Why were villages enclosed?

- After enclosure, all a villager's land was in one place, which saved time and effort.
- Farmers could do as they liked on their own land: they could plant new crops, dig drains, use new methods of farming, like Tull's Seed Drill, Townshend's four-field rotation or Bakewell's selective breeding.
- In the open fields, land was wasted because there were footpaths and tracks; the commons could not be used effectively.

- It led to a big increase in production, sometimes as much as ten times.
- The population of Britain rose rapidly from about 1750. This meant that more food had to be produced.

Until 1750, most enclosure took place by agreement. After 1750 Enclosure Acts were passed for each village that wanted to enclose.

How did this work?

1. The owners of four-fifths of the land had to present a petition to **Parliament** asking for the village to be enclosed.
2. Parliament sent commissioners to find out who owned land and how big each holding was.
3. An enclosure map was drawn up. This redistributed the land in the village in the same proportions as before.
4. The villagers shared the costs of the commissioners.
5. The villagers moved on to their new farms. They built fences and farmhouses.

Enclosure was often very unpopular with some people. Why?

- The people who wanted enclosure were usually the richer landowners who could afford improvements. They stood to make extra profits from increased production.
- The poorer villagers sometimes could not afford the commissioners' costs. If this happened they lost their land and had to find work as labourers or leave the village.
- The poorer villagers sometimes ended up with the poorer quality land. In the open fields this had been shared among all the villagers.
- Poorer villagers could not afford seed drills and other improvements.
- Enclosure could destroy villages. The villagers left the centre of the village to live on their farms. They no longer worked together at harvest time.

Was enclosure as bad as it seems?

- Villagers who complained were sometimes inefficient, or they did not understand the advantages of enclosure.
- The number of people employed in farming stayed the same after enclosure was complete. About 700 000 families altogether remained.
- Many of the stories about the bad effects of enclosure were reported by people who opposed it, such as William Cobbett.
- Most commissioners worked fairly, but in most cases the richer landowners must have come off better.
- Enclosure created thousands of miles of hedgerows, which became the habitats for many wild animals.

By 1870 all the villages, except for Laxton, had been enclosed. The process created the patchwork effect that covers much of the English countryside to this day.

ENGLISH CIVIL WAR

The English Civil War began in August 1642 and lasted until 1646, when **Charles I** gave himself up to the Scots. During the first years of the war it seemed that the King would win. His forces reached the outskirts of London in October 1642 and won the Battle at Edgehill in 1643. After that, however, the Parliamentary armies began to dominate and they won the important battles of **Marston Moor** in 1644 and **Naseby** in 1645.

Who supported the King in 1642?

- The aristocracy and landowners supported the King. So did many people who lived in the countryside.
- Anglicans were more likely to support the King. **Catholics** also supported the King.

Who supported *Parliament?*

- Merchants and businessmen were likely to support Parliament.
- **Puritans** supported Parliament.
- People living in towns and ports were more likely to support Parliament.

But it was not as simple as that. Some families were split by the war. Sir Edmund Verney supported the King; his son, Sir Ralph Verney, supported Parliament. Many people tried to avoid getting involved.

Why did Parliament win?

- Parliament controlled London, which was the most important and the richest city.
- Most merchants and businessmen supported Parliament. They were able to raise more money than the landowners who supported the King. By 1644 the King was running out of money. He could no longer afford to pay his soldiers.
- Parliament controlled the main ports, like London and Bristol. This meant that the King found it difficult to bring supplies into the country.
- The New Model Army was much better trained and prepared from 1644. Its leaders, **Fairfax** and **Cromwell**, were better generals.

↔ *Charles I, Marston Moor, Naseby, New Model Army*

ESSAY

An essay is a long answer to a question; this may be several hundred words, or much longer. As you get older, your teachers will ask you to write essays more and more. At GCSE they are more important than at Key Stage 3. If you cannot write good essays, you will not get a high grade.

Essays are also important in other subjects, especially English, but also Geography and Religious Education. If you study subjects at A-level, essays will be very important.

How to write a good essay

1. First, you need to make sure that you **understand the question**. There will be two or three key points in the wording.

   ### Look at these examples
   - Why did **William of Normandy** invade England in 1066?

   The key word here is **why**? The question is asking you to explain some reasons why William invaded England, but you all also need to explain who William was, and why he invaded in 1066.

   So there are three points to remember and to include in your essay:
   1. Who was William?
   2. Why did he invade?
   3. Why 1066?

   - In what ways did the Church in England change in the reign of **Henry VIII**, after his divorce from **Catherine of Aragon**? In what ways did it stay the same?

   The key words here are **change**, in the first part, and **stay the same**, in the second. The question is asking you to explain what did change, but also what did not. **BUT** you will also need to explain something about why Henry wanted to divorce Catherine, and why this led to changes in the English Church.

   > REMEMBER: this question is only about the reign of Henry VIII. Don't fall into the trap of covering anything after Henry died in 1547.

   So again there are three points to include in your essay.
   1. Why was there a divorce?
   2. What changed?
   3. What did not?

   - What effects did the **Second World War** have on the lives of people in Britain during the years from 1939 to 1945?

   The key word here is **effects**. The question is asking you to explain what happened to the lives of people in Britain during the Second World War. But you will also need to consider how the war changed in the years from 1939 to 1945. Did everything happen at once, or did the effects get worse during those years? So this question is also asking you to explain the changes.

   So this is a more complex question. You will need to think more carefully before you begin to write. There are a number of points to take into account.
   1. How did the Germans attack Britain?
   2. What did these attacks do to the lives of people in Britain?
   3. How did the lives of people change from 1939 to 1945?

2. You need to **think** about your answer and **research** it carefully. In history the way to write a better answer and get higher marks is not necessarily to write more, but to think more about what you are going to write. Once you

start writing it is difficult to change what you are writing, unless, of course, you are using a word-processor. If you save your work on disk, it is easy to change it if you find out more information.

3. How to do your **research**.

> *REMEMBER: if your teacher asks you to write an essay you will already have studied that topic in class or for homework.*

- The first place to look will be in your exercise book or your file. Make a note of the pages that cover the topic.
- You can also look in your textbook or the other books you use in class. Use the index or contents page of the books to find out where the topic is covered; again, it helps to make a note of the pages. You will probably not need to go any further than this.

> *REMEMBER: if you need more information, go to your school library or your local library. Ask the librarian where to find the books about history, or use the library index.*

4. **Planning**

Paragraph One: introduction. This sets the scene for your answer. Who was William? Why did Henry want a divorce? How did the Germans attack Britain during the Second World War?

You now need to pick out the points you want to make in the essay, the reasons, or the changes, or the effects. Each of these will be covered in paragraphs Two, Three, Four, etc.

Try to get the paragraphs into an order. This may be chronological order, or you may want to put them into he order of importance.

Try to make sure that each paragraph links with the next one. This will earn you higher marks.

Final Paragraph: conclusion. This is to sum up the points you have made. If you think that one reason or change of effect was more important than the others, this is a chance to explain why. But do not try to add anything which you have not already included in your essay.

> *REMEMBER: always plan your essay before you start to write.*

5. **Writing** is the easy part, if you have planned your essay carefully. Do not start writing until you have worked out what you are going to include in your essay.

If you want to practise writing an essay, turn in this book to the entries for each of the topics that these three essays are based upon. Use the sections to help you plan and write your essay.

EVACUATION

Evacuation took place during the **Second World War**. In an effort to protect children from the effects of German bombing, the government asked parents to allow their children to be sent from the centres of cities to the countryside. Most children went with the other members of their school and their school teachers went with them. Some children went to **Wales** or the west country. Some only went 20 miles or so out of London to Surrey, Essex or Kent. Pregnant women were also encouraged to live away from cities.

⊹ Beveridge, Home Front

EVIDENCE

Evidence is a word which is used to describe the information which historians use to find out about and write about the past. Evidence can come in many forms:

- letters, diaries or books
- photographs or films
- speeches made by people, or interviews with people
- records compiled by people or governments
- buildings, music, plays, paintings, drawings and novels which have survived
- books written by historians about the past.

The role of the student of history is to make use of all the evidence available and try to reach a balanced judgement about what happened in the past and why it happened. To do this you need to ask yourself three basic questions:

1. What sort of evidence is there?
   Diary, a letter, a cartoon, a newspaper article, etc.
2. Who produced or wrote it?
   Are you told anything about the person? Is it somebody you have heard of? What do you know about them?
3. Why was the evidence produced?
   Did the writer or producer have a reason for producing the evidence? Was it intended to try to persuade somebody about something?

> *REMEMBER: the three Ws – What? Who? Why?*

If you have to do a test where you are asked to use evidence, it is a good idea to write the 3Ws at the top of your paper before you start writing. This will help you to answer the questions more effectively.

EXCLUSION CRISIS

The Exclusion Crisis was the attempt by the **Whigs** to prevent **James**, Duke of York, becoming King after the death of his brother, **Charles II**. They objected to him because he was a **Catholic** and tried to pass an Act of **Parliament** to stop him becoming King.

⊹ Charles II, James II

EYEWITNESS

An eyewitness is someone who actually saw something happen. Eyewitness accounts are very useful, as they can help you find out what it was like to be present at events in the past. However, eyewitnesses usually see only part of what happens and can also miss things altogether. You need to compare what one eyewitness says with what others say and then look at what historians have written about the same event.

> REMEMBER: do not assume that eyewitnesses always get things right.

FACTORIES

The word factory is a shortened version of manufactory. It was used in the late-eighteenth century to describe the buildings which held the new machinery of the **Industrial Revolution**.

The first factories were built in 1719 for the manufacture of silk, but the real development of factories took place in the 1770s, when a series of inventions were made which increased the production of **cotton** thread dramatically. These inventions were:

1764   The Spinning Jenny, by James Hargreaves
1768   The Water Frame, by Richard **Arkwright**
1779   The Spinning Mule, by Samuel Crompton

Why were factories built?

- The **domestic system** was inefficient and the thread that was produced varied in quality.
- The Water Frame and Spinning Mule were too big to be used in the domestic system.
- The machines needed **water power**: they were too big to be worked by hand.
- The new machines were very expensive, and the workers needed supervision.

In what ways did factories change textile production in Britain?

- Spinning was mechanised almost immediately, because the spinning machines worked well. The weaving machines were less reliable.
- The cotton industry moved into factories very quickly, because it was a new industry.
- Production of cotton thread rose dramatically.
- In the domestic system the machines that were used needed skilled workers. In factories the workers did not have to be skilled. All they had to do was watch the machines and make sure nothing went wrong.
- Factories used water power. This meant that factories had to be built beside streams and rivers. Most were built on the sides of the Pennines.
- Cotton production became centred in towns in Lancashire. These new industrial towns grew quickly and with few controls.

BUT the woollen industry was much slower to change and weaving did not move into factories immediately. Handloom weavers continued to work in their own homes until the late 1830s.

How did factories change the lives of textile workers?

Historians have disagreed about the effects of factory work on textile workers. Some things are certain:

- Workers were forced to move into towns; these towns were built and controlled by the factory owners.
- Workers had to work regular hours.
- Workers were paid hourly rates and were generally paid more.

BUT did the lives of workers get better or worse?

- The real problem was that before factories, workers had worked in the domestic system. There is very little known about this. Nobody was interested in it at the time. **BUT** we know a great deal about factories: many people visited them and there were several parliamentary inquiries into factory conditions in the early nineteenth century. There is no doubt that conditions in factories were very bad by the standards of the present day, **BUT** were they better or worse than the domestic system?
- Another problem was that the reports were often compiled by people who wanted factory conditions improved, so they may have exaggerated. At least one report, the Sadler Report in 1831, only chose the worst examples of treatment that could be found.
- One way to find out is to look at other evidence. For example, there are records from some factories which tell us how much workers were paid. There are houses which were built by factory owners for their workers, which were often soundly built and are still standing today. From the 1780s the population began to rise, just as more and more people began to move into factories.

So what did happen?

For some workers, factories were a step in the wrong direction. Some factory owners took advantage of their workers and treated them very badly. Others realised that workers would work better if they were well treated. In the nineteenth century, especially when Factory Reform Acts were passed by **Parliament**, conditions began to improve for most workers.

> REMEMBER: there is very little evidence that tells us what the domestic system was really like, but there is a great deal of evidence about factories.

FACTORY REFORM

Factory Reform Acts were first passed in 1802 and 1819, but these were ineffective as they were enforced by the local magistrates. The magistrates were often factory owners or the friends of factory owners, so little was done. From 1833, however, inspectors were appointed to enforce Factory Acts and in 1836 all births had to be registered. This meant that inspectors could find out how old child workers actually were.

1833   No children under the age of nine were allowed to work in textile factories
9 to 13-year-olds to work no more than 48 hours a week
13 to 18-year-olds to work no more than 69 hours a week
Factories had to be whitewashed

1844   Dangerous machinery had to be boxed in
Women were to be treated the same as 13 to 18-year-olds

1850   Hours were reduced to ten-and-a-half a day

As you can see, most attention was focused on child workers, but in 1874 workers were allowed Saturday afternoon off for the first time. This led to the development of the Football League, as workers could attend matches.

FAIRFAX, SIR THOMAS

Sir Thomas Fairfax was the commander-in-chief of the Parliamentary Army at the battles of **Marston Moor** and **Naseby**. When a split developed between Parliament and the Army in 1647, Fairfax found himself isolated and he retired. This left the leadership of the Army to Oliver **Cromwell**.

FASCISM

Fascism is the name given to the political ideas of the dictator Benito **Mussolini** who ruled Italy from 1922 to 1945. It is used to describe all extreme right-wing political ideas, including those of Adolf **Hitler** and the Nazis in Germany.

Fascists believe that personal liberty is less important than the strength of the State. Individuals must be prepared to accept restrictions on their freedom in order to create a strong State. In Italy under Mussolini, women were prevented from having careers and were encouraged to produce as many children as possible. Trade Unions and other political parties were abolished and newspapers and books were censored.

Fascists encourage hatred of foreigners – xenophobia – and other racist policies. Both Hitler and Mussolini built up large armies and tried to build an empire by occupying neighbouring countries.

The word fascism is taken from the Fasces: the bundle of rods and an axe carried in front of a magistrate in the Roman Empire. Mussolini used this as an emblem in Italy.

FEBRUARY REVOLUTION

The February Revolution was the sequence of events in February and March 1917 which led to the abdication of Tsar Nicholas II of Russia on 2 March. The Revolution began without any real planning and took many people by surprise, but the results of the revolution were very serious:

- the seizure of power by the **Bolsheviks** in October 1917
- the murder of Tsar Nicholas and his family in July 1918

- the creation of a communist dictatorship in Russia which lasted from 1918 to 1991.

-4- Lenin, Russian Revolution

FEUDAL SYSTEM

The Feudal System was introduced into England after the **Norman Conquest** in 1066. Something like it had existed in England before the Conquest, but under **William I** it became far more organised.

How did the feudal system work?

- William gave land to his barons and bishops. In exchange, they had to swear on oath to provide him with knights when he needed an army.
- The barons and bishops, known as William's tenants-in-chief, kept some of the land for themselves and gave the rest to knights. In return the knights had to swear an oath to do military service whenever the tenant-in-chief was ordered to join the King's army.
- The knights passed on some of their land to **peasants** and collected taxes from them. The peasants also had to work on the land of the knight for a number of days each week. The knight used the money he collected to pay for his armour, weapons and horses. Peasants had few rights and were prevented from leaving the village where they lived.

The feudal system lasted until the late-fifteenth century, when kings began to destroy the power of the barons and organise a royal army.

-4- Peasants' Revolt

FIELD OF THE CLOTH OF GOLD

This was the name given to a meeting between **Henry VIII** and Francis I of France in 1520, just outside Calais. It was a sign that England was going to play an important role in Europe under Henry. His father, **Henry VII**, had not taken part in events on the continent because he was trying to build up the royal finances. He left £300000 to his son. The Field of the Cloth of Gold was a very expensive event and showed that Henry's inheritance was not going to last very long.

FIRST WORLD WAR

The First World War (known as the Great War until the **Second World War**) began in the summer of 1914. In a matter of a few weeks, most of the major countries of Europe rushed into a war which was to kill 10000000 soldiers. Some of the countries which began fighting in 1914 no longer existed after the war came to an end. It was the biggest and most destructive war in history, yet in every capital in Europe the war was greeted with great enthusiasm. As one soldier who was alive in the 1914 said when he was asked what the beginning of the war was like:

The great emotion was excitement.

So why did the Great Powers of Europe become involved in such a disastrous war?

What were the causes of the First World War?

- Hatred between France and Germany over the loss of **Alsace-Lorraine** after the Franco-Prussian War.
- Two systems of **alliances** built up by France and Germany between 1880 and 1914: the Triple Alliance between Germany, Austria-Hungary and Italy; the Triple Entente between France, Russia and Britain.
- Rivalry between Britain and Germany brought about by Germany's **Navy Laws** of 1898 and 1900; these announced that Germany intended to build a navy large enough to match Britain's.
- The behaviour of Kaiser **Wilhelm II** (1887–1918). He tried to create a German empire in Africa and the Pacific and involved Germany in the **Scramble for Africa**. This led to tension with Britain and France.
- The situation in the **Balkans**, especially the rivalry between Austria–Hungary and Serbia. Austria was allied to Germany and Serbia was backed by Russia, as the Serbs used the Cyrillic alphabet and were Orthodox Christians.
- The behaviour of Tsar Nicholas II of Russia, who was a cousin of both Kaiser **Wilhelm II** and King **George V** of Britain. Nicholas believed that Russia would win the war easily and so he did not try to restrain his government. He paid for his mistake with his life and the lives of his family.

All these tensions and rivalries were brought to a head by the assassination of the Archduke **Franz Ferdinand** at **Sarajevo** in June 1914.

What happened after the assassination?

July 5   The Austrian government asked the German government if it would support Austria in a war if Russia supported Serbia. Kaiser Wilhelm replied by issuing a 'blank cheque'. He said that Germany would support whatever the Austrian government decided to do.

July 23   The Austrian government sent the Serbian government an ultimatum. The Serbians accepted all the conditions except one: that Austrian police should be allowed into Serbia to help stop any further unrest. The Austrian government expected the Serbians to reject this.

July 28   Austria-Hungary declared war on Serbia.

July 29   The Russian army was mobilised.

Aug. 1   Germany declared war on Russia.

Aug. 3   Germany declared war on France.

Aug. 4   Germany declared war on Belgium.

How did Britain get involved?

Britain declared war on Germany on 4 August 1914. The reason was the German invasion of Belgium on 4 August. Belgium had become an independent country in 1839 at the Treaty of Westminster. Two countries had promised to defend Belgium if it was ever attacked: one was Britain, the other was Germany. In August 1914 Germany invaded Belgium. The Belgian government immediately appealed to the British government for help. The British government replied by sending every available British soldier to Belgium, about 120 000 men altogether, the **British Expeditionary Force**. They took up positions near the Belgian town of **Mons** at the beginning of the fourth week of August 1914. The German army attacked, following the **Schlieffen Plan**.

The BEF could not stop the German attack: it was outnumbered ten to one, but it did slow it down. The French army, which had been taken by surprise, had enough time to take up positions along the River Marne. In September 1914 the German advance was stopped at the Marne and the Germans were forced back. Within weeks both sides had begun to dig trenches and for the next four years the two armies faced each other across 'no man's land', hardly moving more than a few miles in either direction.

The main events of the war

October 1914	The BEF arrived in the Belgian city of **Ypres**. First battle of Ypres
March 1915	Battle of Neuve Chapelle
April 1915	First use of poison gas by the German army at Langemarck during the second battle of Ypres
April 1915	Beginning of the Gallipoli campaign
May 1915	The British liner **Lusitania** sunk by a German submarine
Sept. 1915	Battle of Loos
February 1916	Beginning of the battle of **Verdun**
May 1916	Battle of Jutland
July 1916	Beginning of the battle of the **Somme**
April 1917	The USA declared war on Germany
August 1917	Beginning of the battle of **Passchendaele** (Third Ypres)
March 1918	Treaty of Brest-Litovsk, Russia and Germany made peace
March 1918	Beginning of Operation Michael, the last big German offensive
August 1918	The Allies broke through the German defences.

Why did the two sides find it so difficult to win a major victory on the Western Front?

- Both sides expected the war to be fought between fast-moving armies using cavalry. They did not expect to become bogged down in trenches.
- Both sides expected the war to be 'over by Christmas'. They had prepared for a short war and they did not believe that it would drag on for four years.
- The Germans believed they could defeat France in six weeks: they did not even bother to take the British Army into account. The Kaiser described it as a 'contemptible little army'.

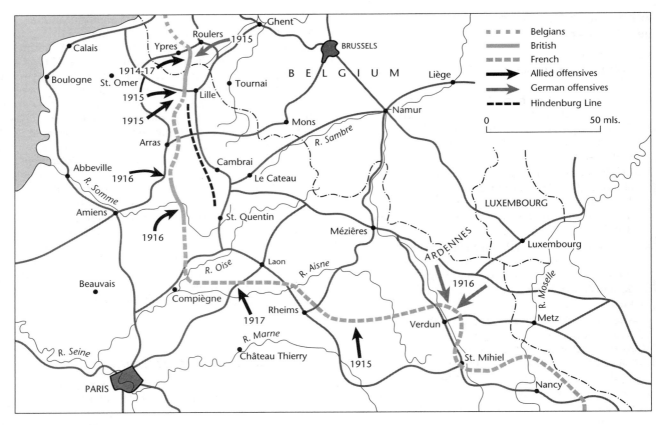

The Western Front

So both sides were expecting a short war and an easy victory. What went wrong?

- Both sides underestimated the effects of two new weapons: the machine gun and barbed wire. Together they made attacking very difficult.

- Both sides overestimated the effects of heavy artillery. Before an attack there would be a bombardment using thousands of guns and lasting up to a week. The commanders assumed this would destroy the enemy defences. It never did. The enemy simply dug deeper trenches and dug-outs and waited for the bombardment to stop.

- The bombardments destroyed drainage systems, especially around Ypres, which was very low-lying. When the British advanced they found that the ground was so muddy that many soldiers drowned before they could get to grips with the enemy. The Menin Gate at Ypres has the names of 54 700 British and Commonwealth soldiers on it, including Indians, Australians and Canadians, whose bodies have never been recovered. They disappeared in the mud around Ypres and still lie there today.

- The British commanders ordered their men to advance at a walking pace, carrying 60 pounds (about 27 kilos) of equipment. This made them an easy target for enemy machine-gunners.

- The British commander-in-chief from 1915 to 1918, Field Marshall Haig, rarely visited the battlefields. When he was taken to the battlefield

of Passchendaele, after the battle was over in November 1917, he said, 'My God, did I send men to fight in that?'

What was it like to fight on the Western Front?

- If you were unlucky enough to get caught in a major battle, life could be very short. The soldiers who went 'over the top' at the beginning of the battle of the Somme on 1 July 1916 were killed almost to a man. But in between battles, or if you were in a part of the front line where there was little action, life was uncomfortable and boring.

- Soldiers normally spent two days in the front-line trenches, two days in reserve trenches and four days behind the lines. While soldiers were in the front line, they were given two pints of water a day, which had to serve for washing, shaving and drinking. The water sometimes had to be carried up to two miles to reach the front-line trenches. Not surprisingly, washing was not a high priority, especially as the trenches could be knee-deep in mud for much of the year.

- Most soldiers agreed that the British trenches were worse built than either the French and German and so were more likely to be flooded. Food was usually cold, if it came at all; so was the weather. For some reason the years 1915 to 1918 produced low temperatures and heavy rainfall. The trenches created two new diseases: 'shell-shock' which was caused by the endless noise of bombardment, and 'trench foot', a fungus which was caused by the mud in the trenches.

- Part of the time spent behind the lines was spent cleaning the dirt of the previous four days and destroying the lice which infested soldiers' clothing.
- If soldiers were unlucky enough to be very close to the enemy front line, as they were at Hooge, just north of Ypres, then lice were the least of their problems. At Hooge the enemy was only 15 metres away. You could hear everything that he did and at any time a mortar-shell or a hand-grenade might come flying over. For this reason trenches always zigzagged: this meant that an exploding shell would have much less effect. If you could dive around the corner away from the blast, you would probably be safe.
- You were not safe, however, if the enemy dug a tunnel under your trench and packed it with explosive. This happened at Hooge in 1915 and when it exploded 500 British soldiers were killed.

Why were the Allies able to defeat the Germans in 1918?

- After the Treaty of Brest-Litovsk, the Germans transferred 1 000 000 men to the Western Front. They launched a big attack on the Allies on 21 March 1918.
- The German attack drove the Allies back 50 miles, but the Germans now had no trenches and defences to make use of.
- In the spring of 1918, US soldiers began to arrive in Europe. Altogether about 1 250 000 came over before the war ended. The German Army was now outnumbered.
- The Allies had learned to use tanks in large numbers as a way of getting across no-man's land and breaking through trenches.
- The Allies began to use surprise attacks without a bombardment.

By October the German army had collapsed. On 11 November 1918, at 11.00 am, the **Armistice** was signed and the guns fell silent.

SELF-CHECK QUESTION 5

Who issued the 'Blank Cheque'?

FRANZ FERDINAND, ARCHDUKE

Archduke Franz Ferdinand, who was the heir to the Austro-Hungarian Empire, was assassinated on 28 June 1914. He was paying an official visit to the Bosnian city of Sarajevo, when he was shot by Gavrilo Princip, a Bosnian Serb student. Princip was a member of the Black Hand Gang, a Serbian terrorist group. Relations between Austria and Serbia had been bad since 1908, when Austria had annexed Bosnia-Herzegovina. Many Serbs lived in Bosnia-Herzegovina and the Serbian government wanted the area to be united with Serbia.

The Austrian government had been looking for an opportunity to smash Serbia and used the assassination as an excuse to issue an ultimatum to Serbia which the Serbian government was bound to reject.

The murder started a sequence of events which led to the outbreak of the **First World War** by the end of the second week in August 1914.

-**|-** *First World War*

FRENCH REVOLUTIONARY WAR

The French Revolutionary War began on 1 February 1793, when Britain declared war on France. France had been at war with other European countries since April 1792, but the British prime minister, William **Pitt** the Younger, had refused to declare war until Britain was actually threatened.

When the French army occupied the Low Countries (Belgium) in January 1793, Pitt went to war. He was afraid that the French would use the River Scheldt as a base for an invasion of Britain. Pitt sent an army to Belgium commanded by the Duke of York. He marched up and down and then came back again, having achieved nothing.

In the same year Britain sent forces to support a rising in the French port of Toulon, in the Mediterranean. But these were also forced to leave before the end of the year.

How did Britain fight the war?

- Britain paid money to Austria and Prussia to fight France. This became known as 'Pitt's gold'. William Pitt the Younger was Prime Minister from 1783 to 1801 and again from 1804 to 1806. A coalition was formed from 1793–5 and a second coalition from 1798–1801.
- To help pay for the war, Pitt introduced income tax in 1798.
- Britain tried to capture France's colonies on the islands of the Caribbean.
- The Royal Navy set up a blockade of the main French ports to try to stop the French Navy putting out to sea. The French and Spanish fleets were defeated at the Battle of Cape St Vincent in February 1797.
- When **Napoleon** tried to invade Egypt in 1798, his fleet was defeated at the Battle of the Nile in August 1798 by the British fleet commanded by Admiral **Nelson**.
- In 1801 Nelson attacked the Danish Fleet at Copenhagen to force the Danish government to withdraw from the League of Armed Neutrality. This had been set up by Napoleon to try to stop British ships from getting into the Baltic. It included Denmark, Sweden and Russia. The League collapsed in 1801.
- In 1802 Britain and France made peace at the Treaty of Amiens. The peace lasted for 13 months. The **Napoleonic War** broke out the following year.

Why was Britain unable to defeat France?

- Britain was an island. She had a strong Navy, but only a small Army.

- France was a much bigger country. The French population was nearly three times the size of Britain's.
- The French army developed new tactics and was very successful. The French fought a series of wars against Prussia, Austria and Russia from 1792 to 1801. The army became very experienced.

- Napoleon proved to be a very successful commander. He was able to defeat every General he faced. The French army had great confidence in him.
- William Pitt the Younger was a very good peacetime minister, but was not so successful at fighting wars.

GALLIPOLI

The Gallipoli campaign (April to December 1915) was an attempt to land Allied forces at Gallipoli in Turkey to try to break the stalemate on the Western Front. The idea was to force Turkey, which had declared war on Britain and France in 1914, to make peace. The Allied forces could then send supplies to the Russian army and attack Germany from two sides.

The landings were a disaster. The Royal Navy began attacking in March, but the landings did not take place for another month. The Turkish army realised what was going on and had time to prepare defences. The British and Australian troops, who did most of the fighting, found themselves bogged down on the coast and were unable to advance in land. There was little water and all the supplies had to be brought by sea. Many troops fell ill.

After eight months the landings were abandoned and the Allied forces were evacuated.

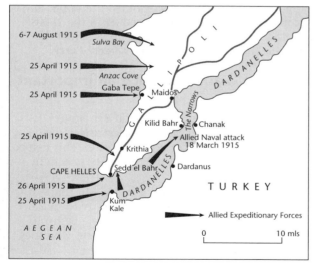

Gallipoli

GANDHI, MOHANDAS K.

✦ *INDIA*

GAUNT, JOHN OF

John of Gaunt, Duke of Lancaster, was the third son of *Edward III*. He commanded the English armies in France from 1372 to 1374 and was very unsuccessful.

By 1374 only five towns remained in English hands. When he returned to England in 1374, he tried to take advantage of the situation and may have hoped that he could become King when Edward the Black Prince died suddenly in 1376. In fact he became the leader of the Council which ruled while *Richard II* was a minor.

When Richard became unpopular at the end of his reign, John of Gaunt organised a plot with his son, Henry Bolingbroke. Henry landed in England in 1399, captured Richard and took the Crown. He became *Henry IV*.

John of Gaunt helped to bring about the rivalry between the houses of *York* and *Lancaster* in the fifteenth century.

GEORGE I, KING, 1714–1727

George I became King in 1714 on the death of Queen *Anne*. He was the first King of the House of *Hanover*. He became King because the Act of *Settlement* of 1701 had stated that if Anne died childless, the Crown should pass to the descendants of Elizabeth, the daughter of James I. This meant the Electress Sophia of Hanover. Sophia died on 25 May 1714, two months before Anne. Anne had had 17 children, but all of them had died before her.

George I was a German, who spoke little or no English. He was also much fonder of Hanover, where there was no Parliament, than he was of Britain. During his reign the position of Prime Minister became more important as George was often in Hanover. In 1721 he appointed Sir Robert Walpole, who remained in office until 1742.

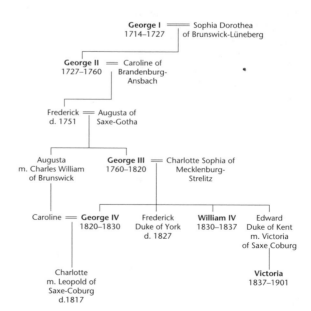

The family tree of George I

SELF-CHECK QUESTION 6

How was George I related to Queen Anne?

GEORGE III, KING, 1760–1820

George III was the first of the Hanoverian Kings to be brought up in Britain and to speak English fluently. He tried to restore some of the influence of the Crown that had been lost in the previous two reigns, but he came to rely on William **Pitt** the Younger, who was the youngest person ever to become Prime Minister when he took office at the age of 24 in 1783.

George III suffered from a rare disease called porphyria. This made him appear to go mad. The first attack came in 1787 and later attacks became more frequent. In 1811 he was permanently affected by the disease. George's son, also called George, took over from his father in 1811 as Prince Regent. This period in Britain is known as the 'Regency'.

George III was a popular King. He built himself a farm at Windsor and was a keen farmer. He wrote articles on farming for newspapers. His nickname was Farmer George. He was one of the first monarchs to show interest in what went on outside the royal palaces.

GEORGE IV, KING, 1820–1830

George IV was the exact opposite of his father. They argued constantly. George IV was always short of money. He gambled and spent a great deal on entertaining. He also bought hundreds of paintings, which are now in the royal collection. George built Brighton Pavilion and regularly travelled there.

GEORGE V, KING, 1910–1936

George V was the son of **Edward VII** and grandson of Queen **Victoria**. At the time of the outbreak of the **First World War** in 1914, he was closely related to both Kaiser **Wilhelm II** and Tsar Nicholas II. The Kaiser was his first cousin and the Tsar was his first cousin by marriage. The three men continued to write to each other right up until the declarations of war. Their letters were signed, 'affectionately Willi', etc.

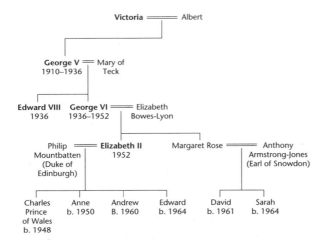

The family tree of George V

GEORGE VI, KING, 1936–1952

George VI became King in 1936, when his elder brother Edward VIII abdicated. George had not expected to be King and was a shy man with a stammer. He was often in ill health. He took his duties very seriously and was King throughout the **Second World War**.

George VI refused to move out of Buckingham Palace during the **Blitz** and often toured the towns and cities of Britain with his wife, the present Queen Mother. He played a very important part in maintaining morale in Britain during the war. He had the same rations as everybody else and when people were asked to have no more than five inches of bathwater, a film was made showing that George VI only had four inches of water in his bath. He died in 1952.

GEORGIAN

The word 'Georgian' refers to the style of art and architecture of the early eighteenth century, the reigns of **George I** and George II. The style was simple and plain. There was little decoration and the emphasis was on balance. Georgian houses are usually made of brick, with rows of rectangular windows.

GLADSTONE, WILLIAM EWART

William Gladstone was one of the most important politicians of the second half of the nineteenth century. He began his career as a **Tory**, but left the Tory Party after the repeal of the **Corn Laws**, when he supported Sir Robert **Peel**. He joined the **Whigs** and became Chancellor of the Exchequer in the 1850s and 1860s and Prime Minister in 1868, when the party had become known as the **Liberal Party**.

Why was Gladstone such an important figure?

- Between 1868 and 1881 he and Benjamin **Disraeli**, the leader of the **Conservatives**, were rivals for the office of Prime Minister. This helped to develop the idea of the two-party system in British politics.
- Gladstone began a series of reforms in the 1870s, which were designed to open the Civil Service and the Army to competition. People began to get appointed on merit rather than on who they knew.
- Gladstone introduced the Ballot Act in 1872. This began to do away with bribery and corruption in elections. In 1883 he introduced the Corrupt Practices Act and in 1884 the Third Reform Act.
- Gladstone was determined to try to solve the problems of **Ireland**. In 1885 he decided that Ireland should be given Home Rule, but he was defeated twice in **Parliament**. If he had succeeded, the history of Ireland in the twentieth century might have been very different.

Gladstone was a very respected figure, although Queen **Victoria** said that he spoke to her as though he was addressing a public meeting. He was Prime Minister four times between 1868 and 1894. He had a very clear idea of right and wrong and was one of the few Prime Ministers in the nineteenth century who tried to avoid further expansion of the British empire.

⊹ *Parliamentary Reform, Ireland*

GLORIOUS REVOLUTION

The Glorious Revolution of 1688 was the sequence of events which brought about the flight of **James II** and the arrival of **William** and **Mary**. William was asked to save England from Catholic tyranny, after the birth of a son to James and his second wife, Mary of Modena.

William landed in Torbay in November and James fled. He was arrested, but escaped to France. Mary was asked to be Queen and William was asked to be Regent. When William refused this offer, William and Mary were invited to be King and Queen jointly in January 1689.

Two weeks later the Declaration of Rights was published. This set out a list of demands that William and Mary had to agree to. The most important demands were:

- Only **Parliament** could make laws.
- A standing army could only be kept with the approval of Parliament.
- Taxes could only be collected with the approval of Parliament.
- Elections to Parliament must be free.
- Parliament should meet frequently.

In December 1689 the Declaration of Rights became law as the Bill of Rights, but Parliament was determined to go further. In the next 12 years there was a series of Acts of Parliament which were intended to make sure that the King could never again behave as **Charles I** and James II had done.

The most important were:

1694 The Triennial Act: Parliament must be re-elected every three years
1701 The Act of **Settlement**.

GREY, LADY JANE

⊹ *Edward VI*

HABEAS CORPUS, ACT OF

The Habeas Corpus Act was passed in 1679 and is still in force today. It has been copied in many countries of the world. The words Habeas Corpus mean, 'you may have the body' and the Act states that if someone is arrested, then after 24 hours they must either be charged with an offence or be released. The Act was passed to prevent people being arrested without any reason.

Today, the Habeas Corpus Act means that the police cannot arrest people without a good cause and if they can find no evidence against them they must be released. Sometimes, in a national emergency, the Habeas Corpus Act is suspended. For example, it was in 1795, during the *French Revolutionary War*, so that suspected French agents could be arrested and held in prison.

HAMPDEN, JOHN

John Hampden was an MP who refused to pay Ship Money in 1637. He was arrested and tried in the Court of Star Chamber. He was found guilty, but became a popular hero. When *Charles I* called *Parliament* in 1640, Hampden spoke out against him. In January 1642, John Hampden was one of the Five Members Charles tried to arrest.

HAMPTON COURT

Hampton Court was a large palace, which was rebuilt by Cardinal Thomas *Wolsey* from 1515 onwards. In 1525 he gave Hampton Court to *Henry VIII*, in exchange for a palace at Richmond. Why he did this remains a mystery. It is sometimes said that it was because Wolsey was becoming unpopular with Henry because he was not able to get Henry a divorce from *Catherine of Aragon*. But Henry did not ask for a divorce until 1527. Another explanation is that Henry was jealous of Wolsey, who was very rich.

HAMPTON COURT CONFERENCE

The Hampton Court Conference was held by *James I* in 1604. It was a meeting between the Bishops of the *Church of England* and the Puritans to settle the differences between them. The *Puritans* wanted the rules of the Church to be relaxed, but James refused. He said the Act of Uniformity must be obeyed. He also banned Jesuits from England. These were *Catholic* priests belonging to the Society of Jesus.

HANOVER

Hanover was a small area in northern Germany, which was the homeland of *George I*. The ruler of Hanover was called the Elector. This was because he was one of the seven people who had, in times past, elected the Holy Roman Emperor.

HAROLD II, KING, 1066

Harold Godwinson became King of England on the death of Edward the Confessor in January 1066. Harold was the Earl of Wessex and was the most powerful noble in England. He had no right to the throne by birth, but he claimed that Edward had appointed him as his successor as he lay dying. Harold was a popular choice and there was no opposition to him becoming King in England. There were, however, two other claimants to the throne.

- Harald Hardrada, King of Norway, was supported by Harold Godwinson's brother, Tostig. He invaded England in September 1066 and tried to take the throne away from Harold. He was defeated and killed at the battle of Stamford Bridge near York. Tostig was also killed.

- *William*, Duke of Normandy, who said that Harold had promised to help him become King, when he landed in Normandy in 1064. William landed in Sussex soon after Harald landed in York. Harold's army had to march south to face William after the battle of Stamford Bridge.

✦ Battle of *Hastings, William I* of Normandy

HASTINGS, THE BATTLE OF

The battle of Hastings was fought on 14 October 1066. It was the last time that an invader defeated the King of England in battle and took the throne. The battle was fought between the forces of King *Harold* and Duke *William*. Each army numbered about 6000 men. Harold's army, which was mostly foot-soldiers, took up a position on a hill. William attacked up the hill with his knights and archers. By the end of the day Harold was dead and his army defeated.

Why did Harold lose the battle of Hastings?

- His army had already fought a battle at Stamford Bridge.
- He had rushed down from Stamford Bridge.
- He did not wait for reinforcements.
- William seems to have pretended to run away, which made the English charge down off the hill. Once they were off the hill, the Norman knights were able to surround the English and kill them.

The story of the battle is told in the Bayeux Tapestry, but this gives the Norman version of what happened. We do not know anything about Harold's plans, or why he decided to fight so quickly. One scene in the Bayeux Tapestry apparently shows Harold being killed by an arrow in his eye: in fact this was almost certainly not the case. Harold is probably one of the figures being cut down by a knight on horseback, but it is a story that people have remembered.

HENRY I, KING, 1100–1135

Henry I was the youngest son of **William I** and he became King on the death of his brother, **William II**. Henry was nicknamed Beauclerc, because he was educated and could almost certainly read and write. He tried to restore the authority of the Crown, which had suffered during William II's reign. He set up royal courts and appointed judges who travelled around hearing cases. His chancellor, Roger of Salisbury, set up the Exchequer, which kept the accounts for all the taxes and income of the King.

Henry also recaptured Normandy, which had been given to Robert, William I's eldest son, when William died. Robert was arrested and died in prison. Henry's only son, William, drowned in 1120, when the ship he was sailing in from France to England sank. Henry wanted his daughter, Matilda, to become Queen when he died, but the throne was taken by his brother-in-law, **Stephen**. This led to a long period of civil war between the forces of Matilda and Stephen. This only came to an end when Stephen agreed that Matilda's son, **Henry II**, would become King when he died.

HENRY II, KING, 1154–1189

Henry II became King on the death of **Stephen**. He was a very strong and successful King, who wanted to restore the authority of the Crown after the civil wars of Stephen's reign.

What did Henry II do?

- He destroyed all the castles which had been built during the reign of Stephen. A castle could only be built with royal permission.
- He issued the Constitutions of **Clarendon**.
- He appointed five professional judges to be the first central court.
- One of the judges wrote the first real law book in England.
- He began to charge a tax (scutage) instead of demanding military service.
- He invaded **Wales** and forced the Welsh to accept him as King.
- He invaded **Ireland** and occupied it for the first time.
- Henry spent more than half his reign outside England building up his empire. By 1189 he controlled more than half of France.

Henry had a violent temper. He quarrelled with his Archbishop of Canterbury, Thomas à **Becket**, and with his wife, Eleanor of Aquitaine, and his sons, William, Henry, **Richard I**, Geoffrey and **John**.

When Henry died in 1189, he was succeeded by Richard. His two eldest sons had already died.

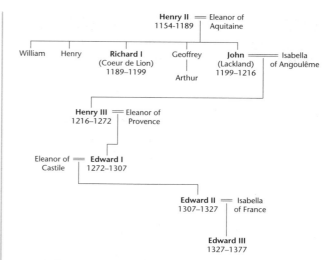

The family tree of Henry II

HENRY III, KING, 1216–1272

Henry III was the son of King **John**. He was only nine years old when he became King and did not begin to rule until 1227.

Why is Henry III's reign important?

- The name **Parliament** was used for the first time in about 1240.
- Henry became unpopular with the barons because he seemed to be going back on **Magna Carta**.
- This led to opposition led by Simon de **Montfort**.
- De Montfort captured Henry at the battle of Lewes in 1265 and called a Parliament. For the first time this included representatives from the counties (knights) and the towns (burgesses).
- During Henry's reign Parliament became more important.

Henry's son, **Edward I**, defeated and killed Simon de Montfort at the battle of Evesham in 1265 and Henry became King again until his death in 1272.

HENRY IV, KING, 1399–1413

Henry IV was the son of John of **Gaunt** and he became King in 1399 when **Richard II** was arrested and put in the Tower. Richard died the following year, almost certainly murdered.

Henry was the first King of the House of **Lancaster**. This was to lead eventually to the **Wars of the Roses** in the second half of the fifteenth century.

HENRY V, KING, 1413–1422

Henry V was the son of **Henry IV** and became King when his father died in 1413. In 1415 Henry invaded France and restarted the **Hundred Years War**. He defeated the French army at the battle of **Agincourt** and occupied most of northern and western France, including Paris. In 1420 he married Catherine, the sister of the King of France. Henry died suddenly in 1422.

HENRY VI, KING, 1422–1461 ▬

Henry VI became King in 1422 when his father **Henry V** died. He was only nine months old. His uncles acted as regents until 1437, when Henry was 15.

Why was Henry's reign unsuccessful?

- Henry was very young when he became King. He had to rely on other people.
- Almost all the lands that his father had won in France were lost.
- He suffered from mental illness more and more as he got older.
- His wife, Margaret of Anjou, was unpopular in England.
- The nobles began to take advantage of Henry's weakness. They set up private armies and this helped to bring about the **Wars of the Roses**, which started in 1455.

Henry was overthrown in 1461 by **Edward IV** and was murdered in 1471.

HENRY VII, KING, 1485–1509 ▬

Henry VII became King in 1485, when he defeated and killed **Richard III** at the battle of **Bosworth Field**. Henry was the last survivor of the House of **Lancaster**. He was a distant relative of John of **Gaunt** and was related by marriage to **Henry V**. In 1471, after the battle of Tewkesbury, he fled abroad, but returned in 1485 to lead a rebellion against **Richard III**. This ended at the battle of Bosworth Field.

Henry was determined to restore the power of the Crown and put an end to the **Wars of the Roses**.

How did he do that?

- Henry married Elizabeth, the daughter of **Edward IV**. This united the Houses of **York** and **Lancaster**.

- He called himself Henry Tudor, which meant that he was neither Lancaster nor York.
- He created the Tudor Rose from the white rose of York and the red rose of Lancaster.
- Henry was very careful with the royal finances. He only went to war once, in 1492, and he made the French pay his expenses.
- Henry collected taxes very thoroughly.
- Henry set up the Court of Star Chamber, which he could use to punish people who disobeyed him. There was no jury and the judges were appointed by Henry.
- Henry executed anyone who stood in his way, for example the Earl of Warwick.
- Henry forced the nobles to disband their private armies and stopped them wearing uniforms. This meant they had less chance of causing trouble by starting rebellions.
- He made sure that his children were well educated.
- Henry tried to arrange important marriages for his children. One daughter married the King of Scotland and the other married the King of France. His sons both married the daughter of the King of Spain.

When Henry died, in 1509, he left his son £300 000 in the Treasury. Henry had gained the reputation of being mean and ruthless, but he was determined to leave England peaceful and prosperous. Henry did not want his son to have to fight for the throne as he had had to in 1485. Henry's reign marks the end of the Middle Ages.

HENRY VIII, KING, 1509–1547 ▬

Henry VIII became King in 1509 on the death of his father **Henry VII**. He married **Catherine of Aragon**, the widow of his elder brother **Arthur**. Henry was very talented. He:

- spoke Spanish, French and Latin fluently

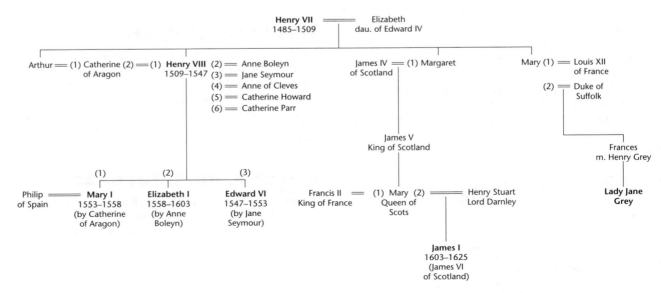

The family tree of Henry VII

- played a number of musical instruments
- composed music, including a very popular song, 'Pastime with good company' and probably the much more famous, 'Greensleeves'
- played many sports including real tennis
- wrote books, including one in Latin defending the **Catholic** Church; the Pope gave him the title 'Fidei Defensor', Defender of the Faith; the letters F D still appear on British coins
- bought many paintings and persuaded the painter, Holbein, to come to England to paint his portraits.

Unfortunately many of the paintings of Henry show him as old and fat. As he grew older he began to suffer from a number of diseases which made him put on weight. Eventually he could hardly walk.

Henry also proved a very successful ruler

- He formed alliances with the Holy Roman Emperor and with the King of France.
- His army defeated the Scots at Flodden Field in 1515.
- He became famous throughout Europe.
- He built up the Royal Navy, including the warship 'Mary Rose', which is on display in Portsmouth.

But the most important event in Henry's reign was his divorce from **Catherine of Aragon**.

Why did Henry try to divorce Catherine of Aragon?

- Only one of her children had survived, **Mary**.
- She was too old to have any more children.
- Henry believed that he needed a son to succeed him.
- He was frightened that his successor might have to fight for the throne, just as his father had in 1485.
- Henry came to believe that he had been wrong to marry Catherine, because she was his brother's widow.
- He fell in love with Anne **Boleyn** and she became pregnant in 1533.

Why did the divorce not go as Henry had planned?

Only the Pope could allow a divorce. Henry had expected the Pope to agree to his request, but Clement VII refused. The matter dragged on for years. When Anne became pregnant, Henry broke away from the Catholic Church and set up the **Church of England**. Henry was then divorced by the Archbishop of Canterbury, Thomas **Cranmer**.

To reinforce Henry's position, in 1534 the Act of Supremacy was passed. This:

- appointed the King as Supreme Head of the Church
- made everyone take an oath of loyalty to Henry as Head of the Church.

Most people took the oath, but Sir Thomas **More**, Henry's Chancellor, refused.

How did the Church in England change after the Act of Supremacy?

- The services of the Church did not change very much. Some prayers were translated into English.
- Priests were still not allowed to marry.
- The Bible was translated into English by William Tyndale. A copy of the Bible was put into every church.
- The **monasteries** were closed in the years 1536–9.
- The 'Six Articles' were passed in 1539; these meant that the Church was still Catholic.

In fact Henry remained a Catholic for the rest of his life. But many people believed he was a **Protestant**. Protestants were people who protested against the Pope and the Catholic Church. In 1536 there was a revolt in the north of England against Henry's actions, particularly the closing of the monasteries. This was called the **Pilgrimage of Grace.**

Henry died in 1547. He left England very poor. He had spent all the money left by Henry VII very quickly. Although he was successful in his early years, as he grew older, many of his plans tended to go wrong. His marriages to Anne of Cleves and Catherine Howard, both in 1540, were unsuccessful. There were several plots against him and his warship, the 'Mary Rose', sank in 1545. Most of all he had created religious problems that would take centuries to sort out.

Arthur, Catherine of Aragon, Thomas Wolsey, Anne Boleyn, Thomas Cromwell

> REMEMBER: Henry VIII remained a Catholic, but people thought he had become a Protestant.

HINDENBURG, FIELD MARSHALL PAUL VON

Field Marshall Paul von Hindenburg was commander-in-chief of the German forces on the Eastern Front from 1914 to 1916. He then became the commander of the German forces on the Western Front until the end of the war in November 1918. After the war he was elected President of Germany in 1925 and was re-elected in 1932, when Adolf **Hitler** stood against him.

In January 1933 Hindenburg was persuaded by Franz von Papen to appoint Hitler as Chancellor of Germany. Von Papen believed he would be able to control Hitler and use the 196 Nazi MPs to create a majority in the Reichstag. Hindenburg did not like Hitler. He did not approve of the violence of the Nazis and their attacks on Jews. Hindenburg knew that many Jews had died fighting for Germany during the **First World War**.

Hindenburg died in August 1934. He was buried with full military honours. His death gave Hitler the chance to create a complete dictatorship in Germany. He now gave himself the title of Führer and combined the roles of chancellor and president.

HIROSHIMA

Hiroshima was the Japanese city on which the first atomic bomb was dropped on 6 August 1945. The bomb, nicknamed 'Little Boy', was dropped by a B-29 bomber from a height of 31 000 feet and exploded 232 feet above ground. Most of the city was flattened by the explosion and about 80 000 people were killed.

At the centre of the explosion, people were vapourised by the intense heat of millions of degrees. Further out, bodies were burnt beyond all recognition. Those who survived were either killed by the tornado, which swept into the centre of Hiroshima at speeds of up to 800 kilometres per hour, or died slowly from radiation sickness, in the days, weeks, months and years that followed.

Why was the bomb dropped?

- The US president, Harry Truman, believed that it would bring the war to an end quickly. He was told that the bomb was ready to be used while he was at the **Potsdam** Conference in July 1945.
- Two Japanese islands had already been invaded and the US Army had lost 28 000 men. Japan is made up of hundreds of islands.
- Truman had been warned by his commanders that an invasion of Japan could cost 1 000 000 lives.
- The Japanese appeared to be ready to fight to a finish. The Japanese Army had 5 000 000 men.
- Few people had much sympathy for the Japanese. They had treated prisoners of war very badly. 60 000 men had died building the Burma–Siam railway.

But some people believe there was no need to drop the bomb

- The Japanese had already sent a message to the Soviet Union saying that they were ready to surrender.
- The bomb could have been dropped on an uninhabited island and used as a warning to the Japanese government.
- Some people believe that the US government wanted to find out what an atomic bomb could do and show the USSR that this weapon existed.
- A second bomb was dropped on Nagasaki on 9 August 1945. This bomb was based on plutonium; the Hiroshima bomb was based on uranium. The US government has been accused of using the second bomb as an experiment to find out what it was like.
- The cost of producing the bomb was enormous. The US government may have wanted to see if it actually worked after all the expense.

There is a lot of evidence that Japan was getting ready to fight to a finish. Kamikaze pilots flew their planes, packed with explosives, into US ships. Soldiers barricaded themselves into caves and refused to surrender. The government had sent out orders for every man to be recruited for the Army and for

schoolchildren to work in factories and coalmines. Schoolchildren were being trained to fight an invasion.

You will have to decide which **interpretation** of this incident is more likely to be true. Was the dropping of the bomb a genuine attempt to end the war quickly, or was it an attempt by the US government to find out how much damage atomic weapons could inflict?

> REMEMBER: you can only interpret Truman's decision to drop the bomb by looking at the situation in 1945 at the end of the Second World War. He cannot be blamed for what has happened since then.

HITLER, ADOLF

Adolf Hitler was born in 1889 in the town of Braunau in the Austrian Empire. In 1909 he moved to Vienna and tried to become an art student. When the **First World War** broke out he joined the German Army and fought throughout the war. He was apparently a brave soldier and won the Iron Cross.

When the war ended Hitler got a job working as a spy for the German Army. He was sent to a meeting of the German Workers Party in September 1919. The party was led by Anton Drexler who was very **anti-semitic**. Hitler joined the party and became its leader in 1921.

Hitler wanted to attract as many people as possible to the Party, so he changed the name to the National Socialist German Workers Party. He hoped that the word National would attract Nationalists who wanted to rebuild Germany after the First World War. He hoped that the word Socialist would attract Socialists who wanted to improve the lives of working people in Germany.

The National Socialists, or Nazis, as they began to be called, were often violent; they would attack their opponents at meetings and this put many people off. The violence was carried out by Hitler's private army, the Sturm Abteilung (Storm Troopers), or SA. They were led by a particularly unpleasant ex-soldier called Ernst **Roehm**.

In 1922 and 1923, **hyperinflation** began to make people's lives very difficult. Hitler tried to take advantage of this in November 1923 and attempted to take power in the city of Munich, the capital of Bavaria. This became known as the **Beer Hall Putsch**. It was a disaster. Hitler was arrested and tried for treason. He was sentenced to five years imprisonment, but was let out before he had served one year.

While Hitler was in prison, he wrote **Mein Kampf** (*My Struggle*), which was a cross between his autobiography and a list of his political ideas. Hitler also decided that he would have to change his tactics and the way that his party was organised.

How did Hitler change the Nazi Party?

- He decided that it must try to gain power by legal means.

- He wanted to set up a proper political party with a national organisation. Before, the Nazis had only been well known in Bavaria. Hitler needed to win as many votes as possible if he was to gain a majority in the Reichstag.
- He set up sections for women and children.
- He appointed Josef Goebbels as head of **propaganda**. His job was to put the Nazi message across as clearly as possible.

Why did Hitler decide to make these changes?

- He knew that if he tried to use violence again and failed a second time, he would be finished.
- At his trial he had gained the attention of a wealthy businessman, Alfred Hugenberg. He offered to finance the Nazis. He also owned 53 newspapers, which he used to publicise the Nazis.

From 1924 to 1929, the Nazis were not very successful in General Elections. Gustav **Stresemann** had managed to get Germany going again after the troubles in 1919 to 1923. But in 1929 Hitler got a second chance.

- On 3 October Gustav Stresemann died.
- On 24 October **Wall Street**, the American Stock Exchange, crashed. This led to the **Depression** of the 1930s, which affected Germany more than any other country.

From 1929, support for the Nazis rose steadily.

1928	12 members of the Reichstag
1930	107 members
1932 July	230 members

Why did support for Hitler and the Nazis rise so quickly?

- The Nazi Party was well organised. It had Hugenberg's money and newspapers behind him.
- Hitler hired a private plane to fly around Germany. He was the first politician to do this.
- Hitler told the German people that the problems of the Depression were not their fault. He blamed the Jews for Germany's problems. He used them as a scapegoat. Hitler said he would be able to solve the problems.
- Hitler said he would do away with the Treaty of **Versailles** which had treated Germany so badly.
- He was always backed up by large numbers of disciplined and uniformed followers. This made it appear that he was a man who could take decisions and sort out Germany's problems.
- Hitler promised different things to different groups of people. To businessmen he promised that he would control the trade unions and deal with the communists. To workers he promised that he would provide jobs.

As the situation in Germany became more and more desperate, people were more and more ready to listen to Hitler's ideas. On 30 January he was appointed chancellor by President **Hindenburg**.

When he took office Hitler was leading a coalition government. There were only three Nazis apart from himself. He immediately called a General Election to try to win a majority. On 27 February, just a week before the election, the **Reichstag** caught fire and burnt down. A communist, Franz van der Lubbe, was arrested inside. Hitler used this as an excuse to arrest many members of the Communist Party.

The General Election took place on 5 March 1933. The Nazis won 288 seats. This was not a majority, but they were supported by the 52 Nationalists. As the 81 Communists stayed away from the first meeting on 23 March, Hitler could now do as he liked.

The Reichstag passed the Enabling Act on 23 March; this made Hitler dictator of Germany for four years. He immediately began to use this power to crush all opposition to him in Germany. All trade unions were abolished and all political parties banned, except for the Nazis. In November 1933, in another General Election in which only Nazi candidates were allowed, 92 per cent of the people supported the Nazis.

Adolf Hitler governed Germany from 1933 to 1945. He committed suicide on 30 April 1945, as the Soviet army closed in on Berlin at the end of the **Second World War** in Europe.

⊹ *Reichstag Fire, Night of the Long Knives, Nazi Germany, Holocaust, Second World War*

HOLOCAUST

Holocaust is a Hebrew word which means sacrifice. It is used to describe the wholesale murder of Jews and other groups by the Nazis during the **Second World War**.

- From 1933 Jews were subjected to increasing persecution in **Nazi Germany**. At first they were banned from some professions: doctors, dentists, the civil service, for example. They also found that their shops were boycotted from time to time.
- Then in 1935 the **Nuremberg Laws** were announced; these made Jews second-class citizens and prevented them from marrying non-Jews.
- In 1938, Jewish synagogues, shops and houses all over Germany were attacked; this was known as Crystal Night. From early 1939 Jews were banned from owning businesses.

The aim of the Nazis was to force Jews to leave Germany. Many did, going to Britain, France and the **USA** in particular. But once war broke out this became more difficult, so Jews were forced into concentration camps and then into ghettos. These were areas of cities which were surrounded by fences. Jews were allowed out in the morning to work, but had to return before a curfew in the evening. The most famous ghetto was in Warsaw.

In 1941, the Nazis began to try to murder Jews, using Einsatzgruppen. These were gangs of armed soldiers who shot Jews in the **USSR** at will. Finally in January 1942 the Nazis decided to set up extermination camps. This became known as the 'Final Solution'. They intended to try to murder all the Jews in Europe.

Altogether at least 6 000 000 Jews were killed by the Nazis, along with more than 1 000 000 gypsies and

4 000 000 Soviet prisoners of war. Many Germans were unaware of what exactly was happening, as extermination camps, like Auschwitz and Treblinka, were built outside Germany. The true story was only discovered when the Allies advanced across Europe in 1945.

Many prisoners of war and Jews were worked to death in concentration camps, such as Belsen and Dachau; these were built inside Germany. These were certainly known about and many German businesses used Jewish workers in their factories. One of these, Oskar Schindler, tried to save Jewish workers. His story is told in the film 'Schindler's List'.

The evidence given by the commandants and guards of the extermination camps at their trials was horrific. Rudolf Hoess, the commandant of Auschwitz, described how he tried to find the most efficient poison-gas to kill the inmates of his camp. He talked of them as though they were nothing better than vermin.

Survivors have described how the fittest and healthiest inmates were allowed to live, as they would be used as slave labour, but the old, the sick and the young were all murdered.

The sympathy that was felt for Jews after this terrible ordeal led to the setting up of the state of Israel in 1948.

HOME FRONT

The Home Front is the name given to the part played by civilians in Britain in helping to win the **First** and **Second World Wars**. The term was invented to encourage people to believe they had an important contribution to make and that the war was not going to be won just by the effort of the armed forces.

During the First World War the most important change came as a result of the very large number of men who joined the army. 2 500 000 volunteered from 1914 to 1916 and another 3 500 000 were conscripted from 1916 to 1918. This led to an increase in the number of women working in industry.

How did the First World War change the role of women in Britain?

- Some 2 250 000 women took up work for the first time.
- Many of these women worked in munitions factories. Before the war many had worked in domestic service as servants in people's houses. They were now paid much more than they had been before the war.
- Women began to work in transport, as bus conductors, lorry drivers and mechanics. The motor industry expanded rapidly during the war and many women found work in it.
- Women also found opportunities in the postal service, the civil service and in office work.
- Many women began to work in medicine. The number of women doctors and nurses increased because of the injuries caused by the fighting in the war.

A poster published in 1916. It was intended to persuade women to join the war effort
Courtesy of ET Archive

However, many women found they were not accepted by men during the war. They were not promoted, they were the victims of practical jokes or tricks, they were given the most dangerous jobs to do and were not paid on equal terms with men.

At the end of the war many women were sacked and their jobs were given to the men who returned from the trenches.

Were there any lasting changes for women from the war?

At the end of the war many women were forced to give up work when men left the armed forces. There were some changes, however:

- In 1918 women were given the vote at the age of 30 if they were householders or the wives of householders; the first woman MP was elected in 1919.
- In 1919 a Sex Disqualification Act was passed, which said that women had to be treated equally in applications for some jobs in some professions.
- In 1922 the State Register of Nurses was set up.
- In 1923 women were allowed to divorce their husbands on equal terms; before it had been more difficult for a woman to get a divorce.
- More women began to become lawyers.

There were also some changes in the ways that women behaved: women began to wear trousers, skirts became shorter, dresses and hairstyles became simpler, women began to smoke in public and go out more on their own. All these changes came about because of the freedom that women had experienced during the war. But these only really affected women who could afford to buy fashionable dresses and had the money to go out and spend. For many women the end of the war removed many opportunities that had opened up in the years from 1914 to 1918.

How did the Second World War change ideas about health and welfare in Britain?

When war broke out in September 1939, the British government expected that the effects on life in Britain would be very serious. Even before September, 38 000 000 gas-masks, 1 250 000 cardboard coffins and 400 000 Anderson shelters had been produced to try to prepare for the effects of bombing.

In the next few months, two more major changes were introduced. First, 1 500 000 people were evacuated. Then, in January 1940, *rationing* was introduced.

What effects did rationing and *evacuation* have on people in Britain?

Many children were evacuated from city centres. The families they went to live with were very surprised at their state of health. Rationing led to an improvement in people's health as they could not eat fatty foods and had to eat more vegetables, potatoes and bread.

These effects made many realise that something should and could be done to improve the lives of the people of Britain when the war ended.

So in 1941 the government asked Sir William *Beveridge* to lead a commission of inquiry to find out what could be done. Beveridge reported in November 1942. It was the experiences of people in Britain during the Second World War and the Beveridge Report which led to the creation of the *Welfare State*.

➡ *Blitz*

HORNBY V. CLOSE

The Hornby v. Close judgement had a very serious effect on *trade unions* when it was made in 1867. The judge said that a trade union could not take legal action to recover money belonging to it, if the money was taken by a union official. This meant that all union funds were at risk of being stolen. The law was changed in 1871 to give trade unions protection.

HUNDRED YEARS' WAR

The Hundred Year's War was fought between England and France from 1338 to 1451. The war was an attempt by the English Kings to defend their lands in France and to claim the French throne. At first they were very successful during the reign of *Edward III*, but lost ground when *Richard II* became King in 1377. *Henry V* then regained all the land lost and his son, *Henry VI*, was the only English King to be crowned King of France.

The main events of the Hundred Years' War

1340	The battle of Sluys: the English navy defeated the French navy
1346	The battle of Crecy: the English longbowmen defeated the French knights
1347	Calais taken by the English
1356	The battle of Poitiers: Edward, the Black Prince, used the same tactics as at Crecy and captured the King of France, his son and many of the French knights
1360	Peace of Bretigny: this ended fighting for ten years. France agreed to hand over Aquitaine and Calais to England. Edward III agreed to give up his claim to the French throne. The Black Prince governed Aquitaine.

Fighting began in the late 1360s.

1371	The Black Prince was replaced by John of *Gaunt*
1372–1375	All English possessions in France were lost except for Calais, Cherbourg, Brest, Bayonne and Bordeaux. These were all coastal towns.

During the reigns of *Richard II* and *Henry IV* there was little fighting.

1415	*Henry V* reclaimed the French throne and invaded France. This led to the battle of *Agincourt*
1419	Normandy reconquered by the English
1420	Treaty of Troyes between Henry V and Charles VI of France. Henry was to become King of France after the death of Charles VI
1422	*Henry VI* became King of England and of France when both Henry V and Charles VI died within a few months of each other
1429	English defeated at Orleans by the French army led by Joanne of Arc
1442	French recaptured Aquitaine
1450	French recaptured Normandy
1453	End of the war: only Calais remained in English hands.

HURRICANE

The Hurricane was a fighter used by the RAF during the *Battle of Britain*. It is not as well known as the *Spitfire*, but was equally successful. In fact 80 per cent of the fighters in the Battle of Britain were Hurricanes, as against 20 per cent which were Spitfires.

The Hurricane was slower than the Spitfire and less manoeuvrable, but it could take more punishment from enemy planes. Some pilots found it easier to fly. When the RAF attacked Luftwaffe formations over Britain, the Spitfire squadrons tackled the German fighters, while the Hurricanes dealt with the bombers and fighter-bombers.

One of the most famous of all fighter-pilots, Douglas Bader, always flew Hurricanes.

HYPERINFLATION

Hyperinflation is the name given to the massive rise in prices which took place in Germany in 1922 to 1923.

Why did it happen?

● The gold in Germany was used to pay the *Reparations* demanded by the Allies at the Treaty of **Versailles**. It was gold which backed up the German banknotes. When the gold was shipped out of Germany, people began to believe that the banknotes were worthless.

- Many Germans did not trust the **Weimar** government as it appeared to have given in too easily to the demands of the Allies.
- After the Ruhr was occupied by French and Belgian troops in January 1923, the German government began to print banknotes and to pay strike pay to German workers who refused to cooperate with the French.

What effects did hyperinflation have? Many people suffered.

- Many Germans found their life-savings were lost.
- People who lived on pensions were ruined.
- Prices rose every day and every hour.
- People rushed to buy goods as soon as they were paid. They bought anything, because otherwise their money would lose value immediately.

- People began to exchange goods (barter) rather than use money.
- Shopkeepers tried to keep their shops closed and avoid selling anything.

But some people gained

- Anyone who had borrowed money could now repay it very easily.
- Some bankers and financiers were able to take advantage of the situation and buy up works of art and businesses.

The confusion caused by hyperinflation led Adolf **Hitler** to believe he could take power in Munich in November 1923, the **Beer Hall Putsch**.

One reason for the lack of support for Hitler was that hyperinflation was already being brought under control by the new German chancellor, Gustav **Stresemann**. He ordered all the old banknotes to be collected and burned. He issued new notes, called Rentenmarks, which were backed by the land of Germany and not by gold. Stresemann was also able to deal with most of the other problems facing Germany in the 1920s and the country seemed to be recovering from the effects of the **First World War**.

INDIA

India has two meanings. It was originally the name given to the area which is now made up of the modern countries of Bangladesh, India, Pakistan and Sri Lanka and also included parts of Afghanistan and Burma. It was an enormous area, nearly 3000 kilometres from north to south and 2500 kilometres from east to west. It stretched from the Himalayan mountains in the north to the tropics in the south.

India in the seventeenth century

When the first English arrived in India in 1603, much of India was governed by the Mughal Emperor Akbar. He was the third ruler of the empire which had been set up by his grandfather, Babar, in 1526. The Mughal Emperors were most powerful in northern India and continued to rule until 1761, but the last Emperor with any real power was Aurangzeb, who died in 1707.

The Mughal Emperors were Muslims. In the late-seventeenth century they were challenged by the Marathas, who were Hindus. When the Mughal Empire collapsed in the eighteenth century, much of India was governed by Maratha princes called Rajahs. They retained their power until India was conquered by the British in the nineteenth century.

The first Englishman to arrive in India was John Mildenhall in 1603. He was a representative of the East India Company, which had been set up in London in 1600. He wanted to gain the right to trade in India. He had to wait until 1608 before he was allowed to trade.

The English and French in India

At first the English were only interested in places on the coast which they could use for trading.

1612   The English occupied Surat in north-west India
1639   The English occupied Madras in south-east India
1661   The English occupied Bombay south of Surat

But in 1664 the situation changed

1664   Foundation of the Compagnie des Indes Orientales, the French East India Company. This led to more than 100 years of rivalry between France and England for control of India
1674   The French occupied Pondicherry in south-east India
1717   British gained the right to trade throughout the Mughal Empire

1740s   In the 1740s and 1750s there was a great deal of fighting between French and British forces in India. The French supported Indian rulers against the British and the British lost control of Calcutta in 1756
1746   French captured Madras
1748   Madras regained by Britain at the Treaty of Aix-la-Chapelle
1757   Robert Clive recaptured Calcutta and won the battle of Plassey
1761   Pondicherry was captured by Clive
1769   Compagnie des Indes Orientales dissolved

Large parts of India, especially Bengal, were now governed by the East India Company. This led to criticism in Britain and there were attempts by the British government to bring the Company under more control. By 1800 a system of government and taxation based on the British system had been established.

Why were the British so determined to take control of India?

- They wanted to get into the spice trade. Europeans had been trying to control it since the fifteenth century.
- They believed that India was very wealthy: there were many stories about gold and silver in India.
- They became convinced that they were bringing civilisation to it. The English thought of the Indians as inferior.
- Many people who went to live in India came to believe they had a right to govern it.
- During the eighteenth century Britain began to acquire a large overseas empire. India became the most important part of the empire. It was the 'jewel in the crown'.
- Many people were fascinated by India. Even in 1851 thousands flocked to see the Indian displays at the Great Exhibition. These included a stuffed elephant, jewels and silks.

Britain and India in the nineteenth century

Until 1858 India continued to be governed by the East India Company, which gradually occupied more and more land. It also began to try to develop India. Universities were founded in Calcutta, Bombay and Madras. A road-building scheme was begun in the 1830s and in the 1850s more roads, railways and canals were built. From 1854 elementary and secondary schools were built.

The Indian Mutiny

In 1857 a rebellion broke out in northern India. It began because Indian soldiers in the army of the East India Company were issued with a new type of cartridge. To use it they had to bite off the end. To make it waterproof it was smeared with grease. The soldiers, called sepoys, believed that it was made from cow or pig fat. To Hindus the cow was sacred and to Muslims the pig was unclean.

To the English the rebellion was treason, but to some Indians it is now seen as the first attempt by

Indians to get rid of the British. It was short-lived, but had long-term effects. In 1858 the government of India was taken away from the East India Company and given to the British government. The Company was dissolved in 1874.

In 1876 Queen **Victoria** was created Empress of India by the Prime Minister Benjamin **Disraeli**. British power in India now seemed to be at its height, but almost immediately changes began to take place.

1885   The Indian National Congress was set up. This was to be the political party which led the campaign for Indian independence in the twentieth century. It led to a series of protests against British rule, some of which included violence.

During the **First World War** about 1 200 000 Indians joined the British armed forces. This led to more demands for self-rule. In 1919 Indians were brought into the government of India for the first time. But in the same year 376 Indians were killed in Amritsar when British troops opened fire on an unarmed crowd. These events led to Mohandas Gandhi beginning his campaign of civil disobedience, or satyagraha.

Gandhi became the most important leader in the campaign to gain independence for India and he campaigned throughout the 1920s and 1930s. He used different methods, all based on non-violence.

- He advocated the production of cotton, which the British government had banned in order to make Indians buy cotton from Britain.
- He led a march to the sea and established salt production, which was also banned by the government, because it wanted to control the production of salt and the profits.

Why did India become independent in 1947?

- India was too big to be governed by Britain.
- Britain was exhausted by the **Second World War** and could not afford to govern India.
- After the war the idea of European countries governing overseas Empires became less and less acceptable.
- In 1947 a Labour government was elected. The **Labour Party** was more ready to allow India to become independent.

But there were also changes in India

- There were large Indian political parties, the Congress Party and the Muslim League, led by Jawarhal Nehru and Mohammed Ali Jinnah.
- Since 1940 the League had called for a separate Muslim country when India became independent. The name Pakistan, meaning 'the land of the pure', had been created for it.
- The Muslim League had supported the war effort. Congress had begun the 'Quit India' campaign, which tried to persuade the British to leave. This led to increasing divisions between the mainly Hindu Congress Party and the Muslim League.

- In 1946 and 1947 there was growing unrest in India between Hindus and Muslims; this led to violence in many parts of India.

In 1947 Viscount Mountbatten was sent to India to organise independence. He announced that India would become independent no later than June 1948. In fact it took place on 15 August 1947. India became a republic with Pandit Nehru as Prime Minister. Pakistan became a republic with Liaqat Ali Khan as Prime Minister.

INDUSTRIAL REVOLUTION

The Industrial Revolution is the name given to the series of changes which took place in industry in Britain in the late-eighteenth century and early-nineteenth century. These changes showed that it was possible to produce goods using machinery in **factories**. Before the Industrial Revolution most goods were produced by hand in people's own homes. This was known as the **domestic system**.

Why did the Industrial Revolution develop in Britain?

There were some long-term reasons:

- Britain depended on trade for much of its wealth. This meant there were people ready to take risks and try out new ideas.
- Britain was a small country with good communications. Roads were built in Britain throughout the eighteenth century and a network of **canals** was begun in the 1760s.
- There was an advanced banking system which enabled money to be borrowed easily. This meant that businessmen could get backing for new ideas.
- In some parts of the country, particularly in **Scotland**, there were schools which specialised in engineering. These produced the inventors who made the new machines.
- Britain was a relatively peaceful country. There was very little warfare in Britain in the eighteenth century. This meant that it was a safe country in which to develop a business.
- Many people were **Protestants**. They were more ready to go into business than **Catholics** and there was less control by the Church.

But there were also important changes in the eighteenth century

- From 1700 and more so from 1750, the population began to rise sharply. More people meant more mouths to feed, more clothing: in fact more of everything.
- From the early-eighteenth century a series of important inventions were made in Britain. These led to new raw materials, such as wrought iron, and new forms of power, such as **steam** and new technology, which enabled products to be produced in large quantities and at much cheaper prices.
- The most important breakthrough came when **cotton** began to arrive in Britain in large

quantities for the first time in the mid-eighteenth century.

The inventions

1709   Thomas **Newcomen** invented a steam engine. It could only be used to pump water, usually out of mines, but it worked and more than 300 were in use by the end of the century.

1709   Abraham **Darby I** developed a method of smelting iron using coal. He found a way of turning coal into coke by smoking it in an oven.

1733   John Kay invented a flying shuttle. This was a mechanism which enabled the shuttle in a loom to be knocked back and forth by hammers. This not only speeded up weaving, but it also meant that wider pieces of cloth could be produced.

1764   James Hargreaves invented his Spinning Jenny, which enabled a spinner to spin more than one thread at a time. The early machines could produce eight threads.

1765   James **Watt** produced an improved version of Newcomen's engine. This worked much quicker and used less fuel.

1768   Richard **Arkwright** produced the Water Frame. This led to the building of the first factories.

1779   Samuel Crompton developed the Spinning Mule. This was the most successful spinning machine. It was a mixture of the Spinning Jenny and the Water Frame, which is why it was called the mule.

1779   Abraham **Darby III** built the iron bridge across the River Severn at Coalbrookdale. This was the first large structure to be made of cast-iron.

1781   James Watt added the Sun and Planet gear to his steam engine, which provided rotary motion. This meant it could now be used to drive machinery. More and more factories were now powered by steam.

1782   Henry **Cort** developed the puddling process. This enabled the production of large quantities of wrought-iron. This was stronger and lighter than cast-iron and could be shaped much more accurately. This was much more suitable for machinery.

1780s   John Wilkinson began to use wrought-iron for new products: furniture, buildings, even jewellery. He also invented machines which could accurately drill holes in machinery. This was to be very important if machines made of metal parts were to fit together properly.

1784   Edmund Cartwright produced the Power Loom. This was a fully mechanised weaving machine, but it was very complicated and did not always work very well. Unlike spinning, weaving did not move into factories quickly.

1793   The Cotton Gin was invented by Eli Whitney, an American. This could take the seeds out of cotton; before this had been done by hand. The supply of cotton reaching Britain increased even more quickly.

The industry which led the way in the Industrial Revolution was cotton. By the late-eighteenth century it was possible to make cotton cloth from start to finish entirely by the use of machinery. This made the cloth much cheaper and also improved the quality. Once the cotton industry showed it was possible, other industries followed.

The machine-tool industry

Once the new machines had been invented, new technology was needed to make and repair them. This was carried out by the machine-tool industry.

1790s   Joseph Bramah and Henry Maudslay invented the lathe. This meant that parts for machines could be made with great precision.

1840   James Naysmith invented the Steam Hammer. This mean that iron could be hammered very accurately.

1840s   Joseph Whitworth invented the micrometer and classified screw sizes. This enabled machinery to be fitted together very accurately and repaired easily.

1856   Henry Bessemer developed the Converter. This could produce large quantities of cheap steel for the first time. Steel was a much better raw material for machinery than wrought-iron.

These inventions meant that machinery could be produced in large quantities, with replaceable parts. From the 1840s to the 1870s, Britain became known as the 'Workshop of the World', because almost all the machinery made in the world was produced in Britain.

It was during this period that the Great Exhibition was held to show off Britain's successes.

What effects did the Industrial Revolution have on Britain?

- Britain became the most important industrial country in the world and remained so for the next century.

- Britain began to export goods around the world: first cotton, but later manufactured goods and then machinery and railways.

- The wealth gained created a new class of people who earned their money from business. These became the **middle class**. At first they were ignored by the upper class and the landed gentry, but the **Whig Reforms** of the 1830s were a sign that their influence was growing. Sir Robert **Peel**, the Tory Prime Minister, was the son of a factory owner.

- In Britain, people began to move to the new industrial towns to find work. By 1851 50 per cent of the people of Britain lived in towns. In 1700 it had only been 20 per cent.

- The new industrial towns became overcrowded and often very unhealthy. In Bolton in 1830 life expectancy was estimated at 17. When cholera appeared for the first time in 1831, the situation became desperate.

- The factories of the Industrial Revolution created a new working class, which for the first time lived and worked closely together. This led to the creation of the first **trade unions** in the 1820s and the **Chartist** movement in the 1830s. This eventually led to the development of new political movements. For example, Karl **Marx** developed his ideas of communism when he was living in Manchester, the centre of the cotton industry, in the 1840s.

Britain's lead in industry began to disappear in the 1870s and by the **First World War** Britain had been overtaken by Germany and the **USA**.

Why did this happen?

- Britain was the first to industrialise: other countries could copy Britain's lead but avoid her mistakes.
- Britain sold machinery to all countries: they were able to catch up very quickly.
- Germany and the USA were both much bigger countries with more raw materials. By the late-nineteenth century, some of Britain's raw materials were beginning to run out.
- British companies tended to be smaller than those in other countries and were sometimes slower to adopt new ideas.
- Education developed more slowly in Britain than in Germany, for example. Industry needed an educated workforce.
- The British governments did not support British companies as much as some foreign governments supported their companies. German governments did not allow British goods to be sold freely in Germany. This was called 'Protection'.

Britain never regained the industrial position that it held in the nineteenth century, but it did lead the world in developing industry and in showing how manufacturing could be improved by the introduction of machinery.

SELF-CHECK QUESTION 7

Which industry began the Industrial Revolution in the 1760s?

INTERPRETATION

An interpretation is an attempt by an historian to explain why or how events have happened in the past. The National Curriculum at Key Stage 3 states that all pupils should be able to explain why historians have disagreed over interpretations of the past.

For example, Christian writers in medieval Europe described the Crusades as attempts to regain the Holy Land from Muslim heathens. Muslim writers at the same time described the Crusades as the Frankish invasions.

You will find that a number of entries in this book have references to different interpretations, including the **Beer Hall Putsch** and **Hiroshima.** If you are going to understand why interpretations of the same event can be very different, you will need to find out:

- Something about the background of the writer. Did they have any political or religious ideas, for

example, were they trying to make a point or prove something? Communist historians give different accounts of the effects of the Industrial Revolution to those written by capitalist historians.

- When was the book written? Would the writer have been influenced by any later events? This has happened since the dropping of the atomic bomb, for example: some writers have been influenced by the after-effects of the bomb. But did President Truman, or anybody else, know about these at the time?
- What sort of book is it? Is it intended to be taken seriously for example?
- What sources of information did the writer use? Did they have access to all the information available?

REMEMBER: most of the books you use at Key Stage 3, or even at GCSE, will be written simply to try to help you understand what has happened in the past. The writer will not be trying to give you their own political ideas.

INTERREGNUM

The Interregnum is the name given to the period from 1649 to 1660 when there was no King in England. The word means 'between reigns'. It began with the execution of **Charles I** in January 1649 and ended with the **Restoration** of **Charles II** in May 1660. This period is also known as the **Republic** and the **Commonwealth**.

IRELAND

Until the twelfth century, Ireland was made up of a number of separate kingdoms. Some of these were Irish descended from the Celts, the original inhabitants of Ireland. One King, the King of Dublin, was Norse and was descended from the Viking invaders who had landed in Ireland in the ninth century. The Kings fought against each other to decide who had the right to be called the King of Ireland.

How did the English become involved in Ireland?

In 1169, Rory, King of Connacht, drove Dermot, King of Leinster, into exile. In 1170, Richard de Clare, nicknamed 'Strongbow', arrived in Ireland to help Dermot fight back. He captured Dublin and then married Dermot's daughter. In 1171 he succeeded Dermot as King of Leinster.

Strongbow, however, had acted without the permission of King **Henry II**. So Henry invaded Ireland and forced Strongbow to accept him as his overlord. When Strongbow died in 1176, his land passed to Henry. He created his son John King of Ireland in 1185. Ireland was governed by a series of lieutenants, or representatives of the King. The first was William Marshal, who married the daughter of

Strongbow. They were responsible for collecting taxes, keeping law and order and meeting the Irish *Parliament* after it was set up in 1264. When *John* became King of England in 1199, he remained King of Ireland as well.

Ireland in the thirteenth and fourteenth centuries

During the reigns of *Henry III* (1216–1272) and *Edward I* (1272–1307), the power of the English in Ireland grew. The barons occupied the south-eastern areas of Ireland, Dublin, Wexford and Waterford, and set up the feudal system. From the early fourteenth century there was increasing trouble between the English and the Irish.

Why did this happen?

- The Irish did not like the feudal system, which went against their tribal or clan system.
- Edward I's laws were extended to Ireland. This meant that English law was being used in Ireland. The Irish wanted to use their own laws.
- English barons in Ireland began to build castles and occupy more land. They became the richest people in Ireland.
- In 1316 Edward, the brother of Robert Bruce, landed in Ireland to try to set up a kingdom of Ireland. He gave up in 1318.
- During the reign of *Edward III* (1327–1377) more and more attention was paid to the wars with France. This led to increased attacks by the Irish on the English.

How did the English react?

1366 The Statute of Kilkenny was passed. This:
- banned marriages between the English and the Irish;
- made English the official language;
- insisted that English law was used in Ireland.

But this did not improve the situation. In the fifteenth century Ireland became more and more independent of England.

1398 *Richard II* led an army to Ireland. This again failed.

1413–1422 During the reign of *Henry V*, about half of the English returned home.

1450s Richard of York agreed that Ireland could be virtually independent and even allowed Irish coins to be minted. The Irish Parliament now began to pass its own laws for almost the first time. The power of the King of England was restricted to the area around Dublin, which became known as the 'Pale'.

Ireland under the Tudors and Stuarts

Henry VII was determined to build up the power of the King after the Wars of the Roses, so in 1494 he passed the Statute of Drogheda, known as 'Poyning's Law'. This tried to bring Ireland back under English control. It said that:

- the Irish Parliament could not meet without the consent of the King of England
- no laws could be passed without the approval of the King of England
- all laws passed by the English Parliament were to be obeyed in Ireland.

But it was one thing to pass a law like this and quite another to enforce it. The King governed through a 'Lord Deputy' who was based in Ireland. In the Pale, around Dublin, the people were English and obeyed the King and followed English law, but elsewhere the situation could be very different. In the east and south of Ireland there were English lordships, owned and ruled by the descendants of the barons who had landed in Ireland in the twelfth century. The rest of Ireland was ruled by Irish lords, who spoke Gaelic and used Irish law.

Orders issued by the Lord Deputy in Dublin would be obeyed in the Pale; they might be obeyed in the English lordships, but would not be obeyed in the Irish lordships.

How did the Tudors bring Ireland under control?

1542 *Henry VIII* was declared King of Ireland. The Lord Deputies began to impose English law on the south and west of Ireland. The north, particularly Ulster, remained Gaelic.

1597 A rebellion broke out in Ireland led by the Earl of Tyrone. He was supported by the Irish lords, but also by some of the English in the south of Ireland. They joined in because they were *Catholic*. The King of Spain sent 3500 men. *Elizabeth I* sent an army to Ireland commanded by the Earl of Essex. He failed to defeat the rebels, but his successor, Lord Mountjoy, had put down the rebellion by 1601. Tyrone surrendered in 1603.

The Ulster Plantation

When *James I* came to the throne in 1603, he decided to try to put an end to the problems in Ireland by replacing the Irish landowners in Ulster by English landowners. They continued the process by bringing over English farmers and giving them land. The newcomers were all *Protestants* and many of them came from Scotland. The Irish were forced to move to smaller farms. Often these were on poorer land. This became known as the 'Ulster Plantation'. The process was continued throughout the seventeenth and eighteenth centuries.

How did the actions of Elizabeth I and James I change the situation in Ireland?

- They made English Catholic landowners angry. They began to be treated as second-class citizens. James I called them 'half-subjects'.
- They made Irish landowners angry, because their land was taken away from them and given to Protestants.

These changes were to be very important in the future. They did not solve the problems in Ireland, but made them much worse.

Why did relations between England and Ireland become worse during the seventeenth century?

- In October 1641 there was a rebellion in Ulster and 3000 Protestants were murdered. The Irish Catholics were frightened that the English *Parliament*, which was controlled by *Puritans*, was about to pass laws against Catholics. *Charles I* wanted to put down the rebellion, but Parliament would not allow him to take control of the army. Before anything could be done, the Civil War broke out in 1642.
- During the Civil War Ireland supported Charles I. When the war ended Parliament was worried that the Irish might support Charles and attempt to put him back on the throne.
- In 1649 Oliver *Cromwell* was sent to Ireland to deal with the Catholic forces. He laid siege to the town of Drogheda and when his soldiers forced their way in, about 3000 Catholics were killed, including many women and children. He blamed the Catholics for the massacres which had taken place in 1641 and was determined to punish them.
- Cromwell then encouraged more Protestants to settle in Ireland and take the land of the people who had been killed. This continued the plan started by James I, the 'Ulster Plantation'.
- The Irish Parliament was not allowed to meet and Ireland was governed from England.

Ireland after the *Restoration*

Relations between England and Ireland improved when *Charles II* was restored in 1660. The Irish Parliament began to meet again and Charles was recognised as King of Ireland. But the situation changed when *James II* was forced to flee in 1688. He went first to France and then to Ireland to try to regain the throne. *William III* invaded Ireland and this led to the battle of the *Boyne* in July 1690. This is still celebrated in Ulster. The *Orange* Order is named after William of Orange, who became William III.

After the battle William agreed that Irish Catholics should have religious liberty and be allowed to enter the professions. This was accepted by the English Parliament, but was rejected by the Irish Parliament, which was made up entirely of Protestants. They passed laws which prevented Catholics from sitting in the Irish Parliament and from holding any public office or being an officer in the army. Catholics were not allowed to worship. This meant that the Catholic and Protestant communities in Ireland were now deeply divided.

To make matters even worse, William III continued the 'Ulster Plantation' begun earlier in the century. Most land in Ireland was now owned by Protestants, but the great majority of the population was Catholic.

The United Kingdom

Until 1801, Ireland was a separate kingdom, with the King of England as its head, but in 1801 Ireland was united with Britain (*Wales* and England had been united in 1536 and *Scotland* and England in 1707) by the Act of *Union*. The country was now known as the United Kingdom of Great Britain and Ireland. The Irish Parliament was closed and Irish MPs began to sit at Westminster.

Why was the Act of Union passed?

In 1793 the *French Revolutionary War* had broken out. In 1796 and 1797 the French tried to land an army in Ireland to support a rebellion by the United Irishmen. This was defeated at the battle of Vinegar Hill in 1798. The Act of Union was passed so that the British government could control the situation in Ireland more easily.

How did the Act of Union change relations between Ireland and the rest of Britain?

The Prime Minister, William *Pitt* the Younger, had wanted to give Catholics the right to vote when the Act of *Union* was passed, but *George III* refused. He said it would break his coronation oath as head of the Church of England. Pitt resigned in protest. Now the Catholics in Ireland were not only being governed by *Protestants*, but also by Protestants in England.

In 1828, Daniel O'Connell was elected MP for County Clare in Ireland. This was illegal as Catholics were not allowed to vote, and also not allowed to hold public office in Britain under the Test Act of 1662 (see *Clarendon Code*). The Prime Minister, the Duke of *Wellington*, decided to repeal the Test Act (1828) and also to pass the Catholic Emancipation Act (1829).

Wellington did not personally agree with Catholic Emancipation (meaning freedom or equality), but ever since the battle of *Waterloo* he had been horrified by bloodshed. He was convinced that if he did not allow Catholics the right to vote and sit in Parliament there would be a *civil war* in Ireland.

Daniel O'Connell hoped to reverse the Act of Union and recreate the Irish Parliament in Dublin, but the British government refused. O'Connell's ideas were taken up by a group who called themselves 'Young Ireland'. They gained a great deal of support when Ireland was hit by the potato famine in 1845.

How did the potato famine affect Ireland?

- In 1845 and 1846 the potato crop failed in Ireland. In western Ireland many farmers depended on potatoes for their livelihood.
- One million people died in the years 1845–47. Another million emigrated, many to the USA.
- The Irish blamed the British government for the famine, because they did nothing to help the starving.

- The **Corn Laws** banned the importing of wheat from abroad, which meant that food could not be sent to Ireland.
- The British government repealed the Corn Laws and sent wheat to Ireland to feed the people, but it arrived to late.
- In 1848 there was a rebellion against the British in Ireland which failed. The two leaders were forced to flee. One, James Stephens, set up the Irish Republican Brotherhood in Dublin. The other, John Mahoney, set up the Fenian Brotherhood in New York. Both organisations were set up in 1858 and wanted to create an independent Ireland free from British control.

The Fenians

The two organisations became known as the Fenians. They were the forerunners of the terrorist organisations in Ireland today. In the 1860s the Fenians carried out a series of attacks. In 1867 they tried to attack Chester Castle to seize weapons which they planned to use in a rebellion. When this took place a month later, most of the Fenians were arrested. Later in the year the Fenians tried to blow a hole in the wall of Clerkenwell prison in London to rescue two prisoners. Twelve people were killed in the blast.

The Fenian attacks had a big impact on William **Gladstone**, who became Prime Minister for the first time in 1868. He decided that he had 'to pacify Ireland', as he put it.

Gladstone and Ireland

1869   The Disestablishment Act: this meant that Irish Catholics would no longer have to pay tithes (taxes) to the Protestant Church.
1870   The Irish Land Act: this said that landlords must pay compensation if they evicted a tenant and for any improvements that a tenant had made. This was an attempt to bring Irish law into line with English law.

Neither of these laws went far enough for the Irish, however, so when Gladstone became Prime Minister again in 1880, he went further.

1881   The Land Act: this guaranteed tenants the three 'Fs': fair rents, fixity of tenure (meaning that a tenant who paid rent on time could not be evicted) and freedom to sell a tenancy to the highest bidder.

The Land Act was just what many Irish tenants wanted, but it came too late. In 1871 a Home Rule for Ireland Party had been set up. In the 1880s the leader was Charles Stewart Parnell. He and his Party wanted self-government for Ireland.

1881   Parnell was sent to Kilmainham prison for trying to persuade Irish farmers not to accept the Land Act.
1882   He was let out after he agreed to cooperate with Gladstone and the Liberal government. This was known as the Kilmainham Treaty.
1882   But only four days after Parnell's release the Fenians murdered a government minister and a civil servant in Phoenix Park in Dublin. Parnell denied all knowledge of the crimes.

The British government replied with an Act which gave the police the power to search and arrest suspects and suspended trial by jury. The Fenians began a series of attacks in Britain.

The effect of this on Gladstone was to convince him that Home Rule for Ireland was necessary. This would mean setting up a parliament in Dublin and creating an Irish government to run home affairs.

1886   When Gladstone became Prime Minister for the third time he introduced an Irish Home Rule Bill. This was defeated in the House of Commons.
1892   Gladstone became Prime Minister for the fourth time and introduced a second Home Rule Bill. This was defeated in the House of Lords.

When Gladstone died in 1898, the problems in Ireland had still not been solved.

In the early twentieth century more and more Irish MPs supported Home Rule. After the General Election of 1906, the Irish Nationalists, as they were now called, supported the Liberal government as it promised to bring about Home Rule. But once again something blocked their way.

Ulster

1912   The Liberal government of Herbert Asquith introduced a third Home Rule Bill. This had a real chance of success as the Parliament Act of 1911 had made it impossible for the House of Lords to defeat a Bill. All it could do was to hold up a Bill for two years. The Bill was passed by the Commons but defeated in the Lords. However, it would become law in 1915, after a two-year delay.
1912   The Ulster Covenant was signed in Belfast. This was organised by Sir Edward Carson, who began the Unionist movement. This was joined by Irish people who did not want to be separated from Britain. Their main fear was that they would be swamped by the Catholics who outnumbered the Protestants three to one.
1913   The Ulster Volunteers were set up. They were determined to fight to keep Ulster in the United Kingdom. They were faced by the Dublin Volunteers. Both sides began to collect arms.
1914   Civil war in Ireland seemed about to break out but, before it could, Britain declared war on Germany on 4 August and Home Rule was postponed.

How did the *First World War* change relations between Britain and Ireland?

At first many Irishmen volunteered to fight in the British Army: altogether about one hundred thousand. But gradually support for Britain began to change.

- In 1916 the Easter Rebellion took place in Dublin. This was led by Sir Roger Casement and Patrick Pearse and organised by the Irish Republican Brotherhood. It was backed by the Germans. The

Rebellion was a failure, but it won support for the IRB when many leaders were executed.

- Ulster regiments were allowed to put the Red Hand of Ulster on their badges. Other Irish units were not allowed anything similar.

- In 1918 conscription (compulsory military service) was extended to Ireland. This made the Irish Nationalists withdraw from Parliament at Westminster.

- In December 1918 Sinn Fein won a large number of seats at the General Election. This new Party wanted a complete break with Britain. They refused to attend Parliament at Westminster and instead set up their own Parliament, the Dail Eireann, and declared Ireland independent.

By the end of 1919 civil war had broken out in Ireland. The British government recruited volunteers from ex-servicemen and sent them to Ireland. They became known as the 'Black and Tans', from the colour of their uniform. They fought fire with fire, replying to Sinn Fein atrocities with atrocities of their own.

How was the civil war settled?

The British Prime Minister David **Lloyd George** decided that Ireland had to be given independence. He passed the Government of Ireland Act, which set up separate Parliaments in Dublin and Belfast. Southern Ireland became a dominion of the Empire, like Australia and New Zealand, while Ulster remained part of the United Kingdom. This situation lasted until 1937, when Southern Ireland (Eire) became independent.

IRON CURTAIN

The Iron Curtain was the name given to the border between East and West in Europe that was set up by Joseph **Stalin**, the ruler of the **USSR**, in the years after the **Second World War**. The name came from a speech made by Winston **Churchill** in 1946.

The Iron Curtain was a 1000-mile fence cutting off the communist countries of eastern Europe from the non-communist West. But it was also a barrier between two different ways of life. It was an attempt to cut off eastern Europe completely from the West.

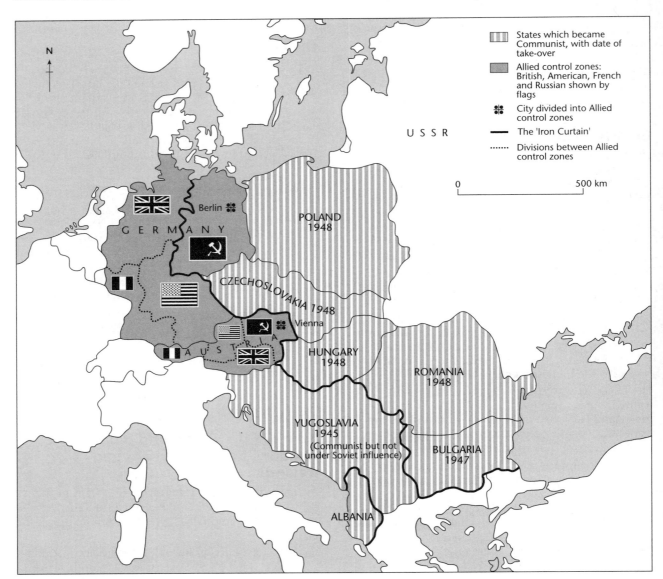

At some points it was a series of fences protected by razor-wire, dog runs, photo-electric beams, remote-controlled weapons and guard towers. The most famous example of the Iron Curtain was the **Berlin Wall**, however. This was built in 1961.

Why did Stalin build the Iron Curtain?

- He wanted to set up a buffer zone of countries in eastern Europe to protect the USSR against another invasion by Germany.

- He did not trust the West, Britain and the USA, because they had invaded Russia in 1918 and had delayed the invasion of France until 1944.

- He was trying to prevent western influence reaching the East and refugees leaving the East for western Europe.

The Iron Curtain collapsed in 1989 and 1990, when the countries of the East threw off Soviet control. But for 45 years it dominated Europe and divided Germany.

JACOBITES

This was the name given to the supporters of the descendants of **James II**, who tried to regain the throne of Britain after James II's death in 1701. There were two main attempts: the '15' and the '45'.

The '15'

In September 1715 there was a rising in **Scotland**. This was brought about by the unpopularity of the Act of **Union** of 1701 and of the **Hanoverian** succession. James Edward, the Old Pretender, landed in December 1715. Although the Jacobites advanced as far as Preston, they were defeated and James Edward escaped to France.

The '45'

In 1745, Charles Edward, the Young Pretender, led an army of highlanders as far as Derby, but he was forced to retreat. His army was defeated at the battle of Culloden in 1746.

⚓ *James I*

JAMES I OF ENGLAND, 1601–1625, VI OF SCOTLAND

James I of England became King at the death of **Elizabeth I** in 1603. He had already been King of **Scotland** since 1567, when his mother, **Mary**, Queen of Scots had abdicated (given up the throne) in his favour. James was the great-great-grandson of **Henry VII** and became King because all of **Henry VIII**'s children died without heirs. Elizabeth I arranged for him to succeed her when she died.

What sort of man was James I?

When he became King of England, James had already been King of Scotland for 36 years. In Scotland he had been very successful, but when he came to England he gained the reputation of being weak and clumsy. Why did this happen?

- James was a foreigner. He behaved differently to the English, who had been used to having Elizabeth as Queen for 45 years.
- James looked strange: his tongue was too big for his mouth and he dribbled when he drank.
- James had very thin legs and wore padded clothes to prevent himself from being stabbed.
- James spoke with a strange accent and used words the English did not understand.

How did James govern England?

James was intelligent and soon realised that England was quite different from Scotland. He showed he was determined to deal with any opposition in England and soon dealt with the religious problems left by Elizabeth. Many **Puritans** believed that James would be sympathetic, as Scotland was Presbyterian, but James was more concerned with royal power than he was with religion.

1604 The **Hampton Court Conference** was held to sort out differences between the bishops and the Puritans. James refused to allow any changes to the laws of Elizabeth I. Both Puritans and **Catholics** were told they would have to obey the Act of Uniformity.

1605 The Gunpowder Plot, which may well have been a set up to discredit Catholics, allowed James to pass laws against Catholics in 1606.

1611 The **Authorised Version** of the Bible (King James Version) was finished. This was an attempt to put an end to arguments about which version of the Bible should be used in church services. In future only this version could be used.

James was less successful in dealing with Parliament. Even so he managed to survive without Parliament for many years and found ways of raising money without Parliament's approval.

Why did James I meet opposition from Parliament?

- He wanted to unite England and Scotland, but Parliament refused.
- He began to collect taxes without Parliament's approval.
- He tried to marry his son, Charles, to a Spanish princess. This was strongly opposed as the princess was a **Catholic**.
- He had favourites, such as the Duke of **Buckingham**, to whom he gave money and gifts.
- He raised money by selling 'monopolies', which allowed people to control the selling of items such as soap.

In 1621 this led Parliament to issue the 'Great Protestation', which accused the King of interfering in the ancient rights and privileges of Parliament. James tore the page from the journal of the House of Commons.

When he died in 1625, James I had begun the major disagreements between the Crown and Parliament which were to lead to civil war in 1642. He had found that he could not govern without asking Parliament for taxes and he had made many people think that he and his son were Catholics. Money and religion were to be the downfall of James' son, **Charles I**. James had realised that he could not push things too far. His son did not have James' common sense and soon began to annoy Parliament.

SELF-CHECK QUESTION 8

How was James I related to Queen Elizabeth I?

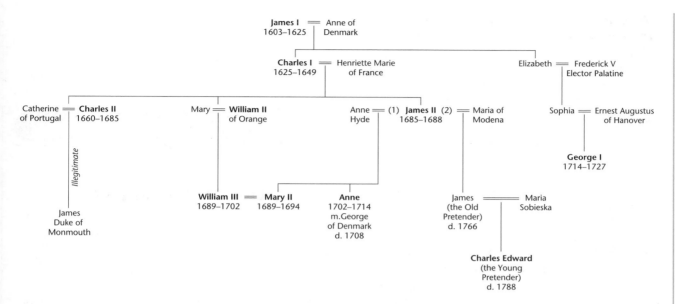

The family tree of James I

JAMES II, KING, 1685–1688

James II was the younger brother of **Charles II** and became King in 1685. He was immediately faced by the Monmouth Rebellion, which tried to place the Duke of Monmouth, an illegitimate son of Charles II, on the throne. The rebellion was defeated at the battle of Sedgemoor. The reason for the rebellion was that James was a Roman Catholic: there had already been an attempt to stop him becoming King during the **Exclusion Crisis** in 1680.

Once he became King, James II began to try to increase **Catholic** influence in England.

- Catholics were appointed to public office and became army officers. This was not allowed by the **Clarendon Code**.

- A Declaration of Liberty of Conscience was announced which allowed people to worship as they wanted.

- Seven bishops were arrested when they refused to permit the Declaration to be read in their churches.

- In 1687 James had a son by his second wife, Mary of Modena, who was a Catholic. He already had two daughters, who were Protestant, by his first wife, Anne Hyde, but he would now be succeeded by his son.

In the summer of 1688 an invitation was sent by the **Whigs** to William of Orange, the husband of James II's elder daughter, **Mary**. He was asked to save England from Catholicism. **William** agreed and landed in England on 5 November 1688. James fled to France, throwing the Great Seal of England into the Thames. This meant that England could not be governed. The following year the throne was offered to Mary, but this was refused. William would not allow his wife to become Queen unless he became King. So Parliament offered the Crown to William and Mary to reign as King and Queen. This was accepted. For the only time England had a King and Queen at the same time.

These events became known as the **Glorious Revolution** of 1688 and were followed by the Declaration of Rights.

What happened to James II?

After the battle of the **Boyne** in 1690, James lived in France. He died in 1701. His son, James Edward, the Old Pretender, landed in Scotland in 1708 and again in 1715, the first **Jacobite** Rebellion. James II's grandson, Charles Edward, the Young Pretender, tried to regain the throne in 1745, the Second Jacobite Rebellion.

JARROW

Jarrow is a town on the river Tyne in Northumbria. In 1936 it became famous because of a march to London by 200 unemployed men. The marchers carried a petition to **Parliament** and it was intended to make people aware of the problems faced by the people of Jarrow.

Until the 1920s Jarrow had been a prosperous shipbuilding town, but it was very badly hit by the **Depression** in the 1930s. Most workers in Jarrow were employed at Palmer's Yard, which was closed in 1932 and pulled down in 1934. This put 10 000 people out of work, out of a population of 35 000.

When the marchers reached London, they presented the petition to Parliament, but nothing was done to bring work to the town.

JINNAH, MUHAMMED ALI

✥ INDIA

JOHN, KING, 1199–1216

John was the youngest son of **Henry II** and became King in 1199 on the death of his brother, Richard I. Even today, historians disagree over what King John was really like.

Why is it very difficult to get a clear idea of what John was like as a King?

- John appears in the legends about **Robin Hood** as an evil prince who makes the people of England pay high taxes.
- John had an argument with the Pope and was excommunicated in 1209. This meant that he was excluded from the Church.
- John lost many lands in France, including Normandy.
- John became involved in a serious disagreement with his barons and was forced to issue the **Magna Carta**.

So what was John really like? How did he get such a bad reputation?

- John was compared with his brother **Richard I**. Richard was very popular, but probably did not deserve this reputation.
- John had to try to put right some of the things that had gone wrong during Richard's reign, when he had hardly been in England and had spent a great deal of money.
- Some writers at the time said that John was intelligent and fair. They said that he was unlucky.
- John was not a good General and was faced by Philip II of France who was extremely able.
- Most of the information about John comes from a book written by Matthew Paris. He based his book on one written by Roger of Wendover. Roger described John as an evil villain. Some of the things that he wrote about could not possibly have happened, but Matthew accepted everything.
- In the nineteenth century, historians made Richard into a hero and John into a villain. They believed everything that Roger of Wendover and Matthew Paris wrote.

> REMEMBER: *do not allow the stories about King John in the legends of Robin Hood to influence you.*

JUSTICES OF THE PEACE

Justices of the Peace were magistrates or judges who were appointed for each county in England. They were first appointed in the fourteenth century and became very important by the end of the fifteenth. Until the nineteenth century there was no police force and no local government in Britain. If any action was needed it was the Justices of the Peace, or magistrates as they were often called, who had to take it. They were unpaid and usually untrained.

- JPs became responsible for local law and order, taking over from the **sheriff**. They were responsible for dealing with the **Peterloo** demonstration in 1819.
- They were responsible for running the **Poor Law**. The Berkshire magistrates set up the Speenhamland System in 1795.
- They had to enforce laws passed by **Parliament**. They were responsible for enforcing the **Factory** Acts of 1802 and 1819.

In the nineteenth century the Justices of the Peace lost many of their duties, but they continued to act as magistrates and to try minor criminal cases.

KENNEDY, JOHN F.

John F. Kennedy became the youngest ever President of the **USA** when he took office in January 1961. He was rich, intelligent and a member of a very influential family from Massachusetts; his father had been ambassador to Britain during the **Second World War**.

Why was Kennedy elected?

- Some Americans believed that a more aggressive policy was necessary to deal with the challenge of Nikita **Khrushchev**, the Soviet Prime Minister. The previous president, Dwight Eisenhower, had allowed the Soviet Union to gain a lead in space technology and the arms race.

- Kennedy was a very persuasive speaker and his family had a great deal of money and influence.

- His opponent in the race for the Presidency was Richard Nixon, who always appeared on television looking as though he had not shaved. This put many voters off. In the end Kennedy won 50.5 per cent of the votes and Nixon won 49.5 per cent.

What did Kennedy try to achieve?

- He set out to try to change the USA through his 'New Frontier', which was an attempt to give equal opportunities to all Americans. This included Medicare and measures to improve housing and education. This was unpopular with some Americans who believed that the federal government should not help ordinary people. They should stand on their own two feet.

- He tried to pass a Civil Rights Act which gave Black Americans the same rights as Whites throughout the USA. This was very unpopular in the southern states. Kennedy depended on Democrats in the south for support.

Kennedy was a very inexperienced politician. He had not been a state governor and did not know how to deal with Congress. For the first two years he was unable to get very much done and all his policies were opposed by people in the USA.

Kennedy also found himself faced by problems abroad

- He increased the number of Americans in Vietnam. Some historians believe that he was responsible for American involvement in the Vietnam War.

- Nikita Khrushchev tried to take advantage of Kennedy's inexperience. This led to the Cuban Missiles Crisis in October 1962. Khrushchev tried to place Soviet missiles on the island of Cuba, where Fidel Castro, a communist, had seized power in 1959. Although Kennedy was able to deal with the crisis very successfully, it made him unpopular with some Americans who wanted to deal with Cuba more strongly. It also angered Americans who had lost money when their property in Cuba had been taken over by the new government.

- When he heard that the Soviet Union had put a man in space in 1961, Kennedy ordered US scientists to get a man to the moon before the end of the 1960s.

All Kennedy's policies led to increased spending and made him enemies. More and more of his measures became bogged down in Congress. Although he had many good ideas, he was not very successful at putting them into practice.

On 22 November 1963 President Kennedy was shot in Dallas, in the state of Texas. The official version of the events, the Warren Commission, stated that he was shot by Lee Harvey Oswald. However, since then there have been many other different explanations. It has become one of the most popular mysteries of the twentieth century.

KING, GREGORY

Gregory King compiled an estimate of the population of England and Wales in 1696. He used **parish** registers of baptisms and bills of mortality, which listed the causes of deaths, and came up with a figure of 5 500 000 people. This is now thought to be about right. The first **census** of 1801 put the population at 11 000 000. This suggests that the population of Britain doubled in the eighteenth century.

KHRUSHCHEV, NIKITA

Nikita Khrushchev became the leader of the **USSR** in the mid-1950s after the death of Joseph **Stalin** in 1953. At first he shared power with other leaders, but he emerged as the most important figure by 1956. In that year he denounced Stalin's methods in his 'Secret Speech'. Unlike Stalin, Khrushchev liked to travel and meet people. He also wanted to prove that the Soviet system was better than the American way. This led him to travel throughout the Soviet Union and visit many countries around the world.

How did Khrushchev change the Soviet Union and its policies?

- He began a policy of 'coexistence' with the West; this meant he was prepared to work with the western leaders.

- He began to visit other countries and meet the leaders of the **USA**, Great Britain and France.

- He began to try to compete with the West in sport, the space race and overseas aid.

- Whereas Stalin had always been very secretive and rarely left the Kremlin, Khrushchev was outgoing and travelled widely.

He promised that the standard of living in the USSR would rise. He said 'What sort of communism is it that cannot produce sausage?'

Did Khrushchev succeed?

- The first satellite, the Sputnik, was launched in 1957. The first man in space was Yuri Gagarin in 1961.
- The USSR began to win more medals at the Olympic Games than the USA.
- Many countries in Africa and Asia turned to communism.

But there were also failures

- Khrushchev's attempts to improve the standard of living in the USSR failed. His Virgin Lands scheme, which tried to increase the production of food, was a disaster. He was not able to change Soviet industry from the methods of Stalin's Five Year Plans. In 1962 there were placards in streets in the Soviet Union which said, 'Turn Khrushchev into sausage meat.'
- He clashed with President **Kennedy** of the USA over Cuba, when he tried to put Soviet missiles there in 1962. The missile sites were discovered by American spy planes and Kennedy blockaded Cuba to prevent any more missiles being landed. Khrushchev had not expected Kennedy to react like that and he was forced to back down or risk the outbreak of a nuclear war. Some other leaders in the Soviet Union saw this as a disaster.

In the end Khrushchev's failures outweighed his successes and he was forced to resign in October 1964.

LABOUR PARTY

The Labour Party was founded in 1900 as the Labour Representation Committee. It changed its name to the Labour Party in 1906.

Why was the Labour Party set up?

- The Labour Party was set up by some trade unions, the Cooperative Movement and the Fabians, who were a group of writers and intellectuals who wanted to bring about change.
- There was a strong trade union movement by the beginning of the twentieth century. They wanted to use the Labour Party to change the law relating to unions. This became very important after the **Taff Vale Case** in 1901.
- The Labour Party was to represent the interests of working people in Parliament. Most working men now had the vote after the **Reform** Acts of 1867 and 1884.

From 1900 to 1914 the Labour Party was allied to the **Liberal Party** but, after the **First World War**, the Labour Party became the most important opposition party in **Parliament** and formed the government in 1924 and 1929.

Both of these governments were shortlived. Why?

- In 1924 the Labour Party was in a minority in the **Commons** and relied on the Liberal Party for support. When it was accused of being communist, the Liberals backed out.
- In 1929 the Labour Party was also in a minority in the Commons. It faced the problems of the **Depression** and was replaced by a **National Government**.

It was not until 1945 that a Labour government was elected with an overall majority. From 1945 to 1950 the Labour government created the modern **Welfare State** and also introduced the **nationalisation** of many industries.

SELF-CHECK QUESTION 9

What was the name of the Labour Party from 1900 to 1906?

LANCASTER

The House of Lancaster was descended from John of **Gaunt**, the third son of **Edward III**. John's son **Henry IV** became King in 1399 when he arrested **Richard II**.

Richard was murdered the following year. The Lancastrians ruled England until 1461, when **Henry VI** was overthrown by **Edward IV**, the descendant of Edward III's fifth son, Edmund. He was a member of the House of **York**.

The battles between the two families are called the **Wars of the Roses**, as the Lancastrians' emblem was the red rose and the Yorkists' emblem was the white rose. These are still the badges of the counties of Lancashire and York.

LANGLAND, WILLIAM

William Langland was a country priest who wrote a long poem called *The Vision of Piers Plowman* in the 1360s. In the poem he defended the poor of England and attacked landlords, the government and the Church. The poem contains the earliest reference to the legends of **Robin Hood**.

LAUD, WILLIAM

William Laud was one of **Charles I**'s closest advisers. He became bishop of London in 1628 and Archbishop of Canterbury in 1633. He soon became very unpopular.

Why did Laud become unpopular?

- Laud published a new Prayer Book and then insisted that everybody should use its exact words in church services.
- Laud also made churches move their altars from the centre of the church, where they had been since **Elizabeth I**'s reign, to the east end of the church. The altar also had to have a rail in front of it to keep people away.
- Laud insisted that priests and ministers should wear vestments (special robes) when they were holding services.

When **Charles I** tried to make the Scots use the Prayer Book he found himself in real trouble, as the Scots invaded England and Charles had to call Parliament and ask for money for an Army.

In 1641 Laud was arrested by Charles on the orders of Parliament and put in prison. He was executed in 1645 at the end of the **Civil War**.

LAW

⬥ *Act of Parliament*

LEAGUE OF NATIONS

The League of Nations was set up at the Treaty of **Versailles** in 1919.

Why was the League of Nations set up?

- It was the idea of **Woodrow Wilson**, the President of the USA. When he arrived in Europe he put forward 'Fourteen Points', which he believed would help bring about a lasting peace. The League was point fourteen.

- The *First World War* had been such a tremendous shock to the countries involved, that they were determined to try to prevent it ever happening again. The League was to be a way of settling disputes in the future. Members had to agree to use peaceful methods.
- The League would offer 'Collective Security', which meant that countries who joined would help each other if they were attacked.
- The League would try to solve the problems left at the end of the war, for example disarmament, health (there had just been a major epidemic of influenza, which had killed 20 000 000 people), trade, etc.

How was the League organised?

- **The Covenant:** this was the set of rules of the League. All members had to agree to the Covenant. The main rules were:
  - to support other members against attacks
  - to agree to accept peaceful solutions to disputes
  - to support decisions of the Council and the Assembly.
- **The General Assembly:** this contained three representatives from each of the member countries. It met once a year. Each member country had one vote.
- **The Council:** this was to have nine members: five Permanent Members and four others which would change from time to time. The Permanent Members were to be France, Great Britain, Italy, Japan and the **USA**. However, the USA did not join the League. This left only four Permanent Members until Germany was admitted in 1926. It became the fifth Permanent Member.
- **The Secretariat:** this ran the League and was based in Geneva. It was headed by a Secretary-General. The first was Sir Eric Drummond, who was British.

How could the League deal with countries which broke the Covenant?

There were two forms of action which the League could take:

- Economic sanctions: this would mean asking members to stop trading with other countries. For example, the League would publish a list of goods which could not be bought or sold and all members were asked to obey this. This happened in 1935 when Italy invaded Abyssinia.
- Military sanctions: this would mean asking members to take military action against other countries. This never happened, because the League of Nations had no army of its own. It had to persuade each member to declare war on a country which broke the Covenant. So in 1931, when Japan invaded *Manchuria*, the League eventually sent a message to the Japanese government condemning its actions. The Japanese ignored the message and left the League.

Was the League a success?

Until 1930 the League had a number of successes:

- Italy was forced to withdraw from Corfu, which it tried to invade in 1923
- a number of border disputes were settled, for example one between Sweden and Finland
- a lot of work was done by the League's agencies to tackle disease
- the League gained considerable respect and many countries joined; in Britain it was very popular.

But there were also weaknesses

- the USA had not joined the League. This meant the most powerful country in the world was not backing it
- the League was seen as a 'club for the victors' of the First World War. Russia was not allowed to join
- the membership was mostly European: it had less influence in other parts of the world
- the attack on Corfu by *Mussolini* was a sign of things to come. What would happen if powerful countries ignored the League in future?

What went wrong in the 1930s?

1933 Japan left the League after the invasion of Manchuria.

1933 *Hitler* withdrew Germany from the League during the Disarmament Conference at Geneva. He claimed that the other Powers were refusing to disarm, when Germany was already disarmed as a result of the Treaty of *Versailles*.

1937 Italy left the League after the invasion of Abyssinia.

What made this all the worse was that these were three Permanent Members of the Council. All of them had broken the Covenant. This left only two Permanent Members: Britain and France. Neither government was ready to take action on its own and both preferred to rely on *appeasement* to try to stop the Dictators.

The League of Nations was finally wound up in 1945. Its assets were transferred to the *United Nations* which was set up in the same year.

LENIN, VLADIMIR

Lenin was the leader of the *Bolsheviks*, the Communist Party which seized power in Russia in October 1917. Lenin was born in 1870 and became involved in politics in 1887. His brother, Alexander, was arrested in St Petersburg carrying a bomb with which he intended to assassinate Tsar Alexander III. He was tried and hanged. When Lenin arrived at university later in the year, he joined a terrorist organisation and was then expelled from university for taking part in a demonstration. He spent four years living at home with his mother and then moved to St Petersburg in 1893. Here he joined the Social Democrats. He was arrested and imprisoned in 1895 and exiled to Siberia from 1897 to 1900.

In 1903 the Social Democrats split into two sections. One, led by Lenin, became known as the Bolsheviks (the majority). The other, led by Julius Martov, became known as the Mensheviks (the minority). In fact there were more Mensheviks than Bolsheviks, but Lenin won one important vote at a conference in Brussels and the names stuck.

During the years from 1903 to 1917 Lenin spent most of his time living abroad. In 1917 he was in Switzerland. When news of the **February Revolution** reached Germany, the German government decided to send Lenin back to Russia to try to stir up a revolution. The Germans hoped this would mean that Russia would make peace. This would allow the German forces on the Eastern Front to be moved to the West.

The April Theses

In March 1917 Lenin arrived back in Russia and immediately issued the April Theses. This was a list of demands which he hoped would attract people to support him. The most important was the ending of the war, but others were:

- all land and banks to be nationalised
- the abolition of the army
- the transfer of political power to workers' committees called 'soviets'
- the withdrawal of support for the provisional government.

Lenin hoped that his ideas would lead to a breakdown of law and order and that he would then be able to seize power. He made speeches and wrote articles trying to persuade people to support him, but this did not work. So, on 4 July, the Bolsheviks tried to seize power by force. This became known as the **'July Days'**.

The July Days was a complete failure. Many Bolsheviks were arrested and Lenin was forced to flee to Finland in disguise. He shaved off his beard and put on a curly wig. It appeared that the Bolsheviks had failed.

The July Days led to the appointment of a new Prime Minister of the provisional government, Alexander Kerensky, who had been a revolutionary and a member of the Petrograd Soviet. In August the commander in chief of the Army, General Kornilov, tried to overthrow Kerensky because he thought that he was going to try to seize power. This became known as the **Kornilov Revolt**. The only way that Kerensky could defend himself was to appeal to the Bolsheviks for help; this meant that the leaders were released from prison and given arms. So Lenin was given a second chance. He was now convinced that the provisional government could be overthrown.

The October Revolution

Lenin and **Trotsky** planned to seize power on 25 October 1917. Trotsky trained the 'Red Guards' and they took control of the bridges and the important buildings in the city centre. The Winter Palace, where the provisional government met, was stormed and Kerensky fled. The following day Lenin became the ruler of Russia.

How did Russia change under Lenin?

- All land, factories and banks were nationalised. Private bank accounts were confiscated.
- All church property was confiscated and religious education in schools was banned.
- The government took control of all shops and set up a system of rationing.
- Other political parties were banned and workers could only join trade unions set up by the government.
- All debts to foreign countries were cancelled.
- Russia made peace with Germany in February 1918 and left the **First World War**.

The New Economic Policy

These changes led to a civil war in Russia from 1918 to 1920, which the Bolsheviks won. But the cost of the war was so great that Lenin was forced to allow some changes to the communist system. Small businesses could be set up and people were allowed to buy and sell between themselves. This became known as the New Economic Policy. It lasted until 1928.

Lenin died in January 1924. He had been seriously ill for some time, partly because he had been the target of at least four assassination attempts. During one, a bullet had lodged in his chest. He left a 'Political Will' naming Leon **Trotsky** as his successor.

✛ *Russian Revolution*

LENINGRAD

In 1924, after the death of Lenin, the city of Petrograd was renamed Leningrad in his honour. It kept this name until 1991, when it was renamed St Petersburg, which had been its name from the beginning of the eighteenth century until 1914. At the outbreak of the **First World War**, the name of the city was changed from the German version, St Petersburg, to the Russian version, Petrograd.

During the **Second World War** Leningrad was besieged by the Germans for 900 days, but the city held out.

LIBERAL PARTY

The Liberal Party developed from the **Whig** Party in the middle of the nineteenth century. With the **Tories** it was one of the two big political parties of the late-nineteenth and early-twentieth centuries. The Whigs and the Liberals had carried out many reforms: the **Whig Reforms** in the 1830s; the reforms of **Gladstone** in the 1870s and 1880s, and the **Liberal Reforms** in the 1900s. By the 1930s, however, the Liberals had almost disappeared as a political force.

Why did the Liberal Party collapse so quickly?

- The Liberals lost the support of the business class to the **Conservative Party**.
- The new Labour Party began to win the votes of working people.

- The Liberals argued among themselves during the **First World War** and were divided into two sections for six years after the war.
- They found they were the third party in a system that only really worked with two, because the House of Commons had two sides: one for the government and the other for the opposition.
- The policies of **Lloyd George** after the war did not help. He was blamed for many of the things that went wrong in Britain in the 1920s, although they were not really his fault.
- By the time that Lloyd George and Asquith had patched up their quarrel it was too late. Many voters had already changed to the Labour Party.

LIBERAL REFORMS

In 1906 the Liberals won the General Election with a huge majority. They had already decided to introduce a series of reforms to give people some protection against poverty, sickness and unemployment.

Why did the Liberals introduce their reforms?

- In the **Boer** War many volunteers for the Army had been turned down because they were unfit.
- A report had been published in 1901 which showed that many people in Britain lived in real poverty.
- The Liberals were supported by the Labour Party, which wanted the reforms.

1906–7	School meals, milk and medical inspections were introduced to try to improve children's health.
1908	Old Age Pensions were introduced.
1911	The National Insurance Act was passed. This gave unemployment benefit for 15 weeks and sickness benefits for 26 weeks.

These reforms were the basis for the **Welfare State**, which was developed by the Labour government after the **Second World War**.

LLOYD GEORGE, DAVID

David Lloyd George was the leading British politician in the first two decades of the twentieth century. He played a very important role in the passing of the **Liberal Reforms** which laid the foundations for the **Welfare State** and he was responsible for organising the war effort in Britain from 1916 to 1918.

1908	He became Chancellor of the Exchequer.
1909	He introduced the 'People's Budget'. This was to help pay for Old Age Pensions and other Liberal Reforms. He raised money by increasing income tax and putting duties on alcohol, tobacco and petrol. This set the pattern for all Budgets ever since.

When the Budget was defeated in the House of Lords, the government introduced the Parliament Bill which reduced the power of the Lords. In future the House of Lords would only be able to delay bills for two years and would not be able to vote at all on bills to do with finance.

This was a very important change in **Parliament**.

1911	Lloyd George introduced the National Insurance Act, which provided unemployment benefit and sickness benefit for the first time in Britain.

When the First World War broke out, Lloyd George remained Chancellor of the Exchequer and had to find ways of paying for the war effort. He did this by increasing income tax and by borrowing money. In 1915 he became Minister of Munitions. He now had to find ways of increasing the numbers of guns and shells produced by Britain. He encouraged women to take up war work in munitions factories and in other jobs.

In 1916 he became Secretary at War, which meant that he was in overall charge of running the war. This led to clashes with the Prime Minister, Herbert Asquith. Lloyd George wanted a more organised war effort. Asquith had tended to let the country continue as it had been in peacetime. Asquith resigned in December 1916 and Lloyd George took his place as Prime Minister. He set up a new coalition government to win the war. Most members of the coalition government were Conservative.

How did Lloyd George change the way the war was run?

- He set up a War Cabinet of five: these ministers had no departments to run and met daily to deal with the war.
- He took over industries and ran them for the war effort: labour, shipbuilding, food production, railways. This was known as 'War Socialism'.
- He set up a Ministry of Information to help boost public morale and undermine Germany by **propaganda**.
- He persuaded businessmen to help the government fight the war: for example, newspaper owners and journalists were recruited.
- He forced the Navy to accept the convoy system, which led to a fall in the number of ships sunk by submarines.
- The Army was forced to accept Marshal Foch, the French commander, as Supreme Commander of the Allied Forces. Until then the two allies had not cooperated very effectively and sometimes not at all.

When the war came to an end in November 1918, more than any other person, Lloyd George could claim to have won the war for Great Britain.

How did the war affect Lloyd George's position in Britain?

- The argument with Asquith split the Liberal Party. Although the split was ended in 1924, the Liberals never recovered. This meant that Lloyd George depended more and more on support from the Conservative Party if he wanted to stay in power after 1918.

- Lloyd George disagreed with most people in Britain who wanted Germany to be dealt with very harshly after the war. He wanted Germany to be allowed to recover.
- He had to deal with the situation in **Ireland**. It was his idea to allow Ulster to remain in the United Kingdom.
- He had to deal with the economic problems created by the war: unemployment, industries worn out, exports lost, debts to the USA.
- Like most people he did not realise how badly Britain had been affected by the war. When he tried to build 1 000 000 new homes and raise the school-leaving age from 12 to 14, he found he could not afford the costs.

Lloyd George remained as Prime Minister until 1922, when he was forced to resign after a revolt by the Conservative backbenchers led by Stanley Baldwin. Even today, the Conservative backbench committee is known as the 1922 Committee. Lloyd George never served as a government minister again. He died in 1945.

LONGBOW

The longbow was the most successful infantry weapon used by the English in the Middle Ages. It was first adopted by **Edward I** after his wars against the Welsh, who had used it very successfully. It was most effective during the **Hundred Years' War** in the battles of Crecy, Poitiers and **Agincourt**.

The longbow was about two metres long and had a range of 800 metres. Arrows fired from it could penetrate chain mail and plate armour. Its use led to the end of the mounted knight in battle.

LONG PARLIAMENT

The Long Parliament was the name given to the Parliament which met in November 1640, the last Parliament before the beginning of the **Civil War**. It was recalled in February 1660, when all the surviving members were summoned to London. This suggested that all the events of the Civil War and the **Republic** had had no legal status and that only the Parliament elected in 1640 could actually take any decisions. The Long Parliament was dissolved on 16 March 1660.

LORDS

The House of Lords is one of the three parts of **Parliament**, along with the **Commons** and the Monarch. It began as the King's council, to which important barons and bishops were invited by **William I** and his successors. The barons began to act as a separate body during the reign of King **John** (1199–1216), when they forced him to accept the **Magna Carta**. During the reigns of **Henry III** (1216–1272) and **Edward I** (1272–1307) the Lords and Commons both began to be summoned.

LUSITANIA

The Lusitania was a passenger liner which was sunk by a German submarine on 7 May 1915. 1198 lives were lost, including 139 Americans. This almost led to a US declaration of war on Germany. The Lusitania was carrying munitions and the German embassy had put an advertisement in papers in New York warning Americans against sailing in her.

MACADAM, JOHN LOUDON

John Macadam was a very successful roadbuilder in the late-eighteenth and early-nineteenth century. Unlike **Telford**, he did not use stone blocks in his roads, but small stones. He laid a bottom layer of stones about seven centimetres in diameter and then a top layer of stones about three centimetres in diameter. Both layers were made up of stones with jagged edges. When these layers were pressed down they formed a hard, compact surface. Later a layer of tar was added to the top to form 'tarmacadam' or 'tarmac'.

Macadam's method was cheap and reliable and was widely used by **Turnpike Trusts**. In 1827 he became the Surveyor-General of Turnpikes in Britain.

MAGISTRATES

✥ **Justices of the Peace**

MAGNA CARTA

The Magna Carta, or Great Charter, was issued by King **John** in 1215. John was forced to agree to the Magna Carta by his barons who were angry at the way they had been treated. The main cause of the barons' complaints was the war that John had been waging against Philip II of France in an effort to regain control of Normandy. The war ended with the defeat of John at the battle of Bouvines in 1214. John had also been excommunicated by the Pope in 1209 because he refused to accept Stephen Langton as Archbishop of Canterbury. John was forced to give in and accept Stephen Langton in 1213.

Why were the barons angry?

- John was already unpopular because he had been excommunicated by the Pope in 1209:
- The barons said that:
  - he had demanded too much money from them in taxes to pay for the war in France
  - anyone who could not pay was unfairly punished
  - there was no way anyone could complain about their treatment.

In 1215 rebel barons, who had refused to fight in France, captured London and John agreed to meet them at Runnymede beside the Thames. After a week of discussion he accepted the Magna Carta. This set out what John could and could not do in the future.

Most of the Magna Carta was concerned with the rights of the barons, but there were some sections to do with ordinary people.

The most important sections of the Magna Carta stated:

- no royal official can take anything from any man without paying for it
- no one can be placed on trial without some form of evidence against him
- no one can be arrested or imprisoned except according to the law of the land
- no one can be denied justice
- the King cannot raise taxes without the consent of the Great Council.

Twenty-five barons were to be elected to form a Great Council. They were to make sure that John kept to the Magna Carta.

Was the Magna Carta important?

Nowadays it is regarded as very important and many other documents have been based on it: the United Nations Declaration of Human Rights, for example. But at the time:

- the barons were only really interested in themselves
- King John immediately broke many of the promises he had made
- the Pope actually said it was illegal
- most of the sections were only restating what was already happening. It was an attempt to make John behave as most Kings already did.

But it was the first time the King of England had been forced to make promises by his barons.

MANCHURIA

Manchuria was a province of China which was invaded by Japan in 1931. This was a clear breach of the Covenant of the **League of Nations**, of which China was a member. The Chinese government appealed to the League for help and the League sent a commission to China to investigate the matter. The League should have ordered military sanctions, but this would have meant member countries declaring war on Japan. Instead the League sent a message to the Japanese government telling it to withdraw. The Japanese ignored the message and left the League.

This was the first example of a Permanent Council Member ignoring the Covenant. It made the League look foolish and encouraged other countries to do the same. It was the first step in the collapse of the authority of the League.

MARLBOROUGH, THE DUKE OF

The Duke of Marlborough was the most successful British General during the war of the Spanish Succession from 1702–1713. He won a series of victories, beginning with the battle of Blenheim in 1704. These battles made sure that Britain made major gains at the Treaty of Utrecht in 1713,

including parts of Canada, islands in the Caribbean and Gibraltar. This was an important stage in the development of the British Empire.

In 1710 the Tories won control of the House of **Commons** and Marlborough was dismissed. He had been supported by the **Whigs.**

MARSHALL PLAN

The Marshall Plan was an attempt to rebuild Europe after the **Second World War**. In March 1947 President Harry Truman offered grants of American money to all European countries. The plan was named after his Secretary of State, George C. Marshall.

Truman intended that Marshall Aid would be made available to all countries in Europe, but in fact only countries in the West accepted it. The **USSR** and other eastern European countries attended the first meetings in 1948, but withdrew when they discovered they would have to join the Organisation for European Economic Cooperation, which would control how the money was going to be spent. This would mean that the **USA** would be able to influence the countries of the East and undermine communism. This was what Truman had hoped would happen.

Altogether 17 countries received a total of $13 750 000 000, which allowed them to recover from the war much more quickly than the countries of the East. This was one of the reasons why Stalin tried to force the West out of **West Berlin** in 1948.

MARSTON MOOR, THE BATTLE OF

This was one of the most important battles of the **English Civil War** fought on 2 July 1644. It ended in defeat for the Royalists and led to the surrender of the cities of York and Newcastle. After this almost all of northern England was in the hands of **Parliament**.

MARX, KARL

Karl Marx was the founder of Communism. His books, *The Communist Manifesto* and *Das Kapital*, influenced many politicians and revolutionaries in the late-nineteenth and twentieth centuries. The most important effects were on the revolutionary parties in Russia, the Social Democrats and the Socialist–Revolutionaries. One section of the Social Democrats, the **Bolsheviks**, seized power in Russia in 1917 and ruled the country until 1991.

What did Marx believe?

- All property should be owned in common by all people.
- No one should make any profit out of the work of another person.
- People should be paid according to the value of the work they did.

These were very attractive ideas to working people in the late-nineteenth century, when many of them were suffering from the effects of the **Industrial Revolution**. This could mean long hours at work, low

pay and dismissal. At the same time some people in society, the owners of industry, appeared to be getting better and better off.

Marx had developed his ideas while he was living in Britain in the 1840s. He had seen the effects the Industrial Revolution had had on workers.

Marxist ideas had most effect in countries where there seemed to be little hope of change or improvement, or where the government was a dictatorship or an autocracy. This helps explain why Russia and China were countries where Marxist ideas took over.

MARY, QUEEN, 1553–1558

Mary was the eldest child of **Henry VIII** and came to the throne in 1553 on the death of her brother, **Edward VI**. She was the daughter of **Catherine of Aragon** and had been brought up as a **Catholic**. She married Philip II of Spain, a Catholic country, in 1554. This was not popular in England.

During Mary's reign England changed back to being a Catholic country. How did this affect people in England?

- The Pope became the head of the Church.
- Church services had to be in Latin.
- The English Bible was banned.
- Priests who had married during the reign of Edward VI were ordered to leave their wives.
- About 300 people were burnt as heretics because they refused to change back to Catholicism. They included two bishops, Ridley and Latimer, and the Archbishop of Canterbury, Thomas **Cranmer**, who had divorced Henry VIII and written the Prayer Book.
- The Six Articles were reintroduced (see **Henry VIII**).

This horrified many people in England. Nothing like this had ever happened before. However, it was nothing like what was happening in other countries of Europe, where thousands of people were killed. Mary refused to allow the Inquisition into England. Nevertheless, she gained the nickname 'Bloody Mary'.

Mary also became involved in a war with France. In 1558 the last English possession on the continent, Calais, was lost. Mary died childless in 1558 and was succeeded by her sister, **Elizabeth I**.

MARY, QUEEN, 1689–1694

Mary was the elder daughter of **James II**, by his first wife Anne Hyde. She was brought up as a **Protestant**. In 1688 she was asked to become Queen. She ruled with her husband William of Orange, who refused to allow Mary to be Queen unless he became King.

✛ *Glorious Revolution, William III*

MARY, QUEEN OF SCOTS

Mary, Queen of Scots, was the mother of **James** VI of Scotland and I of England. Mary was married three

times: first to Francis II of France, then to Lord Darnley and, after he was murdered, to the Earl of Bothwell. In 1567 she was forced to abdicate in favour of her son, James, and fled to England. She asked **Elizabeth I** to protect her. Mary remained in England for 19 years, until she was executed in 1587.

Why was Mary, Queen of Scots, executed?

- She was a grand-daughter of **Henry VII**. Some people believed she had a better claim to the throne than Elizabeth.
- When she was married to Francis II, she had called herself Queen of England and Scotland.
- She was a **Catholic** and there was a series of Catholic plots against Elizabeth in the 1580s. Although Mary may not have been involved, she was tried and found guilty. She was executed in February 1587.

Mary's son, James, was chosen by Elizabeth to be her successor. He was a **Protestant** and had become King of Scotland in 1567 after his mother's abdication.

MEDIEVAL

Medieval refers to the period from about 1000 to about 1500 (it can also be used for the period from about 500 to about 1500). It means 'middle' and historians sometimes refer to the Middle Ages, meaning the period between the Roman Empire and the modern world.

MEIN **K**AMPF

Mein Kampf was the title of the book written by Adolf **Hitler** while he was in Landsberg Prison in 1924. He had been arrested and convicted of treason after the failure of the **Beer Hall Putsch** in the previous year. *Mein Kampf* means 'My Struggle' and later Hitler often referred to his followers as Kampfer, or strugglers.

The book is a mixture of Hitler's life story and his political ideas. He attacked the **Armistice** of November 1918, 'the stab in the back', and the politicians who had signed it, 'the November Criminals'. He also attacked the Treaty of **Versailles**, the 'Diktat'. He then went on to blame Germany's defeat on the Jews.

In the book Hitler clearly explained how he would act if he came to power in Germany. Few people took it seriously, because much of the book is made up of wild accusations and lies. But Hitler said, 'If you are going to tell a lie, tell a big lie.' If the book had been read more carefully, the politicians who had to deal with Hitler in the 1930s, both inside Germany and in Britain and France, would have been much better prepared.

MEMOIRS

The word 'memoirs' is used to describe the writings of politicians or other people in which they describe their careers. They are usually written after they have retired and are based on their diaries and other papers. Memoirs can be very useful as they can help us to understand why people acted as they did. But

sometimes they can be confusing as the writer may try to make out that they were more important than they really were. Some writers even try to distort what really happened to prevent people finding out about mistakes they made.

MIDDLE **C**LASS

Middle class was a term which was first used in the nineteenth century. It described the people who lived in towns and who made their living from business and the professions. These people became much more important after the **Industrial Revolution**. In France the term 'bourgeois' was invented. This means people who live in towns. This was intended to separate them from the aristocracy who owned land.

MONASTERY

A monastery was a religious building where men could go to live; women would go to a nunnery or a convent. Monks had to obey the rules of the order they were joining. The vows were of obedience, poverty and chastity. Most monasteries were built in remote areas and monks lived simple lives. They had to attend seven church services every day and had few meals. The Carthusians only had one meal a day.

Why did people become monks?

- Some men believed it was a way to serve God. Monks spent a great deal of time praying.
- Some boys were sent to monasteries by their families because they were too poor to support them.
- Some rich families would send one of their sons into the church, perhaps to become a monk.
- Although life in a monastery could be very hard, many orders were very wealthy and often very powerful.
- Monks were educated and abbots often played important roles in government.

Monasteries in Britain

The first monks in Britain were Celtic monks in Scotland, but when St Augustine arrived in 597 and became the first Archbishop of Canterbury, he brought with him Benedictine monks. The Benedictines wore a black habit and became known as the 'black monks'. They shaved the top of their head to show they were monks. This was known as the 'tonsure'.

After the **Norman Conquest** (1066) many more monasteries were built in Britain. The Cluniacs set up their first house in 1077. They were a very powerful order from Burgundy in central France. The most important order, however, was the Cistercians. They built many houses in the north of England, mostly in Yorkshire. The founder believed that monks should live in the countryside away from towns. The Cistercians were sheep farmers and made their habits from sheep's wool. They became known as the 'white monks'. The Cistercians became very wealthy and owned large areas of land.

The last monks to arrive were the Carthusians in

1178. They were the strictest of all and ate only one vegetarian meal a day.

The main role of monks was to pray to God, but they also cared for the sick, set up hospitals, looked after the poor and ran businesses and schools.

Why did monasteries become so wealthy?

- The monasteries were usually founded by barons, who gave them land to support themselves.
- Many people gave gifts to monasteries. Often this was land. In return, the monks would pray for the givers of the gifts. They hoped this would help them get to heaven.
- Monks were often very good craftsmen and good at business; they had nothing else to distract them. The Cistercians were very successful sheep farmers.

What happened to the monasteries?

Most monasteries in Britain disappeared in the 1530s. **Henry VIII**'s minister Thomas **Cromwell** suggested that Henry could raise money by taking the lands and wealth of the monasteries. He sent people out to investigate the monasteries. Most of the reports they produced said the monks were breaking their own rules. Cromwell used this as an excuse to close all the monasteries.

Nowadays most monasteries are in ruins. There are many in Yorkshire, such as Rievaulx and Jervaulx.

MONS

The battle of Mons was the first battle fought by the **British Expeditionary Force** in the **First World War**. When the BEF arrived in France, it took up positions near the Belgian town of Mons and was faced by the German Army of 1 250 000 men trying to carry out the **Schlieffen Plan**. The BEF was forced to retreat, but it was able to slow down the advancing Germans to allow the French to counterattack. The battle lasted on and off for five days.

Although there were 120 000 men in the BEF, most of the fighting was done by half of them commanded by Sir Hubert Smith-Dorrien. The other half, commanded by Sir Douglas Haig, became detached and took little part in the fighting. Haig became the commander-in-chief of the British Army in France in December 1915.

MONTFORT, SIMON DE

Simon de Montfort was the leader of the barons' rebellion against **Henry III** in 1265. He captured Henry at the battle of Lewes and then summoned a **Parliament**. For the first time this included two representatives from each shire (knights) and two representatives from each town (burgesses). This was the first time that the **Commons** had been included in Parliament.

Simon de Montfort was defeated and killed by Henry's son, Edward, at the battle of Evesham in the same year, but his idea of summoning the Commons lasted. **Edward I** continued the idea when he became King in 1272.

MORE, SIR THOMAS

Sir Thomas More was well known as the author of the book, *Utopia*, in which he described an ideal country. In 1529 he became Chancellor to **Henry VIII** when Cardinal Thomas **Wolsey** was dismissed. But he resigned in 1532, when Henry began to limit the power of the **Catholic** Church.

In 1534 the Act of Supremacy was passed. This said that everybody had to take an oath to Henry as the Head of the Church. Refusal to take the oath counted as high treason. Sir Thomas More refused.

Why did Sir Thomas More refuse to take the oath of supremacy?

The main reason was he did not believe that Henry was the Head of the Church. More believed that the Pope was still the Head of the Church.

Henry tried to persuade More to change his mind, but failed. More was executed in 1535.

MUNICH AGREEMENT

The Munich Agreement was signed on 29 September 1938. Four leaders signed the document: Adolf **Hitler**, Neville Chamberlain, the British Prime Minister, Benito **Mussolini**, the Italian dictator, and Edouard Daladier, the French Prime Minister.

The Agreement handed over to Germany an area called the **Sudetenland**. Since 1919 this had been part of Czechoslovakia, but most of the people spoke German. In September 1938 Hitler demanded the Sudetenland and Neville Chamberlain visited Germany in an effort to solve the crisis. In the end, Britain and France gave in and allowed Hitler to have his way. The Czech government was told it had to accept the decision and that Britain and France would not support the Czechs if they decided to fight.

The Czechs were particularly angry as the Sudetenland contained about one-quarter of the Czech population, as well as most of their iron and their defences against Germany.

Why did Chamberlain sign the Munich Agreement?

There are two interpretations of his actions.

- Chamberlain believed that if Hitler was given the Sudetenland, that would be an end to his demands. This would mean there would not be a war.
- Chamberlain believed that war was inevitable and so he signed the Agreement to put off war as long as possible. In fact war broke out just 11 months later.

It is difficult to decide which of these two interpretations of Chamberlain's actions is the more accurate: he appears to have changed his mind and wrote different explanations at different times.

MUNICH CRISIS

The Munich Crisis is the name given to events in September 1938 after **Hitler** demanded that the

Sudetenland be handed over to Germany. At the Munich conference the British Prime Minister, Neville Chamberlain, agreed that Hitler should be allowed to take the Sudetenland. The Czechoslovak government was not consulted. This was the final act of **appeasement**.

⬩ **Chamberlain, Adolf** *Hitler*, **Nazi Germany, the Second World War**

MUSSOLINI, BENITO

Mussolini became Prime Minister of Italy in October 1922 and from 1925 he ruled as a dictator.

Why did Mussolini become popular in Italy after the *First World War*?

- Italy had suffered during the war: 460 000 soldiers were killed and the country was heavily in debt.
- Italy had been promised extra land by Britain and France during the war, but when the war ended the land was not handed over. This made it look as if the Italian government had been ignored.
- The governments after the war were weak. They were coalitions (made up of more than one party) and were not able to take decisions.
- There was unrest in many cities and many people became communists.
- Mussolini set up the Fascist Party and promised to sort out Italy's problems. He organised armed gangs who would deal with troublemakers and criminals.
- Mussolini promised to rebuild Italy and recreate the Roman Empire.

In October 1922 Mussolini threatened to march on Rome if he was not appointed Prime Minister. The King of Italy, Victor Emmanuel III, who supported Mussolini, refused to back the existing government and invited him to become Prime Minister.

How did Mussolini change Italy?

Mussolini was the first of the dictators who came to power in Europe in the 1920s and 1930s. Most of the others copied his ideas, but also avoided his mistakes.

- All other political parties were banned, trade unions were banned.
- Newspapers and books were censored.
- Education was controlled and all school books were rewritten. 1922 was renamed the Year One. Children were encouraged to become fit. Boys were expected to become soldiers.
- Women were discouraged from working and from horse-riding and wearing trousers. They were encouraged to stay at home and have as many children as possible.
- Children were encouraged to join an organisation called the Balilla, which trained them to be good Fascists.
- Mussolini began a series of schemes to improve the Italian economy. He called these the 'Battles'. He tried to make Italy self-sufficient in food and to increase the Italian population.

- Mussolini began to build motorways (autostrada) to provide work for Italians during the **Depression**. He also built new public buildings and claimed that he 'made the railways run on time'.

At first Mussolini was very popular. In the 1920s Italy appeared to become more prosperous and more powerful. Many Italians found work in the industries Mussolini set up and Italy seemed to be recovering from the effects of the **First World War**. In 1929 Mussolini even managed to make an agreement with the Pope called the Lateran Treaties. The Pope agreed to accept the Fascists and Mussolini agreed that the **Catholic** religion would be taught in every Italian school. He also promised to pay the salaries of Catholic priests and set up the Vatican City in Rome. This convinced many Italians that they should support Mussolini. But in the 1930s Mussolini began to become less popular in Italy.

Why did Mussolini become unpopular?

- Mussolini tried to build up a picture of himself as a superman. He had photographs taken of himself flying an aeroplane, driving a racing car, playing the violin, winning a chess game, even jogging. Unfortunately, many of these photographs were faked and Italians began to realise that many of Mussolini's claims were not true.
- Many of Mussolini's plans were not well thought out and failed. The Italian population actually fell and, while he grew more wheat, there was less olive oil and fruits which were important exports. He tried to build a new city in southern Italy called Mussolinia, but only a few foundations were finished.
- Most Italians found themselves worse off by the early 1930s. Mussolini's attempts to make Italy self-sufficient made most things more expensive. Wages did not rise as quickly as prices.
- From 1935 Mussolini came more and more under the influence of **Hitler**. Before that Hitler had been the follower and Mussolini the leader. Many Italians did not like this. When Mussolini tried to begin persecuting the Jews, most Italians refused.

To try to regain popularity Mussolini began to build an empire. He invaded Abyssinia in 1935. The Abyssinians did not have a modern army and it was an easy victory. It made Mussolini popular for a time, but it also meant that he came even more under the influence of Hitler. In 1936 they signed the Rome–Berlin Axis.

Mussolini declared war on Britain and France in 1940, but the Italian armed forces were not very successful. He tried to invade North Africa and Yugoslavia, but each time his Army had to be rescued by the Germans. In 1943 the Allies invaded Italy and Mussolini was overthrown. He was rescued by German paratroopers, but in April 1945 at the end of the war he was caught trying to escape and he was shot by Italian resistance fighters. His body was hung upside down in the street.

NAPOLEON

Napoleon Bonaparte became First Consul of France in 1799 and Emperor in 1804. He ruled France until 1814 when he was exiled to Elba. In 1815 he returned to France, but was defeated at **Waterloo** and was then exiled to St Helena in the South Atlantic.

NAPOLEONIC WAR

The Napoleonic War began in 1803 and lasted until the final defeat of **Napoleon** in 1815. The peace brought about at the Treaty of Amiens in February 1802 lasted only until March 1803, when Napoleon declared war on Britain.

From 1803 to 1805 Napoleon planned to invade Britain. He built up an army at Boulogne and tried to carry it across the Channel and land in Kent. To do this he needed command of the sea.

Why did Napoleon's plan to invade Britain fail?

- Napoleon was a great general, but had little understanding of naval matters. He believed that his admirals should be able to win sea battles as easily as he could win battles on land.
- The Royal Navy had blockaded the French ports. This made it very difficult for the French fleets to put to sea. When they did, they were followed.
- The main British admiral was **Nelson**. The French had no one who was able to deal with him.
- The French Navy had lost a series of battles to the British. They did not believe that they could win, even though they were also supported by the Spanish fleet.
- The British ships were better trained than the French: they could fire their guns up to three times as fast.
- When the French fleet escaped from Toulon in May 1805, Nelson guessed what was happening and the French and Spanish fleets were forced back into Cadiz. When Napoleon ordered the French admiral to go out and fight, they were defeated at the battle of **Trafalgar** on 21 October 1805.

By then Napoleon had given up any idea of invading Britain; his armies were already marching east and in the next two years he conquered Austria, Prussia and Russia.

The Continental System

Napoleon now tried to starve Britain by stopping all exports of wheat from the Continent. This became known as the Continental System. Every country in western Europe was forced to join. The effects were severe. Within four years the price of wheat, and therefore the price of bread, in Britain had doubled. There were outbreaks of unrest, including Luddism.

The British government replied by stopping all goods reaching France. This meant that Napoleon found it difficult to produce uniforms for his soldiers.

Why did the Continental System fail?

- Farmers in Britain began to enclose more land. This meant they could grow more wheat.
- The Speenhamland System helped protect people from the worst effects. This gave people who were unable to support themselves money when the price of bread went up.
- Britain sent an army to Portugal and Spain in 1808, which began the **Peninsular War**. This was to last for the next six years. 250 000 French troops were bogged down in Spain trying to defeat the British under **Wellington**. The Spanish supported the British; the word 'guerrilla', meaning 'little war', was invented to describe their methods of fighting.
- In 1811 the Continental System collapsed when Russia withdrew.

Napoleon surrendered after the battle of **Waterloo** in 1815 and was exiled to St Helena in the south Atlantic. He died in 1821.

✦ *Wellington, Peninsular War, Poor Law, Waterloo*

NASEBY

Naseby was the final major battle of the **English Civil War**. It ended in a total defeat of **Charles I**. Most towns which had been holding out for the King surrendered and there was only one large Royalist force left in England. This was defeated at the battle of Stow-on-the-Wold in March 1646.

NATIONAL GOVERNMENT

The National government was set up in Britain in August 1931, when the Labour Cabinet resigned rather than agree to cuts in unemployment benefit. The Prime Minister, Ramsay Macdonald, went to Buckingham Palace to resign, but was persuaded by King **George V** to stay on as Prime Minister and lead a National government. This was made up of four Labour ministers, four Conservatives and two Liberals.

Why was the National government set up?

- In 1929 the **Wall Street Crash** had caused unemployment to rise in Britain; more and more was spent on benefit. By the end of August the government was running out of money and needed to borrow from American banks. They

- would only lend the money if the government reduced spending.
- When the Labour Cabinet discussed the proposal, a majority voted against making the cuts. Ramsay Macdonald and Philip Snowden, the Chancellor of the Exchequer, were among those in favour.
- The King persuaded Macdonald to stay on as Prime Minister because he believed that the crisis would only get worse if there was a General Election.

This is one of the few occasions when the Monarch has become involved directly in politics. This usually happens only during a national crisis. Another occasion was when Neville Chamberlain resigned as Prime Minister in May 1940, during the **Second World War**.

National governments remained in power throughout the 1930s, but they became increasingly dominated by the **Conservative Party**.

NATIONALISATION

Nationalisation is the taking over of businesses by the State and then running them in the public interest. This has happened to some extent in Britain during both world wars, but the main example was during the Labour ministry of 1945 to 1950. In these years coal-mining, gas, railways and electricity were all nationalised.

Why did the Labour government nationalise so many industries?

- To try to guarantee standards of safety. This was important in coal-mining, where some pits were very small and the owners could not afford improvements.
- To provide reliable services for the people of Britain. Most of the industries which were nationalised supplied people with essential services. In the past these had been unreliable.
- To provide essential services as cheaply as possible. The nationalised industries were non-profit-making.

In the 1980s and 1990s many of the nationalised industries were denationalised: that is, they were sold to the public.

NATIONALISM

Nationalism is belief and support for one's own country. This can lead to extreme views, as in the case of the National Socialists in Germany, or the Fascists in Italy. Nationalists are normally right-wing politically and believe that the State should be protected. They also believe that individual people should be prepared to sacrifice their liberties, if necessary, for the good of their country.

NATIONAL SOCIALIST

National Socialist was the name **Hitler** gave to his political party. It was originally called the German Workers' Party, when he joined it in 1919, but he changed the name to the National Socialist German

Workers' Party after he became leader in 1921. The name was intended to appeal to as many people as possible. National would attract, Hitler hoped, right-wing Nationalists, and **Socialist** would attract left-wing Socialists. This worked, but in the long run it caused problems for Hitler as it meant there were people in his Party with very different views. This problem was eventually dealt with at the **Night of the Long Knives**.

NATO

NATO is the North Atlantic Treaty Organisation which was set up in 1949 after the **Berlin Blockade**. It was a sign that relations between the Super Powers were now so bad that some form of military alliance was necessary. Thirteen countries joined in 1949, including Britain and the **USA**. It led to US troops and aircraft being stationed in European countries to protect them against a possible attack by the countries of eastern Europe.

The most important aspect of the Alliance was that if any one of the member countries was to be attacked, all the others would immediately protect it.

Since 1949 most countries of western Europe have joined NATO and recently some of the former communist countries, such as Poland and Hungary, have joined. Since the Alliance was set up, none of the members has been attacked.

NAVAL ARMS RACE

The Naval Arms Race was one of the causes of rivalry between Britain and Germany before the **First World War** and a long-term cause of the war.

Why did the Naval Arms Race begin?

- It began in 1900 after the Second German Navy Law, by which Germany planned to build up a Navy to rival Britain's.
- The British government became alarmed as Germany had only had a small Navy in the past.
- Germany only had a small coastline and few colonies, so it was assumed that the Navy would be used against Britain.
- In 1906 Britain launched HMS *Dreadnought*, a new type of battleship with ten 12-inch guns.
- The Germans replied with Dreadnoughts of their own. Britain then built bigger ships with 13.5-inch guns and later 15-inch guns.

The race to build bigger ships went on until the war broke out in 1914.

NAVY LAWS

The German Navy Laws were passed in 1898 and 1900 and were the idea of Admiral Tirpitz. He wanted to build up a Navy second only to Britain's and started a 17-year building programme. A canal was built at Kiel to enable the Navy to pass from the Baltic to the North Sea.

The Navy Laws were part of a wider attempt by Kaiser **Wilhelm II** to turn Germany into a world power. Germany had already begun to acquire colonies in Africa and the Pacific and had built a railway from Berlin to Baghdad. The Kaiser talked about the 'Drang nach Osten': the 'push towards the east'.

The Navy Laws caused great friction between Germany and Britain and were a cause of the *First World War*.

NAZI GERMANY

Nazi Germany is used to describe the period from 1933 to 1945 when Germany was ruled by the Nazi Party led by Adolf *Hitler*. The word Nazi came from the full name of the party, the National Socialist Party. Hitler always used that name and Nazi was used by his opponents.

How was Nazi Germany governed?

After the Enabling Act was passed in March 1933, Adolf Hitler could govern without the Reichstag, the lower house of the German parliament. This made him dictator for four years. It was only when President *Hindenburg* died in August 1934 that he gained total power and combined the posts of chancellor and president, giving himself the title of Führer.

- All other political parties were banned and all decisions were taken by the Nazis. The Reichstag ceased to have any importance.
- Only Nazis could become civil servants, government officials or teachers.
- A People's Court was set up to try cases of treason, but this could include almost anything. It worked in secret and there was no appeal except to Hitler himself.
- Trade unions were abolished and a Nazi Labour Front was set up. This tried to bribe workers with cheap holidays and exhibitions.
- The Nazi Party took control of every area of life in Germany. A secret police force was set up, the 'Geheime Staats Polizei' (Gestapo).

How did the lives of people change in Nazi Germany?

The biggest changes were in the lives of women and children:

- All schools were single sex. All lessons were based on Nazi ideas and children were taught Nazi beliefs every day.
- Children had to join Nazi youth organisations when they reached the age of five. These held meetings in the evenings and at weekends. The Nazis realised that it was very important for them to win over children.
- Children were encouraged to spy on their parents and report what they did and said.
- Women were forced to give up work when they got married. They were not expected to wear make-up or go out without their husbands.
- The Nazis said that women should look after their husbands and children. 'Church, Children and Cooking' was how the Nazis described women's lives.
- Jews were persecuted more and more.

-+- *Anti-semitism, Holocaust*

Men were less affected, but they lost the right to strike and to express their own opinions. The Nazis controlled all books and newspapers, films and radio programmes. What Hitler was really trying to do was to control people's ideas by limiting what they could read, listen to and watch. Any writers, painters or composers the Nazis did not approve of were banned. These included Mendelssohn, a German composer who was Jewish; Van Gogh, a Dutch painter who was an Impressionist, meaning he did not paint exactly what he saw; and H.G. Wells, a British novelist who wrote a book called *The Shape of Things to Come*, in which he predicted that a *Second World War* would lead to the destruction of the world.

Why did people accept these changes?

- Many people were desperate in the early 1930s. 6 000 000 people were unemployed in Germany when Hitler came to power.
- The changes were introduced gradually; the worst effects only came into force during the *Second World War*. It was not until 1939 that Jews began to be really badly treated.
- Unemployment fell rapidly under the Nazis: by 1938 there were only 500 000 people out of work. Hitler began to build motorways, and rearmament also provided many jobs.
- Most people found themselves getting better off. Wages rose, transport improved, there was more security.
- Germany seemed to be recovering. In 1936 the Olympic Games were held in Berlin and the *Rhineland* was reoccupied.

Who opposed the Nazis?

There were three main groups of people who tried to oppose the Nazis:

- Political parties like the communists and the *socialists*. They were banned from 1933, but they tried to work underground in secret. There was a big communist group called the Red Orchestra which became very important during the Second World War.
- Students. There were a number of student groups who distributed leaflets and organised meetings, but these were usually broken up and the members executed. One group was called the 'White Rose'.
- Religious groups. These were the most difficult to deal with as many Germans would not have accepted attacks on the *Catholic* and *Protestant* Churches. Hitler actually claimed to be a Catholic. The Nazis tried to use churches by putting copies of *Mein Kampf* on the altar and Nazi banners around the church. Many Christians appear to have put up with the Nazis, but many spoke out, like Martin Niemoller and Dietrich Bonhoeffer.

Why did opposition to the Nazis fail?

- One reason was terror: everybody knew they were being watched. In every block of flats there was someone recording when people went in and out and who they met. People could be arrested at any moment and never be seen again. There was no way of protesting or complaining.

- Children spied on their parents. Hitler tried to break down the family and make children loyal to him. He was described as their father in school books.

- But the main reason was simply that the majority of Germans found they were better off under the Nazis and were prepared to put up with Nazi policies as a result.

NAZI-SOVIET PACT

The Nazi–Soviet Pact was signed on 23 August 1939. It came as a great shock to the rest of Europe as the two countries had been bitter enemies since **Hitler** had come to power. Germany promised not to attack the Soviet Union and the Soviet Union promised not to attack Germany. Most people took this as a sign that Germany was about to invade Poland. This happened on 1 September 1939. The Pact also contained secret clauses:

- the Soviet Union would attack Poland from the East and the two countries would divide Poland between them

- the Soviet Union would be free to occupy the Baltic States of Latvia, Lithuania and Estonia.

In reality this postponed a war between Germany and the Soviet Union for nearly two years which suited both countries.

NELSON, VICE-ADMIRAL HORATIO

Horatio Nelson was the most successful British Admiral during the **French Revolutionary** and **Napoleonic Wars**. While he was a captain he lost his right eye and right arm, but he continued his career and played a very important part in the battle of Cape St Vincent in 1797. The Spanish fleet was divided into two sections and Nelson put his ship between them to prevent them uniting. This action could have been disastrous and he could have been court-martialled for disobeying orders, but it led to a complete victory.

In 1798 Nelson, now promoted to Rear-Admiral, was given command of the Mediterranean fleet. He was the youngest commander in the Navy. When **Napoleon** sailed to Egypt, Nelson tracked him down and found his fleet in Aboukir Bay at the mouth of the Nile. He ordered his ships to attack immediately and caught the French fleet completely by surprise. The French admiral was so confident that Nelson would not attack that he had begun to repaint the ships. In the battle all but four of the French ships were captured or destroyed.

In 1801 Nelson was in the Baltic as second-in-command to Admiral Hyde Parker. Denmark had just joined a League of Armed Neutrality organised by the Baltic countries against Britain. Hyde Parker was supposed to force his way into the Baltic and try to make the Danish government withdraw. He sent Nelson with part of the fleet on a scouting mission to Copenhagen. Nelson saw the Danish fleet lined up and decided to attack immediately. When Hyde Parker saw this he signalled Nelson to break off the attack. Nelson was told about the signal, but decided to ignore it. He is supposed to have put his telescope to his right eye and said to his flag-captain, Thomas Hardy, 'You know Hardy, I have only one eye, I have a right to be blind sometimes; I really do not see that signal.'

Nelson's most famous battle took place in 1805. For two years he had been blockading Toulon in the Mediterranean. When the French Admiral, Villeneuve, finally escaped in a storm, Nelson followed him to the West Indies and then back across the Atlantic, sending word ahead that Villeneuve was coming. This was all part of Napoleon's attempt to invade Britain in 1805. Nelson caught up with Villeneuve at Cape **Trafalgar** outside Cadiz in southern Spain. He attacked the French and Spanish fleet head on in two lines, capturing 18 ships and destroying the fleet as a fighting force. The French fleet never left harbour again during the remaining ten years of warfare.

During the battle Nelson was shot by a French sharpshooter. He had refused to cover up his uniform and walked backwards and forwards on the deck in full view of his own men and the enemy throughout the battle. He was carried below and died two hours later. Nelson's body was brought home and buried in St Paul's Cathedral.

Why was Nelson so successful?

- Nelson was very popular with the men he commanded. At a time when discipline in the Navy could be very brutal, he treated his men well.

- Nelson was always prepared to try something new. All his victories involved taking chances. He was quick to seize the initiative, but always planned well.

- Nelson made sure that his captains understood exactly what he expected of them. He called them his 'band of brothers'. Many of them went on to become Admirals.

- Nelson's ships were always well trained. His crews could fire twice or three times as fast as the enemy.

Even today the Royal Navy uses the expression 'the Nelson touch' and sailors have three black lines on their uniforms which represent his victories at the Nile, Copenhagen and Trafalgar. Nelson's flagship at Trafalgar, HMS *Victory*, is preserved at Portsmouth. It is the oldest commissioned warship in the world. It was built in 1758 and is still on active service.

NEWCOMEN, THOMAS

Thomas Newcomen built a steam-atmospheric engine in 1709. This used **steam** power to raise the piston, but allowed it to fall by atmospheric pressure. The engine was very reliable, but slow and expensive, because cold water was injected into the cylinder to condense the steam after each stroke.

Newcomen's engine was used mostly in mines as a pump, because it could only produce reciprocating (up and down) motion. About 300 engines were in operation by the end of the eighteenth century. In 1763 James **Watt** was given a model of Newcomen's engine to repair. This gave him the idea of improving it and adding rotary motion.

NEW DEAL

The New Deal was the name given to the programme started by President Franklin **Roosevelt** to help the **USA** recover from the effects of the **Depression** in the 1930s. The name came from a speech that Roosevelt made during the presidential election campaign in 1932. He said, 'I pledge you, I pledge myself to a new deal for the American people.'

How did the New Deal work?

Roosevelt wanted to restore confidence in the Federal government. He did this by:

- closing all the banks for four days to stop people drawing out their money
- making radio broadcasts, called 'fireside chats', which told the American people what he was trying to do
- ordering that all letters sent to the President should be answered and help given if possible.

Roosevelt then wanted to offer three things: relief, recovery and reform. To do this he set up a series of government agencies, the 'Alphabet Laws' they were called, to offer help to Americans.

- The Civilian Conservation Corps (CCC) gave work in the countryside, clearing wasteland, planting forests.
- The Public Works Administration (PWA) built new public buildings, libraries and hospitals.
- The Tennessee Valley Authority (TVA) built dams to provide electric power and control flooding.
- The Agricultural Adjustment Act (AAA) gave farmers guaranteed prices for their produce.
- The National Recovery Administration (NRA) encouraged employers to pay fair wages and accept trade unions.
- The Social Security Act gave workers unemployment pay.

Did the New Deal Work?

- Roosevelt did manage to restore confidence in the Federal government.
- Unemployment fell from 13 000 000 in 1933 to 8 000 000 in 1940.
- But it was the **Second World War** that really ended the Depression in the USA. When the USA declared war in December 1941, unemployment disappeared very quickly.

NEW MODEL ARMY

The New Model Army was the Parliamentary army set up in 1644 on the lines of the Ironsides, Oliver **Cromwell**'s regiment of cavalry. The New Model Army was set up in response to a series of Royalist victories in 1643. The members were better trained and better equipped than before. It was also helped by the Self-Denying Ordinance, which was passed by **Parliament** in 1644. This said that no members of the Houses of Parliament could be in the Army. This led to completely new commanders. The Earls of Manchester and Essex, who had been the main generals since 1642, were replaced by Sir Thomas **Fairfax**, who commanded the Army until the end of the war.

NEWTON, SIR ISAAC, 1642–1727

Sir Isaac Newton was a mathematician and scientist who played a major role in developing ideas about the universe.

1669   Newton published details of 'Calculus', a form of advanced mathematics, which he called 'Fluxions'. This enabled scientific calculations to be made more accurately.

1675   Newton built the first reflecting telescope.

1687   Newton published his laws of motion, which included the idea of gravity. This said that all bodies in the universe attract each other. This explained why the solar system was held together.

1704   Newton showed that white light could be broken down into different colours by refraction. This enabled more accurate observations to be made. He also laid out the methods which should be used in scientific experiment.

Newton was a very important figure in developing scientific knowledge, particularly about the universe. He proved beyond all doubt that the medieval ideas about a universe with the Earth at the centre were impossible and he was able to explain many of the discoveries made by scientists in the sixteenth and seventeenth centuries. He was regarded at the time as being a genius and when the Royal Mint was set up in 1696, Newton was put in charge.

NIGHT OF THE LONG KNIVES

The Night of the Long Knives is the name given to the murder of many opponents of **Hitler** inside the Nazi Party on 30 June 1934.

Why did the Night of the Long Knives take place?

- The main reason was to get rid of Ernst **Roehm**, the leader of the SA, the Sturm Abteilung (Brownshirts). Roehm had been demanding that he should be made the commander-in-chief of the German army. Hitler did not want to do this as he knew it would be very unpopular with the generals. Until then, Hitler had used as an excuse that President **Hindenburg** would not agree, but by the summer of 1934 it was clear that Hindenburg was dying. Hitler wanted to get Roehm out of the way before Hindenburg died.

- Roehm was also one of the leaders of the **socialist** wing of the Nazi Party. He wanted a social revolution to give working people more influence in Germany. Hitler wanted to set up a right-wing dictatorship.
- Hitler was frightened that Roehm would use the SA to get rid of him and seize power. The SA had at least 500 000 members, although Roehm claimed there were 3 000 000.
- Roehm ordered the members of the SA to go on holiday in July 1934 and called the leaders to a meeting in Munich. This was Hitler's chance. He ordered the SS, the Schutz Staffeln (Blackshirts), to murder the SA leaders while they were unprotected.

Altogether about 400 people were killed, including many leading Brownshirts, but also others Hitler wanted out of the way, such as General Kurt von Scleicher, who had been chancellor before Hitler. The Night of the Long Knives marked the end of the power of the SA.

NON-CONFORMIST

Non-conformist was used to describe anybody who did not 'conform' to the beliefs, services and prayers of the **Church of England**. Usually it is used about the **Protestant** churches which were set up after the Church of England was created in 1534: the Presbyterians and Congregationalists for example.

NORMAN CONQUEST

The Norman Conquest was the invasion of England by **William** of Normandy and his defeat of **Harold** at the battle of **Hastings** in 1066.

How did the Norman Conquest change England?

- It made England part of a growing European empire centred on northern France. The Norman Kings spent most of their time in France and were usually abroad for at least two-thirds of their reigns.
- French became the language of government and the law. Many modern words in English are based on French words.
- Most English landowners lost their land. **William I** gave 50 per cent of the land of England to his barons, 25 per cent to the Church and kept 17 per cent for himself. Only 8 per cent remained in the hands of the English. However, no baron was allowed to have all his land in one block. It was split up into small estates all over the country; this was to prevent one of William's barons building up an Army in one place and then trying to overthrow the King.
- Most senior posts in the Church were given to Normans. By 1090 there was only one English bishop left. The English cathedrals were gradually replaced by new Norman ones, built in a new style of architecture which is now called Romanesque. Some cathedrals, like Elmham, were destroyed and never replaced; some, like

Rochester, were rebuilt on the same site. At Rochester you can see the outline of the English cathedral on the floor of the Norman one.
- Many monasteries were built in England. William's invasion had been backed by the Church. He built abbeys and monasteries as a way of giving thanks. The first was at Battle, in Sussex, the site of the battle of Hastings.
- William I established the **feudal system** in England. This had not really existed in England before 1066. It was a way of controlling the country and providing him with an Army if he needed it.
- During William's reign about 70 castles were built in England. Most of these were wooden at first, but were replaced by stone as soon as possible. They had a central tower called a keep, usually built on a mound called a motte, and a outer wall surrounding a courtyard called a bailey. These castles were known as motte and bailey castles. William built castles at places he wanted to control: Hastings and Pevensey, where he had landed, Canterbury, London (the White Tower at the centre of the Tower) and York. He also built a line of castles down the Welsh border to protect England from invasion.

By 1070 resistance to the Normans had almost come to an end. Before 1066 England had always had Kings and three of them had been Danish. Most people accepted that there had to be a King and there was little choice but to accept William.

NOTES

You will be asked to write notes about something sooner or later in your history lessons, or for homework. This means you are being asked to find out the most important details about the topic and write them down so that you can use them later. It is very tempting to copy down details from a book, even just to copy out whole paragraphs or pages, but this is not a good idea: it does not help you learn and it can take up a lot of time. You might just as well leave the information in the book and read it again later.

What should you do?

Whatever you are being asked to make notes on – whether it is a person, a battle, an organisation or an Act of Parliament – there are four things you need to remember:
- **Dates:** when did it happen, when did the person live, when did the important events take place?
- **Names:** who were the important people involved – husbands, wives, children, leaders, politicians?
- **Places:** where did things take place? Where was the person born? Where did they live?
- **Events:** what were the most important events, the things which really made a difference?

The first three of these will be straightforward. Most history books will give you these details. It is the last one that you will have to think about. It is always better to write down more than you actually need. You can always sort out your information later.

How to take notes

There is no one way to take notes. Some people write in the back of their exercise book or file; some write in a separate book. The most important thing to remember is that notes are there to help you, so if they are very untidy they will not be much use.

- Write clearly. Leave spaces between different pieces of information. Do not try to cram as much information on one page as you can.

- Always write down the book and the number of the page you have used. That way you can go back and check your information and find out more.

- Keep your notes in some sort of order. For example, you could write dates down the margin of a page and fill in details as you discover them. Or you can use a different page for different topics. Some people write information on cards

and then sort them into the correct order later on.

> REMEMBER: notes are there to help you do a piece of work later on – an essay or a project. The more careful you are over your notes, the better your final piece of work will be.

NUREMBERG LAWS

The Nuremberg Laws were published in Germany in September 1935. They stated that:

- Jews were not German citizens and could not vote
- Jews could only marry and have sexual relations with other Jews
- any German who had one Jewish grandparent was to be classed as a Jew.

◆ Holocaust

OATH

An oath is a promise to obey or tell the truth, usually made in a religious building, in the presence of a priest or minister, or using a religious book or object. Oaths were used a great deal when most people were unable to read or write. They were a very important part of the **feudal system**, and the word feudal comes from the Latin word 'feuda', which means an oath. Oaths are still used today in law courts, where witnesses have to swear to tell the truth. Members of the armed forces and MPs also have to swear oaths.

O'CONNELL, DANIEL

✦ **Ireland**

O'CONNOR, FEARGUS

O'Connor was one of the leaders of the **Chartist** movement. He founded the *Northern Star* newspaper in Leeds and led what was called the 'Physical Force' section of the Chartists. However, he never actually used violence himself: he seems just to have talked about it.

ORANGE

Orange is a small area in southern France near Avignon. It was the original home of the family which became the 'stadtholders' of Holland in 1581. William of Orange became King **William III** in 1688 when **James II** fled. The 'Orange Order' is an important part of the loyalist community in Ulster today.

OSBORNE JUDGMENT

The Osborne Judgment took place in 1909. It stated that a **trade union** could not give money to a political party. This had a serious effect on the **Labour Party** as MPs were not paid at the beginning of this century. The only way that working men could afford to become MPs was if they were supported by trade unions.

OVERLORD, OPERATION

This was the name for the Allied invasion of France on 6 June 1944, known as **D Day**.

OWEN, ROBERT

Robert Owen was a factory owner in the 1820s and 1830s. He owned huge factories at New Lanark in central Scotland and believed that his workers should be treated fairly. Owen tried to set up a **trade union** to represent all workers in the country. It was called the Grand National Consolidated Trades Union. He tried to organise a general strike, but it collapsed within a month.

Why did the GNCTU collapse?

- Owen had underestimated the difficulties of communicating with the branches all over the country, and many of the members had no way of supporting themselves when they were out of work.
- The government was frightened that Owen's union might lead to a revolution, so members who were caught were dealt with very harshly, such as the **Tolpuddle Martyrs**.
- Employers forced their workers to sign a 'document' saying they would not join a union. If they did they would be sacked.

Owen was one of the first people to try to set up a trade union to represent ordinary factory workers. When the GNCTU collapsed, many of the members began to support **Chartism** instead.

OWEN, WILFRED

Wilfred Owen was a poet who served during the **First World War** and was killed by machine-gun fire on 4 November 1918, just one week before the **Armistice**. Owen wrote many poems based on his experiences during the war which were published after his death. They had great influence on people in the 1920s and are still very popular today. You may well study some of them as part of your GCSE English course.

Wilfred Owen was appalled by the suffering that soldiers had to endure in the trenches and described it in graphic detail. In *Anthem for Doomed Youth* he imagines a funeral service taking place in the trenches, with the sound of the guns instead of a church choir. In *Strange Meeting* he describes meeting the soldier he had killed the day before his own death.

Owen's most famous poem is *Dulce et Decorum Est*. In it he describes a gas attack on a group of soldiers marching away from the trenches. One of them is caught in the gas before he can get his respirator on. He drowns in the gas.

Because he was only a young man when he died and because his death came so close to the Armistice, Owen's work came to have great influence on people in Britain. He made many believe that war should be avoided at all costs.

PAINTING

Paintings are an important form of evidence for historians before the nineteenth century, when photographs were invented. Sometimes paintings are ignored because they are not exact pictures of what actually happened, but they can give a very good idea of what people wore and what work they did. It is also important to think about why the painting was produced. There is often a reason behind paintings: for example, the Soviet dictator, Joseph *Stalin*, had many paintings produced to make himself look popular. They showed him meeting Soviet people and talking to them, when in fact he hardly ever left the Kremlin in Moscow.

> REMEMBER: paintings give very useful evidence about what people believed was important and what they wanted others to believe.

PALMERSTON, HENRY, VISCOUNT

Lord Palmerston was the most influential politician in Britain in the mid-nineteenth century. He was Prime Minister from 1855 to 1859 and again from 1861 to 1865 when he died at the age of 83. He was also Foreign Secretary for many years and Home Secretary.

Palmerston was very popular in Britain and believed in defending British interests around the world. He often used 'gunboat diplomacy', which meant using the Royal Navy to force other countries to accept British ideas or Britain's wishes. Palmerston was not popular with Queen *Victoria* or her husband Prince *Albert*, who believed that he was too hasty and offended too many foreign governments.

PARISH

Before the late-nineteenth century, the parish was the only local government unit in Britain. It was the area linked to each Anglican church and was organised by the vicar and the church-wardens. In Queen *Elizabeth I*'s reign (1558–1603) the parish was given responsibility for organising the *Poor Law* and until the nineteenth century most schools were parish schools.

Each parish was also responsible for the upkeep of the roads within its boundaries. The churchwardens could force every able-bodied man in the parish to work for six days each year on the roads. In fact this did not work very well. Most parishes spent six days in the summer filling in holes and many people managed to avoid the work.

When local government began to develop in Britain in the second half of the nineteenth century the parish became less important, but there are still parish councils in many parts of Britain today.

PARLIAMENT

In Britain Parliament means the Monarch, the House of *Lords* and the House of *Commons*. All three have to agree before a bill can become law. Parliament first included the Commons in 1265 in Simon de *Montfort*'s Parliament but, in its modern form, Parliament dates from the nineteenth century when it began to include organised political parties and Cabinet ministers.

PARLIAMENTARY REFORM

In the early-nineteenth century there were many unusual things about elections and the House of *Commons*.

- Many new industrial towns, such as Birmingham, Manchester, Leeds and Bradford, had no MPs.
- Many small towns had two MPs, such as Gatton, Bramber, Dunwich and Old Sarum. Gatton only had one voter and the other three did not really exist. Bramber was a ruin, Old Sarum had burnt down in the thirteenth century and Dunwich had fallen into the sea in the fourteenth.
- There was no one way to qualify for the vote. In some places it depended which house you lived in and in others it was whether or not you paid local taxes.
- Many MPs were elected because they bribed their way. In the 1807 Yorkshire County Election, the three candidates spent £230,000 between them.
- Voting was in the open so anybody could find out how somebody had voted and threaten them.
- Only men over the age of 21 could vote and even then they had to own property in one form or another.
- Altogether there were about 300 000 people in Britain who could vote out of a population of about 16 000 000.

In what ways did elections change in the nineteenth and twentieth centuries?

The Great Reform Act of 1832

- In the countryside, every man who owned land worth £2 a year, or who paid £50 a year in rent was given the vote.
- In towns every man who paid £10 a year in rent was given the vote.
- Many small places lost their MPs and 143 seats in the Commons were given to new towns, mostly in the north of England.
- The number of voters increased to about 700 000.

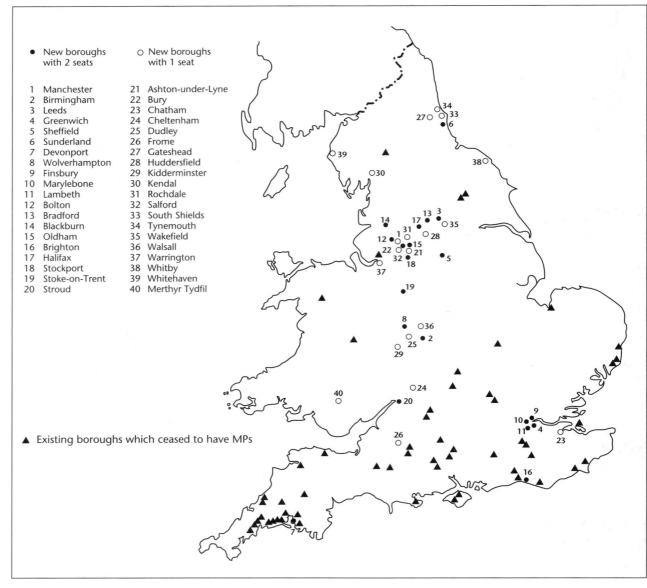

Redistribution of seats in the 1832 Reform Act

Why was the Great Reform Act passed?

- Many factory owners had no vote and no representation in Parliament. They had become very important since the Industrial Revolution.
- In 1830 the Whigs won the General Election. They supported reform.
- There were many protests and disturbances in the years from 1829 to 1831. Nottingham castle was burnt down and so was the centre of Bristol.
- The government was frightened that there might be a revolution in Britain as there had been in France in 1830.

The **Tories**, who controlled the House of **Lords**, voted against the bill. However **William IV** agreed to support the **Whigs** when the House of Lords voted against the Reform Bill in 1831. He said he would create as many Whig members of the House of Lords as would be necessary to get the bill passed. In the event the Tories gave way and the bill became law.

The Second Reform Act of 1867

All male householders paying rates in towns could vote. The number of voters increased to about 2 000 000.

The Secret Ballot Act of 1872

This said that voting must take place in secret so that threats and bribery would not work.

The Corrupt Practices Act of 1883

This banned bribery and limited the amount of money that candidates could spend on elections. It also forced candidates in Parliamentary elections to publish accounts to show how they had spent money. This meant that very wealthy people could not use their money to get themselves elected.

The Third Reform Act of 1884

This abolished the differences between town and country constituencies. All male householders who paid rates could vote. The number of voters increased to 5 000 000.

By the end of the nineteenth century, elections to Parliament were very different from what they had been in 1800. However, there were still two things which had not changed:

- Women were still not allowed to vote.
- The vote was linked to property. If a man had not lived in his own house for a year or more, he could not vote.

The twentieth century

1918 After the **First World War** women were given the vote at the age of 30 if they were householders or the wives of householders.
1928 Women were given the vote at the age of 21.
1967 The age for voting was lowered to 18.

Suffragettes, Suffragists

SELF-CHECK QUESTION 10

Which of these places gained MPs for the first time in 1832? Manchester, Leeds, Birmingham, Sheffield, Wolverhampton, Bolton, Bradford, Brighton.

PASSCHENDAELE

The battle of Passchendaele, or the Third Battle of Ypres, was fought from July 1917 to November 1917 and was an attempt by the British forces in the Belgian town of **Ypres** to fight their way out. The battle was an almost total disaster and the British Army suffered about 400 000 casualties.

Why was the battle of Passchendaele a failure?

- The fighting around Ypres had turned the battlefield into a quagmire. The attackers had to follow ribbons laid on the ground to show them where the solid ground was. If they wandered off the solid ground they could drown in the mud.
- The weather throughout the battle was very bad with heavy rain which made the battlefield even more muddy.
- The British were attacking uphill and the Germans were well dug in. At the top of the hill were five concrete machine-gun posts which were captured on 4 October 1917.
- One month later the British gave up attacking. They had still not reached the village of Passchendaele, which was six miles from Ypres.
- In March 1918 the German army counter-attacked and recaptured all the ground they had lost the previous year. The British were pushed back right into the town.

Field Marshall Haig, who had ordered the attack, did not know what conditions were like on the battlefield. When he visited the site of the battle in November, he is reported to have said, 'My God, did I send men to fight in that?' One soldier wrote, 'I died in Hell, they called it Passchendaele.'

PEARL HARBOR

On 7 December 1941 Japanese forces launched a surprise attack on the US naval base of Pearl Harbor in Hawaii. The US forces were caught completely by surprise, even though they had intercepted radio messages warning them of the attack. 3400 Americans were killed, eight battleships were destroyed and about 300 aircraft, but the main target of the attack, the three American aircraft carriers, escaped; they were at sea undergoing trials. The **USA** immediately declared war on Japan and Germany.

Why did the Japanese attack Pearl Harbor?

- Japan was ruled by a military dictatorship. Politicians had little influence, the Army wanted to build an empire in the Pacific.
- Japan had a growing population and very little inhabitable land: only 15 per cent of Japanese land could be lived on.
- Japan lacked raw materials and had no supplies of oil. In July 1941 the USA stopped supplying Japan with oil.
- The Japanese government believed it would have to fight the USA sooner or later if it was to take control of the Pacific. It decided to attack without warning to try to catch the Americans off their guard.

Overall the attack on Pearl Harbor was a failure. Not only did the Japanese fail to destroy the American aircraft carriers, but it also convinced many Americans, who up until then had not wanted to become involved in the war, that the USA had to take part. Less than six months later the US Navy destroyed three Japanese aircraft carriers at the battle of Midway. This ended any chance the Japanese had of defeating the USA.

PEASANT

The word 'peasant' is used to describe any agricultural workers who had some form of bond between them and a landowner. This usually meant they had to work for a certain number of days on their landlord's land each week, or that they had to pay taxes to him. The taxes would usually be in produce: chickens, eggs, wheat, etc.

In Britain many peasants owned some land and a house, but in some European countries they owned nothing. Peasants in Britain were called 'villeins', 'cottars' or 'bordars'.

When the **feudal system** disappeared in the fifteenth and sixteenth centuries, peasants became members of open field villages and so became landowners themselves. In France, however, peasants still existed in the 1780s and they were one of the reasons why there was unrest which led to the French Revolution in 1789.

PEASANTS' REVOLT

The Peasants' Revolt was a rebellion by peasants in Essex and Kent against the Poll Tax, which was collected in 1377, 1379 and 1380. The Poll Tax was collected to help pay for the costs of the **Hundred Years' War** against France. It had to be paid by every person aged 15 or more. In 1377 all peasants had to pay 4d, in 1379 4d, but in 1380 12d. Many people tried to avoid paying by hiding or lying, so in 1381 commissioners were sent round to find those who had not paid.

Why did the Peasants' Revolt take place?

- The main short-term reason was the Poll Tax. This is what triggered off the Revolt.
- A longer-term reason was the **Black Death**. This had led to a fall in the number of peasants and this in turn made it more difficult for landowners to find workers. This made wages rise, because workers could choose who they were going to work for.
- To try to stop wages rising, the government passed laws limiting wages, but this only made the situation worse.
- Underlying all this was the fact that the feudal system was becoming more and more out of date. Peasants no longer wanted to be tied to landowners and to have to work for them every week.

The revolt began in Essex in May 1381 and then spread to Kent. The rebels in Kent chose Wat Tyler as their leader and released John Ball, a priest, from Maidstone jail. These two led the rebels to London. The rebels from Kent camped on Blackheath and the rebels from Essex camped at Mile End.

The situation was so serious that King **Richard II**, who was only 14, came to meet the rebels. He met the Essex rebels at Mile End. He agreed that:

- serfdom should be abolished
- peasants should no longer have to work for their landlords
- everyone who had taken part in the rebellion should be pardoned.

The Essex rebels accepted this and returned home, but the rebels from Kent attacked the Tower of London and murdered some of the King's ministers.

The next day the King met the rebels at Smithfield. Wat Tyler rode out to meet the King, but he was attacked by one of the King's men. He fell from his horse badly injured. The peasants were about to attack the King when he rode forward and called on them to follow him. He announced that they would all be allowed to leave and would not be punished. The promises made at Mile End would be kept.

In the meantime, however, Wat Tyler had been executed by the Mayor of London. The King soon changed his mind and had the leaders of the revolt hunted down and executed.

What were the results of the Peasants' Revolt?

- Landowners were frightened by what had happened. They gradually gave up trying to make peasants work for them every week.
- Wages were allowed to rise and more and more peasants became paid labourers.

- The number of peasants in England fell and by the sixteenth century they had all disappeared.

PEEL, SIR ROBERT, JUNIOR

Sir Robert Peel junior was the son of the factory owner. He became Home Secretary in 1822 and made a series of changes in the way that prisons were run. He also reduced the number of offences which carried the death penalty. His most famous reform, however, was the formation of the Metropolitan Police Force in 1829. They became known as Peelers, or Bobbies, after Sir Robert Peel. This was the first real police force in Britain.

In 1834 Peel was Prime Minister for a short time and was re-elected in 1841. In between these years he had reorganised the **Tory** Party and was the first politician to issue a manifesto (a list of policies) in 1837. In doing this Peel played a very important role in developing politics and **Parliament**.

When Peel became Prime Minister for the second time in 1841, he was the first man to occupy that post who came from the **middle class**, as he was the son of a factory owner.

From 1841 to 1846 Peel made many changes in Britain

- He played an important role in the development of Free Trade, by abolishing many duties on imports.
- He passed Acts which banned the employment of women and children in coalmines and which forced factory owners to box-in dangerous machinery.
- He passed an Act which controlled the Bank of England and other banks which issued banknotes.

In 1845, when the Irish Potato Famine broke out, Peel became convinced that help had to be given to the Irish. He repealed the **Corn Laws**, which stopped foreign wheat being imported into Britain. This enabled food to be sent to **Ireland**. The repeal of the Corn Laws divided the **Tory** Party and Peel was forced to resign. For four years he led a section of the party in the House of **Commons**, which was known as the Peelites. In December 1850, Peel was killed riding back from a visit to see the Crystal Palace being built in Hyde Park. His horse stumbled and he was thrown from its back.

PEEL, SIR ROBERT, SENIOR

Sir Robert Peel senior was an important factory owner in Manchester at the beginning of the nineteenth century. Peel was one of the first factory owners to believe that workers would work better if they were treated well. He inspected his **factories** regularly and did not allow the overseers to treat workers badly. In 1802 and 1819 Peel managed to pass laws in **Parliament** to make factory owners treat their workers better. But the laws were enforced by the local magistrates and they were often on the side of the factory owners. Most of Peel's efforts came to nothing.

PENINSULAR WAR

The Peninsular War was fought by the British Army from 1808 to 1814. It was an invasion of Portugal and Spain to prevent **Napoleon** conquering those countries. From 1809 the British Army was commanded by Lord **Wellington**. He had only about 40 000 men against 250 000 French. So he tried to wear the French out by marching into Spain every year, then retreating to Lisbon in the winter and hiding behind enormous lines of defence called the lines of Torres Vedras. The French were never able to break through. During the winter Wellington was supplied by the Royal Navy, while the French had to find food in Spain. The Spanish attacked the French forces and destroyed food and animals to prevent them feeding themselves.

In 1814, after five years of fighting, the British Army was able to cross the Pyrenees and advance into southern France.

Why was the Peninsular War important?

- It tied up 250 000 French soldiers in Spain.
- It stretched Napoleon's lines of communication as he was fighting in Austria and then in Russia at the same time.
- It led to large numbers of casualties and many soldiers became disheartened.
- It made Wellington's reputation. He became the Commander of the Allied Forces when Napoleon escaped from Elba in 1815.

PEPYS, SAMUEL

Samuel Pepys was the Secretary of the Navy Board in the 1660s and wrote a diary describing the events of the period. It is one of the most important documents of the **Restoration**. Pepys described in detail the effects of the **plague** in 1665 and the outbreak of the fire in 1666. Pepys developed a form of short-hand to write his diary.

In 1669, Pepys became convinced that he was going blind, so he stopped writing. In fact he did not go blind, but he never began his diary again.

PETERLOO

Peterloo was the name given to a meeting in St Peter's Fields in Manchester on 16 August 1819. A large crowd gathered to hear a speech by Henry Hunt, the MP for Preston. But the meeting turned into a tragedy. The local magistrates, who were watching the meeting from the roof of an inn, panicked and ordered the yeomanry to disperse the crowd. They failed, so cavalry units were ordered to do the job. Within 15 minutes the crowd had been dispersed, leaving at least 11 dead and more than 400 injured.

Why was the meeting held?

- It came at the end of a period of hardship and unrest after the end of the **Napoleonic War**. Many people were out of work and the price of bread was high, partly because of the **Corn Laws**.

- The government had reacted to the unrest by suspending the **Habeas Corpus** Act and trying to prevent public meetings.
- People were demanding reform of Parliament. Only about 300 000 people in the country could vote.
- 'Orator' Hunt was a popular speaker. He had organised the meeting and warned people not to bring weapons or cause any trouble.

Why did the meeting end in tragedy?

- The magistrates panicked when they saw the size of the crowd, which was estimated at 50 000; they would never have seen so many people before.
- The magistrates were untrained. They were frightened that property in Manchester was going to be damaged.
- The yeomanry were unpaid amateur soldiers, who supplied their own horses and equipment. They were completely inexperienced and some had been drinking all morning. They were trapped in the crowd and had to be rescued by the cavalry.
- The cavalry were professional soldiers and the magistrates should have used them first. They cleared the crowd easily.

What were the results of the meeting?

- The government praised the magistrates and blamed Hunt.
- The government passed the 'Six Acts' which gave more power to magistrates.
- The commander of the cavalry said that it was the magistrates' fault.
- To many people this was evidence of the harshness of the government.

PHONEY WAR

The Phoney War was the name given to the period at the beginning of the **Second World War** when there was little or no fighting. The word 'phoney' meant pretend or fake. The Phoney War began in September 1939 when the **British Expeditionary Force** was sent to Belgium and lasted until April 1940 when Germany attacked Denmark and Norway. The main reason for the Phoney War was that **Hitler** had not expected Britain to declare war after the invasion of Poland on 1 September 1939 and he was not ready for a major campaign in western Europe. He used the seven months to build up his forces for an attack in the west.

PHOTOGRAPH

The first photographs were taken in the 1820s, but they began to be important pieces of historical evidence in the late-nineteenth century. A photograph can be very useful in showing what the past was like, but sometimes people in the past have faked photographs for their own purposes. For example, **Hitler** used photographs to show how powerful he was. They showed tens of thousands of uniformed men standing in straight lines.

It is easy to dismiss photographs which have been faked, when in fact all pieces of evidence are important. A faked photograph allows us to see the methods of **propaganda** used by people. They also can help us to understand people's attitudes and how they viewed certain issues.

PILGRIMAGE OF GRACE

The Pilgrimage of Grace was a rebellion which broke out in northern England in the autumn of 1536. It began as a protest against the closure of the **monasteries**, but became much more widespread and included many people who were protesting about living conditions. Eventually an army of at least 40000 marched south, led by Robert Aske.

The marchers were met by representatives sent by **Henry VIII**, who agreed to their demands. Most marchers went home. Henry then had the leaders arrested. Robert Aske was sentenced to death for treason and executed.

PITT, WILLIAM, THE ELDER, EARL OF CHATHAM

William Pitt the Elder was Prime Minister from 1757 to 1761. He played a very important part in Britain's success during the Seven Years' War (1756–1763). In 1759, the 'Annus Mirabilis', four important battles were won against the French: **Quebec** and Minden on land, and Quiberon Bay and Lagos at sea. At the end of the war France gave up all claims to Canada and Spain handed over Florida. In America, France agreed that the Mississippi River would be the boundary between the British Colonies and Louisiana, the French territory.

Pitt resigned in 1761, but was Prime Minister again from 1766 to 1767. His greatest success, however, was as a war leader.

PITT, WILLIAM THE YOUNGER

William Pitt the Younger was the son of William Pitt the Elder. He was the youngest man ever to become Chancellor of the Exchequer in 1783, at the age of 23. The following year he became Prime Minister. Pitt the Younger remained Prime Minister for 17 years until 1801, the second longest term of office ever. Only Sir Robert Walpole (1721–1742) was Prime Minister for a longer period.

Why was William Pitt the Younger Prime Minister for so many years?

- Pitt was supported by King **George III**, who felt that he could trust him. It was important for a Prime Minister to have the support of the King.
- Pitt was an excellent speaker in the House of Commons. This persuaded many MPs to back him.
- Pitt was known to be honest and was not corrupt.
- Pitt was an excellent administrator and introduced a series of important reforms into government.

How did Pitt change the government in Britain?

- He introduced the idea of the budget, where the government explains how it is going to spend and raise money each year.
- He introduced a proper system of accounting in government finances.
- He introduced income tax to help pay for the war against France.

Unlike his father, Pitt was not successful as Prime Minister during wartime. He did not understand military matters as well as he did finance.

In 1801 Pitt resigned. He wanted to introduce **Catholic** emancipation, but George III refused. He said that as Head of the **Church of England** he could not agree to the idea. Pitt became Prime Minister again from 1804 to 1806. He died in January 1806 at the age of 46.

PLAGUE

The Great Plague broke out in London in April 1665 and lasted until early the next year. Altogether about 70000 people died. In fact this was only one of many outbreaks of plague in the seventeenth century: an earlier one had killed 40000 people. The 1665 outbreak is the best known because it was the biggest, and also because it was followed by the Great Fire of London in 1666. It was also described in detail in two books: the diary of Samuel **Pepys** and the novel *A Journal of the Plague Year* written by Daniel Defoe.

In 1665, the plague which hit London was the bubonic plague. It was spread by plague fleas which lived on black rats, although people did not know this at the time. The rats came to England on ships which landed goods in London. For this reason the worst effects of the plague were felt in London. Samuel Pepys, for example, sent his wife to Greenwich, only about five miles away, to escape the effects of the plague. Many people left London and Pepys described the streets as being totally deserted.

The plague was made worse by the narrow medieval streets of the city of London. They were difficult to keep clean and many of the houses were built from wood. In 1666 the city was destroyed by the Great Fire and it was then rebuilt. St Paul's Cathedral and many other churches were designed by Sir Christopher **Wren**.

One place outside London which suffered very badly was the village of Eyam in Derbyshire. The plague broke out here when a roll of cloth was delivered to one of the villagers from London. Concealed in the cloth were plague fleas. When people began to die some families fled, but the majority agreed to stay in the village led by the vicar, William Mompesson. As a result, more than two-thirds of the villagers died from the plague.

This was the last major outbreak of the plague in Britain, although deaths from it were recorded in the eighteenth century.

SELF-CHECK QUESTION 11

Which sort of plague broke out in 1665, bubonic or pneumonic?

PLANTAGENET

Plantagenet was the family name of the Kings of England from 1154, when **Henry II** became King, until **Richard II** (1377–1399). The name apparently came from the plant broom, 'genet' in French, which the family used as an emblem.

PLEBISCITE

A plebiscite is a vote on a single issue. **Hitler** asked the German people to approve some of his actions by plebiscites, the **Anschluss** for example. There were always big votes in favour. This enabled Hitler to claim that his actions were approved by the German people. Dictators in particular have used plebiscites to justify their actions. The word referendum is often used to mean the same thing, but a 'referendum' is normally used in a democracy.

POOR LAW

The Poor Law was the main method of relieving poverty before the beginnings of the **Welfare State**. The first Poor Law was passed in 1601, in the reign of **Elizabeth I**. The government had become worried at the number of **beggars** in England and passed the law to make each **parish** responsible for its own poor and to try to make sure that beggars did not wander around the country. To get poor relief, beggars either had to stay in the parish in which they were born or stay in one place for at least a year.

Under the Elizabethan Poor Law there were two groups of poor:

- 'Impotent Poor': people who were poor through no fault of their own – children, the old, the sick – were to be looked after and the parish could collect rates to meet the cost.
- 'Idle Vagabonds': people who were lazy. They were to be made to work.

It was the responsibility of the church wardens to make sure that this happened.

How did the Poor Law change in the seventeenth and eighteenth centuries?

1662 Parishes were allowed to send 'paupers' back to their home parish.

1723 Parishes were allowed to build a workhouse and make 'paupers' work in it.

1782 Parishes were able to join together to build bigger workhouses.

1795 The Speenhamland System was introduced. This allowed parishes to pay poor relief based on the price of bread and the number of people in the family. This was paid to both idle vagabonds and the impotent poor. This was not compulsory, but about half the counties of England used the system.

The Speenhamland System was a major change in the Poor Law. Why did it take place?

- The population of Britain rose rapidly in the eighteenth century. There were many more people unemployed.

- Enclosure forced large numbers of people away from villages in parts of England.
- The **Industrial Revolution** meant that many people were attracted to towns, where they lived closely together.

These changes meant that the old systems no longer worked in some areas.

The Speenhamland System was abolished in 1834, when the Poor Law Amendment Act was passed. Why was the system abolished?

- People believed it was becoming too expensive. The amount spent had gone up from £2 000 000 to £8 000 000.
- People believed that it encouraged large families, as the amount paid varied according to the number of people in the family.
- People believed it encouraged employers to pay low wages, as workers were paid whether they were working or not.

The Poor Law Amendment Act changed poor relief dramatically

- All parishes were grouped into 'Unions' and were forced to build workhouses.
- Poor relief could only be provided in a workhouse, except for the sick and the old.
- Workhouses were to be made as unpleasant as possible to discourage people from entering. Paupers were forced to wear uniforms. Families were split up and they worked in silence.

The Poor Law remained in force until it was abolished in 1929. Until then the old, the sick and the unemployed could be forced to go into the workhouse if they were unable to support themselves.

POTSDAM

The Potsdam Conference was the last of the conferences between the leaders of the Allies during the **Second World War**. It was held in Potsdam, outside Berlin, after the defeat of Germany.

What was agreed at Potsdam?

- Germany was divided into four zones. Each zone would be occupied by one of the four Allies: Great Britain, France, the **USA** and the **USSR**. Berlin was divided into four sectors.
- The Nazi Party would be dissolved.
- War criminals would be tried and punished.
- There would be free elections in Germany, freedom of speech and a free press.
- Germany would pay **reparations** for the damage caused by the war. Most of this would go to the USSR.
- All the Allies agreed to take part in the **United Nations**.

But there were also disagreements at Potsdam

- The new US president, Harry **Truman** tried to force the USSR to allow free elections in the countries of eastern Europe which had been occupied after the end of the war. He said he wanted to 'get tough with Russia'.

- **Stalin** was angry that the USA had not told him about the atomic bomb which he knew the USA had developed.
- This was the beginning of the **Cold War**.

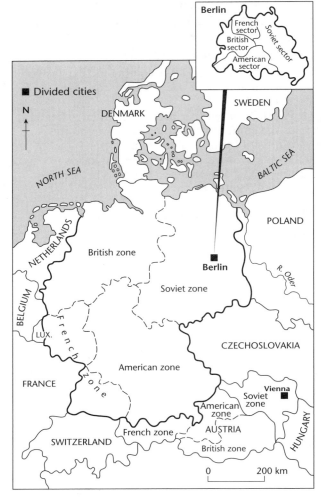

Germany after Potsdam

PRIME MINISTER

Prime Minister is the name given to the most important minister in the British government. Until the eighteenth century the Monarch had much more power and authority than Parliament and chose his or her own ministers, sometimes ignoring Parliament altogether. But after the **Glorious Revolution** of 1688, the Monarch had to make more effort to make sure that Parliament did what he or she wanted it to. Queen **Anne** and **George I** both began to give more responsibility to ministers.

Sir Robert Walpole is usually said to be the first Prime Minister. He was in office from 1721 to 1742, but he depended on the support of George I and George II. The Monarch had a good deal of choice as to who he or she could appoint. In the 1760s, **George III** appointed a series of Prime Ministers, in an effort to find someone he trusted. It was not until the late-eighteenth and early-nineteenth centuries

that Prime Ministers began to be able to act on their own. Even so, in 1801, William **Pitt** the Younger was forced to resign when George III refused to consider **Catholic** Emancipation.

As the two main political parties, **Whigs** and **Tories**, emerged in the nineteenth century, the role of the Prime Minister became more and more important. The Monarch had to appoint the leader of the party which won a General Election as Prime Minister. This meant that the Monarch had little or no choice of who was to be the Prime Minister. It also became accepted that the outgoing minister would recommend a successor to the Monarch when he resigned.

In the twentieth century all decisions are taken by the Prime Minister and the **Cabinet**. The Monarch does not interfere in the running of the country.

PRINCES IN THE TOWER

The Princes in the Tower were the two sons of **Edward IV**, **Edward V** and his brother Richard of York, who disappeared in the summer of 1483. They were taken to the Tower of London by their uncle, Richard of Gloucester, in June and never emerged. At the time rumours began that they had been murdered by Richard, who became King **Richard III** in July. In 1670 two skeletons were discovered in the Tower, both of young boys.

In his play *Richard III*, William **Shakespeare** made out that Richard III murdered the two boys. But this was part of an attempt to persuade people that **Elizabeth I**'s grandfather, **Henry VII**, had been justified in killing Richard and taking the Crown.

> REMEMBER: there is no evidence that the skeletons were those of the two princes and no evidence that Richard III was involved in the murder.

PRINT

A print is a form of picture which was widely used before photographs were available. An engraving was made on a metal plate and then ink was used to produce the print; this could be done over and over again. In the eighteenth century the painter, Hogarth, produced prints criticising life in London. One of the most famous is 'Gin Lane', in which he attacked the easy availability of gin in the first half of the eighteenth century.

Prints were used in newspapers until well into the twentieth century. Newspapers would employ artists who would draw scenes and these would be reproduced for their readers.

Most prints give a fair picture of the scene at the time, but some, like Hogarth's are more like **cartoons**. They caricature life, rather than trying to depict it accurately. However, all forms of evidence are important and Hogarth's prints show us how people felt at the time. They help us understand not only how people behaved, but also how people reacted to life in London.

> REMEMBER: a print is not a photograph

PROPAGANDA

Propaganda is any attempt to persuade people to accept or believe ideas. It is an attempt to control how people think. It can come in almost any form: posters, newspapers, paintings, cartoons and speeches are very common forms of propaganda, but books, films, television and radio can all be used. We often think of propaganda as being a bad form of influence and it can be when it is used by dictators, or others, to increase their hold over their people. **Hitler**, **Mussolini** and **Stalin** all used propaganda to stop people finding out the truth. They controlled the press, education and all forms of art and entertainment. But propaganda can also be used to try to warn people about the side-effects of drugs or other dangers. All governments use propaganda in some form or another.

It is easy to dismiss evidence because it is propaganda and is, therefore, not telling the truth.

But propaganda can be very useful

- It can show what ideas people had in the past and how and why people disagreed.
- It can allow us to understand what methods of persuasion were used in the past and how developed or effective they were.
- It can help us to understand what people were trying to achieve and how determined they were.

> REMEMBER: whenever you look at a piece of propaganda, ask yourself the questions: Who published it? Why was it published? Who was supposed to see it or read it?

PROTECTORATE

The Protectorate was the name given to the period when **Oliver Cromwell** was Lord Protector, 1653–1658.

PROTESTANT

Protestant is used to describe the people who protested about the **Catholic** Church in the fifteenth and sixteenth centuries and then left to form their own Churches. These included the **Church of England**, the Lutheran Church and the Presbyterian Church.

PUBLIC HEALTH

Public health was a term invented in the nineteenth century when people first became concerned about the cleanliness of towns in Britain. Until the early-nineteenth century many people did not connect dirt and disease. They believed that diseases were caused by bad blood. When cholera broke out for the first time in 1831, however, more and more people began to link it with the amounts of rubbish which lay in the city streets in Britain. People began to believe that diseases was caused by 'bad air'; the air became polluted and when people breathed it in they caught disease.

Why did things get worse in the nineteenth century?

- The population of Britain rose very quickly: between 1801 and 1851 it doubled.
- Many of these people lived in towns: by 1851 50 per cent of the people of Britain were town-dwellers.
- The new towns had not been planned: they were built quickly without any proper sanitation or fresh water.
- Many people found themselves living in crowded rooms with no fresh water and very little fresh air. They threw their rubbish into the streets and got their water from the nearest river.

The first Public Health Act was passed in 1848 as a result of the efforts of Edwin Chadwick. He had produced reports which showed that people lived longer if they lived in the countryside. The Act was not a success, however, as it did not force local councils to make improvements and Chadwick was not popular.

In the 1850s, however, ideas began to change. Why?

- In 1854 Dr John Snow proved that cholera was more likely to break out where there was a dirty water supply.
- In 1858, the Thames was so polluted that Parliament had to stop sitting because of the smell.
- In 1861, Prince **Albert** died from typhoid, brought on by a poor water supply.

In the 1850s and 1860s new sewers began to be built in London and a second Public Health Act was passed in 1875. This set up local Boards of Health which had to act. But even then there was much resistance to change.

Why did people oppose changes in public health?

- Some doctors were poorly trained; they did not understand the links between dirt and disease.
- People who owned poor quality housing and made money from it did not want to have to improve it.
- People regarded Chadwick and other reformers as cranks. They did not like being told what to do.
- The worst problems affected working people: They could not vote and few people paid them much attention.
- The rich already had supplies of clean water. Why should they pay to help the poor?

PURITANS

Puritans were **Protestants** who appeared for the first time in the late-sixteenth century. The name came from the word 'pure'; they believed that people should live simpler and purer lives.

What did Puritans believe?

- People should dress and act simply. Puritans normally dressed in black and white.
- Church services should be simple and concentrate on the Bible.
- Churches should not have coloured pictures or decorations.
- Priests should not wear coloured vestments, but dress simply. They should concentrate on preaching sermons based on the Bible.
- Ordinary people should not take part in games or entertainments, especially on Sundays.

- During the **Protectorate**, Puritans closed theatres and stopped many sports and pastimes, including maypole dancing.

After the **Restoration** the Puritans were less important, but some churches still follow their ideas today.

PYM, JOHN

John Pym was one of the most important figures in the arguments between the King and **Parliament** in the first half of the seventeenth century. He was arrested in February 1622 for criticising **James I**. In 1641 he became the chairman of the committee of the House of **Commons** and he was one of the five members whom **Charles I** tried to arrest in January 1642. This started the chain of events which led to the outbreak of war in August 1642.

QUEBEC

The battle of Quebec was fought in 1759. It ended French control of parts of Canada. The French army commanded by General Montcalm was in position on the Heights of Abraham above the river. The British Army was commanded by General James Wolfe. He found a path up the cliffs, which enabled him to attack the French without warning. The battle was a complete victory, but Wolfe was killed. At the Treaty of Paris in 1763, at the end of the Seven Years' War, France gave up all claims to Canada.

RATIONING

Rationing was introduced for the first time in Britain during the **First World War**, when there were limits put on the amounts of food people could buy each week. Rationing became much more important during the **Second World War**, when it was introduced in January 1940. Once again it was food that was rationed first. A committee was set up to work out how many calories were needed by people in different jobs. Workers in heavy industry, like coalmining, got most; office workers got less. Pregnant women and young children also received special rations. Cod liver oil, orange juice and school milk all became important ways of making sure that young children received enough.

Later in the war other items became rationed: clothing, soap and furniture. This was an attempt to try to make sure that materials needed for the war were available.

Some foods were never rationed, such as bread, vegetables and potatoes. Everybody was asked to eat as many vegetables as possible.

How did rationing work?

- Every person was issued with a ration book; this contained pages with squares on them. There was one page for each item which was rationed.
- Everybody had to register with a grocer and a butcher, for example, who would then be provided with enough food for all his customers every week.
- If you went away on holiday, you had to take your ration book with you and give it to the hotel or to the landlady.
- From time to time rations changed: the number of eggs could go up and down. During the war clothing rations fell each year.

Was rationing a success?

- It did provide everybody with enough food to survive, but it was not popular. It was very demoralising to have to eat the same meals over and over again.
- There were many attempts to help people cook different meals with the same foods and to change their eating habits. Lord Woolton was the Minister for Food and he published a recipe for Woolton Pie, which was made of vegetables and breadcrumbs. He also published this verse to try to encourage people not to peel potatoes.

    Those who have the will to win,
    Cook potatoes in their skin,
    For they know the sight of peelings
    Deeply hurts Lord Woolton's feelings.

- One unexpected result of rationing was that everybody got healthier. Rationing meant that people could eat less fatty foods and had to eat more vegetables. They also drank more milk.
- People were asked to grow as much of their own food as possible. Allotments were set up and there were slogans such as 'Dig for Victory'.
- There was also the 'black market'. People in the countryside were not affected much by rationing as they could grow their own food. Sometimes this food was brought into towns to be sold illegally. Butchers also had meat over after a carcass had been cut up. Offal, liver and kidneys were not 'on the ration' and sausages could be made out of what was left over. If you watch *Dad's Army*, Private Jones often secretly gives Captain Mainwaring a small parcel of sausages.

Rationing continued after the war and actually got worse in some ways. Bread was rationed for the first time in 1946. Rationing was not ended completely until 1953.

> REMEMBER: rationing actually made most people healthier.

REARMAMENT

The word rearmament is used to describe the attempts of Adolf **Hitler** to rebuild the German armed forces in the 1930s. Under the Treaty of **Versailles**, Germany had been forced to reduce its Army and Navy and destroy all of its aircraft. In 1935 Hitler introduced conscription and began to build warships and the Luftwaffe, the German airforce. This was the first attempt by Hitler to challenge the Treaty of Versailles. Britain and France adopted the policy of **appeasement** and did little to stop him. This encouraged Hitler to go further.

REFORM

The word reform is used to describe changes which lead to improvements in conditions in an area of public life. For example, in 1832 Parliament was reformed by the Great Reform Act. There were **Factory Reform** Acts in 1833 and 1844 and **slavery** was abolished in the British Empire in 1833.

Reforms are often concentrated in short periods. For example, there were many reforms in the years after 1832. These are known as the **Whig Reforms**. There were also many in the 1870s; these were passed by **Gladstone** and **Disraeli**. There were also important periods of reform in 1906–1914, the **Liberal Reforms**, and in 1945–1950, when the **Labour Party** introduced the **Welfare State**.

REFORM ACTS

The term Reform Acts refers to the three Parliamentary Reform Acts passed in 1832, 1867 and 1884.

•‡• *Parliament, Reform*

REFORMATION

The Reformation is the name given to the changes in the **Catholic** Church in the sixteenth century. These came about because of attacks on the Church by reformers.

Why was the Catholic Church attacked?

- It was claimed that it had acquired great wealth and it was not being used properly, for example to help the poor.
- Popes and bishops were using the wealth and power of the Church for their own benefit.
- There were a number of Popes who had very bad reputations, for example Alexander VI (1493–1502) was a member of the notorious Borgia family. Popes were accused of using bribes to get elected.
- During the fourteenth and fifteenth centuries there had often been two Popes: one in Rome in Italy and the other in Avignon in France. At one point there had actually been three.
- Church services and the Bible were in Latin and could not be understood by ordinary people.

The attacks on the Church began in the late-fifteenth century, but became important in the early-sixteenth century. In 1517 Martin Luther criticised the Church for selling indulgences; these were guarantees that the buyer would go to heaven. This led to breakaway movements in Germany and Switzerland, the Lutheran and Calvinist Churches. In England, the Anglican Church was set up. However, this was more to do with **Henry VIII**'s divorce than reform.

How did the new churches differ from the Catholic Church?

- They did not accept the authority of the Pope.
- Their services and the Bible were translated into the local language. More people were encouraged to join in; in the Catholic Church the priest played the most important part.
- Services and churches were simpler and plainer. There were often few decorations and the priests, or ministers as they sometimes became known, wore few special clothes.
- Beliefs were based on the Bible, rather than on traditional ideas. The new churches often stuck closely to whatever the Bible said.
- The new churches often had no bishops. They were controlled by the members, rather than by a leader, such as the Pope.
- They emphasised that Christians should actually do good works, rather than pray or pay others to pray for them. This had happened in many **monasteries** and chantries. Here people could pay for a monk or priest to pray for them after they died.
- In the **Protestant** countries, as they came to be known – Holland, Germany, England, Sweden – there was much more involvement in business. The new churches said that being successful in business and then using your money for a good cause was a good way of serving God.

What effects did the Reformation have?

- It divided Europe into two parts. Over the next 200 years there were many wars between the two sides. The Thirty Years' War (1618–1648), which destroyed large areas of central Europe, was based on religious differences.
- There were civil wars in France and England.
- The Catholic Church fought back, setting up the 'Holy Office', or 'Inquisition'. This persecuted people who had given up Catholicism. Thousands were tortured and burnt, including 300 people in England during the reign of **Mary** (1553–1558).
- In 1540 the Society of Jesus was set up. The members became known as the Jesuits. The Council of Trent, which met from 1545 to 1563, reorganised the Catholic Church and set out Catholic beliefs.
- Many people were able to take part in their religion in ways that had been impossible in the past. This led to stronger religious beliefs.
- It led to a great growth in business. The strongly Catholic countries, like Spain, were soon overtaken by Holland and England.
- It led to important developments in scientific knowledge. Galileo, the Italian scientist, had been banned from making discoveries by the Inquisition and had been forced to admit that his ideas were wrong. Nothing like this happened in England.
- There were many new schools and hospitals founded in England in the early-seventeenth century. Many of these were built with money provided by Protestant merchants.
- There were many important developments in art, music and literature.

REICHSTAG FIRE

The Reichstag fire broke out on the night of 27 February 1933, at about 9.14 pm. The Reichstag was the lower house of the German Parliament. When the police arrived at the scene, they found a Dutchman, Marinus van der Lubbe, inside carrying firelighters. He was seen running around the building waving his shirt.

Van der Lubbe was arrested, tried and found guilty of treason. He was sentenced to death and executed. But did he actually set the Reichstag on fire?

The background

- **Hitler** had become Chancellor on 30 January 1933 and had immediately called for a General Election; this was to be held on 5 March.
- Hitler wanted to win an overall majority at the General Election so he could be elected dictator. His main opponents were the communists.
- Van der Lubbe was a former member of the Communist Party. He was also mentally retarded.

What happened on the night of 27 February 1933?

Hitler was dining with Josef Goebbels. When they heard about the fire they drove to the Reichstag. They found Hermann Goering already there; he was the Speaker of the Reichstag and the Minister for the Interior, who was responsible for the police force. Goering and Goebbels both announced that the fire was the work of the Communist Party. Four leaders of the Party were arrested along with van der Lubbe and also put on trial.

What happened after 27 February 1933?

The communists were blamed for the fire. Every newspaper attacked them and a book was written called *Armed Uprising*. It claimed that the fire was part of a communist plot to overthrow the government. The trial was delayed until November and, except for van der Lubbe, all the defendants were acquitted, even in a Nazi court. It was in this atmosphere that the General Election took place.

Did van der Lubbe do it?

He certainly must have been involved: he admitted that at his trial. But he could not have done it on his own. In 1942 Hermann Goering claimed that he did it; this was at a dinner party given on Hitler's birthday. But when he was on trial at Nuremberg, after the war, he denied he had had any part in the fire.

What probably happened was the fire was started by the Nazis to try to put the blame on the communists. The man responsible was the leader of the Berlin Stormtroopers, Karl Ernst, with about ten others. Van der Lubbe was used as a scapegoat. Ernst said they had to get him into the building and make him believe he had started the fire all on his own. All the Stormtroopers were murdered afterwards; Ernst was killed in 1934.

At the General Election the Nazis won 288 seats, which was not an overall majority. But the communists had been warned what to expect in the future. They were not present when the Reichstag met on 23 March and Hitler was able to pass the Enabling Act easily.

⊹ Adolf Hitler, Nazi Germany

RENAISSANCE

Renaissance means rebirth. It is used to describe the developments in art, literature and scientific knowledge which took place from the late-fifteenth century to the seventeenth century.

Art

Before the Renaissance many **paintings** were religious; afterwards portraits and landscapes became more and more popular. The renaissance in painting began in Italy with artists such as Leonardo da Vinci, Michelangelo and Titian, but the biggest changes took place in the paintings of Holbein, Van Dyck and Rembrandt. They made their livings by painting for wealthy merchants and the royal family. As more and more chateaux and country houses were built in the seventeenth century, more and more paintings were needed to cover the walls.

Literature

In England in the sixteenth century there were a number of very important developments in literature. The theatre became very popular and many plays were written. Before this there had been almost no performances at all, except for religious mystery plays. The most famous playwright is **Shakespeare**, but there were many others, including Christopher Marlowe and Beaumont and Fletcher.

Another important development was in poetry. This became very popular in the reign of **Elizabeth I** (1558–1603), every Elizabethan gentleman was expected to write poetry, preferably about the Queen. Poetry remained very popular in England throughout the next two centuries.

Scientific knowledge

The most important development in scientific knowledge was the discovery of the nature of the universe. The medieval belief was that the earth was the centre of the universe and that the sun, moon and planets revolved around it on spheres. This explanation had been put forward by Ptolemy who lived in the second century. Although scientists had doubted this for centuries, the **Catholic** Church had supported this idea, as it fitted in with the story of creation in the Bible.

How did ideas change?

1543   Nicholas Coppernick, known as Copernicus, proved that the earth went round the sun.

1609   Johannes Kepler put forward his 'Laws of Interplanetary Motion'. These explained how the planets moved.

1610   Galileo saw through a telescope that a comet went through what would have been one of the spheres.

1687   Isaac **Newton** put forward the Law of Gravity, which explained how the planets and the stars in the universe attracted each other.

REPARATIONS

Reparations is the name given to the sum of money which Germany was ordered to pay to the Allies at the Treaty of **Versailles**. The total amount was set at £6 600 000 000 and it was to cover the cost of the damage caused by the fighting during the **First World War**.

REPEAL OF THE CORN LAWS

The Repeal of the Corn Laws took place in 1846. This meant that it was possible to import corn into Britain freely.

Why was the Repeal of the Corn Laws important?

- It reduced the price of bread and helped create a period of prosperity for Britain in the mid-nineteenth century.
- It was an important step towards 'free trade'; this was the belief that countries should buy and sell freely with one another.
- It showed that the business class, which supported free trade, was beginning to become more influential than the landowners, most of whom had opposed free trade.
- It led to the collapse of the **Tory** Party, which had opposed repeal, for a period of 30 years. From 1846 to 1874, most governments were **Whig** (Liberal).

-+- *Peel, Tories, Conservative Party, Ireland*

REPUBLIC

A republic is a country which has an elected leader, usually called a President. The first large republic was the **United States of America**.

RESEARCH

The word 'research' means to find out about and it is something you will be asked to do many times when you study history.

Why do research?

- There is rarely enough information about a topic in one book; you have to look in a number of books or a CD-ROM.
- It is useful to compare different books to see if they agree. This will help you to explain different **interpretations** of history.
- It helps you to become more skilful at collecting and making use of information.

How to go about research

- You need to have a clear idea of the topic or question which you are trying to find out about.
- You should try to decide what you need to know. For example, if you were asked to research a person, you should try to find out when they were born, what were the important dates and events, what they achieved. In other words, try not to get bogged down in a lot of unnecessary detail.
- You must have some information about the places to look in and how to use them: textbooks, libraries, CD-ROMs, the Internet.
- You must record your information clearly and in an orderly manner. For example, make a note of the books you use and any page numbers, so that you can go back to find out more. If you can, it helps to photocopy the page, but you must only do this if it is to help you study a topic.

> REMEMBER: research is only the beginning of the task. You must be able to make use of what you have found out.

-+- *Notes*

RESTORATION

The Restoration was the name given to the period after the return of **Charles II** on 29 May 1660. After 1660 there was a great outburst of interest in art, music and the theatre, all of which had been suppressed during the Republic. The theatre was the most important feature of the Restoration. Plays were often comedies and could be bawdy. Charles II encouraged this as a way of increasing his popularity. The most popular writers were William Congreve and William Wycherley. The plays tended to be about society and described the situations in which people could find themselves. Often they made fun of people's behaviour.

The first English operas were written by John Blow and Henry Purcell. Purcell was the first major English composer. He wrote a wide variety of music in English. His most famous works were *King Arthur, The Indian Queen* and *The Fairy Queen*. These were all a cross between operas and plays. He also wrote a series of works for the birthday of Queen **Mary**. These are called *Queen Mary's Birthday Odes*.

Another important aspect of the Restoration was the **Royal Society**.

REVOLUTION

A revolution is the overthrow of the government. In 1688 **James II** was overthrown and replaced by William and Mary. This is known as the **Glorious Revolution**. In 1789 the **French Revolution** led to the death of Louis XVI and the creation of the French Republic. In February 1917, Tsar Nicholas II was overthrown and eventually power was seized by the **Bolshevik** Party. This led to the creation of the Soviet Union.

RHINELAND

The Rhineland was an area in western Germany which was demilitarised in the Treaty of **Versailles** in 1919. The Treaty stated that no armed forces or military equipment, including any buildings, could be positioned within 30 miles of the east bank of the river Rhine. It was hoped that this would prevent a German invasion of France. Allied troops were to be stationed in the Rhineland for 15 years, or longer if necessary.

In March 1936 **Hitler** reoccupied the Rhineland. This was the second step in his attempt to destroy the Treaty of Versailles. The first had been **rearmament**.

RHODES, CECIL

Cecil Rhodes was an English businessman who founded the De Beer's diamond mining corporation in 1880. He wanted to bring all of southern Africa under British control, and build a railway from the Cape to Cairo, in Egypt. When gold was discovered in the Transvaal in 1886, Rhodes provided finance for the mining operations and soon controlled many of the mines. In 1889 Rhodes set up the British South Africa Company, which was granted control of most of central Africa by the British government. In 1890 he became Prime Minister of South Africa.

Between 1890 and 1895 Rhodes tried to extend British influence in southern Africa. He built the city of Salisbury and this area became known as Rhodesia in Rhodes' honour in 1895. Today it is called Zimbabwe and Salisbury is named Harare.

Rhodes also built a railway linking Capetown with Johannesburg. The only obstacle in his way was the Transvaal. This was a **Boer** republic, which refused to take part in Rhodes' plans. He decided to try to overthrow the government in December 1895. He planned an uprising in the Transvaal capital, Johannesburg, and an invasion of 660 men led by his friend, Starr Jameson. It was a disaster. The uprising was called off and Starr Jameson was caught on 2 January. Rhodes was forced to resign.

During his lifetime Rhodes was seen as a hero. Today his reputation has suffered. He interfered in the affairs of the African countries of Mashonaland and Matabeleland and tried to undermine President Kruger in the Transvaal. He was an outstanding businessman, but he was too ready to take advantage of others and to use underhand tactics when necessary.

✦ *Boers*

RICHARD I, KING, 1189–1199 ▪

Richard I was the third son of **Henry II**. The year before he came to the throne he became religious and so, in 1189, only a few months after he had become King, he set off for the Holy Land as part of the Third **Crusade**. This was typical of Richard. He was never happier than when he was fighting. This earned him the nickname, 'Coeur de Lion', the 'Lionheart'. To finance the expedition Richard raised all the money he could and then left, leaving Hubert Walter, the Archbishop of Canterbury, in charge. While he was away he sent back demands for more money.

The Third Crusade was the biggest of all. As well as Richard, there was Philip II of France, the Holy Roman Emperor Frederick Barbarossa and Duke Leopold of Austria. The Crusade was not a success, however. Frederick was drowned on the way and Richard and Philip argued. Philip eventually left to return to France. Richard and Leopold became enemies after Richard tore down Leopold's flag from the walls of Acre.

In 1192, on his way home from the Crusade, Richard was taken prisoner by Leopold and held to ransom. He demanded 100 000 gold marks, the equivalent of two years' taxes. The ransom was collected in two years and Richard returned in 1194. The demands for extra taxes may well have helped to bring about the legend of **Robin Hood**.

Within a matter of months Richard left England

again and spent the next five years fighting Philip II in France. He was killed by an archer in 1199.

Richard's reputation

History books used to write about 'good King Richard' and 'evil King **John**'. Even today it is difficult to discover what they were really like.

● Richard was only in England for about six months in ten years. Most people knew nothing about him at the time.
● He gained a great reputation because he went on a crusade.
● He was popular because he was never in England. If things went wrong, someone else got the blame, like his brother John.
● Richard was a romantic figure, always fighting for his country.

But on the other hand

● Richard did very little for England: he merely spent a great deal of money.
● He took no interest in the country.
● He was a cruel fighter: he apparently had 3000 Muslim prisoners killed at Acre.
● He was rash and hot-headed and argued with the other leaders of the Third Crusade.

RICHARD II, KING, 1377–1399 ▪

Richard II became King at the age of ten in 1377 on the death of his grandfather **Edward III**. His own father, the Black Prince, had died in 1376.

Until 1389 England was ruled by a council dominated by Richard's uncle, John of **Gaunt**. Richard was very popular at first, meeting the **Peasants** at Mile End in 1381 and bringing an end to the **Peasants' Revolt**. Later in his reign Richard became more unpopular.

Why did Richard II face more trouble towards the end of his reign?

● He was an unsuccessful general. He tried to attack Scotland in 1385 and Ireland in 1398.
● He tried to raise taxes without **Parliament**'s approval and this led to a major argument with Parliament in 1397. Some of Richard's opponents in Parliament were executed.
● But probably the most important reason for Richard's troubles was the conspiracy organised by John of Gaunt. He arranged for his son, Henry Bolingbroke, to land in England while Richard was in Ireland in 1399. When he returned, Richard was captured and imprisoned. He was almost certainly murdered the following year.

RICHARD III, KING, 1483–1485 ▪

Richard III was the brother of **Edward IV** and the uncle of **Edward V**. He was crowned King in July 1483 after the disappearance of Edward V and his brother Richard of York, the '**Princes in the Tower**'. Rumours soon spread that Richard III had murdered his two nephews, but there is no absolute proof of this. What is certain is that the two boys were taken to the Tower and never emerged.

Richard was a popular King. He was a good general and there appears to have been no opposition to his becoming King in 1483. Later he was described as an evil, cruel figure.

Why did Richard get such a bad reputation?

● Sir Thomas **More** wrote a history of King Richard III in 1513. He was a close friend of **Henry VIII** at the time and wrote a particularly nasty description of Richard. Henry VIII's father, **Henry VII**, defeated and killed Richard at the battle of Bosworth Field in 1485. More was probably trying to explain why this had happened. If Richard was an evil man, then Henry VII's actions would be justified.

● In 1592 William **Shakespeare** wrote the play *Richard III*. In it he describes how Richard murders not only **Edward V** and Richard of York, but also **Henry VI**, who died in 1471. Richard is portrayed as a cripple, with one leg shorter than the other, and a hunchback. In the sixteenth century many people were not very sympathetic to the handicapped. Shakespeare must have known this.

Was Richard III's reputation justified?

● There is no actual evidence that **Edward V** and Richard of York were murdered by Richard, although Richard III took them to the Tower and they never emerged.

● One writer at the time, Domenico Mancini, who was opposed to Richard, admitted he could find no evidence that Richard was involved.

● Most people seem to have accepted Richard's accession readily.

● However, it is very unlikely that Richard knew nothing about the deaths. It seems that the two boys were dead by the end of August and that Richard was involved in one way or another.

Richard was King for two years. He was killed at the battle of Bosworth Field. This brought to an end the **Wars of the Roses**.

ROBIN HOOD

Robin Hood was a legendary figure, who is supposed to have lived during the reign of **Richard I** (1189–1199). According to the legend, Robin Hood lived in Sherwood Forest, robbing the rich and giving the money to the poor. He protected them from the evil Sheriff of Nottingham who collected taxes for Prince **John**. Robin Hood's real name was Robin of Loxley. He was an outlaw who had lost his estates. In the legend he is restored to his rightful position by King Richard I, who returns from the Third Crusade.

Was there a real Robin Hood?

There are two people called Robert Hood in official records.

● One lived in the 1310s and 1320s. He lived in west Yorkshire and was married to a woman called Matilda. He built a house with five rooms. This is written in the records of west Yorkshire.

● The second Robert Hood lived in the 1220s and was an outlaw. The legal records of Wakefield, in west Yorkshire, state that he was on the run from the Sheriff of Yorkshire. He lived in Barnsdale.

Neither of these Robert Hoods sound like the Robin Hood of the legend.

How did the legend develop?

● The legend of Robin Hood existed by the late-fourteenth century and early-fifteenth century. The poem *Piers Plowman*, written in the 1360s, mentions the rhymes of Robin Hood.

● Robin Hood is also mentioned in a number of history books written in the first half of the fifteenth century, one in 1420 and one in 1440. In these books he sounds much more like the Robin Hood of the legend. He robs the rich and does not attack women. He lives with Little John in the forest of Barnsdale.

● In 1521, John Major wrote the *History of Greater Britain*. He puts Robin Hood in the reign of Richard I and says that he lived in Sherwood Forest. This is just like the legend.

So it seems that the story of Robin Hood developed gradually over a long period of time, at least 300 years. The original Robert Hood lived in Barnsdale in the 1220s and he eventually became the outlaw of the legend who lived in Sherwood Forest during the reign of Richard I.

ROEHM, ERNST

Ernst Roehm was an ex-soldier, who became one of Adolf **Hitler**'s earliest and most loyal supporters. He joined the Nazi Party in the early 1920s after Hitler had changed the name from the German Workers' Party to the National Socialist German Workers' Party. Roehm became the leader of the Storm Troopers, the Sturm Abteilung or SA. He played an important part in the **Beer Hall Putsch** in November 1923, taking control of the post office in Munich and holding it while Hitler marched in from the Burgerbraukeller. Eventually, however, Roehm was forced to surrender.

Roehm was attracted to the Nazis because he was a socialist. He wanted to bring about a revolution in Germany and get rid of the existing government and way of life. He did not want to set up a right-wing dictatorship as Hitler did. He often described the generals as 'old fogeys' whom he would replace with a new Army based on the SA. He believed the SA was the basis of the Nazi Party.

In the 1920s Roehm did much of Hitler's dirty work, such as organising demonstrations, attacking other politicians and political parties and beating up Hitler's opponents. He looked like, and was, a violent, sadistic man with a scarred face, who was obviously not frightened of Hitler.

When Hitler came to power in January 1933, Roehm expected there would be some form of socialist revolution. This would mean getting rid of the existing government and giving more power to working people. Roehm wanted to be made Minister for War and Commander-in-Chief of the Army. In fact Hitler had no intention of allowing this to happen. Hitler wanted a right-wing Fascist state and wanted to be able to rely on the loyalty of the Army.

Roehm was eliminated during the **Night of the Long Knives** on 30 June 1934. He was arrested in Munich, given the chance to commit suicide and, when he refused, he was shot.

ROOSEVELT, FRANKLIN DELANO

Franklin Roosevelt was elected President of the USA in November 1932. He was then re-elected in 1936, 1940 and 1944. He was the only man to be elected President on more than two occasions.

What sort of man was Roosevelt?

He was born into a very rich New York family and attended an expensive private school. He then studied at Harvard University and became a lawyer. He served as under-Secretary for the Navy during the **First World War** and was then chosen as the Democrat Party's candidate for Vice-President in 1920.

In 1921 Roosevelt caught polio. This was a crippling disease which affected many people up to the middle of this century. He was paralysed from the waist down and could only walk with great difficulty.

Despite his illness, Roosevelt was determined to re-enter public life: he stood for Governor of New York in 1928 and was elected. In 1932 he was chosen as the Democrat Party's candidate for President and won in a landslide victory.

Why was Roosevelt elected President in 1932?

- His opponent, President Hoover, had done little to help Americans during the **Depression**.
- Roosevelt had organised a number of relief measures as Governor of New York.
- Roosevelt had already suffered personal tragedy and had shown that he could survive it.
- Roosevelt was a very effective public speaker. He devised several slogans which people remembered: 'the **New Deal**', 'the only thing we have to fear is fear itself', 'Relief, Recovery, Reform'.

Most Americans were prepared to back Roosevelt, even though he made few promises and seemed to have few ideas about how to tackle the Depression.

As soon as Roosevelt became President he began the New Deal. This was a massive programme aimed at getting America back to work. By 1940 unemployment had dropped from 13 000 000 to 8 000 000.

To many Americans Roosevelt was a hero, but some Americans hated him. Why was he unpopular?

- Some Americans regarded Roosevelt as a traitor to his own class. As a very wealthy man they expected him to help the rich. In fact he raised taxes on the very rich and ignored their protests. Some people even refused to say his name. They just called him, 'that man in the White House'.
- Big business did not like Roosevelt or the New Deal. They saw it as the government interfering in things that were none of its business. Henry Ford hated Roosevelt. When Roosevelt visited one of Ford's factories during the **Second World War**, Henry Ford hid from him. He only agreed to meet Roosevelt when his son made him.
- Roosevelt was accused by some people of being a dictator. He tried to force the Supreme Court to accept laws and used the President's powers to issue executive orders.
- Others regarded Roosevelt as a communist. They believed he was taking away from people in taxes what they had earned for themselves.
- But to some people Roosevelt did not go far enough. In 1937 he tried to stop the New Deal and he refused to take over businesses for the government until the war made it essential.

Roosevelt and the Second World War

After the **First World War** the US Congress had voted not to join the **League of Nations** and had not ratified the Treaty of **Versailles**. This did not mean that the USA was not involved in European affairs: US banks lent vast sums to Germany in the Dawes Plan and to other European countries including Britain, but most Americans did not want to become involved in another European war. So when the Second World War broke out, the USA remained neutral.

However, after the fall of France in June 1940, Roosevelt became more and more determined to send as much help as possible to Britain. He realised that if Britain was defeated, the USA would be next.

- In September 1940 he signed the 'Destroyers for Bases' agreement. This gave 50 old destroyers to Britain, in exchange for the use of bases in the Caribbean.
- In March 1941 he signed the Lend Lease Act. This allowed American planes, tanks and other equipment to be given to Britain on the understanding that they be handed back as new after the war.
- In June 1941, Lend Lease was extended to the **USSR** after the beginning of Operation Barbarossa.
- In the summer of 1941 US ships began to escort convoys across the Atlantic.
- In August 1941, Roosevelt met Churchill and they signed the **Atlantic Charter**.
- Finally, the USA declared war on Germany on 11 December 1941 and Roosevelt agreed with Churchill that the first aim of the Allies must be to defeat Germany.

From 1941 Roosevelt emerged as the leader of the wartime Alliance. He was determined that a new international organisation should be set up after the war and that the USA should play a leading role in it. He made up the name '*United Nations*' to describe the alliance of countries fighting the Axis and the name became adopted for the organisation which replaced the League of Nations in 1945.

Franklin Roosevelt died on 12 April 1945, just a few weeks after becoming President for the fourth time. He was one of the most influential figures of the twentieth century.

SELF-CHECK QUESTION 12

What was the name of Roosevelt's programme of recovery in the USA in the 1930s?

ROYAL SOCIETY

The Royal Society was set up by *Charles II* in 1662. He wanted to encourage developments of all kinds after his *Restoration* in 1660. The Royal Society held regular meetings and in 1665 it began to publish its own journal, *Philosophical Transactions*. This was the first scientific magazine published anywhere in the world.

All the leading English scientists belonged to the Royal Society.

- Robert Boyle: he invented the pump and put forward Boyle's Law which explained that pressure was related to volume.
- Robert Hooke: he invented the microscope and was able to identify plague fleas for the first time. He was also the first to use the word 'cells' after making observations of the structure of cork. This led to the discovery of micro-organisms.
- The most famous member of the Royal Society was Isaac *Newton*. In 1675 he presented to the Society a reflecting telescope which he had invented.

Charles II also founded the Royal Observatory at Greenwich and appointed John Flamsteed as the first Astronomer Royal. This led to the creation of the Greenwich Meridian from which time all over the world is calculated. If you visit the Observatory in Greenwich Park you can see the meridian marked by a brass line set in the ground. You can stand with one foot on the western hemisphere and one foot in the eastern hemisphere.

RUMP

The Rump was the name given to the *Parliament* which sat from 1649 until 1653. It was made up of the members who had not been excluded during 'Pride's Purge' in 1648. It ruled England between the death of *Charles I* in January 1649 and the setting up of the *Protectorate* in 1653.

✦ Oliver *Cromwell*

RUSSIAN REVOLUTION

The Russian Revolution took place in two stages in 1917. In March, Tsar Nicholas II was forced to abdicate and a provisional government took over. In October the provisional government was overthrown by the *Bolsheviks* and they ruled Russia for the next 74 years.

Why was Tsar Nicholas II forced to abdicate?

There were some long-term reasons: these are things which had been going on for some time and had made people increasingly angry.

- Russia was an autocracy. This meant the Tsar had total power. Although there was a Parliament, the Duma, it had little influence and could only criticise the Tsar's government. So, some politicians wanted to make Russia more democratic.
- Nicholas was, however, a weak and incompetent ruler. He allowed himself to be influenced by people who did not want any changes to take place in Russia.
- In Russia there were huge differences between the rich and the poor. About four-fifths of the population were peasants, many of whom could not read or write. In the towns, workers lived in poor, overcrowded accommodation. Political parties tried to make use of these conditions.
- There were a number of terrorist groups, which used violence. One was the Bolsheviks, led by *Lenin*. In 1881 the Tsar Alexander II was murdered. In 1911 the Prime Minister, Peter Stolypin, was murdered.
- The Tsar's government used violence against the people: Stolypin had 9000 people executed. If there were disturbances in the streets the government would use Cossacks, soldiers from southern Russia, to break up the crowds. Many people were killed.

There were also some shorter-term reasons, which developed in the years before 1917.

- The Tsar's wife came under the influence of Gregory Rasputin. She was already unpopular because she was a German, but her connection with Rasputin made things even worse.
- The Tsar kept dismissing the Duma and then changing its organisation. This made people wary of trusting him.
- But the most important reason was that Russia became involved in the *First World War*.

How did the *First World War* affect Russia?

- The Russian armies were very badly defeated by the German army. Millions of Russian soldiers were captured or killed.
- Russian industry could not produce enough war materials.
- The Russian railway network was very poor and it could not get food to the cities. Prices rose and people began to starve in the big cities of Petrograd and Moscow.
- To make matters worse the Tsar dismissed the Commander-in-Chief of the Army in 1915 and took command himself. This was a terrible mistake. Now he got the blame for everything that went wrong.

- The Tsar now relied on information from his wife about the situation in Petrograd. She often did not tell the truth and made out that everything was fine. In fact by late 1916 the situation was desperate. In December 1916 Rasputin was murdered by Russian nobles and in February 1917 workers in Petrograd began to go on strike. The Tsar tried to return to Petrograd, but his train was stopped. He was forced to abdicate and a provisional government took over.

Why were the Bolsheviks able to seize power in October 1917?

- The provisional government was only meant to be temporary. It was there to govern Russia until a General Election was held. The provisional government did not want to take any major decisions.
- The provisional government did not end the war with Germany, which many Russians wanted.
- The provisional government was unable to take any decisions without the support of the Petrograd Soviet. This was a committee of soldiers and workers which was set up soon after the provisional government. It represented the workers of Petrograd.
- The provisional government lost the support of the Army in August and this led to the Kornilov Revolt. The Bolsheviks had to be asked to help the government defend itself.
- The leader of the provisional government, Alexander Kerensky, became more and more unpopular. He also did not take the threat from the Bolsheviks very seriously.
- The Bolsheviks were well organised and well led by Lenin and ***Trotsky***.

On the night of 25 October 1917 the Bolsheviks seized control of the Winter Palace in Petrograd almost without firing a shot. Kerensky fled to the USA and died in 1971. Over the next two years the Bolsheviks gradually took control of all Russia. Other political parties were banned, newspapers were censored and thousands of people were murdered. So began the Communist dictatorship of Russia, which was to last for 74 years.

SARAJEVO

Sarajevo is a city in the Balkans. In 1914 it was part of Bosnia-Herzegovina, which had been taken over by the Austrians in 1908. The population of Sarajevo was mostly Serbian. It was here that the Archduke *Franz Ferdinand* was murdered by Gavrilo Princip on 28 June 1914. This act started the chain of events which led to the outbreak of the *First World War*.

SASSOON, SIEGFRIED

Siegfried Sassoon was a poet who served on the Western Front in the *First World War*. His poems, such as *The General*, are very critical of the conditions that British soldiers had to endure and he put the blame squarely on the commanders of the British armies. Sassoon was present at the beginning of the battle of the *Somme*, although he did not take part in the fighting. He was part of a unit which was positioned just behind the front line and was responsible for getting supplies to the soldiers in the frontline. If he had been in the front line he would probably have been killed.

Sassoon's experiences made him very bitter. He continued his criticisms after the war, writing his *Memoirs of a Foxhunting Man*.

SCHLIEFFEN PLAN

The Schlieffen Plan was the German plan of attack at the outbreak of the *First World War*. It was developed by Count Alfred von Schlieffen at the beginning of the century. The main aim was to avoid a war on two fronts. This had become more likely since 1894, when France and Russia had signed the Dual Alliance. Germany could now be attacked from both sides at the same time.

How did the Schlieffen Plan work?

- The Plan was intended to knock out France before the Russian Army could get going. It was expected that the Russians would take at least six weeks to mobilise (organise) their Army.
- Most German soldiers would be stationed along the French border; they would attack France immediately war broke out.
- The German advance would go through Belgium to avoid the French Army which would be on the German border. More than a million men would be involved. Belgium was a neutral country and its Army was very small. It would not be able to stop the German advance.
- The German Armies would sweep through Northern France and encircle Paris before the French Army could do anything about it. Once Paris was captured the Germans believed that France would surrender
- At the same time, the French Armies would attack Germany in Champagne to the east: this was known as 'Plan 17' in France. If necessary the German Armies facing the French would retreat to drag the French attackers away from Paris.

Why did the Schlieffen Plan fail?

- After Alfred von Schlieffen died, the German High Command changed the Schlieffen Plan. Some soldiers were transferred from the right wing which would go through Belgium and moved further to the east. This meant that the German Army in Belgium was not strong enough.
- The Russian Army mobilised much quicker than was expected. Within two weeks there were Russian Armies advancing on Prussia in eastern Germany. Soldiers had to be transferred to meet them.
- The Belgian Army put up a stronger fight than was expected. Belgian fortresses at Liege and Namur were difficult to capture. It took two weeks of fighting. This held up the German advance.
- The *British Expeditionary Force* arrived in Belgium by the third week of August. It took up positions at the town of *Mons*. When it was attacked by the Germans it slowed down the advance even more. Kaiser *Wilhelm II* referred to it as a 'contemptible little army', because there were only 120 000 men in it, but they were highly trained professional soldiers. One German officer wrote, 'It seemed as though there was a machine gun behind every tree.' This was a tribute to the accuracy of the rifle fire of the British infantry.
- The extreme right wing of the German Army did not move as quickly as expected and it was forced east of Paris, instead of to the west. The commander of the forces in Paris attacked it from the west.

Eventually the German Army was stopped at the battle of the Marne in September 1914. Here it was counter-attacked by the French and was forced back. Within a few months both sides had dug trenches and the Western Front had developed. Many soldiers were trapped in the same places for the next four years. See map overleaf of the Schlieffen Plan.

SCOTLAND

Scotland was a separate kingdom for most of the period that you will study. Scotland and England were not united until the Act of *Union* in 1707, which created the country of Great Britain.

Scotland and England after the *Norman Conquest*

When *William* the Conqueror landed in 1066, Scotland was ruled by King Malcolm III (often

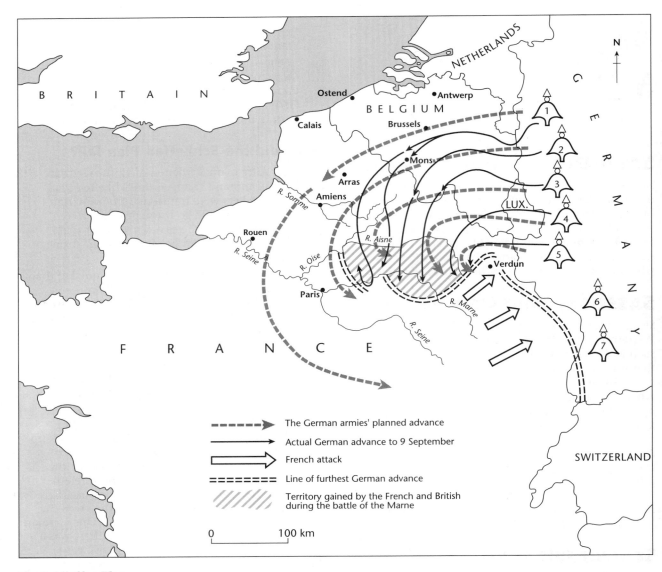

The German armies' planned advance

Actual German advance to 9 September

French attack

Line of furthest German advance

Territory gained by the French and British during the battle of the Marne

0   100 km

The Schlieffen Plan

known as Malcolm Canmore). He appears in William *Shakespeare*'s play *Macbeth*, in which he succeeds his father Duncan when he is murdered by Macbeth. Malcolm defeated and killed Macbeth in 1057 and reigned as King until 1093. Although Malcolm was King of Scotland, he only really controlled the centre and south-east. The western isles were Norwegian; the Highlands and Galloway, the south-west, were beyond his control.

Malcolm was forced to do homage for his kingdom to both *William I* and *William II* and he was married to an Englishwoman. This helped to spread Norman influence in Scotland. This continued when Malcolm's son, Alexander, succeeded him in 1093. He served in *Henry I*'s army in Wales in 1114 and his brother David was given estates in England by Henry. Alexander's sister, Matilda, married Henry I of England in 1100. Both Henry I and David gave land in the Borders to a Norman baron, Robert de Brus; one of his descendants was to play an important part in Scottish history. Other Normans also settled in the Borders.

Why did relations between Scotland and England grow worse in the twelfth and thirteenth centuries?

- During the civil wars in King *Stephen*'s reign, the Scots invaded northern England and occupied land. In 1157 *Henry II* drove the Scots out of England, but in 1175 King William the Lion invaded again and was captured by Henry II. He was forced to accept Henry II as his feudal overlord and did homage for his kingdom.

- During the reigns of *Richard I*, *John* and *Henry III*, the links between Scotland and England became weaker and the Kings of Scotland became more powerful. In 1202 King *William IV* forced the Earl of Caithness in northern Scotland to swear loyalty to him and in 1266, Alexander III gained the Isle of Man and the Western Isles. When Alexander did homage to *Edward I* in 1278, he only did so for his English lands and not for his kingdom.

- Alexander III died in 1286, leaving only his grand-daughter, Margaret. When she died in 1290, the Scottish nobles asked Edward I to choose a new King from a list of 13. Edward chose John Balliol, who was descended from a Norman family which had settled in Scotland during the reign of David I. Edward insisted that John Balliol swear an oath of loyalty to him. The Scottish nobles refused and John Balliol made a treaty with the King of France. The alliance with France was to last until the eighteenth century. This led to wars between Scotland and England.

The wars between Scotland and England

1296 Scotland was invaded by Edward I and John Balliol was defeated. Edward made himself King of Scotland. He took the Stone of Scone to London. This had been used as the throne when Kings of Scotland were crowned. It was returned in 1997.

1297 William Wallace led a rising against Edward and won a victory at Stirling. He was defeated at Falkirk in 1298 and captured and executed in 1305. Edward I united England and Scotland but there was another rising led by Robert Bruce.

1307 Edward I died on his way to attack Robert Bruce.

1311 Robert Bruce invaded England.

1314 An English army invaded Scotland and was defeated at **Bannockburn**.

1323 Treaty of Northampton: Robert Bruce was recognised as King of Scotland.

Relations between Scotland and England in the fourteenth and fifteenth centuries

From 1323 until the early-sixteenth century there were Kings of Scotland. Relations with England varied. In 1363 **Edward III** and David II considered uniting their kingdoms; in 1346 the Scots invaded England trying to help France during the **Hundred Years' War**. They were defeated at the battle of Neville's Cross and David II was taken prisoner.

The Scots invaded England again in 1513, led by James IV. Once again they were trying to support France in a war with **Henry VIII**. It was a disaster. The Scottish Army was destroyed and James IV, who was **Henry VIII**'s brother-in-law, was killed. James was succeeded by his son, James V, and his grand-daughter, **Mary**, Queen of Scots. Her son James VI became King in 1567.

When James VI became **James I** of England in 1603, the two countries had the same King, but were quite separate. This situation lasted until 1707 and the Act of **Union**.

How did relations between Scotland and England change in the seventeenth century?

- The most important change was that they had the same Monarch, but were two separate kingdoms. When James VI came to England in 1603 he found many differences. The legal system was different and so was **Parliament**, but probably the most important difference was the Church. In Scotland the Church was Presbyterian and had no bishops. This was to lead to difficulties later.

- While James was Scottish and spoke with an accent, his son Charles was not. Charles was brought up in England and was an Anglican. He did not understand Scotland as his father had done. He tried to force the Scots to use William **Laud**'s Prayer Book and went to war with Scotland when they refused. He was actually going to war with himself, as he was King of Scotland.

- The Scots supported Parliament during the **English Civil War**, but changed sides in 1647 and tried to restore Charles. This was because Charles promised to support the Presbyterian Church, while Parliament appeared to be trying to attack it.

- The Scots also supported **Charles II** when he landed in Scotland in 1650, but were defeated by **Cromwell** at the battle of Dunbar.

- When Charles II was restored in 1660 he was supported by the Scots.

The Act of Union

After James II fled in 1688, there was a rising in the Highlands to try to restore him. Many Highlanders were Catholic, unlike the Presbyterians from southern and central Scotland. The Highlanders won the battle of Killiecrankie, but the rising died down. All Highland chieftains were ordered to take an oath of loyalty to **William III** by 31 December 1691. Only the leader of the Macdonalds failed to do so, although he did on 6 January 1692. This was kept secret and on 13 February 1692 about 40 Macdonalds, including the chieftain, were massacred by their traditional enemies, the Campbells, at Glencoe.

When the Act of **Settlement** was passed in 1701, it only applied to England, as Scotland was still a separate country. This led to the Act of Union, which united the two countries and also applied the details of the Act of Settlement in Scotland.

How did the Act of Union change relations between Scotland and England?

- Scotland and England became known as Great Britain. Sophia, Electress of Hanover, or her heirs would now succeed to the throne of the United Kingdom.

- There would be one Parliament. Scotland would send 16 peers to the House of Lords and 45 members to the Commons.

- Scottish law was to remain and the Presbyterian Church was not to be changed.

- The crosses of St Andrew and St George were united to form a new national flag, called the Union Flag.

> REMEMBER: from 1603 to 1707 Scotland and England were separate kingdoms with the same Monarch.

Scotland and England in the eighteenth and nineteenth centuries

- There were two more attempts by the Highlanders to restore **James II**'s heirs. In 1715 and in 1745 the **Jacobites** marched south to try to overthrow the Hanoverians. The second rebellion led to the Highland Clearances: vicious attacks on Highlanders who were forced off their land; many emigrated.

- Scottish schools and universities developed rapidly in the eighteenth and nineteenth centuries. In England the **Church of England** had a great deal of influence on education and the main emphasis was on Latin and Greek. In Scotland there was much more emphasis on science and engineering. Many of the inventors and engineers of the Industrial Revolution were Scottish, such as:
    - James **Watt**, who developed an efficient steam engine
    - Thomas **Telford**, who built canals and roads
    - John **Macadam**, who developed a cheap way of repairing roads
    - John Roebuck, who built ironworks at Falkirk
    - William Symington, who built the first working steamship
    - James Nasmyth, who developed the steam hammer.

- New industries developed in Scotland during the **Industrial Revolution**. **Cotton** factories were built in Lanarkshire by Robert **Owen**. Shipbuilding developed on the Clyde, supported by iron, steel and coalmining.

Scotland during the twentieth century

- Many towns in Scotland were badly hit by the **Depression** because much of Scotland depended on heavy industry: iron, steel, shipbuilding, coalmining and textiles. These were the industries which suffered most in the 1930s. Towns like Greenock and Motherwell do not get as much attention as **Jarrow**, but conditions were almost as bad, with unemployment at about 50 per cent. To try to help recovery the Queen Mary and the Queen Elizabeth were built on the Clyde but, as with most places, it was the **Second World War** which really ended the Depression.

- Since the Second World War nationalism has become much stronger in Scotland; this is partly because many Scots feel they have been governed from Westminster for too long. It is also because of the discovery of North Sea oil and the development of new computer industries in Scotland.

SCRAMBLE FOR AFRICA

The Scramble for Africa is the name given to the attempts by the nations of Europe to occupy colonies in Africa at the end of the nineteenth century.

Why did European countries try to acquire colonies in Africa?

- Africa offered raw materials; gold and diamonds were discovered in South Africa. In central Africa there was copper. Many believed there was great wealth to be discovered.

- The writer Rider Haggard wrote novels about Africa, such as *King Solomon's Mines*, which told of gold and silver hidden in Africa waiting to be found. Africa became known as the 'Dark Continent', just waiting to be explored.

- Africans were heathens: many Europeans believed it was their duty to convert them to Christianity. In the 1860s and 1870s, many missionaries went to Africa. The most famous was David Livingstone, who was lost in central Africa for three years. An expedition was sent out to find him.

- Some British people believed they had a mission to develop Africa and other parts of the world. They believed Africans were backward and savage. They talked about the 'white man's burden': the responsibility of Europeans to civilise the rest of the world.

- European countries wanted empires: the bigger the empire, the more powerful the country appeared to be. Britain had gained the Cape in 1815 and occupied parts of West Africa in the 1870s. In the 1880s British forces occupied Egypt and the Sudan. France began to explore North Africa and the Sahara in the 1830s. On British maps the colonies of Britain were coloured red or pink. People talked of 'painting the world red'.

- Britain became involved in Egypt in 1876, when the Prime Minister, Benjamin **Disraeli**, bought shares in the Suez Canal Company. He wanted to make sure the route to India through the canal was kept open to British ships.

- The real scramble began when Germany began to try to find colonies in the 1880s. Until then the German Chancellor, Bismarck, had opposed the creation of a German empire, but when Kaiser

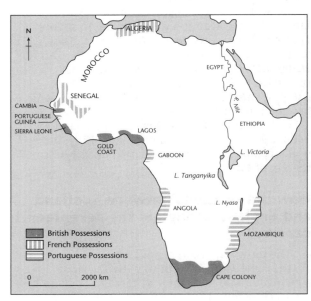

Africa in 1875

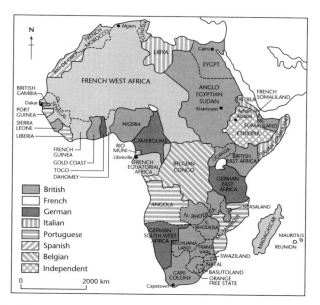

Africa in 1914

Wilhelm II succeeded his father in 1887 this changed. The new Kaiser wanted Germany to have a 'place in the sun'.

By 1914 almost all of Africa had been occupied by Europeans.

Did Africans gain from colonisation?

- Until quite recently it was believed that colonisation was a great benefit to Africans. Today ideas have changed.

- Africans were often used as cheap labour to make goods for Europe. The colonies were seen as a way of making big profits very easily. Raw materials were taken out of Africa without any form of payment.

- Native art and architecture, such as bronzes from Benin in West Africa and Great Zimbabwe in central Africa, were ignored or even destroyed.

- African nations and societies were destroyed by Europeans. The Ndbele, the Shona and the Zulu were all attacked by British Armies armed with modern weapons. At the battle of Omdurmann in 1898, a British Army killed 12 000 Sudanese, some of whom were wearing chain-mail.

- In Africa and elsewhere there was discrimination against natives. In South Africa this eventually led to apartheid, but it was widespread. In many colonies whites and natives led completely separate lives.

- On the other hand African countries did probably develop more quickly under European rule. There were missionary societies which founded hospitals and schools and the slave trade and tribal warfare was reduced. However, the slave trade had been encouraged by Europeans in the past.

- There were many colonial officials who spent their lives trying to do their best for natives. The violence and unfairness which existed in some African societies was brought to an end.

Why was the Scramble for Africa a cause of the First World War?

- It led to increased rivalry between the European powers. Germany occupied South West Africa, now known as Namibia, which was next to British South Africa, and East Africa, which stopped Cecil **Rhodes'** plans for a railway from the Cape to Cairo. Germany also tried to interfere in North Africa in the Moroccan Crises of 1905 and 1911.

- In March 1905 Kaiser **Wilhelm II** made a speech in Tangier, in Morocco, which suggested that Germany was going to try to oppose French influence in Morocco.

- In July 1911 a German gunboat, the Panther, was sent to Morocco. This again made the French and British governments think that Germany was trying to interfere in Morocco.

Although Africa did not directly cause the outbreak of war, it did lead to increased tension between the European countries and in particular between Germany and France.

SECOND WORLD WAR

The Second World War in Europe began on 1 September 1939, when Germany invaded Poland. Two days later, on 3 September at 11.00 am, Britain declared war on Germany. The war in Europe lasted until 8 May 1945 when Germany surrendered. In the Far East, the war began when the USA declared war on Japan on 8 December 1941, the day after the attack on **Pearl Harbor**. Fighting in the Far East ended on 15 August 1945, six days after the second atomic bomb was dropped on Nagasaki.

What were the causes of the Second World War?

- A major cause was the coming to power of Adolf **Hitler** in Germany in January 1933. He used the anger of Germans at the treatment that Germany had received at the Treaty of **Versailles**, and the feeling of despair brought on by the effects of the **Depression**, to build up support for his foreign policy.

- Hitler set out to destroy the Treaty of Versailles and challenge the other countries of Europe. In 1935 he began **rearmament**. He introduced conscription and began to build up the Luftwaffe and the German Navy. In 1936 he reoccupied the **Rhineland**. In March 1938 he carried out the **Anschluss**. In September 1938 he demanded and got the **Sudetenland** at the **Munich** Conference. In March 1939 Hitler occupied the rest of western Czechoslovakia.

- Another major cause was the collapse of the **League of Nations**, which many people and countries hoped would help prevent a second war. Three of the five Permanent Council Members left the League in the 1930s. This left only Britain and France. In these two countries some politicians went on hoping that the League would work until the late 1930s.

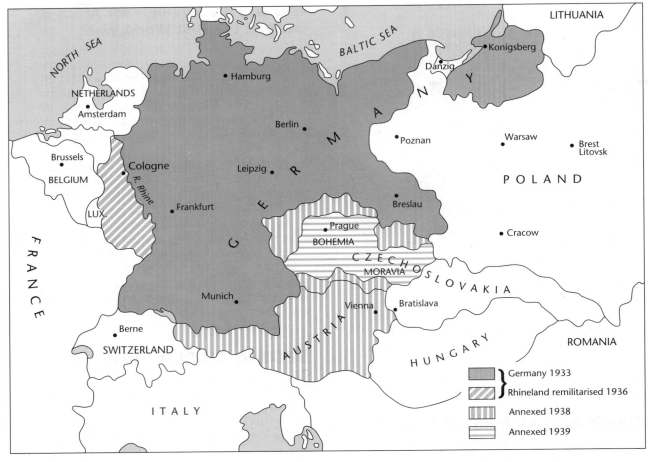

Hitler's actions in the 1930s

- Another major cause was the policy of **appeasement** followed by the governments of Britain and France. They believed that if they gave in to Hitler's demands he would be satisfied and make no more.

- Another major cause was the emergence of other dictators in Europe and around the world: **Mussolini** in Italy and **Tojo** in Japan. Their power depended on military success and their combination with Hitler, the Axis, made war very difficult to avoid.

Why did Britain declare war on 3 September?

At Munich in September 1938, Hitler promised to make no more demands. When he broke the promise in March 1939, the British Prime Minister, Neville Chamberlain, was horrified. He realised that Hitler could not be trusted. He immediately made two alliances with Poland and Romania, promising to defend each country if it was attacked in the future. Poland was the obvious next step for Hitler, as German land had been given to Poland at the Treaty of Versailles to form the Polish Corridor.

When Germany invaded Poland on 1 September, the British government immediately demanded that the German Army should withdraw. If the German government did not reply, Britain would declare war at 11.00 am on 3 September.

Hitler was apparently taken by surprise. He had not expected Britain to react in this way. He did not understand that once the British government had made a promise, it was bound to keep it.

Why was the German Army so successful in 1939 to 1941?

- Germany had started rearming first. By 1939 the German Army was much larger than the British Army, although it was smaller than the French.

- The Germans had developed new weapons, which proved very effective: tanks, dive-bombers, field guns, submarines.

- The Germans used new tactics, **Blitzkrieg**, which took the other countries by surprise. They had practised these tactics during the **Spanish Civil War**. The tactics were based on speed and movement, unlike the **First World War**.

- Britain and France expected the war to be like the First World War. Their armies dug themselves in trenches. The French built a huge line of forts along the border with Germany, the Maginot Line. The Germans went round it through the Ardennes, a hilly wooded area in southern Belgium. The French did not believe the German tanks could get through.

- The French Army seemed to lack the will to fight. Leading figures in France were ready to make peace with the Germans. Some believed that Hitler would protect them from communism.

Why did the Allies win?

- In the first years of the war Hitler made a number of serious mistakes: stopping the German tanks on the outskirts of **Dunkirk**; stopping the attacks on Fighter Command during the **Battle of Britain**; not building enough U boats, which meant that the Allies were able to win the **Battle of the Atlantic**; invading the Soviet Union in 1941 after a delay of two months dealing with Yugoslavia and Greece. Each one of these meant that he missed the opportunity of winning a major victory.

- The determination of the British people in holding on alone from June 1940 until June 1941, when Germany invaded the Soviet Union. This set an example to the rest of the world and showed that the British people were not prepared to give in.

- The effects of Operation Barbarossa, the invasion of the Soviet Union. This destroyed the German Army and led to the destruction of thousands of tanks. It showed that the Germans could be beaten.

- The enormous power of the **USA**. By 1943 the USA was producing four times as much military equipment every month as Germany. Many of the battles fought by the British Army and the Red Army were fought with American-made weapons.

In the end Germany was simply overwhelmed. Attacked on all sides, bombed round the clock from the air and starved of supplies, there was no way that the Germans could win a long war. In the Far East the war was brought to a sudden end by the use of the atomic bomb on **Hiroshima**. There was little chance of Japan winning the war by then, but some experts believed that the war would last for another 18 months or even two years.

SETTLEMENT, ACT OF

The Act of Settlement was passed in 1701. It laid down the succession to the Crown after the deaths of **William III** and Princess Anne, the second daughter of **James II**. The Act was needed because James II had fled in 1688 and neither of his daughters, **Mary**, (1688–1694) and **Anne**, had any surviving children.

What did the Act state?

- When Anne died the Crown was to pass to Sophia, Electress of Hanover, or her heir. She was a grand-daughter of **James I**. Her mother was James I's daughter, Elizabeth.

- The King or Queen must always be **Protestant**.

- The King or Queen were never to leave Britain without the consent of **Parliament**.

- Britain was never to be involved in a war in defence of any land owned by the King or Queen overseas. This was to prevent Sophia using British forces to protect **Hanover**, in northern Germany.

- Foreigners were not to be allowed to hold any offices in Britain and were not to be given money by the King or Queen.

- Judges could not be dismissed unless they did something illegal.

This was a very important Act of Parliament. It was an attempt to put an end to many of the problems which had occurred in the seventeenth century. It is still in force today.

SHAFTESBURY, THE EARL OF

Shaftesbury (until 1851 his title was Lord Ashley) was a member of the Evangelical movement in the **Church of England**. These people believed that Christians should act morally and try to help those in society who were suffering. Shaftesbury took part in many of the reform movements in the first half of the nineteenth century.

- He supported the **Factory Reform** Act of 1833, which banned children from textile factories if they were under the age of nine. He was also a leading spokesman for the Ten Hours Movement, which wanted to reduce the working day of factory workers.

- In 1839 he helped to found the Health of Towns Association, along with Edwin Chadwick; this eventually led to the **Public Health** Act of 1848.

- Shaftesbury's most famous achievement was the Mines Act of 1842, which was passed after an enormous campaign and a report on mines which he had compiled. It banned the employment of women and children underground in coalmines. This is still the law today.

- In 1847 the Factory Act introduced a ten-hour day for women and young persons, although the day was extended to ten and a half hours in 1850.

- Shaftesbury also set up the Ragged Schools, which provided education for poor children and campaigned, unsuccessfully, to ban 'climbing boys'. These were young boys who were used to sweep the large chimneys which were built for wood-burning fires.

When Shaftesbury died the statue of Eros in Piccadilly Circus was built in his memory. The bow held by the figure was aimed at Shaftesbury Avenue, which was also named after him.

SHAKESPEARE, WILLIAM

William Shakespeare was the most important English playwright at the end of the sixteenth and the beginning of the seventeenth century. His plays were performed in theatres in London, like the Globe, which has recently been rebuilt, and drew vast crowds. In the 1590s he wrote a series of history plays which told the story of the Kings of England from **Richard II** to the accession of **Henry VII**. These plays were **propaganda** for the Tudors: they described the successes of the Lancastrian Kings and attacked **Richard III** as an evil murderer. Henry VII is shown saving England from a tyrant.

Shakespeare wrote the history plays to explain why Henry Tudor had seized the throne in 1485, killing Richard III in the process. **Elizabeth I** was also trying to make sure that when she died there was no attempt to prevent **James I** succeeding her peacefully. She wanted people to understand that Henry VII, her grandfather, had been justified in rebelling against Richard III and killing him because Richard had been a mass-murderer, but that there would be no justification in trying to seize power when she died.

Shakespeare was so successful that even today most people's idea of Richard III comes from Shakespeare's play. It is very difficult to find out what Richard was really like.

SHERIFF

A sheriff was a medieval official appointed by the King, who was responsible for a county. The word comes from the Anglo-Saxon term shire-reeve. A reeve was an official and a shire was a county.

Sheriffs were responsible for carrying out the King's orders in their county, collecting taxes and holding courts of law. Each year the sheriff was told how much he had to collect. Sheriffs were also responsible for law and order. They caught criminals and bought them to justice. Sheriffs were the most important royal officials outside the royal court.

In the fifteenth century sheriffs became less important and many of their duties were taken over by the *Justices of the Peace*.

SLAVERY

Slavery is the ownership of one human being by another. It has existed for thousands of years. Slaves were owned in many ancient civilisations. In Rome slave-owning was taken for granted. It existed in Anglo-Saxon and medieval society, but became very rare by the thirteenth century. By Tudor times it had died out in Britain.

The slave trade

In the sixteenth century English ships began to go to Africa and take slaves across the Atlantic Ocean to the Americas. They sold the slaves in the Spanish empire in south and central America. The slaves were used on plantations: huge estates that grew coffee and sugar. When England went to war with Spain in 1585 the trade died out, but it started again in the seventeenth century and by the eighteenth century it had become very important.

Why did the slave trade develop so much in the eighteenth century?

- Sugar began to be grown on plantations in Jamaica, which had been captured in 1659. Sugar became very popular in England and more and more plantations were opened. Slaves were brought from Africa to work on the plantations, because the climate was too hot for white men to work in.

- In the first half of the eighteenth century *cotton* plantations were built in the southern American colonies, particularly Georgia, which was occupied in the 1730s and named after George II. This was a big boost to the slave trade.

The triangular trade

A triangular trade developed. Ships sailed from Britain to West Africa with manufactured metal goods, weapons or iron bars. In West Africa these were exchanged for slaves. The slave traders did not usually catch the slaves themselves; they had often been captured in tribal wars. The slave ships waited for about a month at factories on the coast for the slaves to be brought to them. Then the ships sailed to the Americas. The journey lasted six to eight weeks, with the slaves crowded together below decks. They were only let out on deck once a day and were often chained together. Slave-ship captains reckoned that if half the slaves survived they would make a profit. Conditions were awful. It was said that a slave ship could be smelt seven miles away.

When the ships arrived, they usually stayed for about a week at a small island to allow the slaves to recover from the effects of the journey, so that they would fetch a higher price. Then they were sold at markets. Slaves usually sold for about £20 to £40, but some could cost as much as £200 if they were well educated.

Once the slaves had been sold, the ships were filled with cargoes from the Americas. These were mostly raw materials: sugar, cotton, coffee, tea or tobacco. The ships then sailed for Britain. The whole journey took about 11 or 12 months.

How did the slave trade affect Britain in the eighteenth century?

- It was an enormous source of profit. Up to 50 000 slaves a year were carried across the Atlantic. Most of the ships were based either in Liverpool or Bristol. Liverpool was the more important and its wealth came from the slave trade. It increased in size ten times during the eighteenth century.

- The slave trade also made the *Industrial Revolution* possible. It led to the arrival in Britain of large quantities of cheap cotton. Most of this was landed in Liverpool, which had an ideal climate for cotton-spinning. Most people's lives were improved by the slave trade in one way or another.

- In London a group of merchants appeared who made huge fortunes out of the slave trade. William Beckford, who became Lord Mayor of London three times, was one of the richest men in Britain. Many of the merchants bought country estates and became MPs.

The slave trade, however, led to misery for hundreds of thousands of Africans. After the horrors of the crossing, the 'Middle Passage' as it was called, they could be separated from their family and made to work for the rest of their lives on a huge plantation. Conditions could be very harsh, with cruel punishments like their nose being slit, or ears cut off. Although many slaves were treated very badly, there was little point in paying a lot of money for slaves and then working them to death.

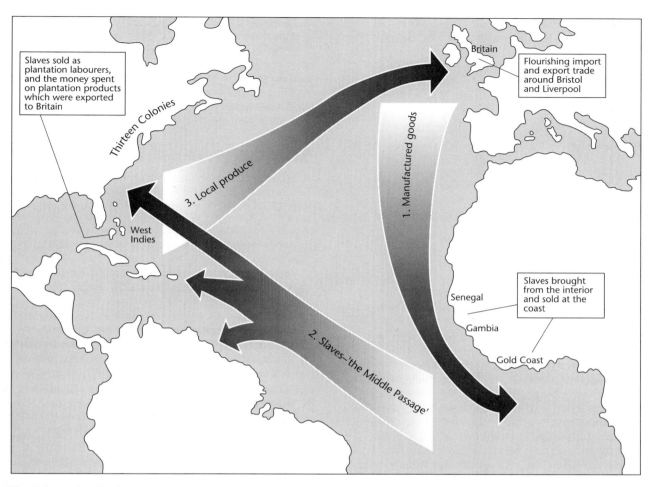

Slaves sold as plantation labourers, and the money spent on plantation products which were exported to Britain

Thirteen Colonies

West Indies

3. Local produce

1. Manufactured goods

2. Slaves–'the Middle Passage'

Britain

Flourishing import and export trade around Bristol and Liverpool

Senegal

Gambia

Gold Coast

Slaves brought from the interior and sold at the coast

The Triangular Trade

Why did people in Britain not protest about the slave trade?

- Many people knew nothing about it. The worst part was the 'Middle Passage' and this took place between Africa and America. It was only when a slave-ship captain, John Newton, began to explain what it was like, that people found out. When an anti-slavery society was set up in 1772, one of the members, Thomas Clarkson, had to have a plan of a slave ship drawn to describe the conditions slaves had to endure.

- Many people stood to gain from the slave trade. It played a very important part in Britain's trade in the eighteenth century.

- The West India Merchants, like William Beckford, were very powerful. Many of them were in **Parliament** and they opposed attempts to do something about the slave trade.

- Many people also defended the slave trade because they believed that slaves became Christians and this was better than remaining heathens in Africa. Some people also believed that Africans were not humans and so did not deserve better treatment.

Why was the slave trade abolished in 1807?

- Charles James Fox, who had just become Prime Minister, was a **Whig** and he believed in reform.

- The Anti-Slavery Society had been very effective. It was led first by Granville Sharp, then by Thomas Clarkson and finally by William **Wilberforce**. They tried many times to get the slave trade abolished. They published leaflets, sent speakers around the country and eventually even convinced some slave owners that they would be better off without the slave trade. Many of the members of the society were 'Evangelicals': this was a movement within the **Church of England** which believed that Christians should behave morally.

- In 1783 the American Colonies had become independent. Only the West Indian islands now depended on the slave trade.

- The West Indian trade had become less important as British control of India developed. Slavery was not used in India.

But the end of the slave trade did not lead immediately to the end of slavery. That was not abolished until 1833.

Why was slavery abolished in 1833?

- The main reason was the Great **Reform** Act which was passed in 1832. This meant that many factory owners and businessmen were elected to Parliament for the first time. They were opposed to slavery, sometimes because they were Christians and sometimes because they believed

111

that slavery was simply out of date. They believed that workers would work harder and better if they were paid.

● The sugar industry in the West Indies was becoming less and less important. In the nineteenth century more sugar was produced from sugar beet in this country.

£20,000,000 was paid out in compensation to slave owners in the West Indies. The only other area of the British Empire where slaves were owned was South Africa. Here abolition led to the Great Trek by the **Boers** in 1833 and to the beginnings of apartheid.

SOCIALISM

Socialism is a political belief that the government should try to help the poorer and less fortunate people in society. Socialism developed after the **Industrial Revolution** in Britain. This emphasised the differences between rich and poor and also created very bad living and working conditions for many industrial workers. The first trade unions were set up in Britain in the 1820s, but these ended with the collapse of Robert **Owen**'s 'Grand National' in 1834. Socialist ideas were continued in **Chartism** and the Cooperative Movement which was founded in 1844. This supplied cheap, good-quality food to working people on a non-profit-making basis.

The Industrial Revolution also led to the creation of Communism and the two words, socialist and communist, are often mixed up. Communists believe the government should take over and run all forms of business; some even believe that all forms of private property should be ended. Socialists believe the poor and weak in society should be helped and not left to fend for themselves. The wealthy should be taxed more heavily to provide help for the poor. Socialists often support some forms of nationalisation. For example, the Labour government in Britain from 1945 to 1950 nationalised certain industries.

Socialism first became important in Britain in the late-nineteenth century, when a number of organisations, such as the Fabian Society, were set up. They wanted to change society so that more help was given to the people who needed it most. In 1892 James Keir Hardie, a socialist, was elected MP for West Ham, and in 1893 he set up the Independent Labour Party. The real breakthrough came in 1900 when the Labour Representation Committee was set up by a group of trade unions and the Cooperative Movement. This changed its name to the **Labour Party** in 1906.

SOCIALIST

The term 'socialist' developed in the nineteenth century and described people who believed that more should be done to try to improve the lives of ordinary people. They thought that the government had a duty to protect the people in society who were not able to protect themselves. Some of the first socialists in Britain were Robert **Owen** and the Rochdale Pioneers, who set up the first Cooperative Society in Britain. This was an attempt to provide working people with cheap, good quality food.

In the second half of the nineteenth century **trade unions** took up these ideas. They began to provide benefits for their members, such as unemployment and sick pay. Trade unions helped to form the **Labour Party** in 1900. Socialist ideas led to the creation of the **Welfare State** and the **Nationalisation** of some industries by the Labour government from 1945 to 1950.

SOMME, THE

The battle of the Somme began on 1 July 1916 and lasted until the second week of November, when it was called off by the Commander-in-Chief of the British Army, Field Marshal Douglas Haig. By that time the Army had suffered about 500 000 casualties and had advanced at best about five miles. Many units were unable to advance at all.

Why was the battle of the Somme fought?

● Haig had become Commander-in-Chief in December 1915: this was his first chance to fight a big battle. He believed that the battle could be won by sheer numbers.

● This was the first time that many of the soldiers involved had been in action. They were the 'New Army' which had volunteered in 1914 and 1915. This meant there was a big increase in the number of men available.

● Haig had originally wanted to fight a battle in Flanders around **Ypres**, but he was forced to change his mind after the beginning of the battle of Verdun in eastern France. The Somme was intended to take pressure off the French army.

How was the battle to be fought?

● A bombardment lasting a week preceded the battle. This was supposed to destroy the German trenches and barbed wire.

● The infantry would then go 'over the top' and cross no man's land. They would capture the German positions and drive through the reserve trenches. Each unit was given targets for the first day. It was intended that other units would then follow and advance even further on the second and third days.

● Once this had happened, the cavalry would charge through and attack the enemy in the rear. This would be the 'breakthrough' that Haig wanted.

What actually happened?

● The bombardment went as planned, but it failed to destroy the German positions. They were either too well dug in or were protected by concrete. Only in one or two places was real damage done.

● When the infantry went over the top they were mown down by machine-gun fire. The infantry had to carry full equipment, weighing 60 pounds, and were forbidden to run. They had to walk at a steady pace. Each unit that went over the top on the morning of 1 July 1916 lost at least one-third of its soldiers. Total British losses were 29 000.

- Although some progress was made, none of the main objectives were taken and there was no breakthrough. The cavalry in reserve was never used.
- Intense fighting went on until August in some places, for example Pozieres, which was captured by Australian soldiers in late August.
- A second attack was made in September and then a third in November. By that time the soldiers were faced by freezing sleet as well as the Germans.

Why did the battle fail?

- A lot of the blame must go to Haig. He had not considered the effects of battles in 1915, such as Loos and Neuve Chapelle, where the British Army had suffered heavy losses. Haig was also a cavalry officer: like many senior commanders, he still believed that cavalry was the key to winning the war. A serious accusation made about Haig was that he went on with the battle long after it had been proved a failure.
- The French had promised 40 divisions to support the British Army, but after the beginning of the battle of Verdun they only provided 16.
- Haig also had to fight the battle with far fewer men than he wanted. He estimated that he actually needed one-third more than he actually had and twice as many guns.
- The bombardment was a complete failure: not only did it not destroy the German positions, but it gave away the time of the attack. When the bombardment stopped the Germans knew the attack was coming.

It is easy to visit the Somme battlefield. It is about two hours by car from Calais and the journey will be easier still when the new motorway from Boulogne to Amiens is finished. The main features of the battlefield are well-preserved and signposted.

SOURCES

Sources is a term used to describe any source of **evidence** used in the study of history at school. You will come across this term frequently.

> REMEMBER: sources must be used in context.

SOVIET UNION

-+- USSR

SPANISH CIVIL WAR

The Spanish Civil War began in 1936 and finished in 1939. It was fought between the Nationalists and the Republicans. Altogether about 700 000 people were killed in the fighting which destroyed large areas of Spain.

Why did the Spanish Civil War begin?

- The main reason for the Civil War was the formation of the Popular Front government after a General Election in February 1936. The Popular Front was made up of socialists, communists and **trade unions** and announced that it was going to reduce the power of the **Catholic** Church and redistribute land. It was also prepared to let Catalonia (north-east Spain) become independent.
- This led to a revolt by the Spanish Army in Morocco which spread to the mainland. The Army wanted to defend the Catholic Church and the rights of landowners and prevent the breakup of Spain.

The leader of the Nationalists was General Francisco Franco, who also became the leader of the Falange, the Spanish Fascist Party.

Why did the Nationalists win the Civil War?

- The Nationalists had the support of the Army and most wealthy Spaniards. They were backed by the Catholic Church which had a great deal of influence in country areas. As a result, Nationalist forces were much better supplied with money and weapons.
- **Hitler** sent the Condor Legion of about 10 000 men to Spain. The Germans used **Blitzkrieg** tactics, dive-bombers and tanks. **Mussolini** also sent aid: about 70 000 Italians altogether. These forces were the best trained and equipped.
- The Republicans received little support; Stalin sent financial aid and some materials, but no soldiers. Britain and France refused to intervene as it was an internal Spanish affair. The Republicans did receive support from foreign volunteers, the 'International Brigades', but they were untrained and of little use.
- The Republicans quarrelled, and even fought, among themselves. The Communists refused to support attempts to bring the war to an end.

Why did Hitler and Mussolini send aid to the Nationalists?

- Hitler wanted to practise Blitzkrieg and also to see how his soldiers stood up to battle conditions. In May 1937 the town of Guernica was destroyed by German bombing.
- Hitler also wanted to get Franco on his side and hoped that he would support Germany when the **Second World War** broke out. This would mean that France would be attacked from both sides.
- Mussolini wanted to make the Mediterranean an 'Italian Lake'. He thought that Spain would be a natural ally of Italy.

In fact Spain did not support either Germany or Italy. When war broke out in 1939, Franco refused to take part and Spain remained neutral. Franco believed that Spain had suffered so much during the Civil War that it could not become involved in another war so quickly.

General Franco ruled Spain as dictator until his death in 1975. After his death, Spain became a Monarchy with a constitution.

SELF-CHECK QUESTION 13

What were the names of the two sides in the Spanish Civil War?

SPITFIRE

The Spitfire was a fighter aircraft used during the **Battle of Britain** in August and September 1940. It became one of the most famous military aircraft of all time. There are still some flying to this day. In fact only one in five of the aircraft used by Fighter Command in 1940 were Spitfires. The great majority of fighters were **Hurricanes**.

The Spitfire was developed in the 1930s by R. J. Mitchell from the Supermarine. This was a seaplane which took part in the Schneider Trophy races, which were held around the Isle of Wight. The Supermarine won the race three times in succession.

Spitfires were very cramped and could be difficult to fly, but they were fast and highly manoeuvrable. They were the most successful fighters of the Battle of Britain. When Hermann Goering, the commander of the Luftwaffe, the German airforce, visited Calais in 1940, he asked if there was anything that was needed. One German pilot is supposed to have said, 'Give me a squadron of Spitfires.' Goering was not amused.

Spitfires were used almost throughout the war, being constantly developed. Only in the last months of the war were they replaced by faster, jet-engined aircraft.

STALINGRAD

The battle of Stalingrad was fought from November 1942 to February 1943, when the remnants of the German Sixth Army surrendered to the Red Army. It ended the attempt by **Hitler** to occupy the oilfields of the southern Soviet Union.

Hitler had ordered the Sixth Army to capture Stalingrad because it was named after the Soviet leader. The Germans broke into the city, but were then surrounded by the Red Army commanded by Marshal Zhukov. Hitler refused to allow General von Paulus to try to break out and instead tried to send supplies by air. After four months von Paulus surrendered: he had only half his army left. Of the 70 000 Germans who surrendered, only about 3000 returned to Germany after the war. The rest died in Soviet prison camps.

STALIN, JOSEPH VISSARIONOVICH

Joseph Stalin was born in 1879. His real name was Djugashvili, but he changed it to Stalin, which meant 'man of steel'. He came from Georgia in southern Russia and started to train to be a priest, but joined the **Bolshevik** party in about 1903. It is difficult to be certain about many aspects of Stalin's

life, because when he became ruler of the **USSR** after the death of **Lenin** he rewrote his own life story, changing it to make himself out to be more important than he actually was.

In 1917 Stalin was the editor of *Pravda*, the Bolshevik newspaper, and he played a minor role in the Bolshevik seizure of power. He resented the fact that Leon **Trotsky**, who had been a Menshevik until 1917, played a much more important role and appeared to be more highly thought of by Lenin.

Stalin gained the reputation of being rather boring and slow. He got the nickname the 'Grey Blur', because he did not speak much and kept himself in the background. When the job of General Secretary came up in 1922 he took it on after all the other leading Bolsheviks had turned it down. Stalin was determined that when Lenin died, he would become the new leader of Russia.

How did Stalin become the leader of Russia?

- Stalin used the post of General Secretary to find out about everything that was going on in the Party and to make sure that all posts were filled by his supporters. He managed to build up support for himself throughout Russia.
- In 1922 Lenin wrote a *Political Testament*. In it he said that Trotsky should become the leader of Russia after him and he also suggested that the other Bolshevik leaders should find a way of getting rid of Stalin. When the will was given to the Bolshevik leaders after Lenin's death in 1924, they decided not to publish it, because they did not want Trotsky to take over. He was unpopular and rude and arrogant. Stalin was saved.
- Between 1924 and 1929 Stalin managed to force most of the other leading Bolsheviks out of power. His main target was Trotsky, who left the Soviet Union (as Russia was now called) for good in 1929. The others, like Kamenev, Bukharin and Zinoviev, retired from their posts. Stalin used his support throughout the country to undermine his opponents and backed one against the other. By 1928 he had total control.

How did Stalin rule Russia?

- In 1928 Stalin ended Lenin's New Economic Policy and forced all peasants to join collective farms. They had to work together with others on large farms which were controlled by the State. Any peasants who objected were murdered. 5 000 000 richer peasants, Kulaks, were killed.
- Stalin began Five Year Plans. These were attempts to modernise industry. All firms and businesses were taken over and run by the State. Each business was told what and how much it had to produce each year.
- Stalin began to get rid of anyone whom he suspected of opposing him. These were the Purges from 1934 to 1938; at least 7 000 000 people disappeared. These included the Bolshevik leaders whom he had forced out in 1925 to 1927,

poets, scientists, managers of industries who did not meet their targets for production and millions of ordinary Soviet citizens, who often did not know what they had done to anger Stalin. The leading Bolsheviks were given 'Show Trials', where they were forced to confess to ridiculous crimes which they could not possibly have committed.

The revision of history

In the 1930s Stalin began to rewrite the history of Russia and the Soviet Union in the twentieth century. He made out that he was much more important than he really had been before he came to power. Textbooks and encyclopedias were destroyed or altered. Children in school had to paste over pages in their books with the new versions of what had happened.

Why did Stalin do this?

- He wanted to destroy the reputations of the other Bolshevik leaders. This would explain why he had put them on trial and had them executed. He picked on Trotsky, in particular, because Lenin had chosen him as his successor. He accused him of treason and said he had done nothing to help Russia. Stalin claimed he had been responsible for the successes in the Civil War in 1918 to 1920.

- He wanted to make out that he and Lenin had been very close friends and that only he knew what Lenin had intended to do in Russia. This would explain why Stalin had become the leader and would make Russians accept him. He had made sure that Lenin's body was preserved in a huge mausoleum in Red Square and encouraged Soviet citizens to visit it.

- He wanted to build himself up to be all-powerful and stop anyone opposing his ideas. This became known as the 'Cult of Personality'. Stalin made out that he was a superman who never made any mistakes.

How did Stalin change the Soviet Union?

On the face of it the results were impressive. Industrial production rose by about 400 per cent in the 1930s. Education and housing improved and women were given equality for the first time. The numbers of doctors rose and medical treatment improved.

The real facts were very different. The Five Year Plans increased production, but not quality. Fifty per cent of tractors broke down. Managers of plants cheated any way they could, because if they did not reach the target figures they might be shot.

Agricultural production fell as Kulaks destroyed their crops and animals, rather than hand them over. In 1932 to 1934 there was a massive famine which killed 5 000 000 people.

People who objected found themselves in slave-labour camps, called Gulags. These were often in Siberia or in northern Russia, where the weather in winter was very cold. Here they worked with little food for ten years or more. Many died from exhaustion.

Stalin made sure that everyone knew about his successes. He used many forms of **propaganda** to pass on the news, but his favourite form was **paintings** and sculptures. These appeared all over Russia. They showed Stalin meeting smiling people, opening factories and dams, and he always looked rather taller and fitter than he actually was.

Stalin and the *Second World War*

In August 1939 Stalin made a pact with **Hitler**: the **Nazi–Soviet Pact**. This put off war between the two countries until June 1941. But when the war began, Stalin was taken by surprise. The Germans advanced deep into the Soviet Union in a massive three-pronged attack, Operation Barbarossa. To win the war, Stalin ordered the countryside to be destroyed as the Red Army retreated. He also appealed to Soviet citizens to defend their motherland. He called the war the 'Great Patriotic War'. Whole factories, even towns, were moved further east out of the reach of the German Armies. The key turning-point was the battle of **Stalingrad**.

During the war the Soviet people suffered terribly, 26 000 000 died altogether. This made Stalin determined that this should never happen again. When he met the leaders of the other Allies at Teheran in 1943 and **Yalta** and **Potsdam** in 1945, he wanted to make sure there was a buffer-zone between him and Germany. It was this which led to the creation of the **Iron Curtain** and the **Cold War**.

Stalin's reputation

Stalin was the most successful of the dictators who came to power in the 1920s and 1930s. He died in March 1953 at the age of 73. He had ruled the Soviet Union for more than 25 years. When he died he was given a hero's burial and his body was placed alongside Lenin's in the mausoleum in Red Square. This did not last long, however. In 1956 Nikita **Khrushchev**, who succeeded Stalin, spoke out about the way Stalin had ruled and about the numbers of people who had died. Soon Stalin's body was removed from Lenin's tomb and the places which had been named after Stalin all had their names changed again. Stalingrad was renamed Volgograd.

With the collapse of the Soviet Union, Stalin's reputation has fallen even further. Historians have recently been able to read the records of all the Purges and the activities of Stalin's secret police. For all his success in helping to defeat Hitler, he was vicious, unpredictable and completely without any feeling for the millions of people he persecuted and killed. More than any other one person, he was responsible for the misery which many peoples in the Soviet Union and in the countries of eastern Europe have had to endure since the 1930s. He was also responsible for the distrust and hatred which developed into the Cold War in the years from 1945 to 1991. No one person has had so much influence on so many people's lives around the world this century.

SELF-CHECK QUESTION 14

What nickname did the other Bolsheviks give Stalin after the Revolution?

STEAM

Steam power played an important part in the *Industrial Revolution* in Britain. It meant that factories did not have to rely on water power and could be built away from rivers and streams. It also led to the development of a new form of transport.

How did steam power develop?

- In the late-seventeenth century Thomas Savery built a steam engine which Thomas *Newcomen* copied and improved. Newcomen's engine was used in mines to pump water.
- In 1763 James *Watt*, a scientific instrument-maker at Glasgow University, was asked to repair a model of Newcomen's engine. He found he could improve it by adding a separate condenser. This meant the cylinder did not have to cool down every time the steam was condensed. This made the engine faster and it used less fuel.
- In 1781 Watt improved his engine again, by adding the sun and planet gear. This made it possible for Watt's engine to turn a wheel. This engine was used to drive factory machinery and to winch trucks at coalmines.
- Later in the 1780s Watt also developed the centrifugal governor which automatically controlled the speed of the engine and parallel motion which reduced wear on the cylinder.
- One of Watt's workers, William Murdoch, built a model locomotive, but Watt refused to allow him to continue work on this. He did not believe that his engine could be used for transport.
- In 1801 Richard Trevithick produced his steam car, which he drove from Cornwall to London. He built a four-and-a-half mile railway in south Wales in 1804 and a semi-circular track in London in 1808. His engine, 'Catch-me-who-can', pulled passengers around the track for a fee of one shilling.

Richard Trevithick was the inventor of the locomotive, but now his name is hardly known at all. Why did other people get the credit?

- Trevithick was a poor businessman. In 1811 he left Britain for South America and only returned in 1827. He was also unable to make rails strong enough to support the locomotives. None of his railways were successful.
- These problems were solved by George *Stephenson*, who built the Stockton to Darlington railway in 1823–5 and the Liverpool to Manchester railway in 1825–9.

In the 1830s and 1840s railways were built to all parts of Britain. They not only helped to make the Industrial Revolution a great success, but also made it possible to hold the Great Exhibition. Not only did the parts to construct the Crystal Palace arrive by train, but so did most of the 6 000 000 visitors.

Steam locomotives were a great success story for Britain during the nineteenth century. They were sold all over the world and helped Britain gain the nickname 'the workshop of the world'.

How did railways change the lives of people in Britain?

- They made day trips to the seaside possible. Seaside resorts began to appear. Thomas Cook began his business in 1840. He made a fortune out of the Great Exhibition, offering a return ticket and entrance for one price.
- They enabled better, fresher and cheaper food to be sold in cities, especially milk and vegetables. They reduced the prices of manufactured goods by carrying them more quickly and in greater bulk.
- They made possible the setting up of a modern postal service, which started in 1840, because mail could now be delivered much more quickly.
- National newspapers also became more important as they could be carried around the country.
- It was railways which made possible the development of the FA cup in the 1870s and League football in the 1880s.
- People could now live further away from their work. Suburbs began to develop around big towns.

All in all railways made people's lives easier and offered greater variety of entertainment and an improved standard of living.

STEPHEN, KING, 1135–1154

Stephen was the nephew of *Henry I* and tried to seize the throne when his uncle died. Henry had made the barons accept his daughter, Matilda, as Queen before he died and this led to civil war from 1135 to 1153, when an agreement was reached that Matilda's son, *Henry II*, would become King when Stephen died.

During Stephen's reign there was a breakdown in law and order, which Henry II tried to put right.

- The Scots invaded and occupied northern England.
- The Welsh attacked across the border.
- Many barons built themselves castles without asking the King's permission.
- Church courts began to hear more and more cases involving clergy.

When Henry II came to the throne he was determined to tackle all these issues and this was one of the reasons why he clashed with Thomas à *Becket* when he became Archbishop of Canterbury in 1162.

STEPHENSON, GEORGE

George Stephenson was the most famous railway engineer of the early-nineteenth century. Like Trevithick and others, he began as an engineer in a coalmine. Here he saw stationary engines which were used to haul coal trucks along rails. This helped to give him his ideas for the development of railways and he built his first railway at the Killingworth Colliery in 1814.

The Stockton to Darlington railway which opened in 1825 was 11 miles long and was the first public railway anywhere in the world. Its success persuaded the merchants of Liverpool to ask Stephenson to build the Liverpool to Manchester railway, which he completed in 1829. This was opened in September 1830 with the Prime Minister, the Duke of **Wellington**, among the guests.

The Liverpool to Manchester railway was 30 miles long and carried passengers regularly on a fixed timetable. It also linked two major cities and proved that a railway could be built over difficult countryside, including a marsh and a range of hills.

Why was George Stephenson so successful?

- Stephenson was able to make strong rails and develop boilers which could withstand high pressure. At the Rainhill Trials in 1829, which were held to decide which locomotive would be used on the line, Stephenson's 'Rocket' easily beat all the opposition.
- Stephenson's son, Robert, was an excellent engineer. It was he who built the railway lines, while his father designed the trains. In 1839 he finished the London to Birmingham railway, which was more than 100 miles long.

George Stephenson's gauge of four feet eight-and-a-half inches became adopted as standard gauge. This meant that all railway lines were built to this size. The only exception were the lines built by Isambard Kingdom **Brunel**, which were seven feet and a quarter of an inch. But in 1846 standard gauge was adopted for all track. By 1892 all broad-gauge track had been converted.

George and Robert Stephenson became national figures. When the committee to advise Prince **Albert** about the Great Exhibition was chosen in 1848, Robert Stephenson was asked to be a member. Naturally he said yes.

STRESEMANN, GUSTAV

Gustav Stresemann became Chancellor of Germany in 1923 and then Foreign Minister the following year. He was the most important minister in the **Weimar Republic**. Stresemann was able to rescue Germany from the effects of **hyperinflation** in 1923 and get Germany going again in the 1920s.

How did Stresemann get Germany going again?

- In 1924 he borrowed money from the USA to help Germany pay **reparations**: the Dawes Plan.
- In 1925 he persuaded Belgium and France to agree not to occupy any parts of Germany: the Locarno Pacts.
- In 1926 he got Germany into the **League of Nations**, becoming a Permanent Member of the Council.

Stresemann died suddenly on 3 October 1929, just three weeks before the **Wall Street Crash** which led to the **Depression**.

SUDETENLAND

The Sudetenland formed part of the new country of Czechoslovakia at the Treaty of **Versailles**. About 3 000 000 German speakers lived in the Sudetenland and it was one of the territories which **Hitler** wanted to reoccupy in order to overthrow the Treaty. He demanded it in September 1938 and this led to the **Munich Crisis**.

SUFFRAGETTES

Suffragettes was the name given to members of the Women's Social and Political Union, which was set up in 1903. It was founded by Emmeline Pankhurst to try to gain the vote for women. Women had been campaigning for the vote for about 30 years; the National Union of Women's Suffrage Societies, led by Millicent Fawcett, had organised petitions, marches and meetings. Mrs Pankhurst wanted to step up the campaign and in 1905 the Suffragettes began to use new tactics. Christabel Pankhurst, Mrs Pankhurst's daughter, began shouting at a meeting during the General Election campaign and was arrested along with another Suffragette, Annie Barnes.

The Suffragettes were a small organisation made up mostly of **middle-class** or even upper-class women. Many were university students. One member was Lady Constance Lytton, who, when she was arrested, was released by the magistrate. She committed the same offence again and this time gave her name as Jane Wharton. She was sent to jail. In jail Suffragettes went on hunger strike and were force fed by a two-metre rubber tube which was pushed down their throat. At least one died when the tube went into her lungs.

The Suffragettes operated in small groups controlled from the centre. Over the next five years they chained themselves to railings outside the Houses of **Parliament**, interrupted debates in the House of **Commons**, staged demonstrations and gradually became more violent. When a proposal to give some women the vote was dropped in 1910, the Suffragettes stepped up their campaign. Pillar boxes and post offices were set alight, railway stations were burnt down, **paintings** were slashed, houses belonging to politicians were set alight and golf-course greens were destroyed with acid. At the Derby in 1913, Emily Wilding Davison ran on to the course and stood in front of the horse belonging to King **George V**. She was knocked down and died four days later.

Why did the Suffragettes take such violent actions?

- They believed that peaceful methods used by the **Suffragists** had got nowhere.
- The Prime Minister, Herbert Asquith, opposed votes for women: so they were trying to force him to change his mind.
- They were trying to show how committed they were to their cause.

But their actions had the opposite effect. Politicians refused to give in to violence. They said that if this was how women acted they did not deserve the vote.

When the **First World War** broke out the Suffragettes stopped all their actions and offered to help in the war effort. In 1915 Christabel Pankhurst organised a 'Right to Serve' campaign to try to persuade the government to let women play a more important role in the war. These changes helped to persuade the government to give the vote to women for the first time in 1918.

Were the Suffragettes successful?

- They certainly got people's attention and convinced the government that this was a matter that had to be taken seriously.
- They probably prevented any form of votes for women before 1914 because of their actions.
- The government, even Herbert Asquith, was very impressed by the way that women worked during the First World War.
- The government may have wanted to try to avoid a repeat of Suffragette activity after the war and so gave the vote to many women over the age of 30 in 1918.

SUFFRAGISTS

This was the name given to members of the National Union of Women's Suffrage Societies which was set up in 1897 by Millicent Fawcett. She wanted to unite all of the organisations which existed around the country into one big group so that they could try to put more pressure on the government. The NUWSS had about 500 000 members; many of them were men. It only used peaceful methods and had the support of a large number of MPs, particularly in the **Labour Party**.

What arguments did the Suffragists use?

- Women could vote in local council elections and for school boards and local health committees.
- Women could vote in Australia and New Zealand. Most of these women had come from Britain.
- Women had to pay taxes and one of the slogans in the eighteenth century had been 'no taxation without representation'. Women claimed they had to pay taxes but had no say in **Parliament**.
- Women could go to university and become doctors. If men could trust their lives to a woman, why not trust her to vote?
- Highly educated women could not vote, while uneducated men could.

Why were the Suffragists unsuccessful?

- Many men were simply prejudiced. They believed that women were incapable of taking serious decisions.
- Some people, including some women, believed that a woman's place was in the home, bringing up children.
- The Suffragettes made people claim that if that was how women acted they did not deserve the vote.
- Queen **Victoria** was opposed to women having the vote.

We shall never know whether the Suffragists would have succeeded. The main reason why women were given the vote was the First World War.

TAFF VALE CASE

The Taff Vale Case took place in 1901. The Taff Vale Railway Company sued the Amalgamated Society of Railway Servants, a trade union which represented many railway workers, for damages after a strike. The decision went against the trade union and it was forced to pay £51 000 in damages and costs.

Why was the Taff Vale Case important?

- Once a decision like this was reached, other judges would reach the same decision in similar cases.
- This meant that trade unions could no longer afford to go on strike: although strikes were legal, they would have to pay for all the costs of a strike.
- It persuaded many trade unions to support the Labour Party to try to get a law passed to cancel the effects of the decision.
- It was a very serious blow to trade unions and led to the **Labour Party** and the **Liberal Party** reaching an agreement in 1903: the Macdonald–Gladstone Pact. The Labour Party promised to support the Liberals at the next General Election if the Liberals would promise to pass a law which would state that trade unions could not be sued for damages after a strike.

The Liberals won the 1906 General Election with a huge majority and immediately passed the Trade Disputes Act. This said that trade unions could not be sued for damages after a strike.

SELF-CHECK QUESTION 15

Which group of workers was involved in the Taff Vale Case?

TELFORD, THOMAS

Thomas Telford was a Scottish engineer, who built roads, harbours, bridges and canals. Telford was born in 1757 and came to England in 1786 to become surveyor of the Shropshire roads. He built roads which had large blocks of stone in the foundations, more than 20 centimetres square. This made the roads very long-lasting, but also very expensive. Telford was therefore only employed to build major roads; his most famous was the London to Holyhead road, the modern A5, which was built to enable Irish MPs to get to and from London.

Telford also built the Caledonian Canal in Scotland and the Pont Cysyllte aqueduct in Wales. Altogether he built 1000 bridges and more than 1000 miles of roads. He also designed a single-span bridge to cross the Thames, although this was not built.

Unlike other roadbuilders at the time, Telford was a civil engineer and became the first President of the Institute of Engineers. He played a very important part in developing engineering in Britain, as well as in developing an efficient transport system.

TITHES

Tithes were taxes paid to the Church in medieval times. Each villager was supposed to give one-tenth of his income to help support the **parish** priest. The word tithe means tenth. The taxes would have been paid in kind: that is, in produce or animals. It would probably not have been one-tenth, but would have been measured in so many animals or measures of wheat, for example.

Tithes remained in force in **Ireland** until the nineteenth century and were very unpopular. Irish Catholics were forced to pay tithes to support the Church of Ireland, which was **Protestant**. Tithes were abolished in Ireland in 1869 when the Irish Church was disestablished. This meant that it was no longer linked to the State and therefore was not paid for by the people of Ireland.

TOJO

General Hideki Tojo was appointed Prime Minister of Japan in November 1941. This meant that the Army had great influence in Japan. He declared that the influence of Great Britain and the **USA** in Asia should be destroyed and ordered the attack on **Pearl Harbor** in December. Tojo was responsible for the war policy of Japan until he resigned in July 1944.

TOLPUDDLE MARTYRS

The Tolpuddle Martyrs were six Dorset labourers who were arrested and sentenced to transportation for seven years in 1834. They were sent to Australia, but returned to England after a public outcry.

Why were the Tolpuddle Martyrs treated so harshly?

- They were members of the agricultural section of Robert **Owen**'s Grand National Consolidated Trade Union, which had organised a general strike. **Trade unions** were legal, because the Combination Acts had been repealed in 1825. But the authorities were keen to crush the strike and the union.
- They had taken an oath when they had joined the union. It was illegal to take an oath in secret. This had been banned by the Secret Oaths Act of 1797, which had been passed to try to prevent any more mutinies in the Royal Navy. Two had broken out in 1797.
- There had been a great deal of unrest in the early 1830s. The local magistrates did not want any more trouble, so they used the Illegal Oaths Act to punish the six labourers as severely as possible.

When the case became known, there was a public outcry and the six were brought back to England.

They became heroes of the trade union movement. If you go to Tolpuddle today, you can still see the Martyrs' Oak.

> REMEMBER: the Tolpuddle Martyrs were sentenced for swearing an illegal oath.

TORIES

Tories was the name given to the supporters of **Charles II** and his brother James, Duke of York, during the **Exclusion Crisis** in the 1680s. They were MPs who supported the Crown and traditional ideas. Their opponents were called **Whigs**. Both words were terms of abuse.

In the eighteenth century, after the **Glorious Revolution**, when the Whigs invited **William** and **Mary** to become King and Queen, almost all politicians called themselves Whigs. To be a Tory meant that you were an MP who was not interested in public office. William **Pitt** the Younger, who became Prime Minister in 1783 at the age of 24, was a Tory, but the Tory Party was really created by Sir Robert **Peel** in the 1830s. He was the first politician to try to persuade people to vote for him by publishing a manifesto.

In the nineteenth century the Tories became known as the **Conservatives**. They believed they should conserve the traditional ideas of the Crown and the Church in Britain. The Conservative Prime Minister Benjamin **Disraeli** reorganised the party in the 1870s and tried to attract working people to the party for the first time; until then the Conservative Party had mostly been supported by landowners, farmers and the better-off in Britain.

TRADE UNIONS

Trade unions are organisations formed by workers to protect themselves and to bargain for better pay and conditions. Before the **Industrial Revolution**, when most workers worked in the **domestic system**, it was almost impossible to organise a trade union. But when **factories** were built, unions, or 'combinations', as they were called at first, began to develop.

Why did trade unions develop after the Industrial Revolution?

- In factories large numbers of workers worked together in one building, or in groups of buildings. They often lived closely together in rows of terraced houses. It was easy for them to meet and discuss.
- Early factories sometimes had very poor conditions and the owners could treat workers very badly. This gave workers something to complain about.
- Some factory owners, like Richard **Arkwright**, made their workers learn to read and write. This meant they could read newspapers and pamphlets for the first time.
- In the 1810s and 1820s there were many demands for reform of **Parliament** from factory

owners and the **middle class**. Workers became involved in this.
- In 1825 the Combination Acts were abolished. These had been passed in 1799, during the **French Revolutionary War**, to try to stop working men causing unrest.

The first trade unions were set up in cotton-spinning in 1826. This had been the first industry to move into factories in the 1770s. These early unions were united in Robert **Owen**'s Grand National Consolidated Trades Union set up in 1834, but this collapsed very quickly, especially when the **Tolpuddle Martyrs** were transported to Australia. For the next 17 years the Cooperative Movement and **Chartism** took over from trade unions.

Why did trade unions reappear in the 1850s?

- By the 1850s Britain had become very prosperous. It was the 'workshop of the world'. The workers who had helped to make Britain successful began to form 'societies'. The first was the Amalgamated Society of Engineers in 1851.
- The 'new model unions', as they became known, were formed by skilled and well-paid workers, who wanted to save money and protect themselves against sickness and unemployment. Other unions were formed by bricklayers, carpenters, joiners and boilermakers.

How were the new model unions different from earlier unions?

- They were formed by well-paid, skilled workers.
- They charged high membership fees: one shilling a week.
- They were less interested in striking than in protecting their workers against unemployment, sickness and providing for pensions.
- They had offices, usually in London, and paid officials who looked after their members' interests.

The new model unions received a setback when the **Hornby v Close** decision was made in 1867, but this was reversed in 1871 by **Gladstone**. However, to get the bill passed he had to ban peaceful picketing where a strike was taking place. Picketing was standing outside a factory holding banners and trying to persuade workers not to go in and work.

Disraeli made peaceful picketing legal in 1875. This was an example of Gladstone and Disraeli competing against each other. It was a sign that the two-party system of politics was beginning to work in earnest.

In the 1870s and 1880s the 'new unions' began to develop. These were unions of unskilled workers who were employed in the new industries which began to emerge in the late-nineteenth century. The first to be set up was the Agricultural Labourers Union in 1879, but the most successful were the Gasworkers and the Dockers, who went on strike in 1889 for the 'Dockers' Tanner' – sixpence an hour – and won.

In 1892, James Keir Hardie was elected as the first Labour MP, but at first many trade unions took little interest. They either supported the **Liberal Party**, or did not want to get involved in politics. Even when the Labour Representation Committee was set up in 1900, only 300 000 trade unionists joined in the first year. By the end of 1901, however, membership had jumped to over 1 800 000, because of the **Taff Vale Case**.

After Taff Vale almost all large unions supported the **Labour Party**, except for miners' MPs who remained separate until 1910. Unions gave money from their funds to the Labour Party so that the MPs could be paid. But in 1909 the **Osborne Judgment** made this illegal. In 1911 the Parliament Act gave MPs a salary of £400 a year and in 1913 trade unions were allowed to give money to political parties, providing that individual members had the right to withdraw their contributions from the donation.

When the **First World War** broke out in 1914, the links between the Labour Party and the trade unions were firmly established. This was to be one of the reasons for the fall in popularity of the Liberals after the war.

TRAFALGAR, BATTLE OF

The battle of Trafalgar was fought on 21 October 1805 and was the most important naval battle of the **Napoleonic War**. In 1804 **Napoleon** had begun to collect an Army near Boulogne for an invasion of Britain. His plan was to gain command of the Channel and then carry 150 000 French soldiers to Kent in barges: but to do that the French Navy had to escape from harbour and evade the Royal Navy.

At first the plan went well. Villeneuve, the Commander of the Toulon fleet, escaped and set sail for the West Indies; **Nelson** followed him, but found out that he was heading back to Europe. Nelson sent a message to warn the Admiralty and Villeneuve was forced to turn south and put into Cadiz. Here he was trapped by Nelson. Finally Napoleon ordered Villeneuve to sail out and fight.

Nelson divided his fleet into two sections and sailed straight at the enemy. This meant that the British ships were fired on for about an hour-and-a-half, but could not return fire. Finally the two sections of the British fleet crashed through the enemy fleet, cutting it into three parts. The British ships were able to capture 18 of the enemy, but Nelson was killed during the battle.

Why was the battle of Trafalgar important?

- It ended any threat of an invasion of Britain. Britain could now concentrate on trying to defeat Napoleon on the continent.
- The French fleet never left harbour again during the war. This gave Britain complete command of the sea and meant that the Army in the **Peninsular War** could be kept supplied.
- It forced Napoleon to turn east for more conquests. This led him to invade Russia, which proved disastrous.

TRANSPORTATION

Transportation was a punishment for criminals that was used in the eighteenth and nineteenth centuries. It meant that prisoners were sent to serve a sentence in a British colony overseas. The first colony was Georgia in America, which was founded in the 1730s. When the American colonies were lost in 1783, convicts were sent instead to Australia. The first were sent in 1788. The most famous convicts to be transported were the **Tolpuddle Martyrs** in 1834.

TRENCH WARFARE

Trench warfare developed on the Western Front during the **First World War** from 1914 to 1918.

Why did Trench warfare develop?

- After the defeat of the Germans at the battle of the Marne in September 1914, both armies 'raced to the sea' to try to outflank the other. When this failed, the German Army and the British and French Armies faced each other over 400 miles from the North Sea to Switzerland. Neither side could find a way through.
- Both sides had expected a war of movement, where cavalry would be the most important weapon. They had not studied the type of fighting which had taken place during the American Civil War from 1861 to 1865, where there had been fighting in trenches.
- Neither side realised that the machine guns and barbed wire made defence much easier than attack.

So the two sides built up lines of trenches, which became more and more complicated over the next four years.

TRIANGULAR TRADE

⊸⊷ *Slavery*

TROTSKY, LEON

Leon Trotsky played a very important role in the **Bolshevik** seizure of power in Russia in October 1917 and in the winning of the Civil War between 1918 and 1920. Until 1917 Trotsky was a Menshevik, a member of the 'minority' section of the Social Democratic Party, but in 1917 he became a Bolshevik. He was a key figure in the Petrograd Soviet, which ran the city from March to October 1917, and he was able to take advantage of the weakness of the provisional government after the Kornilov Revolt.

How did Trotsky help the Bolsheviks gain control of Russia?

- Trotsky became an important figure in the Petrograd Soviet, which had great influence in Russia in 1917.
- Trotsky planned the Bolshevik seizure of power in October 1917. He controlled the Bolshevik forces

and moved Army units which were loyal to the provisional government out of Petrograd.

● He negotiated the Treaty of Brest-Litovsk in March 1918, which brought to an end the war with Germany. This enabled the Bolsheviks to concentrate on the Civil War.

● During the Civil War from 1918 to 1920, Trotsky moved around from one battlefield to another, bringing supplies and urging the Red Army to fight. He had a special train in which he used to travel.

Trotsky was named by **Lenin** as his successor in his political will, which he wrote in December 1922. But after Lenin's death, Trotsky was forced out of Russia in 1929.

Why did this happen?

● Trotsky was not popular with the other Bolshevik leaders: he was arrogant and rude. They could not face the prospect of him being in control of Russia.

● Trotsky paid little attention to what was going on in Russia – he was more concerned with what was going on abroad. He did not realise that other leaders were building up support for themselves.

● Trotsky and **Stalin** disagreed over how the Bolsheviks should act after the Civil War. Trotsky wanted to try to start revolutions in foreign countries; Stalin wanted to build up communism in Russia first.

Stalin hated Trotsky and was determined to get rid of him. Why?

● Trotsky had been a Menshevik until September 1917. He had then become the second most important member of the Bolshevik Party and a close friend of Lenin.

● Trotsky was very popular with the people of Russia: he was a serious rival to Stalin.

● When Stalin found out what was in the political will, he realised he would have to get rid of Trotsky if he was to rule Russia.

After 1929 Trotsky lived abroad. He tried to overthrow Stalin, but it was impossible. He had to move from place to place, because Stalin wanted to kill him. In November 1940, he was murdered with an ice pick by Ramon Mercador, one of Stalin's agents who had worked his way into Trotsky's organisation.

✦ **Russian Revolution**

TRUMAN DOCTRINE

The Truman Doctrine was published by Harry Truman, the President of the **USA**, in March 1947. He offered to help any country that was being threatened either from within or from without its own borders.

Why was the Truman Doctrine published?

● Truman wanted to help the countries of Europe recover from the effects of the **Second World War**. He had seen the devastation the war had caused and he wanted the USA to play a part in recovery. The **Marshall Plan** was announced at the same time.

● Britain had just informed the US government that it could no longer afford to provide money for the Greek government, which was fighting communists. Truman agreed to help, but offered to support any other country at the same time.

● Truman was trying to stop any other countries in Europe becoming communist. The **Iron Curtain** had already cut Europe in two; he did not want that to go any further.

● Truman also hoped he might be able to persuade some of the countries of eastern Europe to break away from communism. Marshall Aid was also intended to help here.

● While the Truman Doctrine did not actually mention the Soviet Union, it was obvious that it was intended as a warning to Stalin that Truman was not going to let him get away with any more attempts to take control of Europe. Truman had said he was going to 'get tough with Russia': this was one example of his policy.

✦ **Cold War**

TURNPIKE TRUSTS

A turnpike trust was a method of improving roads. A group of local people, usually landowners, took over a stretch of road and charged tolls to people who wanted to use it. The money was used to repair and improve the road. They put a gate with spikes on it at each end of the stretch of road. This was often known as the 'toll-bar'. Beside the toll-bar was a cottage where the toll-keeper lived. Outside the cottage was a list of tolls. Travellers were charged according to the size of the vehicle, or the number of animals using the turnpike. Between 1700 and 1820 about 1000 trusts were set up.

What effects did turnpike trusts have on road transport?

● In some cases very little. Travellers, like Arthur Young in the 1770s, wrote that nothing had been done to improve the road. There was no way of forcing trusts to spend the money they raised. Some turnpikes were too short, or did not raise enough money.

● Most main roads were improved. The journey from London to Brighton by stagecoach was completed in one day for the first time in 1762. **Telford** built the London to Holyhead road in the 1820s. This was probably the greatest achievement of turnpike trusts.

● Turnpikes made coaching possible. In 1784 John Palmer started a mail coach service from London to Bath. By 1830 there were 3000 stagecoaches in Britain and 300 a day travelled along the Hyde Park Corner Turnpike.

● Turnpikes increased the speed of journeys. In 1700 the journey from London to York took seven days; by 1830 it took only 20 hours.

Turnpikes and coaches were very good at carrying people and mail. Stagecoaches could average 12 to 14 miles an hour, although galloping was not allowed as it could do too much damage to the road surface.

- Many turnpike trusts employed John **Macadam**, or used his methods of roadbuilding. In 1827 he became Surveyor-General of Turnpikes in Britain.

By then about one-sixth of all roads had been turnpiked: 20 000 miles out of 120 000.

But turnpikes could not compete with railways. They could carry people, mail and heavy goods at much greater speeds than stagecoaches. The golden age of turnpikes and coaching was the 1820s and 1830s. From the 1840s they gradually closed. The last disappeared in the 1890s.

UNDERSTANDING

To do well in history at school you will have to show understanding of the topics you have studied. Understanding is often connected with knowledge, but they are not the same. Knowledge can be gained by just memorising details. For example, you could look at any of the entries in this book and learn them off by heart. But that would not mean that you understood the topic.

To prove that you understood why something happened, you would have to be able to explain why things happened in a particular order; why one thing led to another; or why the event happened at a particular time.

For example, if you were asked the question, 'Why did Henry VIII divorce Catherine of Aragon in 1533?', you would need to look at a number of entries in this book – **Henry VIII**, **Catherine of Aragon**, the **Church of England**, **Henry VII**, Thomas **Cranmer**, **Mary** – and then try to put together the information from all of these in a way that made sense. If possible you would need to be able to explain Henry VIII's personal motives, as well as the concerns he had about England and the succession. Working like this will make the task harder, but more rewarding. It also means that you are much more likely to be able to remember what you have learned. If you just learn it off by heart, you will probably find that you forget the details very quickly.

UNION, ACT OF

This is the name given to the Acts of Parliament which have united England and **Wales** (1536), England and **Scotland** (1707) and England and **Ireland** (1800).

UNION OF SOVIET AND SOCIALIST REPUBLICS

The USSR was the name by which Russia was known from 1924 to 1991. It is often abbreviated to the Soviet Union. The name was meant to suggest that there were separate republics within the USSR which were equals; after the **Second World War** there were 15 altogether. But in fact this was not true. The USSR was dominated by Russia, which contained half the population of the USSR and about two-thirds of the land area. All appointments in the other republics were made from Moscow and opposition to Russia was suppressed. For example, Nikita **Khrushchev**, who succeeded **Stalin**, had spent a great deal of time in the Ukraine, crushing opposition to Russia.

After the Second World War three more republics were added to the USSR: Lithuania, Latvia and Estonia. These had all been independent countries before the war but had been liberated by the Red Army in 1944–5. As they had been Russian in the nineteenth century, Stalin simply kept them under Soviet control. These were the first of the Soviet Republics to revolt when the USSR began to break up in the late-1980s.

To be accurate, you should use the term Russia about events before 1924 and USSR or Soviet Union from 1924 to 1991. However, you will find that some history books get this wrong, perhaps even some of the ones you are using at school.

UNITED NATIONS ORGANISATION

The United Nations Organisation was set up at the end of the **Second World War**. Fifty countries met at San Francisco in 1945 to plan the organisation and the first meeting took place in London in January 1946. In April 1946 the **League of Nations** was closed and all of its assets were transferred to the UN.

In fact the term 'United Nations' had been in use for some time. Franklin **Roosevelt**, the US President, had invented it to describe the alliance of nations fighting the Axis powers during the war. In 1943 and 1944 a number of UN organisations were set up to plan for reconstruction after the war.

How is the United Nations organised?

- The **General Assembly** has representatives from all member countries: it holds discussions and votes on proposals. Each country has one vote.
- The **Security Council** has five permanent members: Russia, the USA, France, China and Britain, and ten temporary members. This meets whenever there is a serious issue to deal with, it can send observers or armed forces to any part of the world, or order member countries to stop fighting, or order members to stop trading with another country. All decisions have to be agreed by all the permanent members of the Security Council.
- The **Secretariat** does all the day-to-day work of the UN and carries out the decisions of the Security Council. It is headed by the Secretary-General.
- The **International Court of Justice** has 15 judges from different countries and decides on legal disputes between members.
- There are also many **agencies**, such as the Food and Agriculture Organisation (FAO), the World Health Organisation (WHO) and the United Nations Commission of Refugees (UNCR).

Why was the United Nations set up?

- The United Nations was based on the **Atlantic Charter**, which was drawn up by Franklin **Roosevelt** and Winston **Churchill** in August 1941.

Roosevelt was determined that the cooperation of the Allies should continue after the war. **Stalin**, the leader of the Soviet Union, and Churchill both agreed that their countries would join the UN.

The aims of the UN were given in its charter: to maintain international peace; to develop friendly relations between nations; to solve international problems by cooperation; and to encourage respect for human rights.

In what ways is the UN different from the League of Nations?

The USA and the USSR both joined the UN. Neither had joined the League. This gave the UN much more authority.

Almost all the nations of the world have joined the UN. There are now nearly 200 members. The League usually had less than 50 members and many countries left.

The UN has an Army. It can ask for forces from members and they serve in UN uniforms. They wear light blue hats and badges. Their equipment is also painted light blue or white. This is meant to make them stand out and show they are not taking sides.

The Secretary-General of the UN is always chosen from a small country: this helps it to appear neutral. The first Secretary of the League was British and this made people think that the League represented the big European countries.

In 1952 the UN moved to a site in New York. The USA gave the land to the UN.

But the UN has not been without problems

Some members do not pay membership fees.

Members ignore decisions of the Security Council.

UN peacekeeping forces are distrusted and accused of taking sides.

Food supplied for famine relief goes missing, or falls into the hands of the wrong people.

Decisions are blocked by one of the permanent members of the Security Council.

But overall, the countries of the world seem to believe that it is better to keep on talking than to stop, so the number of members keeps growing.

UNITED NATIONS UNIVERSAL DECLARATION OF HUMAN RIGHTS

In December 1948 the General Assembly of the United Nations agreed the Universal Declaration of Human Rights. This set out the way that all people should be treated in every country in the world. For example:

All human beings are born free and equal.

Everyone has the right to life, liberty and security.

No one shall be tortured.

Everyone has the right to freedom of thought and religion.

The UN hoped that all countries would follow the Declaration, but although the General Assembly accepted it, it has proved very difficult to put it into practice.

UNITED STATES OF AMERICA

The USA grew out of the 13 colonies which broke away from Britain in 1783. The Constitution was drawn up in 1787 and the first President, George Washington, was elected in 1789.

How is the USA governed?

The Federal Government is headed by the **President**, who is elected every four years and can be re-elected once. The only exception to this was Franklin **Roosevelt**, who was elected four times. The President governs the country and is Commander-in-Chief of the armed forces.

Most decisions of the President have to be agreed by **Congress**, the American **Parliament**. There are two houses, the House of Representatives and the Senate. In the House of Representatives each State has one representative for every four hundred thousand voters. In the Senate, each State has two senators. This is intended to give the bigger States more say in the House, but protect the smaller States in the Senate. In 1919 President **Woodrow Wilson** put forward the idea of the **League of Nations** at the Peace Conference at **Versailles**, but Congress would not agree to US membership of the League. He also signed the Treaty of Versailles, but Congress refused to back him. The USA never joined the League and never ratified the Treaty of Versailles.

The **Supreme Court** decides whether or not the President is acting constitutionally. The USA has a written constitution, which sets out the rights of ordinary citizens and each section of the government. The nine judges of the Supreme Court, headed by the Chief Justice, have the job of looking at the actions of the President and can declare them illegal.

Each **State** has its own State Congress and controls law and order, education and transport. States do not like the President or the Federal Government interfering in their affairs.

VERDUN, THE BATTLE OF

The battle of Verdun was fought from February to December 1916 during the *First World War*. It was an attack by the German Army on the city of Verdun in eastern France. The Germans were trying to 'bleed France dry'.

Why did the Germans attack Verdun?

- Verdun was in a salient, which was a place where the French front line jutted out and was surrounded on three sides by the German forces.
- It was very difficult to send supplies to the city as there was only one road in. This became known as the 'sacred way' (la voie sacrée).
- The French had removed many of the guns from the fortresses which defended Verdun to get ready for the battle of the *Somme*.
- The Germans believed that the French Army would defend Verdun to the last man and they hoped to cause massive casualties.
- The Germans believed that if Verdun fell, it would destroy French morale.

At first the battle went very well for the Germans: some of the forts were captured and the French found it very difficult to keep Verdun supplied. There was a stream of lorries and men going up the sacred way. But the Germans also suffered very heavy casualties and eventually the French counter-attacked and drove the Germans back. As in many battles of the First World War, both sides ended up more or less where they had started. Both sides suffered more than half a million casualties.

One effect of the battle was that the French were unable to provide as many soldiers for the battle of the *Somme*. They had originally promised 40 divisions, but were only able to give 16. This made Haig's task more difficult.

VERSAILLES, THE TREATY OF

The Treaty of Versailles was signed on 28 June 1919, exactly five years, almost to the minute, after the assassination of the Archduke *Franz Ferdinand*. The main leaders were Georges Clemenceau, the Prime Minister of France, David *Lloyd George*, the Prime Minister of Britain, and *Woodrow Wilson*, the President of the USA. The fourth leader at the beginning of the conference was Orlando Vittorio, the Prime Minister of Italy, but he left when he discovered that promises made to give Italy land on the Adriatic coast were not going to be kept.

What did each of the leaders try to achieve?

Clemenceau wanted revenge for all that had happened to France in the four years of fighting and for the loss of Alsace-Lorraine in 1871. He wanted Germany to be made to pay and made to suffer and he wanted France to be completely protected from any possibility of an attack by Germany in the future. To achieve this, Clemenceau demanded that the Rhineland should be handed over to France. That would stop any more attacks.

Woodrow Wilson wanted a just peace. He believed that the war had partly been caused by the way the Powers had acted in the years before. He came to Europe in December 1918 with his 'Fourteen Points'. These suggested ways of trying to avoid wars in the future. As the *USA* had hardly been affected by the fighting, he was not interested in revenge.

Lloyd George found himself in between the other two. In Britain, people wanted to 'make Germany pay' and 'squeeze her until the pips squeaked', but Lloyd George believed this would only lead to more trouble in the future. He wanted Germany to be allowed to recover after the war, so he opposed Clemenceau's demand for the *Rhineland*.

The terms of the Treaty

- **Land:** Germany lost about 10 per cent of her land. *Alsace-Lorraine* was given back to France. The Polish Corridor was created to give the new country of Poland a way out to the Baltic and Germany also lost land to Belgium, Denmark and Czechoslovakia.
- **Colonies:** all German colonies were taken away and handed to Britain and France to look after until they were ready for independence.
- **Armed forces:** the German Army was reduced to 100 000 men and conscription was banned. The Navy was reduced to six ships and submarines were banned; the Airforce was to be completely destroyed.
- ***Rhineland*:** this was to be demilitarised: no soldiers or military equipment were to be kept within 30 miles of the east bank of the river. The Allies would occupy it for 15 years.
- **Saar:** this was to be occupied for 15 years and France would be able to mine coal in it during that time.
- ***Reparations*:** Germany was to pay for the damage caused by the war. The full cost would be worked out by 1921; it eventually came to £6 600 000 000. This would be paid for the rest of the twentieth century.
- **War Guilt:** Germany was to accept the blame for the war, alone.

The Treaty was very unpopular in Germany. Why?

- The Germans had expected they would be treated much more leniently because they had heard about Woodrow Wilson's 'Fourteen Points'.

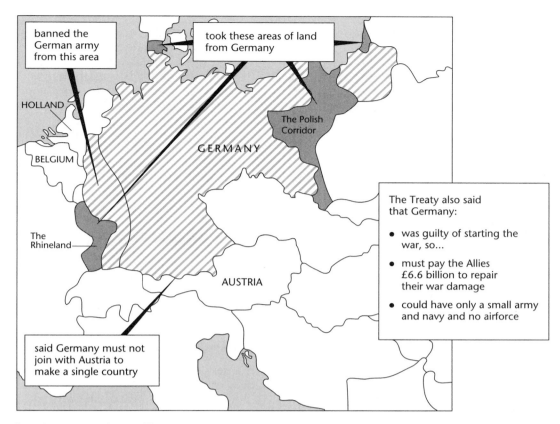

banned the German army from this area

took these areas of land from Germany

HOLLAND

BELGIUM

The Polish Corridor

GERMANY

The Rhineland

AUSTRIA

The Treaty also said that Germany:

- was guilty of starting the war, so...
- must pay the Allies £6.6 billion to repair their war damage
- could have only a small army and navy and no airforce

said Germany must not join with Austria to make a single country

Germany after the Treaty of Versailles

- The German government had not been allowed to take part in the negotiations; it was presented with the final version and told to sign it or else.

- Large areas of Germany with German-speaking populations were taken away. The Polish Corridor cut Germany into two sections. East Prussia was surrounded by Poland.

- The Reparations were very severe and the German government did not believe it would be able to pay. In fact, it managed one year's instalment then gave up.

- The War Guilt clause was regarded as very unfair. The war had been sparked off by the murder of an Austrian by a Serb; Germany had only been one of the countries which became involved. Many Germans believed they were being used as scapegoats for all the other countries.

- Many Germans did not believe that Germany had actually been defeated. They had been told that the war was being fought to protect Germany and the country was never invaded.

What were the effects of the Treaty?

- There was opposition to the terms of the Treaty almost immediately. From 1919 to 1923, there was a series of attempted revolutions in Germany, some by communists, who hoped to take advantage of the situation and follow the example of Russia; others by right-wing nationalists, who blamed the government for accepting the Treaty and tried to overthrow it.

The most famous rebellion was the **Beer Hall Putsch** led by **Hitler** in Munich in November 1923.

- When the **Depression** hit Germany after 1929, Hitler was able to use the Treaty as a way of gaining support. He talked about the 'Diktat' and the 'stab in the back'; as the people of Germany became more and more desperate, they became more and more ready to listen to Hitler's promises to do away with the Treaty.

- British and French politicians in the 1930s came to believe that the Treaty had been too harsh. When Hitler began to break the Treaty from 1935 onwards, they did little about it. They believed that Hitler was justified and should be allowed to get away with it.

The Treaty of Versailles was one of the long-term causes of the **Second World War**.

VICTORIA, QUEEN, 1837–1901 ◼

Queen Victoria came to the throne in June 1837, when her uncle **William IV** died. She was 18. She died in January 1901, when she had been Queen for 63½ years.

Why was her reign so important?

- One obvious reason was its length. She outlived most of her Prime Ministers and her servants. She reigned longer than any other British Monarch and only two European Monarchs have reigned longer: Louis XIV of France and Franz Joseph II of Austria-Hungary. When she died, nobody could

- remember what the coronation service was like, so it had to be reinvented.
- During Victoria's reign, Britain became the most powerful country in the world. The **Industrial Revolution** was completed and Britain became the 'workshop of the world'. The Great Exhibition of 1851 showed how powerful and dominant Britain was. The Royal Navy controlled the seas and people talked about a 'Pax Britannica'. This was a reference to the 'Pax Romana' (Roman Peace) during the Roman Empire. The British **Empire** reached its peak and many people compared it to the Roman Empire.
- Queen Victoria had a very large family: nine children altogether. Most of them married members of other European royal families, which made Victoria a very influential figure. When she had a birthday party it would be attended by Nicholas II, the Tsar of Russia, who was married to her grand-daughter; Kaiser **Wilhelm II** of Germany, who was her grandson; and members of the Norwegian, Danish, Romanian and Spanish royal families. While she lived, a major European war was unlikely. When Kaiser Wilhelm II heard she was dying, he rushed across Europe to be by her bedside when she died on 22 January 1901.

The reign of Queen Victoria fell into three parts

- **1837 to 1861:** during these years she took a keen interest in politics, which became stronger after her marriage to **Albert**, the Prince Consort in 1840. She appeared regularly in public and visited the Great Exhibition 23 times. She was encouraged to do these things by her husband who believed they should try to improve the lives of the people of Britain in as many ways as possible.
- **1861 to the 1880s:** after the death of Albert in 1861, Queen Victoria went into mourning and did

not appear in public for more than 20 years. She always dressed in black and took little interest in events in Britain. By the early 1880s some people were openly criticising her and suggesting that the Monarchy should be abolished.

- **1880s to 1901:** from the mid-1880s Queen Victoria began to appear in public once again, still dressed in black, and she became more and more popular. Her golden jubilee was celebrated in 1887 and her diamond jubilee in 1897. This was the first occasion that a member of the royal family was filmed. By the time she died in 1901 Queen Victoria was one of the most popular British Monarchs ever.

VICTORIANS

Only during two reigns have the British people been known by the name of the Monarch. The first time was the reign of Queen **Elizabeth I**; the second and the much more important was the reign of Queen **Victoria**.

What were the Victorians like?

It is very difficult and dangerous to generalise; only the wealthy and famous were really Victorians, but they were also the most influential and the most powerful.

- Victorians believed that Britain was the most important and the best country in the world. They tried to make other countries, especially in the Empire, use British methods of education, justice and government.
- They conquered and occupied large parts of the world, especially in Africa, and named them after themselves and their Queen: the State of Victoria in Australia, the Victoria Falls in Africa and the city of Victoria in Canada.
- Victorians travelled the world, exploring, converting people to Christianity, building roads,

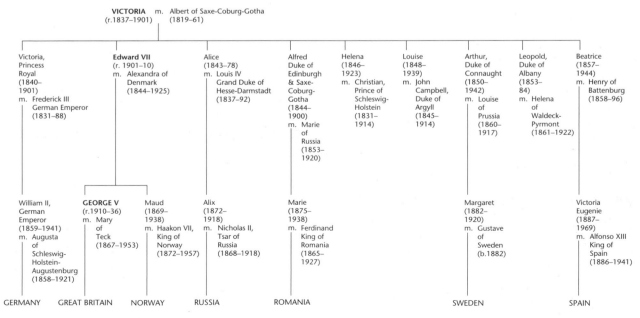

railways, schools and hospitals. They believed they had the duty to give the benefits of British civilisation to other peoples around the world.

In the nineteenth and early-twentieth centuries it was taken for granted that the Victorians were right. Today people have different views.

Why have ideas about the Victorians changed?

- The Victorians used force to compel other people to accept their views. African nations were crushed and their cultures destroyed.

- The Victorians could be very intolerant, even racist. They did not see other peoples as equals.

- Colonies were sometimes exploited: Indians were forced to buy **cotton** from Britain, instead of making it themselves.

But Britain's former colonies, almost without exception, remain on good terms with Britain. They are almost all members of the **Commonwealth**; South Africa has rejoined and Namibia has also joined, although it was not really a colony. As in many cases, people remember the good things and forget the bad.

WALES

The Welsh are descended from the British, the original inhabitants of Britain when the Romans arrived. They were driven back into Wales by the Anglo-Saxons and were ruled by several Princes.

Wales and England in the eleventh and twelfth centuries

When **William** the Conqueror landed in England in 1066, he did not try to conquer Wales. He built a line of castles along the Welsh border and gave land along the border to barons whom he could trust. This was meant to protect England from attacks by the Welsh. These barons became known as the Marcher Lords because the borders were called the Marches.

During the reign of **Stephen** (1135–1154) the Welsh began to raid England because the Marcher Lords were involved in the civil wars between Stephen and Matilda. When **Henry II** became King he sent armies into Wales and encouraged the Marcher Lords to occupy more land. By the end of the century most of south Wales was occupied by Norman barons.

The rest of Wales was controlled by a number of Princes. In the twelfth century the most powerful was Rhys ap Gruffydd, Prince of Deheubarth. When he died in 1197, Llywelyn ap Iorwerth, King of Gwynedd, united his kingdom with Powys and Deheubarth. He called himself Prince of North Wales. His grandson, Llywelyn ap Gruffydd, called himself Prince of Wales. This title was recognised by **Henry III** in 1267.

Wales during the reign of *Edward I*

When Henry III's son, Edward I, became King in 1272, he was determined to bring Wales under English control again. He invaded Wales and defeated Llywelyn ap Gruffydd in 1277. When Llywelyn rebelled in 1282, Edward invaded again and Llywelyn was killed. Edward built castles in north Wales to control the area. Caernarfon, Conwy, Beaumaris, Harlech and others were meant to overawe the Welsh.

In 1284 the **Statute of Wales** divided the country into three parts:

- the area conquered by Edward I in north and west Wales was divided into shires which were controlled by **sheriffs**. This became known as the Principality
- in Powys the Welsh rulers were allowed to retain control, but were forced to become feudal barons under Edward

- the eastern borders were still occupied by Marcher Lords.

In the Principality English law was used, but elsewhere the barons often used Welsh law which was different. This situation lasted until the reign of *Henry VIII*.

Owain Glyn Dwr

For the next 100 years Wales was under English control, but in 1400 Owain Glyn Dwr led a revolt against *Henry IV*. By 1403 he controlled most of the country and even called a Welsh *Parliament*. But Henry IV was too powerful and by 1410 Owain Glyn Dwr was on the run and he died in hiding.

England and Wales in the reign of Henry VIII

The Acts of **Union** of England and Wales were passed in 1536 and 1543. The first was the more important and was the work of Thomas **Cromwell**.

- All of Wales was divided into shires.
- Welsh law was abolished and replaced by English law.
- The Welsh were allowed to send MPs to Parliament at Westminster.
- The Marcher Lordships were almost destroyed.
- *Justices of the Peace* were appointed for Wales. These were all Welsh, and law courts were set up to cover the whole country.
- The use of the Welsh language was protected.

Since 1543 Wales has been part of Britain and later the United Kingdom. There have been no rebellions, as there were in Scotland and Ireland in the seventeenth and eighteenth centuries. Wales played a very important part in the *Industrial Revolution*: one of the most famous ironworks in the country was built by Richard Crawshay at Cyfarthfa in south Wales.

During the *Depression* in the 1930s, south Wales suffered very badly. Merthyr was the second worst hit town in the country; only Jarrow had a higher rate of unemployment.

WALL STREET CRASH

The Wall Street Crash was the cause of the *Depression* which hit the *USA* in October 1929 and then spread to most countries in the world. On 24 October and again on 29 October, share prices on Wall Street, the New York stock exchange, fell dramatically.

Why did the Wall Street Crash happen?

- In the 1920s share prices in the USA rose year after year. Many Americans believed they could make money very easily by investing in shares.
- Share prices went up because companies encouraged people to go on buying on credit. Hire purchase was easily available, but few people realised it was very dangerous to go on selling on credit. Eventually people would not be able to make the repayments.

- The selling and buying of shares was almost uncontrolled in the USA. Many people bought shares without realising they could lose all their money.
- Some companies in which people invested their money were bogus; they simply did not exist. Other companies did not tell the truth. It was difficult for investors to know what they were buying.
- The US government did not believe it had any responsibility for what was happening. The Presidents in the 1920s, Warren Harding and Calvin Coolidge, believed it was not their job to interfere.

Some Americans predicted that a crash was coming, but very few people took them seriously. Most people believed that the USA was so wealthy and so powerful that it could not happen.

WARSAW PACT

The Warsaw Pact was a military alliance of the communist countries of eastern Europe. It was the communist equivalent of **NATO**. The Pact was set up in 1955, because in that year the Federal Republic of Germany (**West Germany**) was allowed to join NATO. The **USSR** was very concerned at this, as Germany had invaded Russia twice in the twentieth century. The Warsaw Pact was an attempt to protect the USSR by drawing the countries of eastern Europe closer together.

The Warsaw Pact lasted until the late 1980s, when it collapsed.

WARS OF THE ROSES

The Wars of the Roses took place from the 1450s to the 1480s and were fought between the Houses of **York** and **Lancaster** to decide which House should rule England. The wars began in 1455 and were brought on by the insanity of **Henry VI**. In 1455 the Yorkists defeated the Royal Army at St Albans and then won the battle of Northampton in 1460. **Richard** of York was declared the heir of Henry VI.

Later in 1460, however, Richard of York was defeated and killed by Margaret of Anjou, the wife of Henry VI. Her success did not last long. In 1461, Edward, the son of Richard of York, defeated the Lancastrians twice and became King **Edward IV**. Henry VI was captured and imprisoned.

From 1469 to 1471, the Earl of Warwick (Warwick the Kingmaker) tried to put Henry VI back on the throne, but the Lancastrians were defeated at Stamford in 1470 and then at Barnet and Tewkesbury in 1471. Henry VI was almost certainly murdered in the Tower in the same year.

In 1485, Henry, Earl of Richmond, defeated **Richard III** at the battle of Bosworth Field. This brought the Wars of the Roses to an end. Henry became **Henry VII** and created the Tudor rose out of the red and white roses of Lancaster and York.

What effects did the Wars of the Roses have?

- On the people of England the wars had very little effect. The battles were fought between the great families of England and their private armies; most of the country and most of the population were not involved.
- The wars convinced Henry VII that he must avoid the same thing happening again at all costs. He called himself 'Tudor', rather than Lancaster or York, and got rid of anybody who stood in his way. He married Elizabeth of York, the daughter of Edward IV.
- The descendants of most of the people who had taken part in the wars were eliminated. The son of the Earl of Warwick was executed. Leaders of revolts against Henry VII were executed.
- Henry VII forced the nobles to give up their private armies, which had been one cause of the trouble. In future only the King could keep a soldier in uniform in England.

WATERLOO

Waterloo was the last battle of the **Napoleonic War**. It was fought on 18 June 1815, between the Allied Army of 65 000 (about 29 000 British), commanded by **Wellington** and the French army of **Napoleon**, which numbered 70 000.

The battle was fought from about 12.00 pm until the evening. Wellington's plan was to hold on until the Prussian army commanded by Marshal Blucher arrived, so he made no attempt to attack the French. He took up position on a long, low ridge, with three farmhouses in front of it. When the French attacked, Wellington ordered his infantry to form squares over the top of the ridge, out of sight of the French.

Although one of the farmhouses was captured, the Allied Army held on until the Prussians arrived at about 7.00 pm. At that point Wellington ordered the Allied Army to advance. The French Army broke and ran. Napoleon fled and surrendered to the captain of a British warship.

WATER POWER

Water power played a very important part in the development of the **Industrial Revolution**. When Richard **Arkwright** produced his spinning frame, it was too heavy to be operated by hand. He tried at first to use two horses to work the machine, but this was too unreliable. The horses walked at different speeds and they needed to be fed and changed from time to time; a better form of power was needed. Water was the answer.

How did water power change the textile industries?

- Water power meant that **factories** needed to be built to house spinning machines. Water could be collected behind dams and used to drive water wheels.
- But factories had to be built near to a supply of flowing water. The Pennine hillsides were perfect. Many of the earliest factories were built in remote areas on the Pennines. These developed into the new industrial towns – places like Keighley and Blackburn.

● But water power had its disadvantages. Water could be unreliable. In the winter it could freeze and in the summer it could dry up. Dams could collapse and factories could be flooded.

While water power served its purpose, it was not the answer. When James **Watt** developed rotary motion, factories moved from the Pennine hillsides to the centres of the new towns.

WATT, JAMES

James Watt was a very important figure in the development of **steam** power in the eighteenth century. In 1763, while he was working at Glasgow University, he was asked to repair a model of **Newcomen**'s engine. In 1765 he produced an improved version, with a separate condenser and a valve box. This meant the engine worked much quicker and used far less fuel.

In the 1770s Watt went into partnership with Matthew Boulton and began to build very reliable engines. In 1781 he developed the 'Sun and Planet' gear, which enabled his engines to turn a wheel and he later added 'Parallel Motion' and the 'centrifugal Governor'. These improvements led to steam power being used in almost all textile factories.

After these inventions Watt showed no further interest in developing steam power. He did not believe that steam could be used for transport and he prevented his workers from experimenting with locomotives and steamboats.

WEDGWOOD, JOSIAH

Josiah Wedgwood was a member of a family which made pottery in the eighteenth century. When **canals** were built by the Duke of Bridgwater and James Brindley, Wedgwood realised how they could help his business in the west Midlands. Canals could bring supplies of china clay from Cornwall and carry his pottery away from his **factories**. He decided to invest money in canals and helped Brindley complete his 'Grand Cross'. The result helped Wedgwood's business considerably. He found that breakages were reduced by two-thirds when his pottery was carried by canal.

WEIMAR REPUBLIC

The Weimar Republic was the name given to Germany in the years from 1919 to 1933. It got the name because the government of Germany was moved to the town of Weimar from Berlin to escape the unrest and violence which broke out there.

WELFARE STATE

The Welfare State is the system of benefits and support, which has developed this century, and which is intended to protect the people of Great Britain from the effects of unemployment, sickness, poverty and old age. The two main parts of the Welfare State are National Insurance and the National Health Service.

The Welfare State was begun by the **Liberal Reforms** before the **First World War** and was continued after the **Second World War** by the Labour government of 1945 to 1950. It put into practice the ideas put forward in the **Beveridge** Report of 1942.

WELLINGTON, THE DUKE OF

The Duke of Wellington was the most successful Commander of the British Army during the **Napoleonic War**. He commanded the British Army during the **Peninsular War** and the Allied Army at **Waterloo**. After Waterloo he retired from the Army and entered politics. He became the leader of the **Tory** Party and was Prime Minister from 1828 to 1830.

Wellington, then Sir Arthur Wellesley, took command of the army in the **Peninsular War** in 1808. He realised he could not defeat the French in a major battle so he used hit-and-run tactics. Each year he advanced into Portugal and Spain and attacked parts of the French Army. Each winter he retreated to Lisbon and hid behind the lines of Torres Vedras, which he had constructed around the city. This lasted until 1813, when he was strong enough to drive the French back across Spain. The following year he invaded southern France.

After the battle of Waterloo, Wellington retired. He had been sickened by the bloodshed on the battlefield and he was determined to avoid any repeat. When violence seemed likely in Ireland in 1828 after Daniel **O'Connell** was elected MP for County Clare, he gave in and agreed to **Catholic** emancipation, although he did not support it.

As a politician Wellington opposed most of the reforms which were introduced in the first half of the nineteenth century. As well as Catholic emancipation, he was also against the Great **Reform** Act and the Repeal of the **Corn Laws**. He represented a very right-wing section of the Tory Party.

Wellington is supposed to have solved a major problem just before the opening of the Great Exhibition. There were birds nesting in the trees in the centre of the Crystal Palace and no one could get them out. The story goes that Queen **Victoria** mentioned the problem to Wellington, who said 'use sparrowhawks, ma'am'. They did the trick by catching the birds and the Great Exhibition opened on time.

Wellington died in 1852 and was buried in St Paul's Cathedral. He was given a State funeral. The next person to be given a State funeral who was not a member of the royal family was Sir Winston **Churchill** in 1965.

WEST BERLIN

When the Allies met at Potsdam to decide how to govern Germany at the end of the **Second World War**, they agreed to divide the country into four zones, one each for the **USA**, the **USSR**, Britain and France. Berlin, the capital of Germany, was inside the Soviet zone, so this was also divided into four sectors. West Berlin was formed by the US, French and British sectors in Berlin from 1945 to 1991. West Berlin was very awkward for the Soviet Union and East Germany. It allowed people behind the **Iron Curtain** an opportunity to see what life was like in the West.

At first travel between the four sectors in Berlin was easy; people could live in one sector and work in another. But after the **Berlin Blockade** many East Germans began to try to escape from the Soviet zone to the other three. In 1961, Nikita **Khrushchev**, the Soviet Prime Minister, tried to stop people escaping by building the **Berlin Wall**. This divided West Berlin from East Berlin.

West Berlin and East Berlin were reunited when the Berlin Wall was knocked down in 1990.

WEST GERMANY

At the **Yalta** Conference in 1945, the Allies decided to occupy Germany and divide it into four zones. They agreed to unite the four zones in the future, but this proved more and more impossible. In 1947 the British and US zones were joined together in 'Bizonia' and the French zone was added in 1948. After the **Berlin Blockade** the Allies decided to create the Federal Republic of Germany, with its capital at Bonn in the Rhineland. This became known as West Germany.

West Germany existed as a separate country from 1949 to 1990. It became a member of the **UN** and was admitted to **NATO** in 1955, although it was never allowed to have nuclear weapons. The Allies continued to occupy it and there are still British forces in Germany today.

WHIG REFORMS

The Whig Reforms were a series of Acts of **Parliament** in the 1830s, which made major changes to life in Britain. The reforms showed the influence of the middle and business classes in the **Whig** Party. All the reforms brought changes which the **middle classes** wanted. The only exception was the Factory Act, which was passed after a number of reports to Parliament showed how badly some factory workers were treated.

1832   The Great **Reform** Act: this gave the vote to the **middle class**
1833   The Abolition of **Slavery**: many of the middle class opposed slavery
1833   **Factory Act**
1834   **Poor Law** Amendment Act: this was intended to save ratepayers money
1835   Municipal Corporations Act: this set up town councils in many parts of Britain which were to be elected by the ratepayers. This meant that the middle class could now control the towns they had founded during the **Industrial Revolution**.

WHIGS

The Whigs were originally the opponents in **Parliament** of **Charles II** and his brother James, Duke of York, in the 1670s and 1680s. The term 'Whig' meant a bandit, as did the term 'Tory'. They had used them as terms of abuse about each other. In 1688 seven Whigs sent an invitation to **William** of Orange to save England from **James II**. They were determined to protect the **Protestant** religion and the position of Parliament.

In the late-seventeenth and early-eighteenth centuries the Whigs were very wealthy and very powerful landowners. All the Prime Ministers after the arrival of **George I** in 1714 were Whigs. But in the late-eighteenth and early-nineteenth centuries many factory owners and businessmen joined the Whigs. They believed the Whigs were more likely to bring about the sort of changes they wanted to see in Britain. They were right, but it took a long time for this to happen. The Whigs did not get into power with a large majority until 1830. They then introduced the '**Whig Reforms**', as they came to be known. These gave much more power and influence to the middle class which had been created by the **Industrial Revolution**.

In the middle of the nineteenth century the Whigs became known as the **Liberal Party**. That name survived until the 1980s, when they united with the Social Democrats to form the Liberal Democrats.

WILBERFORCE, WILLIAM

William Wilberforce was the last leader of the Anti-Slavery League. He led the fight against **slavery** after the deaths of Granville Sharp and Thomas Clarkson. Wilberforce introduced a bill into **Parliament** to abolish the Slave Trade in 1789 and in every year after that until 1807, when it was abolished. It was Wilberforce who organised the Anti-Slavery League after 1807. He published pamphlets, held public meetings and raised as much money as he could. Slavery was abolished in 1833, the year of his death.

Wilberforce, who was elected MP for Yorkshire in 1807, showed much less sympathy for factory workers in the textile industries. Some people made fun of him because he seemed to care much more for slaves in the West Indies, than he did for factory workers who had to put up with poor conditions in Yorkshire.

WILHELM II, KAISER OF GERMANY, 1887–1918

Wilhelm II became Kaiser after the death of his father, Frederick III. Wilhelm was a grandson of Queen **Victoria**; his mother was her eldest daughter, also called Victoria. At birth Wilhelm's right arm was dislocated and it never grew properly. This prevented him from joining the German Army, which most members of the royal family usually did.

When Wilhelm became Kaiser, the Chancellor of Germany was Otto von Bismarck. He had been Chancellor for 25 years and had been successful. He had united Germany and had created a powerful Army. He had also made Germany wealthy by developing German industry and an efficient railway system. The Kaiser and Bismarck soon disagreed, however, and Bismarck was forced to resign.

Why did they disagree?

Bismarck was always cautious in foreign policy. After 1871 he tried to maintain good relations with as many countries as possible. He tried to prevent France from gaining any allies, as he expected that it would try to recover **Alsace-Lorraine** at some point.

He did not want to fight more than one country at a time.

Bismarck did not try to build up an empire as other countries in Europe did. He did not try to build up a Navy, as he thought that Germany did not need one. Wilhelm insisted that Germany must have an empire and a large Navy. The German **Navy Laws** were passed in 1898 and 1900, and in 1905 Wilhelm visited Tangier, in Morocco, to make a speech. These actions made the British and French governments suspicious.

After the assassination of the Archduke **Franz Ferdinand**, the Austrian government sent a message to Berlin asking for German support if Austria went to war with Serbia. The German reply, which came from Wilhelm and his Chancellor, became known as the 'blank cheque'. Germany simply promised to support Austria whatever happened. This encouraged the Austrian government to go ahead and attack Serbia.

Kaiser Wilhelm II was vain and lacking in judgement. He often did not realise, until too late, where his actions were going to lead himself and Germany. Although he did not cause the **First World War** he could have done more to try to prevent it. When at last he realised what was happening in 1914, it was too late to do anything about it.

WILLIAM I, KING, 1066–1087

William, Duke of Normandy, was descended from Rollo who conquered part of northern France in 911. Rollo was a Norseman or Viking, so the part of France he occupied became known as Normandy, the land of the Norsemen. The Vikings had been travellers and fighters and so were the Normans. From the eleventh to the thirteenth centuries the Normans travelled all over Europe, conquering Sicily and parts of southern Italy, the Holy Land and even Byzantium. It was no surprise that William took the opportunity to invade England in 1066.

Why did William invade England?

- On 5 January 1066, King Edward the Confessor died without any children. The English nobles made Earl **Harold** Godwinson King. He was the most powerful of the nobles. William claimed that Edward had promised the Crown to him when Edward was in Normandy. Edward's mother had been a Norman and he had grown up in Normandy.

- William also claimed that Harold Godwinson had promised to help him become King. He said that Harold had been shipwrecked on the coast of France in 1064 and had sworn an oath to William.

- The Pope backed William and even gave him a banner to carry when he set sail.

William was taking a big chance. The English Army was strong and experienced. England was a much bigger country than Normandy and much more powerful. William was not strong enough to invade on his own. He persuaded other barons to support

him: Count Eustace of Boulogne, Alain of Brittany and William's brother Bishop Odo of Bayeux. He said he would reward them with land in England when he won.

At first things did not go well. William's army was held up for six weeks waiting for the wind to change, he was only able to sail on 27 September. In fact this was very lucky for William. When his ships set sail they found that the English Navy had gone away. If they had sailed earlier they would have been attacked at sea.

Another stroke of luck was that William's invasion took place at the same time as another invasion, by Harald Hardrada, the King of Norway. He landed in Yorkshire before William and King Harold Godwinson marched north to meet him. This meant that William was able to land at Pevensey unopposed. When Harold's army did arrive at **Hastings**, the soldiers had already fought a major battle and marched about 500 miles in two weeks.

What sort of man was William I?

- Like all Normans William loved fighting. He spent most of his reign trying to extend his land. He was killed in 1087 fighting in the valley of the river Seine.

- William was ruthless. He put down all the rebellions in England against the Normans and used violence wherever he thought it necessary. All important offices were taken away from the English and given to the Normans.

- He preferred Normandy to England and spent most of his time there. This may have been because England was easier to govern as it had been one kingdom for nearly 200 years.

- William loved hunting and kept about 17 per cent of the land of England for himself. He planted the New Forest to hunt in.

- William was a good administrator. He organised the **Domesday Book** to find out all he could about England. He established the **feudal system** in England. He refused to allow the Pope to appoint bishops in England. No messages from the Pope could be sent to England unless William approved.

When William died in 1087 England was a wealthy and peaceful country. There was very little opposition to the Normans.

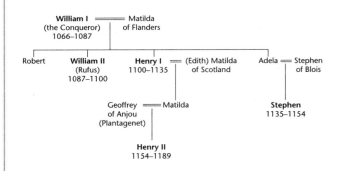

The family tree of William I

WILLIAM II, KING, 1087–1100

William II, or William Rufus as he is also called, was **William I**'s second son. His eldest son was Robert, who became Duke of Normandy. William II was very like his father. He loved hunting and fighting, but he could also be cruel and greedy. When the Archbishop of Canterbury died in 1089, William refused to appoint a new one for four years and kept the income of the cathedral for himself. William became unpopular and was killed by a crossbow bolt in the New Forest in 1100 while he was hunting. He may have been murdered.

WILLIAM III, KING, 1689–1702

William III was the husband of Mary, the elder daughter of **James II**. He was invited to become King after landing in England to drive out James. The **Whigs** had wanted **Mary** to be Queen, but William refused to allow that unless he became King as well.

William's reign was very important as it contained all the Acts of **Parliament** which made up the **Glorious Revolution**. These meant that the power of the Monarch was reduced and that of Parliament was increased. The most important Acts were:

1688   Mutiny Act: this allowed the King to have an Army and had to be renewed every year. This meant he had to call Parliament every year

1689   The Bill of Rights: this made the Declaration of Rights a law

1694   This meant that there had to be a General Election every three years

1701   The Act of **Settlement**.

During William's reign there were also very important changes in the way the country was run.

1693   The National Debt was started. This allowed the government to borrow money from individual people

1694   The Bank of England was founded

1698   The London Stock Exchange was set up, the first one anywhere in the world.

These developments helped the government to borrow money when it needed it. They also helped to make possible the **Industrial Revolution**. Merchants and businessmen could raise money for new inventions or new companies much more easily than they could in other countries.

Was William III popular?

At the beginning of his reign William was very popular. He defeated the forces of James II in Ireland, winning the battle of the **Boyne**; the flower 'Sweet William' is supposed to have been named after him. But after the death of Queen Mary he became less popular. Why?

- William brought over Dutch friends to whom he gave posts and money in England.
- He began to get involved in wars on the continent, mostly in The Netherlands. People thought he was using his position as King of England to defend Holland.
- In the Act of Settlement both of these were banned.

In 1702 William III was killed when his horse stumbled and he was thrown. His horse was supposed to have been frightened by a mole. **Jacobites** raised their glasses to the 'little gentleman in black' and called the flower 'Stinking Billy'. He was succeeded by his sister-in-law, **Anne**.

WILLIAM IV, KING, 1830–1837

William IV became King on the death of his eldest brother, **George IV**, in 1830. The next eldest of the brothers, Frederick, the 'Grand old Duke of York', had died in 1827. William IV's accession led to a General Election. This always happened in the eighteenth and early-nineteenth centuries as it gave the Monarch the opportunity to choose a Prime Minister. This was ended in 1867. The General Election was won by the **Whigs**. This led to the Great **Reform** Act.

William IV played an important part in the passing of the Act, because the **Tories** voted against it in the House of **Lords**. This meant that the Act could not be passed. The Whig Prime Minister, Earl Grey, asked William to create enough Whig members of the House of Lords to get the Act passed. William eventually agreed, but the Tories backed down and passed the Act.

When William died in 1837 he had no children, so the Crown passed to the daughter of his younger brother. She became Queen **Victoria**.

WOLSEY, CARDINAL THOMAS

Thomas Wolsey was **Henry VIII**'s Chancellor from 1515 to 1529. This made him the second most powerful man in England after the King. As well as being Chancellor, he was also a Cardinal, the highest rank in the **Catholic** Church below the Pope and the Archbishop of York. He was also the Papal Legate: the Pope's special representative in England. Wolsey became very wealthy and built himself **Hampton Court**, which he gave to Henry VIII in 1525. At the time people said that he was richer than Henry VIII.

Wolsey was very ambitious. He wanted to be Archbishop of Canterbury, but the post was occupied, and to become Pope. He also wanted more power in England, so when Henry VIII wanted to divorce his first wife, **Catherine of Aragon**, Wolsey said he would arrange it. He failed. Pope Clement VII was in the power of the Holy Roman Emperor, Charles V, who was Catherine of Aragon's nephew. Wolsey was dismissed from the post of Chancellor in 1529 and was summoned to London the following year. He collapsed and died on the way.

WOODROW WILSON

Woodrow Wilson was President of the **USA** from 1913 to 1921. He was responsible for the US declaration of war on Germany in April 1917.

What were US attitudes to the *First World War* before 1917?

- In 1914 and 1915, the great majority of Americans wanted to stay out of the war. The US government had said in 1823 that it would never interfere in European affairs. They wanted to keep to the Monroe Doctrine as the statement was known.

- Many Americans came from Europe, some were from Britain, others from Germany; it seemed easiest to remain neutral.

Why did attitudes change?

- The *Lusitania*, a passenger liner, was sunk by a German submarine in 1915; there were Americans on board.
- In 1916 German submarines began to sink ships on sight without warning. Although the US government protested, American ships were sunk.
- In March 1917 the Zimmermann telegram was published by the US government. This showed that Germany was trying to persuade Mexico to join in a war against the USA.
- During March 1917 several US ships were sunk without warning by German submarines.

How did Wilson react?

- Wilson tried to avoid declaring war. He said on many occasions that it was nothing to do with the USA.
- In December 1916 he tried to bring the war to an end by acting as a mediator. He suggested it should be 'peace without victory'. But Britain and France put forward proposals that Germany and Austria did not accept. Britain and France were now led by *Lloyd George* and Clemenceau who wanted an all-out victory.
- But finally in April 1917, Wilson asked Congress to declare war on Germany.

When the war ended, Wilson did not want to return Europe to the state it had been in before the war. He drew up his 'Fourteen Points' before he came to Europe in December 1918.

What effects did the 'Fourteen Points' have?

- They persuaded the Germans to agree to the *Armistice*, because they thought they were going to be treated leniently.

- They annoyed Orlando, the Italian Prime Minister, because they prevented him from gaining the Adriatic coast which Italy had been promised by Britain and France.
- They led to the setting up of the *League of Nations* which was Wilson's idea.

But having played a major role in the conference at *Versailles* and the setting up of the League of Nations, Wilson was unable to persuade Congress to accept the Treaty or to allow the *USA* to join the League.

Why did this happen?

- Woodrow Wilson was away from the USA from December 1918 to July 1919. No President had ever been out of the country for so long. Many Americans were angry and some accused him of becoming too European.
- Many Americans felt they had sorted out the problems of Europe. Now they wanted to go back to the Monroe Doctrine and not be involved.
- Wilson was not easy to get on with. He appeared to be rather arrogant and he made enemies easily. He put many people off and his health gave way when he tried to go around the country making speeches.
- Many Americans wanted a compromise: there were parts of the treaty and the League which they liked and parts which they did not. To Wilson it was all or nothing.

So in the end the USA did not accept the Treaty of Versailles and never joined the League of Nations.

WREN, SIR CHRISTOPHER

Sir Christopher Wren was the architect who was responsible for rebuilding the city of London after the Great Fire in 1666. His most famous work was St Paul's Cathedral, which was finished in 1710, but he also built Greenwich Observatory, the Royal Naval College and more than 50 churches.

YALTA

In February 1945 **Roosevelt**, **Churchill** and **Stalin** met at Yalta in the southern Soviet Union to plan the end of the **Second World War**.

- They agreed to divide Germany into four zones: each one would be occupied by one of the Allies. Stalin agreed to accept France as one of the powers. Berlin would also be divided into four sectors.
- Poland would be given land in the west, which would be taken from Germany, and would lose land to the **USSR**.
- The USSR would declare war on Japan three months after the end of the war with Germany.
- Stalin promised to allow free elections in the countries of eastern Europe which had been occupied by the Soviet Army.

Roosevelt believed that Stalin would keep his promises. He also believed that the Soviet Army would be needed in the final attack on Japan, so he was prepared to leave the Soviet Union in control of eastern Europe. Churchill did not think this was a good idea. By the time of the **Potsdam** conference in July, it was clear that Churchill had been right. The new President, Harry **Truman**, who took over when Roosevelt died on 12 April, took a much tougher line with Stalin.

YORK

The House of York was descended from Edmund, Duke of York, the fifth son of **Edward III**. His grandson, Richard of York, was Regent during **Henry VI**'s periods of insanity in the 1450s, but was replaced by the Duke of Somerset, the grandson of John of **Gaunt**, a **Lancastrian**. Richard of York defeated and killed Somerset at the battle of St Albans, in 1455; this began the **Wars of the Roses**.

Richard was killed in battle in 1460, but his elder son **Edward IV** became King in 1461. The House of York reigned until 1485, when **Richard III** was defeated and killed by **Henry VII** at the battle of Bosworth Field. Henry was a grandson of the Duke of Somerset.

YPRES

The Belgian city of Ypres (Ieper in Flemish) was occupied by British forces from October 1914 until the end of the **First World War**.

The first British soldiers arrived by train. They were the survivors of the British Expeditionary Force who had fought the German army at **Mons** and had then retreated into France. After the battle of the Marne they were sent north to occupy a gap in the line between the French and Belgian armies.

Ypres (called Wipers by the British) was in a salient, a stretch of the front line which jutted out into the German trenches. So it was surrounded by the Germans on three sides. What made things worse was that the Germans occupied low hills from which they could see the spires of the fifteenth-century Cloth Hall in Ypres and the cathedral. It meant that Ypres could be a very dangerous place, because the Germans were never more than a few miles away and the city was an easy target. In October 1914 a British headquarters in a large white farmhouse just outside the town was destroyed by shellfire. This was during the First Battle of Ypres. The city was also very low-lying, the countryside had to be drained by canals and streams. These were soon destroyed by shelling and the ground became more and more boggy.

In April 1915 the Germans attacked Ypres again, the second battle. This was the first time that poison gas was used near Langemarck to the north-west of the city. Eight thousand Allied soldiers were killed. There is an enormous German cemetery there now with the remains of more than 40 000 soldiers. At Hooge, where you can see mine craters and trenches from 1915, the two front lines were no more than 15 metres apart.

Hooge was on the Menin Road. This was the main road out of Ypres to the east. It runs to the town of Menin (Menen in Flemish). Throughout the war Menin was in German hands. Most of the reinforcements and equipment had to travel along the Menin Road; it was extremely dangerous as German gunners on the hills in the distance could see everything on the road. The most dangerous spot of all was over the brow of a low hill as the soldiers left Ypres. Here there was a junction and a railway line. This meant the Germans knew the range exactly. It was so dangerous that it was impossible to move past this point in daylight. It became known as 'Hell-Fire Corner'. If you visit it today, you will find that the railway line has gone and the corner is now a roundabout, 'Hell-Fire Roundabout'. At the roundabout you go straight on to Hooge or turn right to Hill 60.

In 1915 and 1916 the British tried to fight their way out of Ypres to the north east at Hill 60. This was the scene of underground fighting as both sides tried to dig mines under each other's trenches. If you visit Hill 60 today, you can see a mine crater that was exploded by the British and a machine-gun post which was captured in the fighting.

There are more trenches to visit at Hill 62. This is along the Menin Road just before you reach the Hooge museum. Turn right at the end of the houses and take the road to the Canadian Memorial. The area was called Sanctuary Wood by the first soldiers who arrived there as the trees gave some protection from machine-gun fire. If you look at some of the trees you will be able to see the holes made by machine-gun bullets. The sanctuary did not last very long.

A photograph taken at Hill 62 showing trenches used during the First World War

The Third Battle of Ypres was fought in 1917: it is usually known as *Passchendaele*. It was fought to the north of the city. The British Army made about five miles of ground to the top of the ridge before winter set in. There is an excellent view of the battlefield from Tyne Cot Cemetery, the largest cemetery around Ypres. There are 8700 soldiers buried here including three Germans. The Cross of Sacrifice stands on the site of a blockhouse captured by Australians on 4 October 1917.

Near the centre of Ypres stands the Menin Gate. This is a memorial to all the soldiers who died there and whose bodies have never been recovered. They disappeared in the mud which was churned up after years of shelling.

When you stand in the centre of the city today, it is difficult to realise that it was almost totally destroyed between 1914 and 1918. All the buildings were reconstructed from plans and photographs after the war. In the Cloth Hall museum and at Hill 62 there are photographs of Ypres at the end of the war. There was hardly a building left standing.

It is possible to visit Ypres for the day if you live in the south east of England. It is 100 kilometres from Calais and can be reached easily by car in about one hour. Take the motorway from Calais to Dunkirk and turn off at junction 28. Ypres is signposted. This is the A25 motorway to Lille. Turn off at the Steenworde junction and follow the signs to Ieper. All the sites are signposted in English and there is a tourist office in the middle of the town in the Cloth Hall.

ANSWERS TO SELF-CHECK QUESTIONS

1 Autobiography
2 Parliament to be elected every year
3 Cast Iron
4 The Longbow
5 Kaiser Wilhelm II
6 He was the grandson of Princess Elizabeth, the sister of Charles I
7 Cotton
8 He was the great, great, grandson of Margaret, the sister of Henry VIII
9 The Labour Representation Committee
10 They all did
11 Bubonic Plague
12 The New Deal
13 The Nationalists and the Republicans
14 The Grey Blur
15 Railwaymen